Fighting Bob Evans

EDWIN A. FALK

NEW YORK

JONATHAN CAPE & HARRISON SMITH

Courtesy General Cornelius Vanderbilt

REAR ADMIRAL EVANS ABOARD THE *MAYFLOWER* WITH PRESIDENT
AND MRS. ROOSEVELT AND COMMODORE CORNELIUS VANDERBILT
DURING FLEET MANOEUVRES

PRINTED IN THE UNITED STATES OF AMERICA
BY THE CORNWALL PRESS, INC., AND BOUND
BY THE J. F. TAPLEY COMPANY

FOREWORD

~~~~~~

I ALWAYS shall be happy
that I had the privilege of knowing "Fighting Bob" Evans.
While I was in college and in the years following my
graduation, Admiral Evans was very distinctly one of our
active living national heroes who was especially close to the
hearts of Americans in every part of the country. There
was something about his personality that made people recognize him not alone for his courage or for his technical naval
qualifications, but more especially for his gift of leadership.
I am glad that this book has been written, because the
two volumes which came from the pen of Admiral Evans
himself were primarily biographies relating events and the
part he took in them; and it must be remembered that auto-
biographies by naval officers of necessity contain elements
of restraint and a lack of personal touches which result from
a lifetime of conformity to official restrictions.
His particular lifetime covered three definite phases of
the history of the American Navy. As a Midshipman, and
during his early service he was an active participant in the
largest and most efficient naval organization of the world
—a Navy actually engaged in warfare, a Navy making
history with the introduction and use of weapons of offense
and defense hitherto untried.
He then passed through the second phase, an ordeal in
which his profession saw the Navy of the Civil War reduced to the status of a third-rate power. It is hard for us

to realize that from 1865 almost to 1890 the officer personnel of our Naval service maintained their *esprit de corps* and scientific attainments in spite of a national policy which gave them no new ships and no new guns.

Evans was fortunate that in the later years of his active service he was able to take a definite part in the building of the New Navy; first the small protected cruisers, then the armored cruisers, then the coast defense battleships, then the torpedo boats.

He saw the Spanish-American War bring home to the American people a realization of the need for a first-class Navy, and he became Commander-in-Chief of the Fleet at a moment when we first had a well-rounded Fleet to command.

His will always be a household name among those of us who love the Navy and its glorious record; his will always be a personality which will live in the traditions of the Service.

History will record that for half a century after steam replaced sail there was one great question-mark in the minds of the naval service and of the public as well: could the fleet protect both our coasts? To Admiral Evans it was reserved to answer that question. Under his command not a squadron, not a division, but a complete "fleet in being" passed successfully from our Atlantic ports to our Pacific ports. His name always will be associated with those of the great naval commanders of the United States.

FRANKLIN D. ROOSEVELT

CONTENTS

ILLUSTRATIONS

ACKNOWLEDGMENT

of deep appreciation is due to three in particular of the many persons who rendered substantial assistance in the preparation of this biography. Rear Admiral Bradley A. Fiske, U. S. Navy, retired, and Rear Admiral Edwin A. Anderson, U. S. Navy, retired, both of whom served brilliantly under Admiral Evans and knew him intimately, read the manuscript with painstaking care. Commander Holloway H. Frost, U. S. Navy, preëminent in the younger generation of American writers upon naval affairs and a distinguished officer of our present-day Navy, who is now engaged in writing a naval history of the Civil War, read the part dealing with the Civil War, before going abroad.

Most but not all of the suggestions made by each of these authorities have been gratefully adopted, but the author alone is responsible for the contents of the book.

E. A. F.

1

UNDERWAY

~~~~~~

SUPPLYING the spark needed to detonate the pent-up emotions of San Francisco, renascent after the travails of the seismic fire, there emerged through the light haze, on a spring morning of 1908, the United States fleet that had just rounded South America. In perfect formation, the battleships and their auxiliaries steamed through the Golden Gate as through an arch of triumph, while countless thousands of people, thronging every point of vantage about the enormous amphitheatre that surrounds the harbour, cheered with spontaneous frenzy.

For months this day had been awaited while the fleet was making its long cruise. During the preceding night, the searchlights outside of the capes had flashed assurance that the visitors were ready to enter at the appointed hour. Now they were standing in.

What mattered it that the capital ships, with their shining bright work, spotless white paint and formidable guns, had been rendered obsolete by the successful trials of Britain's latest addition to her navy? The crowds knew nothing of the significance of the *Dreadnought* nor would have cared just then if they had. The American ships might be relatively less powerful than they looked, but, paradoxically, the Commander in Chief, whose flag at the main truck gave them their greatest prestige, personified the New Navy, the Navy of the future that was not yet launched, but within a generation would be ready for the World War and then graciously condescend to parity with the Mistress of the Seas.

Sufficient for the occasion was the fact that the fleet coming into view was the greatest ever assembled under the Stars and Stripes, that it was commanded by the prime favourite of contemporary heroes, and that now, ships, men, officers and Fighting Bob himself, belonged to their beholders. San Francisco was on a patriotic spree. The occasion was, of course, a general holiday, and the elaborate festivities were to continue while the fleet remained.

As the *Connecticut* led the imposing column toward the anchorage, the "old man," whose personality pervaded the entire fleet, was not at his accustomed station, but in the emergency cabin on the after bridge. His physique was winning its half century of rebellion against one of the most indomitable wills that ever had ruled a quarter deck. Partly sheltered from the dampness, but in acute pain, Old Gimpy watched every move of his ships, stretching away in the flagship's wake, as they smartly executed his signal orders. He had arisen from a sick-bed to exercise his command for the last time, and the fleet was giving him its very best.

Thirteen thousand miles, he had brought the fleet in a voyage unprecedented in naval history. Now, one after the other, the sixteen battleships, safe and sound, were passing Point Lobos exactly as, before Christmas, they had stood out of Hampton Roads saluting President Roosevelt in the Mayflower. The civilized world had closely followed the progress of the armada. Through daily press despatches it had watched the transit by the cumbersome battleships, blinded by fog, of the hazardous Straits of Magellan, and the mad tossing of the small destroyers in ocean storms. Finally, as the lookout in the *Connecticut* had sighted the first California landmark, it had heard him sing out "God's country, ahoy!"

The four divisions, followed by two battleships that had

joined company outside the harbour, were nearing the city. Up snapped the flag hoist "Anchor in berths previously assigned"; the job was nearly done. It was the end of the task and the end of the career.

By unanimous acclamation, afloat and ashore, this was Bob Evans' day.

Other landfalls of other times must have crowded his memory, especially those at this same western portal of the country he had served so long. Here he had returned in the Yorktown in '92, after the Chilean crisis, to find himself renamed Fighting Bob. Here he had returned from the Bering Sea patrol. From this same harbour he had set forth to hoist his admiral's flag in the Asiatic Fleet. San Francisco knew him well. His life and spirit were after its own heart. Now, upon the eve of retirement, it hailed him with an admiring affection never before or since equalled in its history of generous welcomes.

There must have been thoughts of distant places, too. The aching legs must have recalled Fort Fisher in '65, the gala reception must have suggested the victory parade up New York Bay after Santiago, the evolutions of the fleet must have evoked pictures of squadrons under sail.

The recollections of the Admiral went back to a childhood in pre-Civil War Virginia, where the Industrial Revolution scarcely had made itself felt. He was born on August eighteenth, 1846, and, as if to anticipate the doctrine of parity, the Fates paired this event with the birth in Ireland that same year of the great British officer Lord Charles Beresford, one of Evans' life-long friends. Admiral Cervera was a boy of seven, Lord Fisher five, and Grand Admiral von Tirpitz was not to be born for three years.

The Naval Academy at Annapolis had been established the previous year, and Captain Sumner of the American merchant marine was preparing his pamphlet on lines of position (Sumner lines) that were to revolutionize celestial

navigation. The tottering government of Louis Phillippe
was skeptically examining the plans of Dupuy de Lome for
an armoured frigate designed to employ steam as her principal motive force and to use sails only as auxiliary—
obviously the impractical contraption of a crank.

President Polk and Sam Houston were waging their
Mexican War, in which Robert E. Lee and Ulysses S. Grant
were winning minor military distinction. A couple of weeks
before Evans saw the light of day, there was elected to the
Thirtieth Congress from Illinois one Abraham Lincoln, and
the triumvirate of Clay, Calhoun and Webster still reigned
supreme in the Senate.

Like George Dewey, who was then a lad in Vermont,
Evans was the son of a physician but whereas the former's
father had a comfortable small town practice in Montpelier,
Dr. Samuel Andrew Jackson Evans, whose name dates and
somewhat locates him, treated patients, many gratuitously,
scattered about a wide area within the radius of a long
night's saddle ride over the mountains. This region was the
Shenandoah Valley south of Roanoke and below the part
soon to acquire renown in the bloody sixties. While politically Virginian, Floyd County was economically and socially
much more like the sparsely settled pioneer country to the
westward than the long cultivated tidewater or upper river
counties that had bred the aristocracy for which that State
was chiefly distinguished. Dr. Evans' associations were
also those of the Tennessee pioneers rather than of the
famous Virginia families which for generations had graced
the pages of our history. It is, however, not to be inferred
that Dr. Evans was a self-educated poor white. On the
contrary, he had been graduated from the University of
Virginia and the name Robley Dunglison that he gave to his
first son was that of a distinguished teacher to whom he
credited much of the inspiration that held him on the path to
learning. He had a small farm in the valley, a few negroes
who were always referred to as servants and never as slaves,

represented his district from time to time in the state legislature and lived modestly upon a scale somewhere between the simpler standards of the rough communities over the mountains and the gentler mode of the landed aristocracy along the great rivers to the east. There was no caste where young Robley was brought up, no mint julep sipping on shady verandas, no breeding of negroes for the New Orlean's slave markets; and there was no scarcity of books, no rude improvisations of the frontier, no instability of insecurity. The Evans family was maintained by its land. The doctor practised his profession because it was the natural thing to exercise one's competency, not because it added substantially to his income. The accumulation of money was not uppermost in the minds of those southwestern Virginians. Industrialism had barely seeped through the passes between the hills. Life went on pretty much the same year after year.

Young Robley was a sturdy boy, short for his years but well set up and coordinated. He could use his hands and his feet and his eyes.

The nearest neighbours in that region could not hear each other's dogs bark and the social life was meagre, usually limited to revival meetings in the summer and an annual visit to Lynchburg in the fall to sell the tobacco and apple crops and buy the winter's supplies. The winters were not at all the kind suggested by the name Virginia. Snow and ice and cold winds brought to the valley much more nearly the kind of winters through which young George Dewey was skating in Vermont, although spring broke much earlier and afforded a glorious season of gradual melting into summer that is almost unknown in the North. Robley was always partial to warm weather, even as a boy before his physique rebelled painfully against low temperature or dampness. Fortunately, a great part of his career was spent in tropical and temperate zones, although duty was to call him upon several occasions into almost the shadow of the Arctic and Antarctic Circles.

Dr. Evans died when Robley was ten. Mrs. Evans, having the sole responsibility of educating the children, moved the family to Fairfax Courthouse, where a good school was accessible. This lay in the county directly across the river from Washington. It was the county of Mt. Vernon and Arlington and the great Fairfax Estate; the Potomac Valley of the Washington's, Custis's, Lee's, Madison's and Monroe's. It was the Virginia of fact and legend; the Virginia that had made the name renowned when Floyd County was still a wilderness. The fatherless Evans family emerged from its obscure and familiar mountain home into the rolling hillsides of the stronghold of aristocracy and tradition. To Robley it was the threshold of the world. A year later he crossed the threshold and entered the world itself. His father's brother resided in Washington and took the eleven year old youngster into his home, where he became a happy member of the family. Just as Dr. Evans had not relied upon his practice for a livelihood, Robley's uncle was a lawyer by profession but a government clerk and newspaper man by vocation.

When Robley took up his residence in the national capital, it was still a provincial and unattractive town of about fifty thousand people of whom a quarter were negroes, variously characterized by European diplomats and American office-holders obliged to live there as "Wilderness City," "Capital of Miserable Huts," "City of Magnificent Distances" and "A Mudhole Almost Equal to the Great Serbonian Bog." It was a living mockery to the ambitious efforts of Major L'Enfant who had drawn its plans and Andrew Ellicott who had laid it out. Between the White House and the unfinished Capitol stretched the poorly paved Pennsylvania Avenue, the only pretentious thoroughfare, which contained shops unable to compete against the up-to-date ones of Baltimore and houses that varied from presentable structures to pigsties. There were churches and saloons scattered about the city and some elegant private homes near slave "livery stables," where the negroes were herded for exportation to the cotton belt. A city that had been made to order and had not grown, it was a queer, sprawled out area of streets without houses, with almost open country between well built-up sections. It had few of the modern conveniences of northern cities and none of the charm of the South; all of the disadvantages of urban life and none of its compensations; and every once in a while some disgusted Congressman would advocate the removal of the seat of government to a less unworthy place.

To the Evans's it was of no concern that the White House, socially austere enough under Polk, had passed into the aging bachelor hands of Buchanan. They were not of the elite and had no social aspirations. Mr. Evans came in contact, however, with many of the statesmen, lesser statesmen and would be statesmen of the day. This was soon to enable Robley, who all his later life had a wholesome abhorrence of politicians and any resort to their influence, to enter the naval service, not by pulling any wires but simply as the result of a fortunate acquaintanceship.

Mr. Evans had entered his nephew in a public school that was one of the bright spots in the backward city and the boy for the first time received some formal education, to which he responded most satisfactorily. His shortness of stature, however, was his undoing. It deceived a larger fellow into cowardly throwing a rock at Evans' first command, a toy boat he was trying to sail in a pool of rainwater in the school yard. This was the only craft ever commanded by him that sank. It was a prophetic incident. More powerful aggressors than this bully were to learn the consequences of failing to respect any ship belonging to Fighting Bob. This older boy was carried home, wiser, meeker and temporarily *hors de combat*. Robley was expelled and, characteristically, felt no remorse for his acts and no grievance against the authorities but only regret at having to leave the school.

He entered Gonzaga College, a preparatory school for Georgetown College, and studied the classics, which were then and for many years to come considered the *sine qua non* of a gentleman's education. Evans undoubtedly had the mental equipment to master these scholarly subjects but his active temperament found the academic halls too narrow and the air of libraries too musty. The most lively place in Washington was the Capitol and Evans found himself in and about the noisy machinery of government at every opportunity. He was liked by the Congressmen and their satellites on the Hill and became a familiar figure in committee rooms, along the corridors and even in the House itself. For many of the men he there saw and heard he had a sincere regard and a friendly feeling but never after did the administration of public affairs hold any glamour for him. There was, however, one spot in the city that thrilled him: the river front, where the romance of the sea touched the tip of a long, slender finger up the winding Potomac from Chesapeake Bay. Sail boats of light draught conveyed a mere hint of the great watery beyond, which the mountain lad had never seen. There, he felt, was to be found the freshness, the breadth of horizon, the lure of adventure which the genial Evans household, the classrooms and the legislative workshops completely lacked. There lay a man's career! Robley Evans felt the urge, it became stronger, very soon irresistible and his mind was made up. His reference in his memoirs to this formulation of his life ambition is striking because of the unaffected emphasis of understatement: "I had never seen salt water; and I don't think I knew a single naval officer; but somehow it came to me that I should like a sea life, and from this time on the idea was never out of my mind."

In all the vicissitudes of his half century behind the Union Jack, he never for one second regretted his choice of profession or questioned the wisdom of it. If ever was born a natural sailor, who after one faint whiff of a thinly diluted salt breeze sought the water with the instinctive directness of a duck, it was Robley D. Evans of southwestern Virginia, the son of a country physician-farmer, the namesake of a scholar and the favoured nephew of a white collared bourgeois. The route he was obliged to follow, however, was hardly that of a duck. The Naval Academy, about his own age, was then as now situated at Annapolis, less than thirty miles from the capital, and Evans travelled over four thousand miles to reach it. He was destined to behold salt water for the first time many days' trip from the nearest seaboard.

The youth's infatuation naturally prompted him to depart for Baltimore or Norfolk, by land or water, and sign up on the first available ship. Sensing what was transpiring in the boy's heart and possibly at the solicitation of his uncle, one of the latter's acquaintances in governmental circles offered Robley an appointment to the Naval Academy. This good angel hailed from the Land of the Saints, where appointments to Annapolis were no more in demand than sage-brush or Indians. Mr. Hooper was the delegate sent to Congress by the Territory of Utah. He was delighted to oblige Mr. Evans and young Robley with this appointment for which he had no other conceivable use, unless Brigham Young was contemplating the eventual establishment of a Mormon Navy on Great Salt Lake. The appointment was so unbelievably wonderful to Robley that he probably would have been willing to credit it as a Mormon miracle, had the tenets of that Church been familiar to him. Anything so good must have some condition, some fly in the ointment, and it immediately developed that the appointment of Mr. Hooper was limited to residents of his remote Territory. Very well; Robley would become a resident, even if he had to go to Utah to do so. If residence at the North Pole had been necessary, he probably would have essayed that too. In four days he was bound for the Naval Academy via Salt Lake City.

The railroads had penetrated the West as far as the Missouri River and Robley made the journey in a day coach to St. Joseph. George Mortimer Pullman was then at work on his invention of the sleeping car and his Pullman Palace Car Company was not to be organized for another ten years. Dining cars were also conveniences of the future. As a matter of fact, the trains moved so slowly and made so many protracted stops that the delays occasioned by permitting the passengers to take their meals at stations were relatively insignificant. Time was not as greedily hoarded in those days, when people still did their short distance travelling on horseback or in horse-drawn vehicles, and steam railroads seemed to have a speed that some reactionary old sceptics avowed was in defiance of nature and divine intentions. The Baltimore and Ohio train jogged along at what Evans regarded as such a remarkable velocity that he hardly had time to observe the scenery. After several days of steaming through the mountains, through the Middle West, across the Mississippi and over the prairies, he reached the rail head on the banks of the muddy Missouri, where the East definitely and fixedly terminated. Robley's uncle had arranged to have him at this point meet a party of five people who were setting forth on the great transcontinental adventure bound for California. On the one side of the river were the locomotives and rolling stock of nineteenth century industrial civilization; on the other side were the covered wagons and supply depots of the untamed frontier. It was the decade of "Bleeding" Kansas. The famous or infamous Kansas-Nebraska Bill was five years old and the bitter contest to determine whether Kansas would become a free or slave State had been raging ever since. Robley Evans first gazed across the turgid Missouri at Kansas, at the most critical time in her history. The border warfare between the pro-slavery Missourians and the free soil immigrants from Massachusetts had attracted the attention of the nation. The names of Kansas and Nebraska had been shouted again and again in the halls of Congress, repeatedly appeared in newspaper headlines and were heard at every political rally. Only three years had passed since the savage sacking of the little anti-slavery town of Lawrence the very day before the dastardly assault by Preston Brooks upon Charles Sumner in the Senate Chamber, a concatenation of outrages that had inflamed the North to furious indignation and the most violent Free State men in Kansas to the retaliatory Pottawatomie massacre. The fanatical abolitionist who in his zeal for negro freedom had thus butchered his way to national notoriety, was now in the East organizing the attack on Harper's Ferry where, not long after Evans' crossing of the Missouri, he was to be captured by Colonel Robert E. Lee and hanged into martyrdom, fame and the battle song of the Federal Army. The lawlessness in Kansas, which interested the young traveller very slightly, had been almost entirely suppressed by Governor Geary but was within two years to have an overwhelming effect upon the former's life and almost nip it in the bud. As he met his companions for the great trek and attended to the many details of preparation, Kansas was drafting the Wyandotte Constitution under which it was subsequently admitted to statehood, but, for all Evans cared at the time, Kansas might have anarchy or an emperor if only the passage of his wagon train was assured. After all, he was a normal boy of thirteen.

The party of six finally had bought its horses and covered wagons, loaded the latter with blankets, clothing, food and other necessary supplies, including plenty of extra ammunition, selected the riding mules and the guns and was ready to cross the prairies.

The route lay northwest into Nebraska Territory, which at that time extended north to British America and west to the Rockies, and westward along the Platte River and its south fork. This was the Oregon Trail, the Old California Trail and the Old Salt Lake Trail—the great highway to the West—later the route of the pony express and eventually of the Union Pacific, the first transcontinental railroad, and the Lincoln Highway, the first automobile thoroughfare from coast to coast. This broad interior stretch had been settled long after the more inviting country beyond it and, even in 1859, had a very small white population, confined almost exclusively to the river and trail posts. Early explorers and fur traders had brought back unalluring descriptions of a monotonously unscenic arid wilderness fit only for the coyote, the bison and the less discriminating of the Indians. The summers had been reported as oppressively torrid with only tornadoes and hail storms to punctuate the heat waves and the winters as long and severe, a desert where spring and autumn refused to linger. These disparaging impressions that filtered eastward in the early decades of the century were declared by later travellers to have been grossly exaggerated and at one time the prognostications of a future Garden of Eden that required only feasible irrigation, went to the other extreme. The Mormon pilgrimage of the late forties, the California gold rush, the overland migration to the Northwest Pacific section left small settlements in their wakes. These, however, were few and far between. A hundred and fifty miles from the Missouri River or any point out of sight of the trail was as free of white population as before Columbus discovered America. Along the one travelled route, however, the deep wagon ruts evidenced the increasing volume of traffic between the railroad terminus and the Rockies. This distance is so great that a modern express train requires all day to traverse it and hundreds of covered wagons could be lumbering along its undulating extent and still leave it a desolate route to each party. The Indians swooped down upon these travellers like pirates upon the ships that followed definite courses. The troops from Fort Kearney could not be everywhere. Whenever possible, the pioneers would move in long caravans for mutual self-protection and frequently even such groups were attacked and massacred by the plundering tribes. To cross the plains in those days was a hazardous undertaking.

What impressed young Evans more than anything else about the prairies were the teeming thousands upon thousands of buffalo.

The trail naturally struck the Platte River at a passable ford. This negotiated, the party pressed on into the country that is now Wyoming and was then inhabited by even fewer white people than the region just traversed. The Indians were, if anything, more predatory and the soil more arid. Kit Carson had blazed the trail and Fort Laramie, the next objective of Evans' party, had been established but no pioneers had settled in this forbidding region. A Mormon outpost on the Green River had been abandoned at the approach of United States troops under Colonel Albert Sidney Johnston two years before.

Nearing Fort Laramie, Evans beheld the glittering snow topped Rockies with an ecstasy no modern tourist behind a railroad car window can experience. After weeks and weeks of slow progress by day and laborious camping by night, after having seen more buffalo than he thought there could be flies in the whole world, after despairing that the rolling prairies had a western boundary, the great mountain range suddenly raised itself majestically out of the continent and pushed its peaks into the clouds. In comparison to these towering giants, the familiar mountains of southern Virginia were mere hills.

To behold this magnificent spectacle was one thing; to penetrate the monster barrier and reach the destination beyond was quite another.

At Fort Laramie new supplies were obtained and also first hand accounts of the wonders of the transmontane country. Here were soldiers and traders who gossiped of affairs in California, Utah, Oregon, and troubled themselves less about negroes than about Indians, less about na-

tional elections than about rattlesnakes, less about cotton
than gold. This was, at last, the West. Before cowboys
or rodeos entered the Wyoming scene and at about the same
time as the inauguration of Buffalo Bill's pony express,
Robley Evans saw the real Wild West that within his own
span of life was to evanesce into a romantic memory.

So far the party had escaped the Indians. Every unfamiliar sound at night or moving object in the distance by
day had been suspected as the indication of trouble but in
each instance happily had turned out to be a false alarm.
Young Robley, however, could not repress a desire to see
these much dreaded red men in action. Shortly after the
journey was resumed at Fort Laramie, this curiosity was
satisfied. The trail, which for a surprisingly large part of
the distance had been in good or fair condition, melted into
a bog that caught one of the wagons tightly in its grip. The
combined shoulders that were put to the wheel failed to
extricate it. Darkness fell and camp was made for the night.
A tablet may some day be placed in a boulder at that spot
to mark the scene of Fighting Bob's first battle. A group
of hostile Pawnees abroad with the dawn surrounded the
party and attacked with bows and arrows. The half dozen
white men, counting the thirteen year old Robley as a man
because he could do the work of one, found cover and used
their firearms. There was a sharp skirmish. The Indians
burned the covered wagons. The defenders sustained no
casualties and retained their horses, mules and enough food
to enable them to return to Fort Laramie for new supplies.

Well, Evans had seen the Indians. He now had his own
experiences to relate upon this second visit to the Fort. No
new wagons were procurable but the fresh supplies were
placed on pack animals, better adapted to this mountainous
part of the trail.

There were several more skirmishes with the Indians
but the party was able to continue on its way. A few guns
courageously handled could counterbalance a great prepon-

derance of numbers in favour of the aborigines. In one fight, the arrows flew thick and straight before the marauders were driven off and a missile stuck in Evans' ankle, the precursor of more serious wounds to be inflicted by people of his own race and nation.

By the time the party reached Fort Bridger, its members were full fledged Indian fighters. They had now clambered through pass after pass of the Rockies to eminences from which they beheld peaks and valleys beyond number and on either side the table-land stretching away in the distance below, and they had descended into canyons that saw the sun for only an hour a day and through which cascades foamed with the roar of locomotives. The width of what later became the State of Wyoming was now behind them and the next leg of the trip would bring Evans to his destination.

At Fort Bridger the Old Oregon Trail branched off to the right, the California and Utah routes keeping to the left fork. This was for many the parting of the ways. The left trail, which, of course, Evans' party took, reached Green River at a certain ferry, which was called Robinson's because a Frenchman of that name operated a boat crossing and trading port there. His chief merchandise seems to have been whiskey, which made the Ferry a drinking hole sought by every thirsty throat in the vicinity.

A detour now occurred which constituted by far the most exciting of all of Robley's experiences with the Indians. What money was to the industrial East and slaves to the South, horses, of course, were to this land of plains and mountains. The coin that the members of the party carried in concealed belts under their clothing was relatively valueless compared to their animals, which required constant and vigilant protection. One day some Indians, simulating friendship, managed to enter the corral at Robinson's and suddenly rode off at full speed with all of the horses. Washakie and his Snake tribe soon happened to come along and, upon learning of the stampede, gave a war whoop, dashed off in pursuit and within a week brought back the stolen mounts. The party was now under the heaviest obligations to Chief Washakie and it was necessary not only to hold a series of whiskey powwows but accede to any requests he might be graciously pleased to make, drunk or sober. Robley was a favourite with his own companions and the other men at Robinson's Ferry. The big Chief now also took a fancy to him and was struck by a whim to show the lad life among the Snake Indians. A ten day visit was the "invitation" but until the visit was over Robley wondered whether or not he was ever to be released from the tribe. There was anxiety as to Washakie's intentions but Robinson knew his Indians and assured Robley's escorts that a chief who would restore stolen horses certainly could be trusted with a mere human being. The discussion was academic. The powwows over, Washakie and his followers departed up the river, taking Robley without manifesting any interest in his inclinations or the consent of the white men. He proceeded to learn more of the American Indian on this trip than a lifetime of study from the outside would have taught him. By day he rode and hunted with the band, by night he stifled in the fetid air of the Chief's own wigwam. He ate their food and wore their garments. He mastered the art of throwing the lasso, became skilled with bow and arrow and such a good all around young Hiawatha that Washakie expressed his willingness to adopt him permanently into the tribe. When Robley politely declined this honour and could not be moved even by the prospect of some day taking one of the Chief's daughters as his squaw, the old warrior was at a loss to comprehend such a perverse discard of opportunity. For a stirring few days it looked as though the boy's future indicia of rank would be feathers instead of gold braid. To an outsider he would not merely have looked like a promising young Pawnee; he would have been taken for one. True to his promise, however, and Robinson's faith, Washakie galloped in to the Ferry at the end of the stipulated period and delivered his guest, all the better for his adventure. The adults of the party could hardly believe their eyes; they thought they had seen their young comrade for the last time and were reluctantly preparing to proceed without him.

Doffing his buckskin clothing with its elaborate beaded trimming that had been made to measure by the squaws, Robley once more became a pioneer and headed westward.

The continental divide was still to be crossed. As the party picked its way along the mountain passes, much new scenic splendour was unfolded and many strange flowers, birds and other animals were observed. With dramatic suddenness, when the trail finally curved between the high steep sides of Echo Canyon, a bend was reached from where the party saw spread before it over a wide stretch of country far below, that very panorama which a dozen years earlier Brigham Young, looking up from the sick bed in which he was being transported, identified as the long sought Promised Land. There in the distance at the feet of the Alpine ranges lay the Great Salt Lake, blue and sparkling and immense. No wonder the name of its discoverer had been given to Fort Bridger. No wonder General Fremont had been enthusiastic about its beauty. No wonder the Latter-Day Saints had here established their headquarters, then called the City of the Great Salt Lake, which Evans could see laid out in checkerboard regularity, a green patch on the dusty brown plain. From one of the very few planned cities in America, he was changing his residence to another. The sight of his new home delighted him. This was a place one could be proud to represent as its first midshipman. It looked particularly attractive at a distance.

Coming down Echo Canyon, Evans had noticed the breastworks thrown up two years before by the Mormons, ready to defend their Thermopylae not against the Indians, but the United States Army. The Leonidas of the West had, however, substituted for a martyr's death on a hopeless battlefield the more agreeable fruits of successful diplomatic chicanery. The development of Utah is one of the most amazing chapters in the history of the West. It has stamped upon its every page the incredibly grotesque titan who sprang out of the Old Testament via New England, became second President of the Church of Jesus Christ of Latter-Day Saints and then the Moses of its exodus to this remote refuge.

Brigham Young had led his flock, pariahs in the East, to a land he thought immune from American persecution, only to find that the Treaty of Guadalupe Hidalgo at the close of the Mexican War ceded it to the United States, which then organized the Territory of Utah. True enough, Young had been named Governor. He proposed to run affairs strictly in accordance with the principles of Home Rule. The American flag might fly over Utah but when Washington presumed to set up a Federal judiciary there and nominate another person and a non-Mormon at that as Governor for the next term, it was going altogether too far and would have to be summarily stopped. Young shouted defiance at the United States, aroused the hostility of the Indians against the Government and prepared to resist any attempt to subdue him by force. This remarkable audacity was bound to merit the admiration of the future Fighting Bob when he heard the story of Utah and, as its future representative in the Navy (even if only lately the enemy Navy!), called upon the great bearded patriarch himself.

The cause of the trouble between the Utah Mormons and the rest of the country was, of course, due to polygamy. It had been practised for some time before Brigham Young openly proclaimed it as a tenet of the Church. The moral indignation of the country seized avidly upon an object in crusading against which the North and South could passionately unite. The emotional forbears of the Anti-Saloon Leaguers and the censorship hounds warned the shocked masses that western civilization was endangered by these

Turks of the American plains, that family life was being degraded into domestic promiscuity. The fear, envy, lust and self-righteousness of the officially monogamous majority were appealed to with success. The agitators waged a "harem-scarem" campaign that took on the uncompromising animosities of religious warfare. It was the great newspaper sensation of the day. Feeling became so intense that violence was apt to break out wherever and whenever the paths of Mormon and Gentile crossed.

After many such occurrences, turning Utah into a dangerously hostile region for all but Mormons, and after Colonel Albert Sidney Johnston had been forced into winter quarters with his Federal troops, it became obvious that the armed revolt against the United States was about to meet disaster. The resourceful Young, through the medium of a supposedly neutral party who was really a secret Mormon agent, achieved a treaty of peace with President Buchanan. When Evans arrived, Young and his adherents had been pardoned and the troops withdrawn. There had been a formal genuflexion to Federal authority and things went on merrily as before. Brigham Young had made the President ridiculous and there are many who believe that the subsequent defiance of the South was encouraged by this show of governmental weakness in Utah. Colonel Johnston for one saw that the Stars and Stripes could be flouted with impunity. For not distinguishing, however, between Buchanan and Lincoln, he was to pay with his life at Shiloh.

Young had a talent for administration that amounted to genius. When in 1847 upon closer inspection, the land of milk and honey had proved to abound in voracious wolves and alkali dust, he imposed his dream upon the reality. Let the sanctimonious Puritans inveigh against polygamy. Where among them was a prophet who could match Brigham's feat of miraculously evoking out of the air over the Lake the white gulls of heaven which devoured the swarming clouds of destructive locusts and grasshoppers? Who among their pedantic engineers had by irrigation converted a desert city into a flowering oasis?

Robley was, of course, enormously impressed by this Mormon Utopia, which was not only a garden to behold but a comfortable community in which to dwell, where Young's schemes of equal land distribution eliminated poverty and the necessities of the passing emigrant trains produced prosperity. The young visitor—or new resident—was welcomed at the home of Mr. Hooper and his fellow-travellers continued on their way to the coast. Robley was supplied with plenty of mounts and enjoyed himself riding and hunting over the plains and into the canyons.

The people seemed to be earnest, simple folk, much like other pioneers except that they took their church and its affairs more seriously. They gossiped about the number of Brigham Young's wives, a dark secret that lent an added lustre to the sturdy old oak from whose acorns grew a forest of family trees. (His spouses totalled twenty-seven.) So mild and devout seemed the inhabitants of this frontier town, that it was hard for Evans to realize that they had been ready to resist the United States Army at Echo Canyon. He knew that they must be made of rugged fibre. Not for many years, however, was Evans to learn how cruelly ruthless they could be if crossed. He was a man of thirty before the truth was unearthed that the Indians who perpetrated the flagitious 1857 Mountain Meadow Massacre of California pioneers that did not spare the women, the sick or the young and horrified the nation, was plotted and aided by Mormons high in the church hierarchy who, with greased faces and plumed heads, were more sadistic than the savages they led.

To Evans, this sojourn at Salt Lake City was simply an agreeable visit among pleasant people. He was, however, eager to complete his period of required residence and enter upon his career. The Navy was always in his mind. As he rode over to the Great Lake, one may be sure that he gazed wistfully across its saline cobalt and dreamt of the seven seas he was to roam.

At last came the time to leave for the East, a fully qualified resident of Utah. The requirements of the statute had been satisfied. It was the early summer of 1860 when the lad took his seat on the overland coach for the long return journey. This rapid transit system had just been organized. There was no serious trouble with Indians on the way, although many bands of them were encountered. There were, however, hail and rain storms and one of the most devastating specimens of the Kansas tornado.

After several weeks of rough riding from one coach station to the next, Evans again saw the brown opaque Missouri River and felt that he was restored to the nineteenth century. The train ride to Washington completed the trip home.

It was now August and the country was in the throes of the presidential campaign. Even a lad uninterested in politics could not shut his ears to the excited arguments in the trains, at the lunch counters on the way and at the capital, upon the burning issues of the day and the rival candidacies of Stephen A. Douglas and Abraham Lincoln.

In mid-September Robley Evans reported at Annapolis for his entrance examination. He passed.

"The trail of the land was over, the trail of the water began."

2

THE BROOD

~~~~~~

AT the age when boys of to-day are entering high school, these young landlubbers from every Congressional district in the country, who constituted the new fourth year class, were marched past the barracks of their seniors to the end of a long wharf and over a gangplank into the heart of the Navy. Moored alongside the pier was the U. S. S. *Constitution* and in these quarters the lads studied, drilled, messed and slung their hammocks. The fame of *Old Ironsides* had penetrated every local school room in the land. These youngsters knew of her trim lines, her tall masts, her exploits and above all the gallant sea fighters who had manned her. Now they were actually aboard of her, climbing the rigging and scrubbing the "deck once red with heroes' blood" as reverently as neophytes dusting an altar.

John Masefield has said that "there has been perhaps, no such beautiful thing on earth, the work of man's hands . . . . " as one of these old frigates with sails set and flags flying. Ever since her launching during the year of Washington's retirement from the presidency, the *Constitution* had brought prestige to our young nation when and where it was most sorely needed. She had been one of those rare ships that are born with a personality and live with character, attracting to her service the stoutest hearts and strongest hands, and sending them forth stouter and stronger—or to a sailor's grave. The Barbary Pirates and the Royal Navy had tasted her prowess. From her mizzen truck had flown the broad pennant of Commodore Edward Preble, who had made the Stars and Stripes more respected along the North African Coast than the flags of the maritime powers of Europe. Stephen Decatur had sailed in his ketch from her side to burn the captured *Philadelphia*, aground under the Bashaw's guns at Tripoli—and to *Old Ironsides* had he returned when the mission had been heroically accomplished, a feat which Nelson acknowledged as the boldest of the age. It was she that had whipped the *Guerriere* (every lad in the class was familiar with the famous picture), reduced to captivity the *Java, Cyane* and *Levant,* and seized many an enemy prize. When the infant republic had struggled for the right to commercial existence, this invincible frigate had been our most cogent argument. When the British had misunderstood English with an ex-colonial accent, the guns of *Old Ironsides* had spoken another common language more readily understood.

Faithful to her name, the *Constitution* had been fired upon, damaged and overhauled, but never destroyed—a truly symbolic "eagle of the sea." Her rosters read like scrolls of honour. If ghosts of ocean warriors return to the scene of their noblest deeds, what crowds of distinguished spectres must have haunted these decks during the midwatch! Isaac Hull, William Bainbridge, Charles Stewart, Charles Morris, John Cushing Aylwin and many, many more.

In these hallowed surroundings, inhaling tradition with every breath, Robley Evans embarked upon his career under the wholesome and inspiring influence of a corps of able officers, who took the lads in hand and made of them seagoing midshipmen. All through later life Evans realized that the Rodgers brothers had been enormously effective in shaping his adolescent mind and nature. Lieutenant Christopher Raymond Perry Rodgers and Lieutenant George Washington Rodgers came of a family that stood in the

Navy for what the Adams family did in New England
statesmanship and the Lees in Southern aristocracy. They
were the sons of George Washington Rodgers the elder,
nephews of Commodore John Rodgers and of Commodore
Oliver Hazard Perry of Lake Erie fame, and cousins of
Rear Admiral Rodgers. After them were to come other
Rodgers to perpetuate the family tradition in naval annals. Names, however weighted with celebrity, were never
more to Evans than cards of introduction. These brothers
won the youth's confidence by their patent excellence and
sterling demeanour. Frequency and intimacy of contact
increased his respect. They were superiors to obey, friends
to trust and fortunate he was to have them in the soul-
stirring months ahead.

This, of course, was the year of the impossible, when
the fruit of ancient despised black cargoes was to drive a
wedge between parts of an indivisible nation. The South
was determined to prolong and extend slavery and make the
North like it; the North was not inclined to extirpate the
institution but revolted at the insistence that it must be
flaunted and blessed. The issue was created by Northern
abolitionist minorities, made a fanatical sacred cause of
righteous principle by the South and reluctantly accepted by
the complacent majority of the North as an alternative to
dissolution of the Union. Because of the inability of his
opponents to agree upon a common candidate, Abraham
Lincoln was in November elected president by a mere plural-
ity. The intransigeant South screamed with anguish before
it was hurt. Just as the Russians mobilized in 1914 as a
nervous precaution and thereby frustrated all efforts to prevent the war, the cotton States in 1861 anticipated trouble—
and brought it. They unreasonably saw fit to accept the election of Lincoln as the curfew of their hopes for a square deal
within the Union. Over two months before he was inaugurated—during that stultifying interregnum which modern

presidents-elect devote to fishing parties or good will tours—
that stormy petrel among the States, South Carolina, announced that it would eat its Christmas pudding as a foreign
sovereignty. Old Hickory was no longer there to spank the
naughty insubordinates as he had done at the time of the
Ordinance of Nullification. There was in his place the
timid old gentleman who had trembled at the defiance of
Brigham Young and was now mumbling prayers with his
eye on the White House clock, hoping against hope that he
would be able to turn over the presidency to his successor
before any overt hostility broke forth. Peace at any price!

Encouraged by South Carolina's leadership, other Southern States fell into line during January of the new year and,
a month before Lincoln was to be sworn in and deliver his
conciliatory first inaugural, the worst fears of Daniel Webster, now nine years gone, were realized. The Confederate
States of America sprang into abortive existence.

On all sides was heard the reassuring chant that war in
those modern civilized times, war that was fratricide, war
between kith and kin over the status of illiterate Africans,
was unthinkable. The South was confident that the border
States would all secede, that Europe would insist upon its
cotton and that the North would not be so misguided as
to resist the inevitable. The North believed that the way-
ward sons would orate themselves hoarse but stop short of
violence. Fort Sumter disillusioned both sides.

The Naval Academy was a cross section of the country,
with its midshipmen from every State and Territory, together dropping their respective colloquialisms for the uniform vernacular of the sea. The Southern lads seemed to
have the current events constantly at heart while those from
the other sections thought of them only when the subject
was thrust upon their attention. The former could no more
discuss the situation than they could their religion or their
mothers' virtue; the latter at least attempted to approach it
rationally. There was in the one group the absolute con-

viction that there was a Right side and that they were on
it, in the other, a variation of opinion and a lack of concur-
rence except upon the final issue   None of the boys was
the least concerned with slavery or with any abstract constitutional theories of secession   The Southerners responded
emotionally to what they regarded as the call to defend their
very firesides, the Northerners quietly and slowly developed
a determination to stand by the Union if assailed from
within as loyally as if assailed from without

The rules were not as strict in those days regarding
confinement to the Academy grounds and the midshipmen,
especially on week ends, mingled in the charming social
circles of the old uncommercialized town of Annapolis,
whose many surviving colonial homes are still architectural
models of that period   Here the sentiment was more south-
erly than the latitude   There were frequent hops to which
the girls of the community were invited and their attitude
was Southern

As the refractory States one after another seceded,
their respective representatives at the Academy found themselves in the anomalous position of being in the Navy of a
nation to which they had suddenly become alien   The
members of the Faculty, officers and civilian instructors, appreciated only too well from their own dilemmas the trying
times that these lads were undergoing as the latter received
mail from far-off plantations and heard colours being
sounded   Home or country   What a wretched choice
What a barren decision for lads at the outset of their
careers   By tacit consent of young and old, resulting from
the common understanding bred of the predicament of the
Southerners and the personal attachment of their Northern
comrades that transcended all sectional schism, the bitter
subject in the minds of all was on the tongues of none   Occasionally as another Act of Secession was announced, there
would be a private appeal of advice to one of the officers, a

deeply touching farewell and one more young passenger on a train headed beyond the Potomac.

The case of Robley Evans, native son of Virginia, was remarkable not only for his ultimate decision but for the fact that he made it himself. When his own State broke away from the United States, instantly carrying Lee and so many other distinguished naval and military leaders along with her, when Robley learned that his younger brother had joined the Confederate Army, he felt the same tug on his loyalty to the flag that had pulled away so many of his classmates. His loyalty, however, seemed to be of sterner stuff. Still short for his years, he stood before his mentor Lieutenant George Rodgers, looked at him with those clear unflinching eyes whose splendour excited the admiration of all who ever beheld them and was reassured in the counsel he had already taken with himself. After all, Robley had burst the bonds of provincialism. Was the transcontinental pioneer who had ridden with the Chief of the Snake Indians and was as much at home in a Mormon settlement or a Nebraska trading post as in a Floyd County village or the national capital to restrict his patriotic devotion to one particular star on the flag? In his own instinctively sound respect his outlook was as broadly national as that of George Washington, John Marshall or Abraham Lincoln, although by no means as conscious and not at all philosophical in origin. If there was in all the land a native American, it was Midshipman Evans. The deliberation had been brief; already he had the admiral's gift of quick decision; and, once formulated, this important decision was unalterable. For ever after, until draped with it at the very close of the adventure, he and the flag were inalienable allies.

Mrs. Evans did not take kindly to the failure of her oldest son to assume what she profoundly believed to be his father's place. She yielded her younger boy, literally a boy, to the Great Defense and suffered the cruel misfortune

of seeing her children bear arms against each other. To
her the war of brother against brother was no oratorical extravagance. From her point of view, from her depth of
emotion, Robley was betraying his father's memory, his
family, his home and his better traditions. That this was
the grief of his mother he well knew but the die was cast.

Robley was still far from attaining the age at which his
own contractual undertakings would be binding. His
mother tried to condone his "treason" as the waywardness
of a youngster under evil influence. He would not return
to his home and duty? Very well; she would see. Much
of Robley's spirit had come from this lady. She took command of the situation and, just as she might have frustrated
the elopement plans of a daughter in her early teens, she
sent her son's resignation to the Navy Department. The
first he knew of this was upon receiving notification of its
acceptance. He was actually out of the service. Again he
turned to his confidential adviser, now, by virtue of wartime promotions, Captain Rodgers. The telegraph was not
yet in very general use but this seemed exactly the sort of
emergency for which it was adapted. Captain Rodgers
spared no words in his message of explanation to Washington and in twenty-four hours the name of Robley D. Evans
was restored to the register. His mother, at the bedside of
her seriously wounded younger son, was furious when she
learned that Robley was once more in the Yankee Academy
but this time left him to his fate, contenting herself with
writing "a very severe letter" which was transmitted by a
blockade runner. After the war, she did not withhold a
mother's unreserved forgiveness. Her other son recovered
and ended the war as a Captain on Lee's staff. Between the
brothers there never was the slightest hard feeling; there
rarely is between opposing active combatants; often, in fact,
it has to be artifically stimulated to brutalize the morale.

By the spring, when a great man had taken over the
deck on the ship of state and Fort Sumter had been fired

upon, the remaining plebes had become handy seamen, adept aloft or on deck, skilled with a marlinspike, seagoing in stride and speech. The two most important subjects in the curriculum were seamanship and gunnery: how to sail a ship and how to fight her. That was the educational doctrine of the old school of oak and hemp, and throughout his career Evans retained the conviction that it was the one best calculated to produce worthy leaders. This was still the age of sail and the midshipmen were drilled in the expert handling of every piece of canvas, every line, every part of the ground tackle, every detail of the boats. They were competent at all the tasks of mariners, experienced in the use of the clumsy ordnance then constituting ship armament and versed in the drills and the martial exactions of the naval service. Discipline was strict as indeed it must be in any efficient military organization. Evans learned to obey and his subordinates in later years rarely ventured upon any test of his tolerance to disobedience in others. President Taft once praised him as "a rigid disciplinarian" but no one who ever was his ship-mate considered him a martinet. He needed no arbitrary regulations or military system to compensate for a lack of the qualities that make for natural leadership. He was inherently competent to wear his insignia of rank and too proud to forget his duty to those who had more stripes or fewer or none at all.

This class that entered in the Fall of 1860 was a notable one. Its members became veterans before they became adults. Trained in the traditions of 1812, they were to have their baptism of fire before graduation and in their prime fight a modern steam and steel Navy to a victory over Spain. The hard-boiled school of sail and cutlass was in this Civil War period evolving into the mechanically propelled, long range school of the twentieth century. A glance at the pictures or models of the queer looking hybrid craft of this transition period shows that there was neither complete confidence in sail nor in steam. As late as 1892, Evans was to use canvas to augment his engines when pressing the *Yorktown* to Valparaiso upon the occasion of the crisis with Chile. He and his contemporaries constituted the generation that linked the navies of John Paul Jones and Nelson with the navies of Sims and Beatty, equally at home in the frigate or the dreadnought. Not many Annapolis midshipmen have been able to do their undergraduate laboratory work in a real war and then, upon attaining command rank thirty years later, find at hand another war in which to earn that military distinction which peace so seldom confers.

The youngsters in *Old Ironsides* with Evans were to wear service emblems of a great war even before they could grow the whiskers and beards then in vogue. In middle age they were to make the most of the opportunity to win a place for their country among the world powers, at the expense of the historic maritime prestige of Aragon and Castile. Many of their names were to grace the pages of history. Together they became famous as "The Brood of the *Constitution*."

Two of them were Sigsbee of the ill-fated *Maine*, who may be said to have acted the part of involuntary prologue to the Spanish War, and Dick Leary, who fired the last shot therein. Others were Harry Taylor of the *Indiana*, Charlie Clark of the *Oregon*, Jack Philip of the *Texas*, Cook of the *Brooklyn* and Chadwick of the *New York*, in command when these vessels fought alongside Evans' *Iowa* at the Battle of Santiago. Dewey's "You may fire when you are ready, Gridley" and his Chief of Staff Lamberton were of that group and also Dyer of the *Baltimore*, Wildes of the *Boston* and Jolly Joe Coghlan of the *Raleigh*, whose ships, with the *Olympia*, were the four largest in the line of battle at Manila Bay. Many ships that happened to miss both battles of that war were commanded by other officers who as midshipmen had slept and messed in *Old Ironsides* with

Bob Evans and he had other classmates in the equally responsible leading posts at the Department.

After the Spanish War, several of these lads of the early sixties attained flag rank but, as the ascent in the hierarchy brought them to narrower and narrower strata, the time came when one among them would have to be selected for supreme command. There was no disappointment among those other competent brothers in arms necessarily passed over because the choice gratifyingly fell upon Robley D. Evans.

When the Civil War opened, Captain Blake, Superintendent of the Academy, felt considerable anxiety as to the safety of his institution, situated in a region that was unfriendly, to say the least. A rumour had reached him that, as a great stimulant to the morale of the South, its new flag would be hoisted for the first time over the water on *Old Ironsides* herself. That would have been a feat indeed. The sentimental value of the aged frigate made her a more desirable prize than a modern steamer. To have started off with a coup as dramatic as the breaking of the Stars and Bars at that very gaff where her "tattered ensign" had so gloriously survived many a mortal combat would have seemed to the Confederacy to augur well for its success. How the news would have flashed over the South!

The plebes aboard were ready to defend the grand old ship against any and all assailants, but to positively ensure that "her shattered hulk should sink beneath the wave" rather than submit to capture, her magazines were mined. Now the drills took on a vital meaning. The drabness of studies and recitations gave way to the business of actual war measures.

During one mid-watch in April the look-out reported a mysterious craft standing in astern. General quarters sounded. Out of their hammocks tumbled the boys and manned the after batteries. Captain Rodgers hailed the ap-

proaching stranger as she drew nearer, silently, without
lights and seemingly with intent to board the *Constitution*
in a surprise attack. This was even more thrilling than
fighting Indians! Shades of the mighty past. Descendants
of Preble and Hull stand by! Each lad felt himself a
Decatur.

Captain Rodgers had been warned that the same
rowdies who a few days earlier had attacked the Sixth
Massachusetts Regiment in the streets of Baltimore might
undertake a bold sally of this sort. As his "ahoy" went
unanswered, the tension became acute. The command to
fire was awaited with taut lanyards. Another second and
Old Ironsides would blaze forth as of yore. W. H. Parker,
the officer in charge of the howitzer, was a Southerner
awaiting the acceptance of his resignation to join the Confederacy. He dreaded the order to fire upon his own
partisans. Years later he wrote of this horrible suspense:
" . . . . I do not hesitate to say, however, that had we
been attacked I should have stood by my guns and performed
my duty by the school. I was still an officer of the
Navy. . . . " Then—just in time to avert a tragic mistake—the vessel was identified as the ferry *Maryland*, carrying the Eighth Massachusetts Regiment. These troops had,
to avoid Baltimore, gone to Havre-de-Grace and seized the
first available means of coming down the bay. As Evans
expressed it, "what one may fairly call the variegated career
of General Benjamin F. Butler would have been very short
and inglorious had the *Constitution* opened fire."

That shrewd politician who had by virtue of his prominence in Democratic party circles obtained a brigadier gen-
eralship in the militia of his State, where previously his
vocation had been the practise of criminal law, was in command of the Regiment. When Evans first saw him under
these unusual circumstances, he was setting forth upon a
career that was to be marked by achievement but not success, by notoriety rather than fame, and was to keep him as a

cinder in the public eye until his death in 1893. A heavy
set burly man, then forty-two, with a flowing black mus-
tache, he issued his orders in the same pompous and bluster-
ing manner that had intimidated witnesses and hoodwinked
juries. Probably no Yankee was to earn deeper hatred in
the South than this rough despot and his conduct was to be
deplored even in all but the most radical Northern circles. It
was Ben Butler who was to capture New Orleans and rule
it as a conquered province, stamping contemptuously upon
the much vaunted Southern chivalry by his famous General
Order, issued it is true after some provocation, that if any
woman should "insult or show contempt for any officer or
soldier of the United States, she shall be regarded and shall
be held liable to be treated as a woman of the town plying
her avocation." Upon removal from New Orleans, he was
to meet alternately with minor gains and major losses in
his subsequent campaigns until recalled by Grant. Evans
was to see him again at Fort Fisher.

Typifying the sordid in politics and unable to clear his
name of repeated charges of corruption during wartime in
profiting from illicit trading by his relatives, he was to become the most savage of Thaddeus Stevens' bloodhounds
and, as one of the House Managers at the impeachment trial,
lead the prosecution of President Johnson before the Senate.
A character which does not mellow in retrospect, he yet
possessed a forcefulness and cunning that accomplished
things. Secretary of the Navy Welles characterized him as
"reckless, avaricious, unscrupulous." The midshipmen's
first impression of the civilian army that was rising to save
the Union was that made by this swaggering lawyer-general.

Upon reaching Annapolis, instead of being chagrined at
his awkward and almost catastrophic manner of arrival, he
characteristically proceeded to tell Captain Blake just how to
defend the Academy. Using his improvised transport to tow
the *Constitution* away from the wharf and thus place a moat
between her and the shore, the ferry was run aground with

the troops still aboard. Here they were marooned while Governor Hicks of Maryland, whose official residence was just outside the Academy grounds, vehemently insisted that no more Massachusetts regiments should enter his State. While Hicks and Butler shouted at each other and the Northern militiamen continued to sit on the mud off shore, the steamer *Boston* came along and landed the illustrious blue-blooded Seventh New York Regiment. Then, Hicks or no Hicks, the *Boston* rescued the insulated Bostonians and dumped them also on the Academy's front lawn.

This invasion broke up the routine of the institution. The soldiers swarmed over the place. As many as could be squeezed into the barracks and halls were quartered there; the rest camped outdoors. While the debarkation had been in progress, the midshipmen covered the operation against any possible interference. Deploying as per their infantry drills, the boys again beamed with a sense of importance but no opposition was offered. They were placed on sentry duty. School was suspended; the middies were playing soldier in a real game.

Maryland was on the border where Yankee met rebel. It was here that the sections overlapped and one could not be sure which way one's neighbour would jump. The secession of the South was regarded here as a *fait accompli* and beyond the possibility of the North to nullify. All the circumstances were conducive to disorder and unorganized violence; they quickly disrupted the serenity of peace. Among many other destructive deeds of less strategic significance, the railroad tracks leading to Washington had been ripped up in many places. The damage to the road-bed itself, however, had not been serious. The repair of the right of way was just the sort of task to which General Butler's driving executive ability was suited. The soldiers energetically set to work, the trains were soon in operation and the national capital reconnected with the North.

In its rapid expansion, the Army had to raise its handful of West Point graduates to high rank and hand important commissions to such outsiders as Butler, many of whom,
if men of higher moral calibre, had less ability. With the
Navy it was entirely different. You could not make even
an ensign over night. The officers needed afloat by both
sides had to be recruited chiefly from the ranks of the Navy,
which was splitting asunder like the rest of the country,
although a larger proportion than in the Army or civilian
walks of life was standing by the Union. As in most great
conflicts of world history, the armies were to occupy the
centre of attention only to have the issue eventually determined by the inexorable pressure of sea power, wielded
by these relatively few officers of the naval service. Every
defection from it was costly. The first Superintendent of
the Academy, one largely instrumental in helping Bancroft
establish it against the reactionary advice of the old timers,
Commander Franklin Buchanan, went over. There were
other serious withdrawals, over three hundred in all. Each,
of course, counted double: the Navy's loss was the South's
gain. It all had a much more personal aspect than the corresponding defections ashore.

Admiral Dewey later wrote: "The leaders on the other
side were men bred to the same traditions as we were.
Officers fought officers with whom they had gone to school,
and with whom they had served and had messed. The
recollections of old comradeship, while softening the ameni-
ties of a civil conflict, also touched us the more deeply with
the sense of its horrors and waste, and brought to its conduct something of the spirit of professional rivalry. Unlike the officers of volunteer infantry who marched South
to meet strangers against whom a strong sectional feeling
had been aroused, we knew our adversaries well. We were
very fond of them personally. To us they had neither horns
nor tails. We felt that they were fine fellows who were in

the wrong, and we knew that they entertained the same feeling toward us."

Before April was over, war had come to the Academy. Its grounds had been converted into a camp. Ten of the first year class were ordered to report for active duty. All of the other midshipmen were now quartered aboard the *Constitution* and Captain Blake pointed out to the Department the importance of transferring the school to a safer place. He recommended Newport and Secretary Welles adopted the suggestion. The books, furniture, models, movable apparatus, together with the Faculty and its families, were loaded on a steamer and, under the guidance of C. R. P. Rodgers, transported to Narragansett Bay, whither *Old Ironsides* was slowly towed via New York and moored alongside a wharf at Goat Island, midshipmen and all.

Rodgers reorganized the school despite the most vexatious obstacles. At first the officers and civilian professors were stowed away in the dank casemates in Fort Adams, at which they properly protested. A large hotel was then obtained for the use of the Academy and here it was lodged. More orders to active duty arrived for the older midshipmen. Soon there were left only the envious plebes and enough upper classmen to maintain discipline. Within a few days, however, the indefatigable Rodgers had the transplanted Academy—or what remained of it, in full operation, with the fourth year recitations and drills proceeding as usual. Had there been left at the school but one plebe and a dinghy, Captain Rodgers undoubtedly would have carried on as nearly as possible the normal curriculum. It is not to be wondered at, that forty years later the then Rear Admiral Evans wrote of the inspiring leadership of the Rodgers brothers: " . . . to them I owe everything in my professional life."

The lads worked hard, eager to be adjudged qualified for war service. They studied ashore and were drilled on

the *Constitution* and other training ships brought to Newport for the purpose. Every day saw them further advanced.

Bob Evans was popular with his classmates. His personality had made itself felt from the outset. He was not
the most brilliant at his studies but that indefinable quality
of ready adaptation to the service was obviously his. It was
not necessary to subdue his ardent spirits within the bounds
of military discipline; without any sacrifice of their buoy-
ancy, they naturally readjusted themselves to the new mode
of life. Of course, these healthy young cubs were known
to commit infractions of the rules. There were few facilities for recreational physical exercise and no organized
athletics; the surplus animal vigour had to find release where
and how it could. Fights were frequent, quickly stirred up
and quickly forgotten. An unprovoked aggression upon
members of another class would be enough to start a fistic
battle between the entire two classes. Evans gave a good account of himself whenever engaged in such combats. His
short body was all muscle and agility. He never hung back
when a fight was pending. Interfering to save another
small chap from the beating of an immense bully he brought
upon himself the proverbial fate of a peacemaker and spent
several days thinking it over in the undisturbed tranquillity
and darkness of the brig before the Commanding Officer
heard the whole story and moved the bully into Robley's
cell, restoring the latter to duty. This escapade occurred while
the school was still at Annapolis and is narrated by his classmate, Midshipman Morgan, who subsequently served in the
lost cause and lived to write *Recollections of a Rebel Reefer.*
"Occasionally we had a little excitement on board of *Old
Ironsides.* One day 'Fighting Bob' Evans, not known by
that sobriquet in those days, gave us a thriller. Two boys,
one big and the other small, had an altercation. Bob had
nothing to do with it, but *con amore* proposed to the big
boy that he would help the little one lick him. The little

boy like a goose said that he did not want anybody to help him, that he would cut his antagonist with a knife if he was touched. An officer passing by heard the remark, and thinking that it was Evans who made it, promptly put him under arrest and marched him to the captain's cabin, and preferred the charge against him. Under the midshipmen's code poor Bob could not squeal on his comrade.

"Captain Rodgers arose from his seat. His wrath was majestic—'And so, sir!' he said to Evans, 'you propose to raise a mutiny on board of my ship. I will let you know, sir, that a midshipman has hung to a yardarm for mutiny before this, and you dare try to raise one and I will hang you!' And turning to the officer said, 'Confine him below.' To one ignorant of the annals of the service this hanging business would have sounded like an empty threat, but it must be remembered that the hanging of Midshipman Spencer, son of the Secretary of War, on board of the brig *Summers* was at that time an affair of comparatively recent date, and worse than that the captain of the *Summers,* Alexander Slidell McKensie, was a 'Rodgers,' and Bob did not know but what the hanging of midshipmen ran in the blood.

"The wardroom of the old frigate was away down below the water line and the after staterooms were as dark as Erebus. Bob was confined in the darkest of them. He stood it for about twenty minutes and then requested that he should be allowed to write a letter. Permission being granted, he was taken into the light, and pen, ink, and paper furnished him, and this, according to the story which filtered down to us midshipmen, was the letter he wrote to his uncle, a lawyer in Washington:—

'My Dear Uncle:—
I have committed mutiny and they are going to hang me. If you want to see me again come quickly to your affectionate nephew, ROBLEY D. EVANS.'

"Poor little Bob, he was only fourteen years of age and of very small stature for his years."

The same volume mentions that, many years after the war, these friendly enemies again met under circumstances that permitted Evans to perform a valuable favour for his old classmate.

The course of transcendent importance was seamanship. It was learned by the practical method of first making the future officers able-bodied seamen. Later classes studied the "Sailor's Bible," the standard text book on seamanship written for the maritime world by Stephen B. Luce. No one seems to a student more exalted in authority than the author of the written word that must be mastered. Post-war midshipmen deferentially looked up to "the man who wrote the book." He seemed the fount of nautical knowledge. In 1861, however, he had not published his great opus and was just a capable officer and inspiring teacher. After distinguishing himself in the opening naval engagements of the war, he came to Newport to assist in the training. Still a young man, he impressed the lads as a sage of ripened years, a veritable Father Neptune, with prematurely greying side whiskers, clean cut features and officer-like bearing.

All week the drills and studies would be pursued and then, on Saturdays, trespassing upon the week end liberty, Luce would take his charges out in the sloop-of-war *Marion* and let them put into execution the fruits of their learning. They would rotate in all the positions aboard ship from deck officer to deck hand.

Evans wrote: "Everything must be done with our own hands, and thus we learned, and learned thoroughly, what a man had to do in every position on board a sailing ship, from passing a close reef to sweeping down the quarter-deck."

The famous tenor voice of Luce could be heard giving the commands as the old sloop stood out each Saturday morning into Narragansett Bay. How the families of these lads, scattered all over the country, would have marvelled at the spectacle of their son's membership in this apparently salt-born crew as it made and lowered sail.

"Loose sail! Up top gallant and Royal Yards!"

"Aloft sail loosers! Set taut! Sway out of the chains!"

"Man the clewjiggers and buntlines!"

There was a poetic rhythm in this age of sail that accounts for the reactionary resistance to the substitution of steam.

Had this been a group of young Breton fishermen or New Bedford whalers, an observer would have remarked that blood will tell.

Luce was not content with proficiency under normal conditions. His youngsters must also be able to handle a ship in any emergency. Often, for example, he would select a soft sand bar and deliberately beach the *Marion* so that the midshipmen could learn how to float a grounded vessel.

Luce was "the master of his trade," as Evans said, and had the ability to impart his knowledge. The handsome Academy building now devoted to seamanship is appropriately called Luce Hall. A destroyer that rendered valuable service in the World War was named for him.

This great teacher was to outlive his renowned pupil. At the age of ninety, five years after Robley Evans passed away, the grand old man of the American Navy was to end a life of marked achievement. The Naval War College, for whose organization he was responsible, had become a flourishing institution and an important part of the Navy, the United States Naval Institute was the vastly better for his eleven years' presidency and he had set a high standard for American naval seamanship that endures to this day; all in addition to an active career afloat, including supreme command of the Fleet.

Bob Evans was one of the most expert among his classmates at the science and art of Luce seamanship. In the summer of '63, the midshipmen were embarked on a combination training cruise and blockade patrol, as was the habit during the war. Luce took some of the men across the Atlantic in the *Macedonian;* the others were in Long Island Sound in the *Marion* and the converted yacht *America,* none of which craft had even auxiliary engines. Lieutenant Commander "Pat" Matthews, commanding the *Marion,* wrote in a report to Luce:

"During the night, the wind freshened and we beat through the Race having all hands on deck. Midshipman Evans (acting Lieutenant) had charge of the deck while beating through and worked ship beautifully, displaying a perfect knowledge of the value of the different sails in steering a ship in a strong tide-way. He also reefed the topsails during his watch with little or no assistance from me."

The previous summer Evans and his classmates had been on a similar cruise in the sloop-of-war *John Adams,* which took them down the coast and into Chesapeake Bay, where they came into close contact with the peninsula campaign. This whetted Robley's curiosity to visit the front and he devoted his leave to so doing. Two features of army life disgusted him: the slowness of the operations and the general inefficiency of the organization, as evidenced by the numbers of stragglers and deserters behind the lines as well as the sloppiness of everything he saw. Nothing seemed "ship shape." He always disliked soldiering, as most naval officers do, and this distaste was engendered before he met with dire injuries while fighting ashore as an infantryman a couple of years later. The Army seemed to lack the clean, hard, expert dash and *esprit de corps* of his beloved service. It must also be remembered that Evans entered the Navy to go to sea and not, as George Dewey, for example, who first sought an appointment to West Point, in order to enter a branch of the military.

While in Washington, Robley thought that he recognized

a familiar enemy in civilian garb. Neither made a sign or spoke a word as the encounter was in a public place and identification of the Southerner would have proved fatal. Yes, Robley realized, as his heart almost stopped beating, it was his own brother!

3

FORT FISHER

~~~~~~

ADMIRAL Sir Cyprian Bridge, appraising the Civil War with the perspective of time and distance and the detachment of non-partisanship, has observed that " . . . peace had been re-established for several years before the American people could be made to see the great part taken by the navy in the restoration of the Union. . . . "

In the midst of the campaign, when the rival armies were absorbing popular attention, Lincoln reminded the North of the vital importance of "Uncle Sam's web-feet."

"At all the watery margins they have been present. Not only on the deep sea, the broad bay, and the rapid river, but also up the narrow, muddy bayou, and wherever the ground was a little damp, they have been and made their tracks."

The sound strategy for the North was simple enough, if like many simple matters it was at first not so obvious. The agricultural Confederacy with its wealth concentrated in land and slaves, both devoted to the cotton industry, must be commercially isolated. To accomplish this, the boundaries on land and water must be closed. The Mississippi must, as Lincoln expressed it, "flow unvexed to the sea," thereby depriving the South of all supplies, chiefly of foodstuffs, from the West. The Federal troops must crush ever southward the sectional frontier and eventually beat into submission the rebel armies. Lastly, the extensive coast line from the Rio Grande around Florida to the capes of Chesapeake Bay must be shut in by a wall of sea power. This would smother the South while the control of the sea would permit the North to maintain its international trade without interference and transport troops from point to point along the enemy coast to meet the ever changing military requirements.

The South had cotton. It was rich in cotton. Let the rebels, reasoned Lincoln, eat their cotton, shoe their soldiers with it, use it to construct artillery, to substitute for sulphur and nitrate.

This was the program, more or less clear in the minds of the Federal Government at the outset and becoming increasingly so as the war continued. It was carried out. It was based upon sea power. Lee's brilliant manœuvres deferred the evil day but, as Mahn said of Napoleon, he was at last vanquished by "far-distant, weather-beaten ships" that silently starved his commissaries, cut off his munitions and reduced the equipment of his men to the barefoot hardships reminiscent of Valley Forge. Like Washington's, Lee's genius shone brightest in the sustenance of his army's morale despite its sufferings, while the decision was being rendered afloat. Only in Lee's case there was no Admiral DeGrasse with a French Fleet to turn the scales his way.

Writing of the strategy of the Confederacy, Major-General Sir Frederick Maurice, the celebrated military scientist, said: "There could not be any question of the conquest of the Union States or of the subjection of their people. These were both militarily and politically out of court. The object of the Southerners was to convince the Northerners that it was not worth while to force them to remain in the Union."

Thus to win the war, the South needed only to keep alive; to do this, however, it was necessary to break down the Navy's control of the sea; this required alien assistance;

and Jefferson Davis hoped almost until the bitter end that
the fleet of either England or France would come to the
rescue.

A few days after Sumter, Lincoln signed the death
sentence of the Confederacy when he announced the blockade. It was a bold step that could have been taken by only
a courageous leader. It disregarded the embarrassment of
impliedly recognizing a state of belligerency with an enemy
whose national existence was denied. It did not stop to
calculate the force necessary to render the blockade effective—to render it more than a mere paper blockade of the
calibre we had ourselves protested against during the Na-
poleonic Wars.

The proclamation had been carefully drafted by Secretary of State Seward and was issued at Washington without
a smile. The South, however, laughed aloud. It was
sanguine that the edict would be impossible to enforce and
that the result of interfering with the exportation of cotton
would be to antagonize England and France to the breaking
point. Surely the British would not endure privations in
order to preserve a foreign Union. (To the everlasting
credit of its textile workers, Lancashire was ready to actually
hunger when the war later became partly a crusade to free
the slaves.) Well, the South laughed first——.

H. W. Wilson, a noted British naval historian, has
thoughtfully concluded that "the blockade was by far the
vastest naval operation attempted down to the date of the
Civil War."

The coast to be blockaded was about three thousand
miles in length. This policy having been adopted, it now devolved upon Gideon Welles to carry it out. He had assumed
the Secretaryship of the Navy upon Lincoln's inauguration
and found that the Buchanan Administration had turned over
this arm of the government in no better shape than the
others. There were altogether less than a hundred vessels
in commission, all far inferior to the newer warships of the

European maritime powers. Only forty were steamers and of these not one was armoured, eight were totally ineffective, a few others unfit for immediate duty and twenty-four were scattered over the world as though the domestic skies had been cloudless.

Welles set about his task from the keel up. The superannuated veterans who solely by virtue of survival congested the higher grades of the Navy were weeded out by appropriate legislation. The independent bureaus were virtually placed under a Chief of Staff by the brilliant designation of Lieutenant Fox, a naval officer, as Assistant Secretary. The personnel of the entire service was increased. Every shipbuilding resource was exploited to the utmost.

The South was never ocean-minded and, although the officers who forsook the Navy to defend their States did everything humanly possible to counter the growing sea strength of the North, their courage, toil and ingenuity were unable to do more than delay the inevitable.

David Dixon Porter, later Admiral, descended the Mississippi with gunboats and controlled the river as far as Vicksburg. Farragut bravely forced his way up from the estuary to New Orleans and took that leading Southern metropolis. Grant joined both jaws of these pincers and the river flowed "unvexed to the sea." The first part of the major strategy had thus been completed when this campaign was brought to a successful termination in the summer of '63, the summer that Gettysburg checked the advance of Lee and threw his Army, in want of food and supplies because of the effect of the blockade, back across the Potomac never to return.

Under international law, the blockade proclamation was invalid because no blockade existed in fact; it was a mere declaration of intention. The sea gates of the South were wide open and at the outset vessels encountered no interference when passing through them. Welles and Fox were working quietly but diligently. As the first war summer approached, single United States warships appeared off Hampton Roads, Pensacola, Charleston, Savannah, Mobile and New Orleans. Then they were sighted in squadrons. The fence was being erected but it had wide spaces and few posts. Blockade running was simple. There was just enough danger to attract the adventuresome and the enterprising. Traffic was soon impeded to an extent that affected prices but did not threaten its extinction. The importation of manufactured products was curtailed sufficiently to stimulate the resourceful Southern women to devise all manner of ingenious substitutes but this situation was at first no more serious than a game that broke the monotony of wartime loneliness and gave the players a gratifying sense of active participation in the great event. Nassau and Havana boomed with the contraband commerce. Profiteers flourished.

Then more and more vessels flying the Stars and Stripes patrolled the Gulf and South Atlantic coasts. "Ships will win the war" was cried in the yards during the sixties as well as during the World War. The hammers flew. The ironclad *Merrimac* of the Confederacy inspired not only the *Monitor* but all manner of other armoured vessels of almost every conceivable size and shape. The harbour entrances of the South became more and more crowded with the units of this mushroom Navy. The far flung ships had all been recalled and refitted. The waters were now teeming with Federal craft.

Blockades do not assault with dramatic strokes; they squeeze with an ever increasing constraint, whose gradual application is no more visible than the motion of an hour hand. Four years it took to throttle the South and, with the vastly changed materiél and resources of a half century later, it again took four years to throttle the Central Empires. The strongest link in the latter was forged by the same Navy that had not balked at the three thousand mile blockade order. It was the Americans who in the World War conceived and for the most part lay the North Sea mine barrage from Great Britain to Norway, while the older powers were saying it could not be done.

The South was ill suited to withstand a blockade. The only necessary element it possessed for such a defence was the fortitude of its population. It soon felt the pinch in every corner of the beleaguered district and in every hour of the day. Not a habit was immune from ruthless violation; not a want was adequately satisfied; not a man or woman, child or invalid, soldier or civilian escaped. The South had relied upon its rivers for inland transportation and the railroads were therefore few and poorly equipped. They utterly failed in the time of need. The few supplies within the lines could not readily be shipped to the points of direst need. Each town, almost each plantation, was thrown pretty much upon its own meagre resources. There were no raw materials, no plants, no goods and the cream of the manhood was under arms. Like lost Arctic explorers rich only in ice that might be worth its weight in gold on the equator, the Southerners were glutted with cotton, piled in heaping bales on the lifeless wharves, until the very sight of it was revolting to them. Ironically, the Southern people and the Lancashire people were both in poverty because huge quantities of this commodity were in the wrong place.

As it became more and more difficult to elude the ships on patrol, the price of cotton in Liverpool and of necessaries in the South reached such staggering figures that the rewards tempted more adventurers to take the risk. Many blockade runners penetrated the lines, some even in sail boats, but gradually, as year followed year, the barrier became increasingly impassable and the isolation of the Confederacy was bringing it to its knees.

England and France did not obtain cotton and did not interfere. Louis Napoleon wavered; Palmerston threatened; Gladstone, Chancellor of the Exchequer, committed his famous indiscretion by saying at Newcastle, in the heart of the textile district:

> "We know quite well that the people of the Northern States have not yet drunk of the cup—they are still trying to hold it far from their lips—which all the rest of the world see they nevertheless must drink of. We may have our own opinions about slavery; we may be for or against the South; but there is no doubt that Jefferson Davis and other leaders of the South have made an army; they are making, it appears, a navy; and they have made what is more than either, they have made a nation."

This rekindled Jefferson Davis' hopes that the Royal Navy would bring deliverance. Charles Francis Adams, however, was on the Saint James's diplomatic front and the new monitors inspired British respect.

The North did not drink of Mr. Gladstone's cup.

The Federal forces afloat increased until there were over six hundred ships in commission. They captured, burned, sank and drove ashore fifteen hundred and four vessels that attempted to run the blockade, the value of which, including the cargoes, exceeded thirty-one million dollars.

The North, with its handful of officers as a nucleus, had developed a great Navy under the pressure of struggling for the survival of the Union.

The strategy of the North was succeeding not only in the blockade but also in the other anticipated attributes of its control of the sea. After romantic gestures like the cruise of the *Alabama,* the ocean lanes were almost freed of Confederate craft. There was relatively more damage to Federal commerce than the dramatic exploits of the *Emden* and the *Seeadler,* in the early days of the war against Germany, inflicted upon allied trade, but the net effect upon the outcome of the war was no greater.

Meanwhile, the United States armies could and did throw reinforcements up and down the coast as the situation dictated. This was a particularly important factor in the peninsula campaigns.

Lee's early victories were Pyrrhic. What availed a few miles of barren territory when the South needed an open seaport? What availed a respite of a few more months when there was no means of supporting the country during the period thus gained?

Farragut was making naval history in the Gulf and his victories, in contrast to Lee's, were substantial as well as brilliant.

Bob Evans' war services were performed in the Atlantic zones in connection with the blockade. This blockade consisted of two major kinds of operations: the interception of blockade runners and the seizure of the principal Confederate coastal strongholds.

During most of the war, Evans was still at the Academy, part of the time on practise and patrol cruises, the balance at Newport. At Fort Fisher he would in 1865, at the age of nineteen, become a man and know a man's suffering, but before that he was still every inch a boy. One night he saw some classmates in the park being spied upon by a watchman who evidently was eager to apprehend them in the act of violating a minor school regulation. This kind of sneakiness never found favour with Bob and he ended the offensive sleuthing by a well aimed stone. The watchman went to the hospital and his assailant to the brig. The prisoner, far from being chastened into submissive passivity, hit the sentry guarding him because the latter insisted upon rigidly enforcing the rule that the place must remain in darkness. This convinced the commanding officer that a severe punishment was in order and it was a fortnight before the culprit was restored to duty. Unlike most of the judges of criminal courts, Evans in after years understood exactly what he was doing when imposing a sentence of confinement.

After the summer cruise of the *Marion* referred to in the

preceding chapter, Captain Matthews was so pleased with the ability displayed by this midshipman that he had no hesitancy in recommending him as an acting lieutenant to help officer the *Governor Buckingham,* one of the new war steamers, which was commanded by a salty naval veteran of the old school and had a combination Navy and merchant marine crew. The latter were to work the ship during the daytime; the former at night; a most unusual and difficult arrangement which never could have been conceived excepting under the stress of war and to meet its exigencies. Bob Evans looked even younger than he was and it was made only too clear to him at the outset that he would be cursed from, above and ignored from below unless he established his authority. This he made up his mind to do at the very first opportunity, which the circumstances indicated would not be long in presenting itself. The ship coaled. This was a task at which all hands were expected to turn to. One of the men had imbibed more than his share of grog and, instead of being stimulated by the liquor to work with increased vigour, he was fortified by it to ignore Evans' orders and just sat down. Unfortunately for him, he relaxed one deck too near the water. Evans was standing on the deck above with a brass voice trumpet in his hand. Lieutenant and trumpet descended together, the trumpet striking the sluggard's head. While the rest of the men gaped in respectful astonishment, Evans bandaged his victim, tied him securely to prevent any further trouble and continued coaling ship. His prestige was now assured.

After this cruise, he took a short but thrilling one in command of the converted yacht *America.* The thrill was derived from the fact that this ship with her crew of fellow midshipmen constituted his first command. Enemy craft were vainly sought off Cape Cod.

On October first, 1863, Evans and his classmates were commissioned acting ensigns. He was ordered to the steamer *Powhatan,* a side-wheeler whose spread of canvas almost obscurred her smoke stack. The Captain was thoroughly disliked and every one was delighted when his tyrannical dictatorship was subordinated to the seniority of Admiral Lardner, who shifted his flag to the *Powhatan* in the West Indies. Evans has given us a vivid description of the Admiral: "To a naturally fluent tongue the admiral added a vocabulary of oaths so fine that it was musical, and when aroused he did not hesitate to speak his mind in the language all seamen understand. At the same time his black eyes shone like fireflies, and his white moustache bristled, each hair standing on end. He certainly was a darling, and much beloved by all of us."

Among other things, Evans took full advantage of this post-graduate course in nautical profanity and his shipmates all bear testimony to his conscientious efforts in keeping alive and even reinvigorating this "language all seamen understand."

These were days of iron men, all right. Liberty was infrequent and the crew indulged in almost daily brawls. That the deck hands and "black gang" would fight each other was to be expected but the atmosphere became so unruly that members of these factions even fought among themselves. These were by no means the orderly boxing bouts that occur to-day beneath the flood lights during a "happy hour" on a modern battleship; far from it, these altercations resulted in serious injuries and, when a few terminated with loss of life, even the old Admiral thought that the lads were getting somewhat too rough. As a remedy, he put in to what were then the Danish West Indies and now the Virgin Islands to grant liberty.

This did not prove to have the desired pacific effect. In addition to plenty of the place's celebrated rum, there was an English squadron in port. The feeling between the respective crews was not of the best. A short time after the starboard watch had shoved off from the *Powhatan*, the British Admiral sent a frenzied message that several of his men had

U. S. S. *POWHATAN* IN A STORM

been killed in a fight between them and the Americans. Admiral Lardner shouted a volley of oaths and, far from recalling the liberty party, sent ashore the port watch! The Danish garrison made matters worse by attempting to stop the riot. The native negroes sided with the English and the *Powhatan's* crew had a strenuous afternoon before the general recall signal was hoisted. Evans went to the landing in charge of one of the running boats and, as he approached, saw the fighting still in progress. Before he realized what was happening in the boat, the crew leaped ashore, stretchers in hand, and jumped into the fray. He followed, also with a stretcher, to chase his men back into the boat, but his temperament triumphed and, upon seeing an American sailor being attacked by three or four natives, he also was swinging his weapon. An oar came down over his shoulders and he replied with a stone that knocked out his assailant's front teeth.

The *Powhatan's* casualty list was three dead and many badly hurt. There was no more liberty that trip for the crew. They had to content themselves once more with internal fighting. The medicine had proved worse than the disease.

The officers, however, became acquainted with several of the West Indies. Evans saw Hayti in its most turbulent era and Havana when it was prospering as the result of the blockade running traffic. Here he indulged in big black cigars almost as long as he was.

When in November 1864 the *Powhatan* anchored in Hampton Roads, the war was entering upon its final phase. The well supplied cohorts of the North were facing Lee's ragged and hungry remnant of an army. Grant was preparing to deliver the *coup de grace* in the spring (but then other Federal generals had been equally sanguine about other springs). Sherman was menacing the rear. Atlanta, the strategic centre of the Confederate interior, had fallen before his army, possibly the best equipped in the world at that time. The March to the Sea was under way. Sheridan's cavalry was riding up and down the Shenandoah Valley. Those were the operations that engrossed the attention of the populace while the unobtrusive and, from a distance, undramatic power of the Navy bore down upon the South more heavily each week, an irresistible tide sweeping in from the sea, creeping into the bays and harbours and up the navigable rivers.

The life-blood of the South was being dried up by this salty intrusion. Jefferson Davis was no longer the peerless leader. The Richmond Government was losing the confidence of the Confederacy. A revolution within a revolution was far from impossible.

The Mississippi and every Gulf port were now in Federal hands and the national flag flew over every principal harbour on the Atlantic excepting only Charleston and Wilmington. The former was effectively closed by the blockading patrol but the thirty ships guarding the two entrances to Wilmington, North Carolina, were unable, because of the conformation of the coast at those points and the fog and storms that were so steadily encountered there, to prevent runners from slipping in and out. Here, where the Cape Fear River emptied into the sea, the Confederates had endeavoured to establish impregnable fortifications that would ensure the protection of this key position. The only way to bottle up Wilmington was to reduce these defences. That would shut the last gap in the blockade wall.

At Cape Hatteras the coast of North Carolina makes a sharp turn and falls away to the southwest in two concave arcs, terminating in headlands that are respectively known as Cape Lookout and Cape Fear. Off this shore tosses one of the nastiest stretches of water in the North Atlantic.

Cape Fear is at the southern extremity of Smith Island, on the sides of which lie the two deep entrances to the Cape Fear River. This is the greatest of the streams that rise

in the Piedmont plateau and, flowing southeast wholly within
the State, drain the coastal plain region. For over one hundred miles from its mouth, the river is navigable and for
thirty miles of the way has a channel deep enough to permit
the passage of large ocean-going vessels. As early as 1730
a settlement was located at this head of commercial' navigation, named New Liverpool and then New Town. In nine
years, having grown to a size that entitled it not only to
incorporation but the name of a British nobleman, it was
rechristened for the Earl of Wilmington. This, however,
did not mollify its indignation at the Stamp Act nor its
chagrin at the British occupation during the Revolutionary
War, when Lord Cornwallis here established his headquarters.

Wilmington was a city of about fifteen thousand when
the Civil War broke out; about half the population were
negroes. Sprawled along the banks of the river whose
estuary became the most difficult of all Southern rivers to
effectively blockade, it soon thrived with the contraband
commerce. It was the runner's delight. The very hazards
to navigation that harassed mariners off Cape Fear, shielded
the elusive little craft that could dart quickly past the patrol
squadrons and disappear through one of the two channels
into the lee of Smith Island. These channels were only
six miles apart on a straight line but the dangerous Frying
Pan Shoals that constituted a submerged extension of the
island separated the two gateways by a forty mile sea route.
Wilmington thus had to be guarded as though it were two
distinct ports. Each entrance was protected by strong coast
fortifications: the southern by Fort Caswell and the eastern
(New Inlet) by Fort Fisher, on Federal Point. These batteries obliged the two blockading forces to keep out of
range. Each of the latter was deployed in a semi-circle, ten
miles or more in length, with the extremities near the beach.
If a ship ventured too near the entrance, the guns ashore
quickly would render the position untenable.

Coming in, the runners would plan a landfall at sundown, wait for pitch darkness, dash through the lines and soon be under the wing of one fort or the other. Leaving, they would descend the river from Wilmington by daylight, lie off Smithville, behind the island and midway between the entrances, until night and then sneak out through the channel which at the time seeemed least alertly watched. Of all the Confederate seaports, Wilmington was the best designed for blockade running, and here that actvity made its last stand. Despite the ever increasing size of the squadrons and the utmost vigilance of the lookouts, it seemed impossible to catch all of the runners as long as both forts remained in the hands of the enemy. When the other ports had been sealed, Lee depended upon Wilmington for his irreducible minimum of supplies. British naval officers on leave were among the skilful navigators who plied this blockade-running trade. Under assumed names, they sought the excitement and the one thousand pound bonus offered for a successful round trip. Various expedients were adopted by the North to stop this and no pains were spared in the application of experience but it was recognized that there was no wholly satisfactory alternative to the reduction of the land batteries.

Admiral Porter assured the Government that this latter was feasible. His opinion carried weight. The son and grandson of distinguished American naval officers, the brother of two others and the foster brother of Admiral Farragut, he had recently been voted the thanks of Congress for "opening the Mississippi River" by his notable achievements at Vicksburg. The name Porter had in the service a connotation similar to that of the name Rodgers, and David Dixon, the third in direct line of renowned David Porters, had already given it added lustre.

To him was entrusted the naval command of the expedition. In wretched contrast, the Army sent no more worthy leader to coöperate in the joint operation than General Ben

Butler, commanding Fortress Monroe. General Weitzel, a military engineer, was sent along.

Elaborate plans were drawn up. Admiral Porter assembled at Hampton Roads, that pivotal point in so many American naval campaigns, the greatest armada that had ever flown the Stars and Stripes. Every kind of warship from the largest ironclad steamer to the smallest converted yacht, representing almost every age and every theory of shipbuilding, was among those present. All were overhauled, refitted and put in first class battle trim. Then they were sent to the drill grounds in the Bay for target practise. It was obvious that a monster project was in the wind. Every sailor had his guess as to what it might be and there were rumours on each ship, authenticated as "straight from the scuttle-butt." The ladies ashore were positive that they knew and the secret disclosures whispered by them to dancing partners mentioned as the fleet's certain destination almost every place along the enemy coast.

Admiral Porter and his staff, who alone knew the plans, kept their mouths shut and, when movement orders were finally issued, they were in sealed envelopes to be opened at sea. One day in December the great expedition got under way and stood out of the Roads, past the Rip-Raps and between the Capes, in three imposing columns, the crowded troopships and supply vessels under General Butler in the centre. From the *Powhatan* flew the broad pennant of Commodore Schenck, commanding the third division of the fleet. Bob Evans was setting forth to battle.

After a remarkably smooth passage to the southward, the Army transports were anchored along the North Carolina shore near New Inlet and the naval forces about twenty-five miles off that entrance, to seaward. The mystery was solved. Those omniscient sailors who had proclaimed Fort Fisher as the objective went about the decks boasting "I told you so." This then was the mission: nothing less ambitious than the storming of the Gibraltar of the Confederacy.

Well, mused the Navy, if Butler holds up his end, Porter can be depended upon to hold up his.

In command of the Fort was Colonel William Lamb, one of the really distinguished officers of the South, who combined a thorough military erudition with a genius for leadership. Ordered to Fisher on July fourth, 1862, he designed a modern coast fortification to replace the indefensible old works then on the point. Despite almost every conceivable obstacle he proceeded to build in accordance with these plans and by the winter of 1864 had accomplished wonders. A soundly devised system of batteries and fortifications had sprung up out of the sand and marsh grass as if by magic. There were forty-four large guns. The land face of the Fort was almost half a mile in extent; the sea face over a mile. The outer works and the intricately arranged interior were the product of the commander's rich knowledge of the subject. He profited by the recorded experience of military history. When Admiral Porter eventually inspected Fort Fisher, he pronounced it vastly superior to the famous Malakoff Fortress which he had seen shortly after the then recent Crimean campaign and which the French and British had told him was the world's strongest citadel. Under the handicap of very limited matériel and unskilled negro labour, Lamb had surpassed the structural achievement of the Imperial Russian Government with all its military tradition.

A heavy gale raised havoc with the exposed fleet and transports, scattering them over a large area and delaying operations until they could be reassembled. Finally the forest of masts over the horizon indicated to the Fort what was about to happen.

The naval bombardment was delivered on Christmas Eve and Christmas Day, in accordance with the carefully formulated General Order drafted by the Admiral before leaving Hampton Roads. An old vessel was loaded with two hundred and fifteen tons of powder, driven directly towards the Fort in the middle of the night and set off with a terrific detonation about four hundred yards off shore. When the smoke cleared away and nothing remained but a mass of floating débris, the Fort was still intact. This powder boat had been a pet scheme of Butler's which, like its creator, turned out to be all sound and fury, signifying nothing.

One of the officers in the fleet later wrote: "At the anchorage, twenty-five miles from the powder-boat, there was the appearance of distant lightning on the horizon; then came, after a lapse of time, a dull sound, and after a couple of hours a dense powder-smoke that shut out the view and was an hour in passing."

The explosion, however, was the signal for the fleet to close and the divisions stood in toward New Inlet, keeping station despite the diversity of their types. Colonel Lamb and his nine hundred men who constituted the garrison watched the approach of what looked like the navies of the world, past and present, raising their hulls out of the water against the dawn of the eastern sky. Porter proposed to fight at short range and the vessels headed straight for the muzzles of the coast batteries. In the van came the *New Ironsides* leading the first division, then the second division headed by the *Colorado,* whose Executive Officer was young Lieutenant George Dewey, and then the rest of the armada.

Bob Evans was thrilled at the spectacle of such a huge naval force swinging into action. The *Powhatan* anchored at the exact spot specified in the plan and brought her full starboard broadside to bear on the Fort, less than a mile away. Her line of sight becoming blocked by the *Brooklyn,* however, Commodore Schenck moved into shallower water even closer to the Fort and now every salvo hit the target. His official report tallied over three hundred shots. The rest of the fleet, now spread in a gigantic arc around the Fort, was doing as well, and never before had a coastal battery been subjected to such a tremendous bombardment. Porter's order had emphasized the elementary doctrine of gunfire: accuracy first, rapidity second. The Southerners withstood the shells as long as they possibly could. Everything inflammable went up in smoke. The garrison was finally forced to take refuge in the bomb-proofs under the traverses.

In the meantime, the troops were landed up the beach and it looked to all in the fleet as though Porter would certainly attain his desire to give Fort Fisher to the Government as a Christmas present. The garrison, huddled in the bomb-proofs, bravely hoped for a miracle. Many of them felt that the end had come. Not so, however, Colonel Lamb. He strode the broad parapet watching the gigantic fusillade, supremely confident that his foresight and efforts of the past two and a half years had achieved results that the fleet could not overcome. He saw that the fire was diffused and that for every shell that struck the Fort, a great many whistled harmlessly overhead or fell short. He was not to be disturbed merely by noise and to his great relief the day passed without many vulnerable spots being struck. The ships were not concentrating upon any definite objective, while the Colonel slyly diverted many shots by setting up at the extreme wings of the Fort tempting flags upon which the Northerners wasted a great deal of perfectly good ammunition.

As the cannonade from the sea continued, the infantry deployed down the peninsula. When the ships ceased firing to avoid hitting these Federal troops, the foremost skirmish line crept to within fifty yards of the Fort. The landward parapet was now manned by the garrison, which had just emerged from the bomb-proofs upon the cessation of the naval fire. An officer and three or four of the Northern men, in a frenzy of enthusiasm, rushed across the intervening space to the slope of the landward parapet. They returned with a horse and the flag of the Confederacy. This gave rise to an exaggeration that had an important effect at the time and has been handed down into history, where it now seems to be permanently entrenched.

Butler has only himself to blame for the misunderstanding. Accepting camp gossip at its face value, he boasted in his letter to Admiral Porter that his men had captured this horse inside the entrance of the Fort and that one of them had wrenched the flag from its staff on the top of the parapet. Colonel Lamb, who was an eye witness of the whole performance, positively denied that any Federal troops had been that close to the Fort. He said that the horse belonged to a courier who had left the enclosure with a message and was shot well within the Federal lines and that the flagstaff had first been shattered by an enfilading shot from one of the ships and then had fallen to the lower palisades toward the leading Federal skirmishers. The credible testimony of other persons present is in accord with this version, which, although contradicting Butler, extracts some of the odium from his next move.

This particular stage of the fighting, whether or not any of the assailants reached the Fort, marked the point of furthest Federal advance on the land side. The miracle for which the less sanguine members of the garrison had been praying now came to pass. The Army of the North withdrew! When General Butler realized that the little garrison was still alive and offering resistance, when night came on and with it a wild storm, he precipitately fled. Victory— so painstakingly planned on such a huge scale and so vital a part in the strategy of the cause—was cast away when seemingly within reach. Colonel Lamb insisted for the remaining years of his long life that lasted well into the twentieth century that Fort Fisher could never have been taken in that first attack. He corroborated Butler's opinion that the barrage of the fleet had not done sufficient damage to reduce the defences to an impotence that rendered possible its capture by the soldiers. Butler's story of how near

he came to success proved a boomerang, as the story was believed, and his withdrawal accordingly condemned.   In the
haste to escape, he recklessly re-embarked the troops while
a heavy surf was breaking, and in the confusion left several
hundred of his men stranded on the beach.

All hands in the fleet from Admiral Porter down were
furious and disgusted at this astounding denouement of the
carefully hatched plot.

Butler's letter to the Admiral said:

> "Upon landing the troops and making a thorough
> reconnaissance of Fort Fisher, both General Weitzel
> and myself are fully of the opinion that the place
> could not be carried by assault, as it was left substan-
> tially uninjured as a defensive work by the Navy fire."

So the Navy was to be blamed!
Porter pointedly replied:

> "I wish some more of your gallant fellows had fol-
> lowed the officer who took the flag from the parapet,
> and the brave fellow who brought the horse out from
> the fort.   I think they would have found it an easier
> conquest than is supposed."

This was reasonable enough in the light of Butler's own
account.

The Admiral reported the miserable affair to Secretary
Welles and urged that "the right man" be sent with troops.
Butler and his legions were already *en route* to Hampton
Roads.

General Weitzel previously had neglected to display courage at Sabine Pass, Baton Rouge, Fort Jackson and Fort
St. Philip; Butler's record was notorious; were these the
best leaders the Army could send to assist the sister service
in a major operation of prime importance?   If the undertaking was as difficult as these two generals reported, it surely
merited the ablest leadership available.

Porter would have liked to dispense altogether with the Army but it seemed foolhardy.

"We all know very well," he wrote to Welles, "that a fort on shore, unless attacked by troops at the same time ships are bombarding, will always hold out against the ships, that is, the enemy will leave the works (and let the ships fire away), and enter again when the ships have gone. We know, from the history of this war, that in no case have we failed to take a fortification where the troops did their share of the work; and this is what the troops under the command of General Butler failed to do."

Grant realized that the Army had not exactly covered itself with glory and he urged Porter to "hold on where you are for a few days and I will endeavour to be back again with an increased force, and without the former commander" (who shortly thereafter was sent home to resume his practise of the criminal law).

The Admiral had no intention of doing anything but hold on. He was determined to take Fort Fisher. "If I can't do better, I will land the sailors. . . .". Eventually that is just what he did and the rest of Bob Evans' life was radically affected thereby.

The ships loaded ammunition and supplies in the exposed waters off Beaufort, the task rendered exceedingly onerous by almost continual gales, and made ready to renew the attack.

The Navy had at least the satisfaction of knowing that it had performed its part well. Evans' commanding officer reported that "every officer and man on board this ship . . . did his duty nobly."

The Confederates naturally capitalized this so-called great victory of the garrison for all it was worth in bolstering the sorely tried morale of the South. Its one avenue of access to the supplies of the outer world remained open.

General Sherman was now at Savannah, his trans-

Georgian sweep an historic fact. Porter despatched Captain Breese to him with a letter asking for one of the conqueror's divisions. There were other plans in the latter's mind and the request was denied. Grant, however, true to his word, sent back Butler's troops to redeem themselves and the Army, "properly commanded." The new leader was Major-General Alfred Howe Terry, who had acquitted himself creditably throughout the campaign. Later he was to become the Military Governor of Georgia and in 1876 one of the Indian fighters of the Northwest in the struggles against Sitting Bull and Crazy Horse.

Once more the transports headed south, the rank and file eager for the opportunity to storm the spithead of alleged impregnability under a general who could be depended upon not to recall them if and when the parapet was reached. Confidence was in the air.

Butler was in Washington before the Congressional Committee on the Conduct of the War, elaborately demonstrating with the authoritative tone of a Napoleon, that Fort Fisher could not be carried by assault. The legislators listened with respect to the pedantic military exposition by the fluent jury spellbinder. Presiding was Benjamin F. Wade, the Ben Wade who tried to unseat from the Chief Magistracy first Lincoln and then Johnson. A newsboy passed along the corridor crying an "extra" and, being called into the room and asked by Wade what had happened, replied: "Fort Fisher done took!"

The statesmen roared with glee. It was a grand joke on Ben Butler. Fortunately for them, however, Admiral Porter was not present to witness this jovial reception to the news. He might have been provoked into the utterance of non-Congressional expletives as burning as the powder flashes of his batteries. He was, at the moment, counting his casualties.

Fort Fisher had indeed been "done took" but it had been no laughing matter to those thousands involved. The capture was a grim business in which the brave garrison had exacted from the assailants the last drop of the bloody price. Among the injured lay Robley Evans.

Upon this second occasion the Army and Navy had worked together smoothly. The forces had met at a rendezvous off Beaufort and once more set course for Cape Fear. During the night of January twelfth the soldiers had disembarked under cover of a detachment of the fleet, within range of Fisher's batteries and amid their fire. Evans had participated in this difficult manœuvre, the naval officers directing the handling of the boats through the breakers, a feat of seamanship requiring the highest skill. Thousands of infantrymen, some field pieces and the bulky supplies had been landed after many hours of arduous toil, as the shells splashed around in the darkness and morning twilight.

At break of day, the bombarding squadrons had stood in from the eastward for the encore that they positively guaranteed would constitute their very last appearance on that stage. They opened fire when within range and the Fort responded. The salvos from the heavier vessels soon drove the gunners on the hill into their bomb-proofs, as upon the previous occasion, and they could do nothing but remain there while the pounding continued with relentless persistence. All day it kept up and all night. As darkness fell, the exploding shells made brilliant star-bursts against the blackening background. The Federal troops organized themselves for the advance down the peninsula. Throughout the following day, the cannonading tore asunder the air over New Inlet and the vicinity. In a steady stream, the magazines of the ships poured their destructive contents out of the gun muzzles into the enemy stronghold. The smoke hung in low, odorous clouds that frequently screened the Fort from the fleet and then drifted clear again. The garrison had no meals, no chance to sleep and was seldom able to venture near the batteries, which accordingly inflicted little damage. The ships suffered less from enemy hits than from the bursting of several of the new Parrott rifled guns. Rifled guns were in their infancy.

All the following day and that night the firing continued without intermission. It seemed as though there never had been silence in that vicinity and as though there never would be. Hell itself seemed to have broken loose. This time the fleet was aiming straight for the bull's eye. Disregarding flags and all other irrelevant objects, the thousands of shots were crashed against the landward side of the Fort, to blast an entrance for the Army. The ships in front of the Fort delivered a direct fire and those on both sides an equally devastating enfilading fire. All but one of the twenty guns on that side of the Fort had after the three day and two night barrage been dismounted. The torpedo wires had been cut, the palisades breached, the outer works pulverized and the rear slope rendered practicable for assault. At a conference aboard the flagship the night of the fourteenth, Porter and Terry decided that the land attack should be made the following afternoon.

January fifteenth was a clear winter day. The visibility was high, the atmosphere crisp. A forenoon of naval bombardment, and, at last, the awaited moment came for the volunteer landing party to shove off on its perilous mission.

Although the Admiral had faith in his new Army colleague, he knew that a naval landing brigade would irrevocably commit the Army to stop nowhere short of the interior of the Fort. It was arranged that while Terry's troops bore down upon Fisher from the rear, a picked party from the fleet would scale the heights on the seaward side. This was a daredevil enterprise but, if it served only to divert the attention of part of the small defense group in the Fort, the Army would be materially aided. The Admiral ordered his party to "board the fort on the run in a seamanlike way," which one of his officers, who after the war became an historian of the event, remarked "was more easily said than done."

That any considerable number of the officers and blue-jackets in this suicide sally could reach the top of the hill unscathed seemed impossible. Porter called it "a forlorn hope." To the call for volunteers, nearly all hands responded.

Evans had the deck when the message arrived and, even before summoning an orderly to carry it to the Commodore, placed his own name at the top of those offering to represent the *Powhatan*. He had three classmates aboard and they all volunteered. Of these four young officers, only two were needed. The choice of one of these two places finally lay between Evans and a New Yorker. Evans refused to toss a coin. Arguing, with a pathos of which he was entirely unaware, that what he considered the irreparable dissolution of his family ties left him unattached and one whose absence would not be missed, whereas his classmate's death would bring grief to his devoted domestic circle and friends, Evans obdurately insisted that he should be selected. The matter was submitted to a senior officer, whom Evans finally won to his viewpoint. When the boats rowed over at mid-day, one of them contained this intrepid lad, then about to freely use his legs for the very last time. He was growing up, a lithe, graceful young man of eighteen, not above medium height, striking in his easy, genial, forceful manner. He seemed to exude salubrity and vigour. A sound physique seemed to be a portion of his inalienable birthright. Yet within a few hours, his life would hang by the thread of his nerves, a stout enough thread, and his future would be inextricably intertwined with the sufferings and frustrations of impaired mobility of limb.

The garrison sent as many men as could be spared to the parapets with muskets and every inch of the Federal advance was going to be resisted to the utmost. Colonel Lamb himself stood on the parapet directing the fight.

To the Navy had been assigned the task of scaling the forty-five degree slope on the seaward side that had not been damaged by the long bombardment. Sixteen hundred seamen and four hundred marines were ready to attempt the impossible. The plan had been for the marines to reach certain previously dug rifle pits and, at least to some extent, to cover the advance of the bluejackets armed with pistols and "well sharpened" cutlasses, who were to scale the heights as of old.

At exactly three thirty in the afternoon, there was a blast on the whistle of the flagship. The ships ceased firing and the naval landing party leaped forward. Calmly and deliberately the musketeers on the parapet sent down a murderous fire. The marines could not reach the rifle pits alive. In the face of this deadly volley, the four battalions of sailors hurriedly were grouped into one uneven line and urged forward by their officers, among whom none advanced with more bravery than Bob Evans. They could not move forward more than a few seconds at a time against the torrent of shot that was being poured down upon them. The dead and wounded fell on all sides. Three times the seamen started up and three times they were driven back. Evans later spoke of Colonel Lamb's total disregard of danger as he directed the defence from his conspicuously exposed position. The Colonel, whose standard of courage was the very highest, on his part watched with astonished admiration the "heroic bravery" of the naval officers on the open sand below, oblivious to the fact that their distinctive uniforms made them easy targets for the sharpshooters.

The casualties of the landing party as it again and again tried to storm the parapet reached a tremendous percentage. A few men managed to scramble to the top but the line as a whole could not get through the musket fire alive.

The whole attack lasted fifteen minutes—the longest quarter of an hour through which any of the survivors had ever lived.

The Navy did not get over the top but the manœuvre was successful. It diverted the attention of the garrison from the simultaneous advance of the Army in the rear. Absorbed by the desperate effort of the sailors to board the seaward parapet, the waves of Northern troops approaching from the land side were not noticed until they were almost across the battered outer works. There was now no stopping the Army.

Colonel Lamb said: "That magnificent charge of the American Navy upon the centre of our works enabled the Army to effect a lodgment on our left with comparatively small loss." Still the garrison fought on. Night fell and Colonel Lamb was seriously wounded. General Whiting, who was present as a volunteer, was also shot. They were both carried off to a safer place. Lee had sent word that if the Fort fell he could not maintain the Army and so Lamb left orders as he was being lifted out on his stretcher that the Fort was not to be surrendered.

The garrison made a final stand and for a few minutes seemed to be driving back the assailants in the dark. Again the Navy intervened. "Just as the tide of battle seemed to have turned in our favour," Lamb later said, "the remorseless fleet came to the rescue of the faltering Federals." The Admiral flashed the signal to again blaze away and the big guns threw shrapnel into the Fort that caused great havoc among the men exposed.

Entrenching themselves closer and closer, the Northern troops realized that very little further resistance was to be encountered and at about ten o'clock at night made a dash into the Fort that carried everything before it.

Fort Fisher had at last fallen. The end of the war was now only a matter of weeks.

As the news reached the fleet, the whistles blew, the crews shouted back the cheers that reached them over the water from the Army, the bells were rung, sky rockets were set off and every yardarm was illuminated with the Costen night signals. It looked and sounded like the Fourth of July.

Admiral Porter was naturally elated at the conquest of

"the largest stronghold of the enemy." He said that ". . . The surrender of the defences of Cape Fear River is one of the most, if not the most, important event of the war. . . ." That this was no exaggeration becomes increasingly clear with the passage of time.

Secretary Seward was correct when he said: "The capture must figure in history as one of the most brilliant achievements of the war."

Among the seriously wounded carried back to the ships was Robley Evans.

Ten years before at Balaklava on the Black Sea, the famous charge of the Light Brigade had in twenty minutes cost the British two hundred and forty-seven gallant cavalrymen out of a total of six hundred and seventy-three engaged. No classic poem has immortalized the sailor's assault of Fort Fisher. Its fifteen minute toll was staggering. Every officer of the *Powhatan* in the volunteer corps was hit by a bullet. Of the sixty-two men in Evans' company, fifty-four were killed or wounded. The repulse from the bastion had turned into a massacre. In the chronicle of the Civil War it should be mentioned with Pickett's charge at Gettysburg.

Evans had been struck several times. While firing his revolver at the figure of Colonel Lamb himself, he was cut across the chest by a bullet from a sharpshooter who kept blazing away at this young officer advancing against the volleys of musketry. The hastily formed line of sailors, marines and officers, all mixed together indiscriminately, made its first rush to within five hundred yards of the parapet and then together dropped flat on the ground as the air above filled with flying lead. The officers rallied the prostrate brigade and it dashed forward another two hundred yards, dropping again under a fusillade of grape and canister. The distance so gained was strewn with naval uniforms that wriggled in agonized contortions or lay as lifeless as the sand.

It was at this second stop that Bob Evans received the grazing wound. At first it seemed to him as though the bullet had penetrated his breast above the heart. "I knew, of course, that if a bullet had gone through this portion of my body I was done for; but that was no place to stop, so I went on at the head of my company."

The muskets barked louder as these heroic volunteers ran towards the tongues of flame and smoke that made it absolutely impossible to remain erect in front of them. A hundred yards were now all that divided the forces. The parapet loomed closer every second. Forgetting his wound, Evans shouted to his few surviving men to rush still faster. Then, of a sudden, down he went on the sand. His left leg burned. Three inches below the knee it had stopped a bullet. A classmate saw what had happened and the two ensigns applied rapid first aid with a silk handkerchief that temporarily stopped the flow of blood. Then they both jumped up and pressed ahead, Evans doggedly dragging the injured leg, which was becoming numb. The stockade was reached, he saw a breach in it and tore through with seven sailors. They dashed for the base of the parapet. A veritable shower of metal came crashing down the slope. The colour bearer, proudly carrying the flag of Evans' company, was one of this heroic octet and he waved his banner in the enemies' faces until struck dead halfway up the last incline. The other seven were likewise brought to earth. Evans, his left leg now in serious shape and his chest also bleeding, was again shot, this time through the right knee. He tried to rise but it was beyond even his will power to stand on a pair of shattered limbs. As he ruefully sank back to the ground, he saw that the charge of the naval brigade had been blasted to destruction. In their zeal, all of the officers had rushed to the front of the assailants and the men in the rear, without leaders, had fallen back in the face of the withering fire.

Evans now could go neither ahead nor behind. As he lay weak and helpless, a sharpshooter thirty-five yards away continued to fire at him and finally hit him in the foot, taking off the end of a toe and causing excruciating pain. The future Fighting Bob was aroused by this attempt to finish him off when obviously non-combatant and, with a final exertion of strength, aimed his revolver and fired just as his antagonist's musket had been reloaded. The Southerner rolled over dead.

A marine, seeing the plight of this young officer, carried him to a place of comparative safety, screened from the Fort's fire. The fleet, however, was now resuming its bombardment to lay the final barrage for the Army and the heavy shells were dropping dangerously close to Evans' new cover. The same marine again picked him up and deposited his torn body in a deep shell hole, just before falling dead himself from a bullet in the neck.

This was the moment that the Army went over at the landward face of the Fort. As the garrison made its last stand to save the Fort, Evans lay asleep or unconscious in his sand pit, weak and desperately wounded. The incoming tide aroused him and he had to extricate himself from that position to avoid drowning. It was a difficult feat. The bullets were still whistling overhead and spattering on the sand but with the help of another and less fearless marine, whose aid had to be conscripted at the point of a wet and useless revolver, he managed to find cover above the tide.

The beach was a dreadful stretch of no man's land, the naval landing party lying about in shattered heaps as far as the eye could see, dead or moaning for water. A brave medical officer whom he knew gave Evans a drink. The youth begged the doctor to lie prone to avoid the fire but the latter shook his head and was starting for the next wounded sufferer when he fell a corpse.

As the sun set at last upon this bloody day, the wounded were carried out of range of the Fort and placed in the warmth of a beach fire, where the crudest kind of surgical treatment was administered, conspicuous for its lack of prophylaxis. The evacuation of these tortured casualties from the peninsula was painfully effected during the night. Evans was lifted into a boat, his legs dangling over the stern, and the coxswain sat on his damaged knees as the breakers were negotiated and the crossing completed to the side of one of the rolling vessels. The heavy seaway made the transfer from boat to ship another problem but by this time nothing mattered to the mangled sailors who a few hours before had been the pick of the Navy. Well, almost nothing mattered—but when the victory outburst rent the air, their faces smiled too.

The following day, the wounded were transshipped aboard the U.S.S. *Santiago de Cuba*—prophetic name for Evans!—and saw the fleet still in its assault formation with ensigns at half mast for those of the landing party who had been for ever left on the strand of Federal Point.

Death-like silence hung over the open roadstead that the previous day had been wildly alive with the bombardment.

"In the excitement of the charge," wrote Evans, "getting wounded was fun, but" [now] "we had a different problem to solve, and it required real nerve to face it."

If, however, he supposed that the drama was over and that the ensuing struggle would be without thrill, he was gravely mistaken. Never again was he to pass a day without painful consciousness of his injured legs; never again was he to swing along in his boyish sailor's stride. That he was able to use those mutilated legs at all was due solely to his determination that nothing would be permitted to thwart his naval career. The storming of the bastion at Fort Fisher was no less heroic, no less inspiring to his colleagues, than Bob Evans' lifelong mastery of his tragic ailment. One feat took fifteen minutes, the other forty-eight years.

When, after the weird treatment that awaited him, his legs eventually emerged stiff and deformed, he was fortunate to be able to walk even with the limp that earned him the nickname of Old Gimpy. This was a term of endearment and to the present time his former subordinates may be detected trying to conceal a tear when speaking affectionately of Old Gimpy and recalling the uneven pace across the bridge or along the quarter-deck that was his melancholy wound stripe from Fort Fisher.

Just to keep his legs or what remained of them, demanded a lot of the "real nerve" Evans knew would be required from now on. There were in those days no hospital ships, as we know them in a modern fleet. Whiskey and morphine blunted many sharp shortcomings. They made the cruise back to Hampton Roads endurable.

The officers treated their heroes as tenderly as the medical officers did unskilfully. The chaplain, however, made a nuisance of himself with exasperating platitudes about the good fortune that had spared the lives of these injured victims and protected them from worse injuries.

The doctors at the Norfolk Naval Hospital did their best to visit upon Evans the proper retribution for not adopting this holy view of the state of affairs and for not offering thanks that he still had arms and a torso. After a bedside consultation, it was decided to amputate both this young man's damaged legs. Had this been done, it never would have been possible to prove that the drastic measure had not been necessary to save Evans' life. The patient, simulating slumber, overheard the verdict. What a night he must have spent! Without a particle of self pity, the prospect of facing the world without legs was more than he could bear. So this was the result of his adventurous trip across the plains, his arduous apprenticeship under Luce, his years of drills and study. The career in the Navy was to end at eighteen in the operating room of a hospital. There was, of course, no sleep for him and even his physical pain was temporarily forgotten in his mental anguish. He re-

solved that any one who had stood up against that hell-fire
of the bastion on January fifteenth could resist a corps of
mere physicians. Would John Paul Jones or Lawrence or
Decatur have allowed his legs to be chopped off? Once
more, then, advance!

The next morning, the solemn visaged surgeons entered
the ward very much in the manner of a sanctimonious squad
of hangmen. One of the assistants stepped up to Evans'
bed to break the sad news. He looked as gloomy as a chaplain. To his surprise, the marked victim was fully aware of
the proposed amputation and explained that, while death
could be met without a quiver, this butchery was intolerable.
The youth argued, he pleaded, he insisted upon his proprie-
tary rights in and to his own limbs, but the medical czars
were adamant. Shrewdly they touched his sense of discipline:

"You know, Evans, orders have to be obeyed."

Even this appeal did not avail. As a last resort, they
would have to use force. The issue seemed hardly contesta-
ble, with the one lone defender painfully flat on his back,
scarcely able to turn. But Evans was equal to the occasion.
In a perfectly matter of fact way and with an audacity that
was to colour his entire career, he accepted the challenge to
force. Out from under his pillow came the trusty old
service revolver, all that remained of his recent accoutre-
ments of office. The doctor was shocked, then frightened.

". . . I told him that there were six loads in it, and
that if he or any one else entered my door with anything
that looked like a case of instruments I meant to begin
shooting, and that he might rest perfectly sure that I would
kill six before they cut my legs off."

What was this—bravado or mutiny? The head surgeon,
impatiently sharpening his knives, burst in with wrath and
fury. He would teach that young cub not to be disrespectful
when his superiors in the Medical Corps had wisely con-

demned a couple of his legs. Then he too caught Robley Evans' expression.

The amputation party was adjourned *sine die.*

There was an invisible accolade. Ensign arise: you are knighted Old Gimpy; you shall serve your country and glorify your Navy; you shall make for ever celebrated your future sobriquet—Fighting Bob—and bequeath it as a priceless addition to the trust fund of naval tradition.

Then followed long weeks of fever and misery in the ward. The primitive hospitalization of the Civil War is one of its most gruesome chapters. A dirty sponge induced erysipelas in one leg and then came an abscess in the knee. Evans was tortured with almost every kind of pain and ache that is known to the human body. When the *Powhatan* arrived in February, his old shipmates found him "a skeleton." Finally he could not abide the hospital another day. His uncle had moved to Philadelphia and there, on a stretcher, he went. The trip, mostly by water, was naturally one that taxed his strength and patience to the utmost but a warm welcome revealed the almost forgotten joys of home and made the hospital seem far off in a lurid haze.

His "convalescence was slow and very tedious" but he did feel himself improve day by day. The will to recover and his quenchless youth pulled him through. At first the frightfully battered and infected legs would not function at all. Eventually he was able to stand, not firmly or evenly or without crutches, but at least it was something. Not for a long time did walking become possible. Both legs were permanently misshapen and injured. When he tried to force down either foot to take a step "the pain . . . was very severe."

"However," Evans added, "I stuck to it, and after a few months the left leg worked fairly well."

Almost any other mortal would have reconciled himself to being an invalid for life but in Evans there now stirred the craving for the sea of his youth, for the life of his chosen service.

Inevitably, Appomatox followed the closing of Wilmington. Lee's soldier son and namesake, in writing his recollections of his distinguished father, said: "The capture of Fort Fisher, our last open port, January 15th, cut off all supplies and munitions from the outside world."

Sea power had won again. As Hannibal was beaten by the Roman control of the Mediterranean, Lee handed to the Commander-in-Chief of the Federal Armies the sword that had been bent and broken by the Navy of Farragut, Porter and the Brood of the *Constitution*.

4

LEGS AND HORIZONS

~~~~~~

ALTHOUGH, in accordance with Admiral Porter's express orders his Flag Captain, Lieutenant-Commander Breese, had led the charge of the naval brigade at Fort Fisher, the Senior Officer Present, who gracefully accepted this arrangement, was Lieutenant-Commander Parker. In the latter's official report of the attack, he included the following citation, which was more efficacious than medicaments in taking the sting out of ugly bullet holes:

> "Acting Ensign (Regular) R. D. Evans was wounded in the leg just after reaching the end of the palisade; he bound up the wound with his handkerchief, and then pressed on until he fell with a second wound in the knee joint.
>
> "From all I can learn, his bravery and determination to enter the fort were equalled by few and excelled by none."

The Medical Board, seeking to accomplish what their brethren in the hospital had failed to do, placed this young veteran upon the retired list and it was necessary to appeal to Congress, which promptly rectified the blunder. Not only was Ensign Evans' name reinscribed upon the active register but with three of his classmates he was upon the recommendation of a Board of Admirals advanced thirty numbers.

In the summer of '66, shortly before his twentieth birthday, he attained the two stripes of a lieutenant.

As soon as he could manage to get about, Evans applied for duty and was ordered first to the Philadelphia Navy Yard, which assignment enabled him to remain near home, and then to ordnance duty at the Yard near Washington. His right leg was still stiff and he was dependent upon crutches. This was a miserable state of affairs and, wholly aside from the obvious hardships it imposed, if prolonged would have rendered sea duty out of the question. The prospect of serving for ever on the beach in the uniform of a naval officer did not appeal favourably to Bob Evans. He had once risked his life to save his legs; now he would risk his legs to regain their usefulness.

Returning home, he persuaded a surgeon to break his right leg at the knee and re-set it in a manner that offered at least a sporting chance of restoring its flexibility. He was a perfect patient, submitting to all of the doctor's treatment and faithfully performing the most painful exercises. The reward came slowly but it came. He was at last able to hobble about and then, in a peculiar gait of his own, actually to walk.

The Department, however, was far from being convinced that in his crippled condition this young man could fill the place of a lieutenant of the line aboard a man of war. The only way for him to prove that he could, was to demonstrate the fact. The problem was how to obtain the sea orders. Captain Daniel Ammen, a high officer in Porter's fleet at Fort Fisher and one of the most able of the blockading commanders, was at Portsmouth, New Hampshire, fitting out the new *Piscataqua* for a cruise to the Orient. This seemed to present to Evans the logical opportunity. If only he could get a berth aboard, he would soon be far beyond the scrutinizing eye of the Department and would somehow manage to force those old legs to hold him up.

Knowing Bob Evans, Captain Ammen for his own sake

as well as the applicant's was only too glad to ask the Secretary to assign this officer to the *Piscataqua*. Orders were duly issued and in October 1867 the young Lieutenant presented them on the deck of the recently commissioned warship that was to carry to the harbours of the Far East, first the name of a New England river and then the name of the Delaware.

The complement that takes in hand a new craft, moulding out of the raw material of a mere floating vessel a properly coördinated unit of the Navy with her own personality and community atmosphere, has a creative consciousness with regard to the ship that breeds a unique attachment. These initial sailors are the ones who endow the ship with the character that, once formed, she will find it difficult to alter. In this instance the designers and builders had not delivered to the Navy a very impressive product. She took the water like an ugly duckling and the waves seemed ever eager to shake her off their backs. Evans expressed the general opinion when he said: "She had many bad qualities, but no good ones."

The shakedown cruise earned its title and brought the *Piscataqua* to the Brooklyn Yard, where she was docked and the finishing touches applied to prepare her for the long maiden voyage. About Thanksgiving she lay at anchor off the Battery at the foot of New York, flying the two-starred blue flag of a rear admiral. It denoted the presence aboard of Rear Admiral Rowan, who was to assume command of American naval forces on the Asiatic Station. He was another of the naval leaders of the Civil War who, like Captain Ammen, had distinguished himself in the Atlantic coastal operations.

An unusually early snow and wind storm swept down the East River and across the Upper Bay, raising havoc with everything afloat. The *Piscataqua's* decks were buried under a thick layer of frozen sleet and her anchor chains became fouled with those of two schooners violently blown from their berths. The ship's apothecary, evidently dreading a cruise that was commencing so inauspiciously and preferring the uncertainties of the hereafter to those of this awkward ship in the Orient, brewed himself a lethal potion and drained the goblet. His burial was the signal to depart and soon the *Piscataqua* was standing out to sea.

The Suez Canal was not opened for another two years and the cut through the Central American isthmus was still a mere dream of which Captain Ammen had often spoken to his lifelong friend Ulysses Grant. The navigator sailing from New York to China thus had his choice of the Cape of Good Hope or the Straits of Magellan. The *Piscataqua* laid her ultimate course eastward but via Rio de Janeiro. This was Evans' first venture beyond the West Indies.

There was in the steerage a quota of freshly graduated midshipmen and, because of the anomalous disarrangements of the war, some of them were older than the wardroom officers from whom they took their orders and under whose tutelage they pursued the arduous post-graduate course afloat. Evans was in experience almost a generation ahead of these fellows, senior to him in age, and his injuries had sobered him beyond his years, so that his abnormally advanced rank sat well upon his shoulders even though the happy charm of youth was still in evidence.

As a steamer the ship was not a great success and the sail-bred officers had all they could do to make her behave satisfactorily under canvas. After a month of vibrating under power and shivering through the trade-wind belts under spread wings, Evans saw what is perhaps the most magnificently situated metropolis of the world. The beauties of Rio harbour have never failed to arouse the admiration of the most scenically spoiled traveller. Evans gazed with rapture at the richly foliaged mountains on all sides and the radiantly white city gracing an arc of shorefront up ahead. Brazil was thriving under the relatively liberal rule of Emperor Dom Pedro II. Despite being what Captain Ammen called "a city of abominable smells and neglected hygiene," Rio was a favourite naval port when free from fever. Such an interlude was being enjoyed when the *Piscataqua* passed under the lee of Sugar Loaf and all hands hit the beach at the earliest possible moment.

A few days later, a Russian training ship brought in a cargo of midshipmen, who promptly fraternized with their American contemporaries despite the difficulties of language. Many of these fellows met again in maturer years, at the opening of the Kiel Canal and elsewhere, and had many a good laugh over the pranks they had perpetrated at the expense of the haughty Portuguese-South Americans in the most dignified corners of the Imperial Capital.

The great social institution was the opera and that was the phase of civic life which was taken most seriously. The visiting naval officers for the most part were suffering through a long evening of musical drama when suddenly a dozen or more youths in Russian midshipman uniforms swarmed across the stage and took over the further conduct of festivities, in the fashion of Yale freshmen after a football victory over Harvard. The populace was shocked and outraged at the disrespect shown by the Czar's young men for the peerless voices of the operatic stars. Admiral Rowan, however, had a sharp eye that recognized in these foreign uniforms familiar faces that bore no Muscovite caste of countenance. His own midshipmen were summoned to the cabin the next day and informed that the remainder of their stay at Rio would be spent where the vistas of the harbour could be enjoyed to the utmost—aboard ship—and their regalia restricted to American uniforms.

The South Atlantic was crossed in three weeks. "We fairly rolled our way to the Cape," said Evans, the ship describing almost a vertical quadrant in its oscillations. The turbulent weather made him constantly aware that his prayers for sea duty had been granted. He kept to his feet, however, and insisted upon doing more than his duty, as above all other things he dreaded the report of a superior that his injuries hampered him in the performance of his watch and division functions. For many years, he continued to feel obliged stoically to seek the most exacting tasks and the most fatiguing details to prove to his shipmates and to himself that he was earning his seat in the wardroom. Never did he ask or accept the slightest consideration because of his ailments. His one determination was to ignore them and thus compel every one else to do the same. Often he would wince with pain but the old smile would soon return. No masochistic fanatic inflicted more suffering upon himself than did Bob Evans in forcing his diseased knee to bend to exercises casually prescribed by one or another doctor. Wet weather seemed to torture his leg bones and joints as if he were a nonogenarian with the gout.

Ten days were spent in South Africa. The *Piscataqua* lay in the open roads at Simon's Town in False Bay, between the Cape of Good Hope and Cape Town. Here the Royal Navy maintained its regional base.

Several times Evans and some of his mess-mates went over the hills to Cape Town and he beheld the celebrated panorama from Table Mountain.

This was the year of the discovery of diamonds in the Orange and the Vaal Rivers. The era of modern South Africa was about to dawn but Evans saw no signs of this in the quiet British outposts along the southern coast.

The next leg of the journey was to Singapore and, while the ship sailed across the Indian Ocean without aid from her engines, the crew was thoroughly drilled in seamanship and gunnery. The Admiral saw to it that his flagship was smartly trained before reaching her station. Rounding Java Head and riding through the Straits of Malacca, the long crossing was at last completed. As the *Piscataqua* stood in to Singapore, Evans strained his eyes for a token of the East and ironically the first object they fell upon in the harbour was the gallant *Hartford* on whose deck Farragut had uttered his "Damn the torpedoes!" at Mobile. The ships greeted each other with great gusto. One was eager to assume her new command and the other to see her native shores.

When, after the World War, the British Empire decided to establish a powerful and completely equipped naval base in the Orient, Singapore was the logical site. It lies there on the edge of the jungle at the tip of the Malay Peninsula, the strategic centre of the Asiatic-Australian-Pacific zones and the cross-roads of all their important arteries of travel.

Evans saw a strange hot city burning under the equatorial sun and was too much absorbed by the exotic wonders thrust before him to speculate upon the significance of location. This was his introduction to the other side of the globe. His senses became acutely aware of the colours, sounds, warmth, fragrance and tropic delicacies of the story-book lands. He breathed the spice-laden air and watched the queer expressions upon faces of bronze, yellow and brown. There were cadences and moods which he had never before known. Softly these new experiences crept upon him, adventures as stirring in their way as the more striking ones of his young crowded past.

When in later years he sat down to write of it all, the thrill of the East seemed ineffable to him as to so many others who preceded and followed. A few details only of the cruise could be mentioned. There were, for instance, the delights of the table that broke the monotony of the mess at sea. His gastronomic organs had happily escaped the Confederate marksmen and at least his appetite had the unimpaired vigour of his years. From the shades of the then dim bygone evenings his recording pen evoked these epicurean high spots. There were the strongly flavoured repasts of Rio, the fruit and wine of Cape Colony, the curry of Singapore, the English hotel dinners at Hong Kong, the sea food of the Philippines.

Evans and his shipmates were living the lures of a re-
cruiting poster. From Singapore up and down the remote
Pacific waters sailed the *Piscataqua,* visiting most of the
larger seaports. They saw China and Japan and Asiatic
Britain, Portugal, Spain, Netherlands, France. Germany
was not yet a Reich. Nowhere did Evans see an American
outpost. There was none. Manila was indolently basking
in the languorous superficial charm of the Spanish occupation while the Igorotes and the Moros beat the brush in the
interior of Luzon and Mindanao. Hong Kong, perhaps,
seemed the nearest to home. The antipathy towards England that had survived our Civil War was quickly relegated
to the background when American and Royal Navy officers
drank a few whiskeys and soda together at the Hong Kong
clubs.

These visits were not at all like cinematographic tourist
peeps. There usually was a stay of several days or a few
weeks at each place. Life was geared more slowly out
there. A leisurely feeling of relative permanence pervaded
the anchorage of the moment.

After the second sojourn in one of these distant cities,
the officers would come ashore with a sense of easygoing
familiarity that dispelled the consciousness of being total
outsiders. While on the Asiatic Station, the ship's complement did belong in a way to the East and constitute a part
of its shifting life.

Travel of this sort engenders sophistication and Bob
Evans was becoming a man of the world besides progressing
along the lines of his career.

The unconscious changes of settings as the *Piscataqua*
moved about through the calms and typhoons and fair winds
gave to Evans and his companions of recurring shore leaves
that indefinable *savoir faire* of navy men. Wherever their
boat capes hung was home. Somehow, two adventures in,
say, Macao would be two adventures, but one in Macao and
one in Amoy would be in richness of colour the equivalent of

more. The workshop of these sailors was the ubiquitous sea and their playground the cities of the earth.

While on this cruise, word came of his promotion as of March twelfth, 1868. Twenty-one and a half years old, the age at which a midshipman nowadays graduates from the Academy if he is among the younger members of the class, and Robley D. Evans was a lieutenant commander whose service record was already noteworthy and experience varied. The rapid pace of his adolescent years had been sustained.

At Yokohama Admiral Rowan caught up with most of the units of his command, a pretty independent command in those days of meagre communication facilities. Washington had to leave matters to the discretion of the Senior Officer Present whether it liked to or not.

The American Navy in those mid-century years felt that because of its historic part in the opening of Japan to foreign intercourse it stood somewhat in the position of sponsor of the Nipponese Islands before the world—as though Commodore Perry by his epochal visit before the Civil War had proposed the Mikado for membership in the society of nations. This attitude was not at all paternalistic nor did it smack of the smugly condescending. It was on the contrary one of respectful pride at having discovered and presented to the West the most promising nation of the Orient. The Japanese cities were remarkable in that they did not give evidence of having commenced their European importations with large acquisitions of the vices and diseases of the white races. While the Industrial Revolution had not yet converted Japan into the Germany of the East, there were plenty of indications that the seeds of Occidental civilization would blossom very differently on that archipelago than anywhere else in the whole of Asia. The progress since Captain Ammen's visit a generation earlier was almost unbelievable.

Naturally the flagship's eyes first of all were directed towards objects of professional naval interest. At Yohohama, the Captain, in the temporary absence of the Admiral, exchanged visits and salutes with Admiral Ennomotto. Ammen was deeply impressed by the early harbingers of the formidable Navy that later won for Japan an undisputed place near the top of the hierarchy of nations. Speaking of the Japanese flagship, Ammen said: "She was a trim little vessel, with rifled battery and admirable small-arms, had fire-extinguishers of approved types, and, in short, was more thoroughly fitted out than the flagship that I had the honour to command."

The business of salutes was perplexing. Ennomotto's rank was not indicated in any way comprehensible to the Americans as the Japanese barge came alongside nor even on the uniform of the little dignitary as he briskly clambered up the gangway, so the Captain inquired how many guns would be in order. The reply specified a number far in excess of that accorded a naval officer of any rank in our own or any European Navy. Admiral Rowan, known as "a stickler as to guns," being ashore out of sound, Captain Ammen diplomatically resolved that the burning of a little more or less powder could do no harm and accordingly blazed away toward the snowy cone of Fujiyama while Ennomotto beamed in satisfaction and the American bluejackets thought that at least a super-mikado and all his august ancestors had come over the side.

The complicated affair was not yet over. "On his leaving," said Ammen, "I gave him his grand salute, and in reply received only the salute that was due to the flag of a rear admiral by our Regulations. I was about having my gig lowered to send on board to say that in an exchange of salutes between European nations (in the East we were still European) the same number of guns was always returned that had been given; but before the boat was lowered our flag was again run up on board of the Japanese flagship and the additional number of guns fired."

By such incidents, Evans learned, as will be seen, when, in later life, it was well to exact the proper gun honours from a hostile Chilean fleet and when to ignore the rude silence of an ostriching Spanish squadron in an English Channel fog.

The panorama of the Orient and the strange human characters projected against it moved before the young veteran in a rhythm new and deeply impressive. He reacted to every stimulus that reached his sensory centres. Many months of his life was he to spend along those shores, visiting the various and varied harbours and covering the great distances between them. He had seen America first and now he was laying the foundations of a universal acquaintance. There was, however, an ineradicable depth to those first impressions of the magic unrealities from Java Head to the Inland Sea that coloured all the sordid and odorous actualities he subsequently saw beneath the lustrous sheen of glamour.

On this cruise Evans acquired his mascot Jowler, a bull dog known and feared by all the canine waterfront fighters of the Orient. It was a question whether his owner was more proud of Jowler's battle record or of the triumphs of his star crew which had outrowed the fastest racing cutters of all the Asiatic fleets and met defeat only at the best blades of the *Colorado,* when that ship arrived to take over the command. Evans' interest in boat racing endured throughout his career and he was never more excited than while cheering one of his crews in a closely contested race. He was a rowing coach of considerable service renown. When in the years of command rank he took over the captaincy of a ship, the sailors doubled their bets on the next race. His oarsmen were skilled at their sweeps but above all swung with a stroke that was charged with the fiery determination of Fighting Bob.

While boating remained with him an avocation until he for ever left the sea, Jowler passed into the limbo with this particular cruise. He had been a regular member of the ship's company, enjoying free access to the wardroom country and a camaraderie with the men in the forecastle. Often in port, a sailor would ask liberty for Jowler and the application disposed of at the mast along with the other business on the agenda. The galley fed him and, after the more sanguinary dog duels, the sick bay bandaged him. When the ship eventually reached New York, Jowler disappeared and Evans received a confession from one of the crew that he had found it impossible to say good-bye to this friend of land and sea. Whether Jowler shipped over or retired to a landlubber's ease, his bereft owner never found out.

Lieutenant Evans' activities on the beach always proclaimed him essentially a man's man with an inclination toward hunting, fishing and competitive sports rather than the allurements of the ballroom. When he sought a congenial chat, it was usually at a men's club to the clinking of glassware rather than under the tropical moonlight to the accompaniment of the soft music of the East. Evans' surviving shipmates say that he was esteemed by the ladies and that their domains presented new fields in which there was offered every prospect of successful adventure, but he was mildly averse to cutting the social capers and left distinction in those arts to the many other officers who made the most of their uniforms ashore.

When Grant was thrust into the high seat that had been much too hot for his predecessor's comfort and to the misplaced General seemed all too frigid, he summoned his friends to grace the steps of the throne. Among these, Captain Ammen was called to Washington, where he helped hold the President's hand and renewed his activities in promoting the fantastic project to pierce the Isthmus of Panama. He was relieved by Captain Earl English.

The tour of duty went along for the others until in the summer of '69 it came time to expect the arrival of the relief, Admiral John Rodgers in the *Colorado*. The *Piscataqua*, now renamed *Delaware*, sailed over to greet her successor at the same gateway to the East at which she had herself been welcomed by the *Hartford*. After the friends in the various ports had been bidden farewell, Evans and his shipmates cast their minds half way around the world and were eager to be off. The homeward bound pennant was ready, a tremendous streamer from which every man aboard, upon the final splash of the anchor, might cut his souvenir. It was longer than the ship.

The final summer was spent in and around Singapore, watching the harbour entrance for the prow of the *Colorado*. The temperature there on the equator, while no higher than in what was called winter, turned the days into nights and the nights into days. The most satisfactory occupation from the forenoon until just before dusk was sleeping. Then, like the jungle beasts behind the city, foreigners began to stir into social activity and a round of gaiety got under way. It was a lordly white aristocracy based upon the insignificant cost of labour and there were the diversions of such a caste, all hospitably open to the American naval officers. Evans adapted himself to the life of Singapore and enjoyed his visit.

When weeks passed and the relief ship failed to put in her appearance, Admiral Rowan grew impatient to the point where even the heat could not suppress his restlessness. Just to be in motion he cruised over to Batavia, where the ship's company almost bathed themselves in gin, and poked his nose into the Straits Settlement, where the good tidings of Admiral Rodgers having at last reached Singapore were received. Back hurried the *Delaware* and before long her homeward bound pennant was waving good-bye to the East.

Thus did these flagships and their admirals come and go, alert to protect the American interests that usually drifted along well enough by themselves, needing no greater aid from the Navy than the respect induced by the showing of the flag. For the most part there was no emergency and no excitement. Some time there might be both. Indeed one fine day there would be and then the commander of the Asiatic Squadron would sail down from Mirs Bay to Manila and, by virtue of the years of tireless preparation for just such a call, make his republic an empire.

Admiral Rowan had not been destined to encounter a greater break in the routine than was afforded by a civil war in Japan, fought in accordance with the Oriental principle of safety first. He had, however, kept his squadron in battle trim and been ready for whatever crisis might have arisen.

It seemed strange to be leaving this other civilization to which the officers and men so imperceptibly had become accustomed. The western hemisphere was now the one of unreality. In those days before the penetration of industrialism and its commerce into the recesses of Asia, the differences between the two great worlds were even more marked than later, because the superficial manifestations of disparity had not been glossed over.

In later life Evans became renowned as a spinner of yarns, true ones, mostly embracing his own experiences. Leaning back in a big chair in his cabin or on the beach with his legs outstretched, he would puff at a Havana cigar and tell his story in his characteristic terse, direct, blunt manner. His listeners were never bored. Those still living remember those congenial chats with the deepest pleasure and still speak of Evans' outstanding integrity of heart and mind, his eyes and his smile. One of his most distinguished subordinates, Admiral Anderson, has said: "I consider him a great man and loved him. He had the most magnetic personality of any one I have ever met. His face in repose was rather stern but he had the most charming smile I recall on any one's face. Wherever he went and in whatever company he was thrown he easily dominated the interest and attention of all present."

In the moments of retrospection, he would often advert to incidents of this Asiatic cruise. It is interesting to recall the fact that he sailed the China Sea, the Sea of Celebes, the Straits of Formosa at the same period that those distant waters were revealing their mysteries to Joseph Conrad. It is not to be wondered at that Evans too brought back from the Orient a large repertoire of stories. He would commence: "The one occasion upon which I smoked opium, in a flower boat at Canton . . . ," "While a few of us were trying to outwit the fan-tan gambling bank at Macao . . . ," "One day in Yeddo Bay during the struggle between the Tycoon and the Mikado . . . ," "At a Satsuma piece shop in Nagasaki . . . " and so on. The tales were always intrinsically good. There was never a resort to the artificial prop of exotic names for their atmosphere alone. That he had a full mental portfolio was not to be wondered at. Youth and the East collided and almost every shore leave provided its unforgettable adventure. He might well have quoted that merchant sailor-author just above mentioned, whose words will be as lasting as Evans' deeds: " . . . for me all the East is contained in that vision of my youth."

The old familiar West loomed up with a shock at Cape Town. That it should do so at the extremity of Africa, of all places, was one of the oddities of European imperialism. The spell was broken and the Orient once more receded behind its curtain of romance.

St. Helena was a frequent port of call on such voyages and here for a few hours Robley Evans steeped himself in the great French tradition only to suffer the brusque intrusion of news that nephew Louis had somehow failed to make the tradition function smoothly at Sedan. Prussia was marching toward the Versailles coronation. Evans soon would see the rise of German prominence in the Far East and then almost live to see it swept away.

The cruise finally ended in fitting fashion, with the climax reserved for almost the last moment. Steaming past Sandy Hook into New York Bay, the *Delaware,* with her great pennant spreading out behind, passed on opposite courses an American warship bound for Brazil, which commenced firing the salute to Admiral Rowan's flag. The guns barked out sharply at the prescribed intervals until the thirteen shots had been counted and then, to the astonishment of all on board the *Delaware,* there were two more. A shout of acclamation went up spontaneously from all on deck. This was a worthy homecoming. In his absence, as a tribute to his distinguished war record, Rear Admiral Rowan had been promoted to the rank of vice admiral! Officers and men, thrilled at the announcement and the dramatic manner of it, continued cheering until the honoured leader came up from his cabin to acknowledge the applause. Evans' comment expressed the general sentiment: "Once in our history, anyhow, the man who deserved it was made vice admiral." There could be no taint of political influence upon this promotion, made while Rowan was out of communication with any and all wire-pullers. It was a stimulating recognition of patriotic service and the whole ship's company came into port rejoicing.

5

CHARLOTTE EVANS

~~~~~~

In Bob Evans' class, quartered with him in the *Constitution* and working alongside of him at Newport, had been Henry Clay Taylor, son of Franck Taylor of Washington and descendant of General Daniel Morgan of the Revolutionary Army. Throughout their parallel careers and until Harry Taylor's death in middle life, these two Brethren of the Brood remained devoted friends.

In 1871 they were connected by an additional tie. Harry had a sister. Washington was near enough to Annapolis to enable her, then a very young girl, to visit her midshipman brother and inspect the glamorous wonders of the Academy, during his plebe year before the outbreak of hostilities. Charlotte was a classmate's sister who fell into the category of delight, not duty. Her southern loveliness was not readily to be forgotten.

Evans had spent considerable time in Washington since the war. After his return in the *Delaware,* he was ordered to resume at the Yard there, the ordnance duty which he had been performing prior to the Asiatic cruise.

To the young Lieutenant Commander, Washington grew to connote Charlotte Taylor and to acquire an irresistible fascination. Bob Evans was in love with her and she with him, then and for ever after. Although frequently painful, his legs gave every promise of allowing him to duly advance in his service. Their improvement convinced Evans that he properly could yield to the strongest urge he ever had felt. The ceremony took place in June 1871 and the couple had a summer honeymoon in the North.

Theirs was a happy marriage. The attractive bride matured into a charming woman, admired by all who met her. Whenever possible, in all sections of the world, she was near her husband. Often, upon reaching a distant harbour, Bob Evans would find his Charlotte there ahead of him, waiting with children and baggage, and patiently prepared for any disappointing change in Departmental movement orders. Above all, a naval officer's wife must be a good sport. This Mrs. Evans proved to be, always.

They had three children. First came their daughter Charlotte, who married Captain C. C. Marsh of the Navy, then their son Franck Taylor, who adopted his father's profession and retired in 1930 as a Captain, and lastly Virginia, who married Harold Sewall, the only man in the family not in the service.

Naturally, Evans wanted to spend his first years of married life on the beach, and he obtained an appointment to the Faculty of the Academy. Eleven years after his arrival there from Utah, he returned to the same old grounds to assume the rôle of teacher. He remained for two years.

He was one of six assistants to the Commandant of Midshipmen, and an assistant instructor in seamanship, naval tactics and naval construction. Harry Taylor was also there, as assistant instructor in mathematics. The Superintendent was John L. Worden, who had fought the *Monitor* against the *Merrimac*. In Evans' second year, French E. Chadwick, Sampson's Flag-Captain at Santiago, and Charlie Clark, skipper of the *Oregon* upon the same occasion, became fellow-instructors.

One of the midshipmen of the Class of 1873 was Albert A. Michelson, who displayed more proficiency in his mathematics than in the subjects taught by Evans, and who was later to measure the speed of light, upon which is based the Einstein theory of relativity.

Evans liked boys but he had little of the studious temperament, and he found his duties irksome. Demonstrating to prospective seamen how to shorten sail was one thing; quizzing them in a classroom ashore was quite another. Annapolis was a dull place for this energetic young man. Being with Charlotte was a joy, and the hunting was fun, but Evans realized that his professional future lay on the water. As the Class of 1873 was graduated, he was ready and eager for sea duty.

He made inquiries at the Department as to vacancies afloat for an officer of his rank and was assigned to the *Shenandoah*, a sloop-of-war serving in European waters.

In midsummer, Lieutenant Commander and Mrs. Evans, with their first baby, crossed the Atlantic in a passenger vessel. At Gibraltar, in August, the former found his new ship.

6

NAVAL FRONTIERS

~~~~~~

W HEN Evans reported for
duty as navigator aboard the *Shenandoah,* the United States
squadron of obsolete and obsolescent ships constituted a
naval anachronism in the Mediterranean. It gave a quaint
touch of mellow charm to the setting of the modern scene
but that was hardly its function.

Europe was entering upon that well demarcated period
from which it was to emerge at Sarajevo in 1914. The
German Empire had been launched by Bismarck, Cavour and
his successors had effected the unification of Italy, and
France was back to republicanism.

Often profiting by our experience more than Congress
has permitted our own Navy to do, the Royal Navy had led
the way in embodying in its fleets the lessons of the Civil
War as well as those of the Battle of Lissa in 1866 between
the Italians and the Austrians. The European navies were
now composed of armoured steamers mounted with breech
loading rifled guns. The revolutionary transition from sail
had been accomplished and the navies of the future definitely
been born. In twenty years Evans was to see them at Kiel
in all their metal and mechanical maturity.

As has been the case after every crisis of our history in
which a hastily constructed navy has extricated the country
from the threatened disaster, the return of peace left us no
wiser in the law of sea power. Some things we never seem
to learn, not even by costly experience. A few years before

Evans' tour of duty abroad, the American Navy had enjoyed a prestige that made of Admiral Farragut's post-war tour a veritable hail-the-hero procession from one European port to another. His was the first naval name in the world and the flag under which he sailed had come into its own. The government, however, let the Navy fall to pieces. The enormous fleet had lapsed into decay and only the spirit of its officers had kept alive the morale throughout the years of physical degeneration.

The European officers would smile at the sight of our old high-masted curiosities standing in and then marvel at the smartness of their trim and the snappiness of their discipline. We had a Navy without a fleet. Those who quietly carried on during these trying years knew that some day before very long the nation again would be obliged to take to the water to insure its independent existence and normal development; they determined to be ready when the Government awoke.

Admiral Dewey has written of " . . . . the period of inertia in the 'seventies, when our obsolete ships were the by-word of the navies of the world . . . " and, in one of his messages to Congress, President Roosevelt said: "At that period our navy consisted of a collection of antiquated wooden ships, already almost as out of place against modern war-vessels as the galleys of Alcibiades and Hamilcar—certainly as the ships of Tromp and Blake."

Evans thus found himself in a squadron that had outlived its own age, in the midst of the new Europe, the Europe that was consolidating its own national entities and their respective imperial extensions.

The *Shenandoah,* like the *Piscataqua,* was a wartime product and not much the superior of the latter except when it came to rolling, which Evans boasted she could do "forty degrees each way twenty times a minute and keep it up for hours at a time." To out-roll the *Piscataqua* was a rare accomplishment.

The officers were a congenial crowd and several were friends of the new navigator. At the Rock the British cordially made things very pleasant ashore. Evans for the first time saw the English Army in its colonial splendour. At Hong Kong there had not been so much emphasis upon the professional soldier's life; here there was little else. He enjoyed the dinners, formal in appearance and jovial in good fellowship, and admired the handsome plate, elaborately furnished quarters and above all the "well-educated and cultured lot of hard-drinking chaps, who seemed ready for any kind of a job that might turn up." With many of the British Army and Navy officers he formed warmly intimate relationships, as those things go, which in later years frequently proved a great delight when recognizing one or another of the familiar faces in unexpected ports after long intervals of separation. It was on this cruise that Robley Evans and Lord Charles Beresford laid the basis for their enduring friendship, just before the latter was assigned as naval aide-de-camp to the Prince of Wales, later King Edward VII, on his trip to India.

The matter of chief naval interest at Gibraltar just then was the Spanish Revolution. The Latins never take their politics quite as seriously as do the Nordic peoples and somehow the antics and capers of the former in their governmental affairs are more obviously ludicrous to the observer on the outside. Spain had its conspicuous charms but the mismanagement of its public business and indeed its private business struck the British and American naval officers as the absurd scrambling of emotional children.

The overthrow of Queen Isabella II and the international embroilments over the choice of her successor had made the Spanish throne the football of European politics. From these manipulations and intrigues had sprung the publication of the famous Ems despatch and the Franco-Prussian War. While her neighbours were thus battling each other, Spain was confining its fighting to intramural limits. The Cortes

and the regency and the unhappy Amadeo had their brief
and luckless hours of nominal rule. Six months before
Evans reached the shores of Spain, Amadeo had abdicated
and, to fill the administrative vacuum, a republic had been
proclaimed. It was to be short-lived and enjoy the distinction of being recognized by no foreign power excepting the
United States, which in those days retained a sentimental attachment to popular forms of government.

To Bob Evans the Iberian scene presented a series of
combats, differing in appearance but alike in nature. There
were the revolting dog fights with their more revolting
baiters, the cock fights with their blood-thirsty human spectators, the bull rings packed with sadistic hoodlums and the
political mêlée that was staged in the centre ring of this
truculent circus, on the plateau at Madrid. He sensed the
colour and the lilting rhythm of the Mediterranean provinces
that he visited as the ship cruised along the coast from Cadiz
and Malaga past Valencia to Barcelona but most of the finer
things of Spain were inevitably beneath the depth of its life
to which a naval visitor had the opportunity to penetrate.
Paradoxically, the ports did not possess even that rare
Spanish loveliness of the white districts of Manila, which
Evans so vividly remembered.

At Cartagena he beheld a clash of British sea power
and Spanish resistance. Admiral Yelverton announced his
intention of removing, for restoration to their owners, two
merchant vessels that had been seized by the revolutionary
government and lay under the guns of the harbour batteries.
The Spaniards defied him and declared that the slightest
move on the part of the English toward the execution of that
threat would be opposed by the instant fire of the coast fortifications and the Spanish ironclads.

The Americans were thrilled at the prospect of seeing
another fight, this time not between ferocious animals but
ships of war. Evans was sceptical. He believed that the
Spaniards of those days preferred to fight vicariously and

that, when it came to firing upon the white ensign of Saint
George, they would think twice. The *Shenandoah* glided
toward the harbour entrance to have a grand stand view.
Admiral Yelverton's statement had specified noon. As eight
bells sounded on one ship after another in the assemblage,
the British column got under way, surrounded the two
steamers in question, and calmly led them to sea.

Evans had been correct in his prognostication.

"The Spaniards stood by their loaded guns. The huge
ironclads sizzled with steam and smoked viciously from their
stacks, but not a shot was fired. Admiral Yelverton had
done his work beautifully."

He watched Yelverton and made a mental note. A generation later, when at Valparaiso in command of a small
gunboat, he would likewise do "his work beautifully" under
the muzzles of fortifications and Chilean warships, whose
garrisons and crews of Spanish blood would suppress their
fiery hostility and drop the lanyards.

At Barcelona there was bad news but it had to be met
sooner or later. There lay the *Wabash,* flagship of the
squadron, and Evans knew what this meant. The navigator's department being relatively idle in port, the officer at the
head of it is selected for all the miscellaneous assignments
from sitting on courts-martial to running the more important errands on the beach. Whatever may arise, the navigator is the one "who will have time for that." The
Admiral now organized a survey party. This resembles a
housekeeper's cleaning of the attic. No government property
may be thrown away. If there is a useless old coffee pot in
the galley, the cook may not simply toss it overboard. There
must be an august inspection, deliberation and condemnation
by a board of survey before the worn-out utensil may be
consecrated to the deep. All officers dislike this sort of
work; Evans positively loathed it. "We surveyed old
stoves, carpets, curtains, pans and pots, until I felt myself
quite competent to run a shop in Chatham Street."

After the general chambermaid activities and the Admiral's inspection in the harbour of Spain's commercial metropolis, the ships weighed anchor and the *Shenandoah* crossed to Tangiers. Here there was much to interest the strangers in the Moorish city and the mysterious hinterland.

With the Captain, he went on a partridge shoot in the desert and this was something new very much under the sun. They had native guides and camels and all of the paraphernalia of the sandy wastes, including Arabian mounts that taught a thing or two of horsemanship to the rider of western mustangs and the once favoured guest of the Snake Indians.

Suddenly the tourists were reminded that the *Shenandoah* was not a yacht. Orders came to hurry to Villefranche, the American naval base in the Mediterranean. The ship headed northeast under full steam and full canvas and ploughed into the night unmindful of storm warnings. The navigator was on deck throughout one of the most violent hurricanes of his career. Before sail could be shortened, half of it was blown away. The ship pitched and rolled in the furious seaway that tossed its enormous waves against the hull with shattering force. Evans felt his old wounds as he always did in dampness and when his legs were subjected to severe strain. It was with difficulty that he kept to his feet and held the almost helpless vessel on her course by means of the feeble engines that just about gave her steerage way. One particularly violent lurch wrenched his hand from the stanchion and threw Evans face down on the deck with a crash that seemed to break every bone in his body. Again the legs took the brunt of the injury and again they were to suffer from the well-intentioned ministrations of the healing agent. When a lull in the storm satisfied the navigator that he could momentarily leave the bridge, he was persuaded to let the doctor examine the damage. His left knee cap had been completely skinned. The physician opened up his medicine case and "before I knew what he was about he clapped a large piece of thick adhesive plaster, which he had melted over a candle, on the raw flesh. It fairly fried me, and caused me intense pain for several days, as well as the use of very strong language." Admiral Lardner's inspiring vocabulary was no doubt drawn upon liberally and it is to be hoped that it salved the pain.

With the frayed remnants of canvas on the yards and in the rigging proclaiming the terrors of the night, the *Shenandoah* reached Villefranche and the officers their families at Nice. The American naval colony at this resort was excited by the probability of war against Spain. The *Virginius* incident had just occurred and it was this that had summoned the *Shenandoah* to the supply base, whence she was to join the rest of the squadron at the Rock and hasten home. That is the life of a naval officer's family. Evans' young wife had with difficulty established herself and the baby at this distant post so that at fleeting intervals the family trio might be together and now Robley was rushing off on the hazardous pursuit of conflict.

That war with Spain was inescapable seemed to the Navy too obvious to require proof. When it would break was the only question. Having seen at close hand the inability of the mother country to govern itself and the rotting of the aged empire at the core, Evans thought it fatuous for our successive Secretaries of State to let their pacific intentions blind them to the patent and ever increasing failure of Spain to reconcile Cuba to her status of dependency. To ineptness of administration Spain was adding a cruel despotism that could not long be exploited almost within sight and sound of our own shore, without involving us in the business.

All wars, however, need for their inception not only the general but the particular. There was in this case a long, vexatious series of items constituting the particular. The *Virginius* affair was one of the links in the chain that came to its bitter end a quarter of a century later when the *Maine* burst into scrap iron under the grimaces of Morro Castle.

The *Virginius* was a vessel used by the ever active Cuban insurgents in conveying arms, ammunition and men to that island. Just as during our Civil War Evans had at Havana seen the illicit traffic in supplies for the Confederacy, for several decades he was to witness the return of these favours by the United States with interest. Ironically, the *Virginius* had herself been a blockade-runner that after capture by the North had been sold to an American citizen who registered her in his name as the undisclosed dummy for the Cuban insurrectionists. With a crew of fifty-two, mostly Americans and Englishmen, and one hundred and three passengers, mostly Cubans, she slunk along in her old familiar way, when over the horizon swept the Spanish warship *Tornado,* which on October 31, 1873, pursued and seized her off the eastern point of Jamaica and brought the captive into Santiago Bay. The Spaniards unleashed their wrathful indignation upon the unfortunate prisoners, who were grimly disposed of by a summary court-martial. The death of no fewer than fifty-three of the defendants, including the American captain and other Americans and some of the British was decreed. The executions were spread over three days of slaughter. On November 8th the sentence of the court had been fully carried out with ceremony worthy of a bull fight. Nothing remained except for Spain to see how Washington would like this display of vigour.

When the news reached the United States, the popular excitement was naturally intense. Hamilton Fish was at the head of Grant's Cabinet and handled the situation most creditably. Displaying a restraint that shone forth in brilliant contrast to the utter lack of any on the part of the Santiago authorities, he nevertheless satisfied the country and the rest of the world that although the work of the firing squads could not be undone, no such outrage would be tolerated. Spain was addressed with a sharp protest that at least temporarily snapped her out of her smug apathy and was duly heeded by the prompt surrender of the *Vir-*

THE "SLAUGHTER-HOUSE," SANTIAGO—SHOOTING OF AMERICANS IN 1873

ginius and the surviving prisoners and the payment of indemnities to the families of the slain Americans (The British Government collected corresponding amounts for the dependents of its victims) Within a week of the final executions, the worst of the war scare was over While it lasted, it was serious Had not Spain submitted promptly to Secretary Fish's demands, she would then and there have been relieved of her overseas possessions, although the condition of the American Navy was far from what it had been in '65 or would be in '98

The newspapers were foaming and the vocal liberators in Union Square and the Boston Common fulminating while the veteran European squadron made its slow way across the Atlantic in response to the somewhat frenzied calls of the Department The *Shenandoah* sailed via Madeira and St Thomas, learning at this West Indies' port that the crisis seemed to have been passed, and then proceeded to Key West, where the pitiful sea power of the United States was assembled, "making faces at the Spaniards ninety miles away at Havana, while two modern vessels of war would have done us up in thirty minutes " Only a genuine democracy could present the anomalous spectacle of an administration headed by a military hero permitting its defences to collapse almost over night The naval mobilization focussed all eyes upon this wretched state of unpreparedness and the first intangible keel block of the new Navy may be said to have been placed

Key West's importance as the springboard of any attack upon Cuba was emphasized at the same time A small island approached by a treacherous channel and without any protected anchorage, Key West lacked a supply depot and was but weakly fortified Some improvements were effected between that time and the actual war period, when Admiral Sampson made considerable use of this base, which again came into naval importance during the World War, as the headquarters of Admiral Anderson's American Patrol Detachment More than ever since its joinder to the mainland by the trestles of the Florida East Coast Railway and by the overseas motor highway, has this island become of great strategic significance in protecting our lines of communication throughout the West Indies, to South and Central America and Mexico and through the Panama Canal. Evans along with the other thinking naval men of the day realized this as they carried out the fleet manœuvres and landing drills made possible on a large scale by the fortuitous concentration of squadrons.

At this gathering of the clans, Evans saw many of his classmates and old shipmates of wartime and the Orient. This part of the conclave was thoroughly pleasant.

The shore operations, however, were particularly irksome to him. Like most of his colleagues, infantry and artillery work seemed drab and dull. When Evans wrote "I have always found soldiering the least desirable part of my profession" he was expressing his feelings with extreme moderation. His legs rebelled against unaccustomed pounding on a military march and he always returned to the ship thanking his stars that he had not gone to West Point. The dirt, the dust, the fatigue were of a nature that seemed less endurable than any of the hardships afloat and far less gratifying in their perceptible accomplishments.

If, unconsciously, he felt that when it came to soldiering he could rest upon the effort and the wounds of Fort Fisher, who can venture one word of adverse comment? Certainly no one who has ever paraded and drilled up and down and across an improvised "grinder" on one of the Florida keys, with cactus underfoot and a tropical sun overhead.

When the war cloud was dissipated, the fleet scattered. The *Shenandoah* went north for a complete overhauling and, to round out his tour of sea duty, the navigator was ordered as executive officer to the *Congress,* bound for the European Station and his family. He relieved one of the most promis-

ing young officers in the service, William T. Sampson, who
later fulfilled this early promise so abundantly.

It is interesting to pause in the recollection of those days
to note that many of the great naval leaders of the Spanish
American War and the period following it were officers who
had stood forth for their ability and personality throughout
their entire careers. Evans was a conspicuous example and
Sampson was another. Referring to the early post-Civil
War days, Dewey said: "Nature had been kind to Sampson.
Not only had he a most brilliant mind and the qualities of a
practical and efficient officer on board ship, but he was, in
those days of his youth, one of the handsomest men I have
ever seen, with a bearing at once modest and dignified. Already he was a marked man among his fellow-officers, who,
in a profession which is so strictly technical, are the best
judges of a *confrere's* abilities."

It was to be expected that Robley Evans found the
Congress in excellent condition when succeeding such an
Executive Officer. That indeed was the case. The ship was
in perfect shape and, as an additional piece of good fortune,
the new Commanding Officer was none other than his last
skipper of the *Delaware,* Captain English.

The executive officer is the line officer next in rank to the
commanding officer of the ship and has complete responsibility for the administration of the personnel, the drilling of
the crew, the functioning of the many departments and the
general welfare of the naval community and its matériel,
subject only to the supervision of the captain, who lives apart
in his own quarters and transmits all orders through the
executive. The latter, according to the Regulations, must
when aboard ship "regard himself as always on duty" and
it is he who presides over the wardroom mess and the internal affairs of the whole ship. Nothing can take place
or be omitted that does not concern the executive.

In the Spring of '74 the *Congress* set forth for the
Mediterranean. Robley Evans looked forward to seeing

his family. Mrs. Evans naturally had breathed more easily since the danger of war had passed and now the young couple eagerly anticipated their reunion.

At Madeira, however, there were unexpected orders. In those pre-radio days, the sailors were well aware that the next port might hold a despatch altering the ship's previously planned course. Captain English showed the despatch to his Executive. There was to be no Nice for the present. The natives of Liberia, as Evans expressed it, had "threatened to barbecue our wards, the coloured American colonists," and the *Congress* was instructed to divert the former's appetites. The American officers could not understand this predeliction for broiled black missionary but, having once helped to emancipate the negroes from American slavery, the Navy turned to the simpler task of saving them from the gridirons of their racial brethren.

Instead, therefore, of heading for the Straits of Gibraltar, the *Congress* was pointed almost due south. She ran on buoyant trade winds toward the Canary Islands, where she made a three day halt at Santa Cruz on the Island of Teneriffe. The high volcanic peaks that rise from their submarine bases and are covered with all manner of luxuriant foliage give the archipelago a natural beauty that fascinated Evans and his shipmates despite the still hostile Spanish inhabitants and the giant fleas. The Executive Officer, enamoured of the scenic splendours, organized a mountain climbing expedition and in old horse-drawn hacks they lumbered up a road that wound its devious way to an elevation of several thousand feet above the ocean. First they passed through dirty villages where the Spaniards, almost wholly illiterate, had learned enough about *Americanos* to scowl and growl at them as they went by. Then the route lay through thick tropical plants of the varieties common in Central Africa, not far away. The *conquistadores* had in the era of their enterprise introduced the coffee tree, the date-palm, the banana, the orange tree and the sugar cane, all of which flourished. When the horses had climbed about fifteen hundred feet the vegetation began to resemble the kinds Evans had seen in southern France and elsewhere along the European shore of the Mediterranean. As the altitude increased, the flora gradually became more and more northerly in species. The party was stirred by the magnificence of the vistas that spread out before them from points of vantage along the road. During his years of travel, Evans saw many breath-taking views. A few of these images survived the keen competition in the contest for most favourable endurance. No subsequently envisaged panoramas in the Straits of Magellan or along the Alaskan coast or in the blue bays of the Mediterranean could dim the recollection of one particular picture of the town and harbour of Orotava framed "in a perfect rainbow."

The skipper was now sick and his Executive had his hands full. The Canaries were physically agreeable and the *Congress* seemed in no hurry to leave. When, however, the mission is to enjoin a threatened banquet upon American citizens, it is well to arrive before the cocktails have been served. Somehow the cannibalism seemed incredibly absurd. The wardroom banter dealt with it in jest. It was too grotesque to be possible. The officers wondered just what they would find when they reached this far-off situation.

The *Congress* sailed down to the Cape Verde Islands in delightful weather, reaching Porto Grande near Mindello on the Island of Sao Vicente.

Here there were memories enough to turn back the thoughts of any American naval officer. In the years when *Old Ironsides* and her contemporaries had roamed the Afric' seas, this had been their local base of operations. Many a historic cruise logged the Cape Verde Islands as a rendezvous or haven. Back in 1812, Porter called here in the *Essex* to take on supplies for his celebrated sweep of the Pacific. Into this anchorage had come *Old Ironsides* herself with her two famous adversaries lashed as prisoners to the wheels of

her chariot, the *Levant* and *Cyane* The remains of several
officers and a number of bluejackets had been buried at
Porto Grande and Evans was outraged when he saw that the
cemetery had been despoiled of its monuments and fences
The matter was duly brought to the attention of the authorities, who previously had been appealed to on the subject by
our government, and they again made the appropriate
promises which it was evident they would forget as soon as
the topmasts of the *Congress* dropped below the horizon
We can visualize Bob Evans courteously but emphatically
protesting against the inexcusable vandalism to the lethargic
Portuguese Governor who would bow almost any assurances
to avoid even an argument in that enervating climate How
accurately the interpreter translated the Lieutenant Commander's remarks is a question but, once the concept that the
American naval cemetery was the topic of the interview was
communicated, we may be sure that the expression and tone
of the speaker conveyed his feelings as plainly as did his
words

The ship now swung toward the southwest along the receding mainland of West Africa This was the equatorial
belt of hot days and light winds and a pellucid sea An
American naval officer who had cruised about this region
earlier in the century on the anti-slave trade patrol, has left
a description of these clear waters through which the *Congress* now took her temporarily well-behaved way

"It is difficult in looking over the ship's side to conceive
the transparency of the sea The reflection of the blue sky
in these tropic regions colours it like an opaque sapphire, till
some fish startles one by suddenly appearing far beneath,
seeming to carry daylight down with him into the depths
below One is then reminded that the vessel is suspended
over a transparent abyss "

At Freetown, capital of the British colony of Sierra
Leone and one of the very few natural harbours on the West
Coast, the *Congress* made a brief stop and then proceeded

along the flat, thickly forested shore to Monrovia, the Capital
of Liberia, named after the same President as the famous
Doctrine. What a strange bit of human history did Evans
here encounter! The descendants of black savages violently
snatched out of the jungle into the slave markets of the new
world were trying, on a narrow fringe between the surf and
the penumbrous depths, to effect a geographical repatriation
near their ancestral haunts. These few thousand American-
ized negroes in their houses and conventional apparel were
hoping to survive the ferocious incomprehensibilities of two
million savages in the region described by the late Sir Harry
Johnston, possibly the greatest modern authority upon
Africa, as the darkest section of the dark continent.

From these impenetrable wilds emerged the weirdest
witchcraft and the most grotesquely mysterious barbarians
of Central Africa, portrayed by Joseph Conrad as *The
Heart of Darkness.*

To this day cannibalism persists and in the nineteenth
century it was notoriously rampant. The fact of its practise by these natives is not so grim as the manner and spirit
of it. Many primitive peoples have assigned to the tasting of
human flesh a part in their religious rituals or tribal ceremonies. It seems impossible, however, to avoid the conclusion that these black folk who lurked amid the thick trees
behind the Liberian coastal settlements ate human flesh
merely because they relished its flavour and nourishment.
Eminent biologists reluctantly have conceded the revolting
possibility that the splendid physique of these negroes was
attributable in substantial measure to this loathsome diet.
The incredulities of the *Congress's* complement were overcome by the unmistakable evidences that slavery was not the
worst fate that awaited unwary strangers captured in the
bush. The missionaries bravely pressed up the stream and
the trails into the menacing hinterland, where they found the
proselyting agents of Islam worthy competitors and where
they often terminated their careers as the *piece de resistance*

of elaborate banquets. Sir Harry Johnston said that these savages enjoy most "the hands and feet, and this very dainty dish is usually set before a king or chief alone." Recently an English official of the Liberian Rubber Corporation found himself in a remote native community far from the beaten jungle track and was terrified to hear the Chief remark upon the whiteness and smoothness of his guest's skin and that dinner seemed to be late. The present British Consul General at Monrovia does not regard an allusion to the pitiless maw of the jungle as a figure of speech.

On the map of Africa, Liberia appears small in extent but the *Congress* was aware of its six hundred mile ocean front as she continued to Cape Palmas, the seat of the threatened trouble. This was close to the equator. Days and nights followed one another without a warning twilight.

Here was another of the settlements of the American Colonization Society. The distant tom toms and the shadowy forests ominously at the back door made the outpost seem an insignificant scratch of the nineteenth century upon the surface of this mammoth mass of ebony. Evans and his shipmates saw little beyond the urbane and cultivated negroes in the foreground. They knew, however, that curious eyes were peering through the verdure to observe all of the activities upon the beach. The magic of gunfire the natives had been made to understand and also in some unaccountable manner the fact that the arrival of this floating fountain of bullets had perilous connection with the proposed feasting upon the Afro-American creed carriers. It can not be denied that the visit of the *Congress* was of negligible significance in the long campaign against Central African cannibalism, a campaign still being fought, but the immediate effect proved to be the direction of the luncheon thoughts of the local Brillat-Savarins toward other viands.

To the Virginia bred Evans, whose intimacy with black people dated from his birth, the spectacle of Africans in Africa was deeply interesting. The dressed-up negroes in

Monrovia and the other towns seemed to him more grotesque than the natives amid their ancestral foliage. He met a fellow-Virginian, President Roberts, born a slave and now a cultivated and widely travelled gentleman of light hue, whose kinky hair alone proclaimed his race, and the other influential Liberians of the day, but they struck him as being miscast. A Southerner may feel ever so kindly toward the negro but he can not regard him as other than a member of the un-skilled labour class. The public dignitaries impressed Evans very favourably but not to be taken quite the same way as the statesmen of other countries—more like the exalted rulers of a coloured fraternal order in the United States.

From Cape Palmas the *Congress* retraced her long course and commenced to climb the latitudes. This time a real visit was paid to Sierra Leone, which in conception and origin was the British counterpart of Liberia. The ship coaled at Porto Grande but her bunkers held only enough for a short trip and it was necessary as well as economical to rely to a considerable extent upon the winds. Evans always wel-comed an opportunity to drill his men in the fundamentals of seamanship aloft. It seemed too revolutionary to be pos-sible that steam would not only augment canvas but within a very few years altogether supplant the natural motive power that for countless centuries had carried the craft of men across the seas. The direct route to the Rock was not followed but one calculated to make the most of the available prevailing winds. First the *Congress* stood out to the west-ward into mid-Atlantic and then veered around toward Madeira.

Throughout these weeks along the African coast the skipper had been on the binnacle list. Upon the Executive Officer, therefore, had fallen the burden of making the cere-monial calls ashore as well as handling the ship and the crew. He worked hard and performed his task in a manner that permitted Captain English to concentrate upon the re-covery of his health. At Funchal, Madeira there was a thorough overhaul while the Captain rested on the beach. When the *Congress* stood out of this lovely place, her Commanding Officer was able to resume his duties and the *Congress* was in shipshape. Evans had risen to the occasion and was now a thoroughly experienced naval officer, qualified to command a capital fighting ship.

For the moment, however, his thoughts were landward. At Madeira there were the first letters from Mrs. Evans in five months and, sailor fashion tearing open the envelope bearing the most recent postmark, he was relieved to read that all was well. The family was in England. He had earned a leave and at Gibraltar one was duly granted. Near the English lake country, in the town of Carlisle, he found his wife and daughter, the latter naturally much changed. They journeyed leisurely to rejoin the *Congress* at Marseilles.

Evans now became acquainted with London and Paris, the London of the ascendancy of Disraeli and the Paris of the decline of Thiers, the London of Browning, Tennyson, Huxley and Herbert Spencer, the Paris of Pasteur, Flaubert, de Maupassant and Bizet. Mr. and Mrs. Evans were energetic tourists, revelling in their holiday together. From Paris they went to the Riviera. Switzerland was left for the next leave, which was a shorter one obtained somewhat later.

After the relaxation of the trip through England and France and into northwest Italy, the brass buttons were shined and the uniform laid out by the mess attendant in the familiar room in the *Congress*. It was now Captain English's turn to run off for a much needed change and Evans completed the work to be done at Marseilles, where the ship's bottom had been scraped and her interior scoured. The men were given their first liberty since leaving the United States and they enlivened the waterfront saloons and quays of the city. When the freedom of terra firma was so seldom enjoyed, the precious minutes on the beach had to be utilized to the utmost. The crew included its quota of rough and tough able seamen and their thirst was intemperate in inverse proportion to the frequency of their opportunities for submerging their heads in the bar-room troughs. Marseilles knows its sailors and the police force marvelled that it could be taught some new tricks by these Yankee bluejackets, who flirted hard, drank hard and fought hard, but, drunk or sober, managed to find their way back to the landing in time to heave themselves into the last boat.

At last the recess was over. With noses losing their portlight tinge and black eyes healing with no questions asked, the *Congress* set sail on her tour of duty about the Middle Sea. There was Barcelona again, the cock fights still packing the arenas and the politicians as turbulent as ever. There was Port Mahon on the Island of Minorca, which in the olden days of American naval activity along the Barbary Coast, had been our base of supplies. Sicily was visited and without haste, then the Ionian Islands, Greece and Crete, the latter still under Turkish suzerainty. In Suda Bay on the north coast of Crete, the *Congress* fired her target practise. Then the ship steamed westward, through the Straits of Messina and into that most magnificent sapphire of all harbour gems, which has made its City of Naples justly renowned. There were, in several of these ports, foreign men of war, French, British, Italian, Russian and others, and Evans was coming into friendly contact with his professional colleagues of these European maritime powers. In ships the United States squadron made a sorry showing but in efficiency of personnel it needed to dip its colours to none.

Again Evans stimulated interest in boat racing and the cutter of the *Congress* won the undisputed championship of the Mediterranean. It became difficult in those days to obtain a bet against any crew coached by this officer who had swept his oarsmen to victory in the Orient and now in Europe.

Before completing her round of the Mediterranean and

returning to Villefranche, the *Congress* cruised along the shores of Asia Minor and North Africa. At the latter ports she looked over the scenes of bygone American naval achievements. The Stars and Stripes, even on antiquated vessels, still inspired respect in those regions.

The winter was spent at Villefranche on the Riviera and the officers disported themselves gaily at Nice and Monte Carlo, so far as their meagre salaries permitted, and with their families enjoyed the social life of the naval colony. Evans found the music of the whirring roulette wheels more fascinating than that of the orchestras. He had a very little to toss to the croupiers and lost that with good humour. The continental resort life was sparkling and, at least on the surface, carefree. The young officers were content to bob their short winters on its surface and take things as they jauntily came along. Evans was making friends among all nationalities, friends who would stand him in cordial good stead the balance of his years, and the mere acquaintanceships he acquired were many times that number. In the seventies Europe and the United States were much less alike than to-day. In Europe's older atmosphere, with every port a different civilization, Evans was becoming a seasoned cosmopolite.

The winter over all too soon, the *Congress* shovelled aboard her allowance of coal for 1875 and broke loose from her moorings at Villefranche, where she must have begun to take on the fixed appearance of a depot ship. At the Rock, now a familiar retreat for him, Evans saw his old English Army friends and had some jolly down-the-hatch bouts at their tables. There were days along the eastern Spanish coast and then the ship once more stepped into the Moslem world across the blue. Those officers who in their school days had been weak in mastering history were benefiting by a post-graduate laboratory course on this cruise of the *Congress*. The previous year had laid an excellent basis. Now they touched at Algiers, Tunis, Carthage, Malta,

Tripoli, Corfu, a study in eras and contrasts. From the ruins of Hannibal's ancient stronghold and the wreck of the *Philadelphia* in Tripoli, the decaying monument of Decatur's exploit, Evans found himself thrust into another Rock. Like Gibraltar, the British officers at Malta maintained a military social life with that perfect blend of the ornately formal and charmingly unaffected whose secret they have learned.

Disraeli's dramatic acquisition of the control of the Suez Canal by his purchase of the Khedive's shares, which was to make Malta the sentry box of the passage to India, was still several weeks ahead. In the meanwhile this strategically situated garrison watched the flow of traffic over the new route. By this short cut the *Hartford,* to which Evans had waved adieu at Singapore five summers before, returned from her cruise in the Orient. She was ordered to meet the *Congress* at Tripoli under the circumstances of one of the most *opera bouffe* crises in our entire diplomatic history.

Had war between the United States and Turkey resulted, the proponents of the economic interpretation of history would have been put to a great deal of perplexing research. The trouble centred about the personality and indignation of one Michel Vidal, one of the organizers of the Republican Party in post-war Louisiana, Congressman from that State in the darkest days of its reconstruction period and for the last six years United States Consul at Tripoli.

His residence in this polyglot city, where Moslem, Christian and Jew, Oriental, European and African, dwelt together in a confusing but picturesque community, had been featured by a widespread unpopularity. As he moved among the flat roofed homes which, with their little gardens, rose in terraces from the seashore, he made his presence felt and disliked. Vidal was an active man of decided opinions and an enormous confidence in his own ability and wisdom. No one ever has charged him with having displayed any tact in the welter of New Orleans carpet-bag politics or in his quasi-diplomatic post from which the United States Minister was far distant, at the Sultan's Porte.

In record time he had succeeded in making himself *persona non grata* in the European colony and in antagonizing all of his consular colleagues and the various *pashas* who, one after the other, had rotated in the office of *vali* of the province. Indeed he was famous in the civic circles. A new arrival of social standing would invariably be asked before long: "Have you met Vidal yet? Just wait!"

Undoubtedly from worthy motives as well as from an irresistible tendency to intrude his sagacity into every situation, he talked vociferously about the necessity of stopping the slave trade between Constantinople and the Soudan via Tripoli and told all who would listen how the Northern abolitionists would make short shrift of such a nefarious business. Then he wrote long letters to Washington urging the establishment of a naval station along the Tripolitan coast. These communications were inadvertently included in a governmental blue book and, upon publication, promptly found their way back to the scene of their inspiration. When Mr. Vidal was observed horseback riding along the shore, the rumour gained credence that he was selecting the most suitable harbour for the United States fleet.

For the summer of 1875, this emissary of American good will had leased the magnificent villa of the grand vizier overlooking the Mediterranean, a short distance from the town. Here he and his family were dwelling in Oriental luxury. On August fourth there appeared off shore the so-called Imperial Turkish Squadron of Evolution. A boat from the corvette *Edirné* landed on the beach nearby to obtain fresh water at a well. The Vidal family was at lunch in a pavilion adjacent to the main building. A housemaid was startled by the sudden sight of a Turkish sailor in the house. The fellow had strolled in from the well to seek a light for his cigarette and, with natural curiosity at the domestic splendours, gaped about. The frightened servant screamed, in dashed Mr. Vidal and out ran the seaman as fast as his legs could carry him, with the consul in somewhat undignified hot pursuit.

The latter lost sight of his man as he came upon the beach and encountered two others from the ship, idly sitting on the boat, one an engineering officer. Out of breath the consul indignantly demanded the whereabouts of the vanished intruder. The Turkish officer tried to placate him and asked of what terrible crime the sailor had been guilty—he had simply sought a match. Inasmuch as these two men were smoking, the explanation did seem unsatisfactory and the irate Vidal let forth a torrent of abuse that would have done honour to any forecastle and was thoroughly understood by the naval officer despite his linguistic limitations. To emphasize his outraged indignation, the consul used his hand. He insisted during the subsequent proceedings that he had merely rested it gently upon the officer's shoulder; the latter swore that he was so violently shaken that his collar was ripped.

It is seldom that enlisted men will stand by while an officer is even touched aggressively and it is rather to be wondered at that the officer's subordinate merely called for help and that the crowd of sailors who quickly gathered did no more than growl and threaten. Not a blow was struck at the consul. The next day, however, he was summoned to appear before a court consisting of five inhabitants, a violation of the treaty guaranteeing certain extra-territorial rights. The *vali* furthermore demanded that Vidal apologize to the Turkish admiral for the disrespect shown his officer. The consul on his part demanded elaborate reparation for the "surreptitious and violent entry" of his home which, with unconscious ludicrousness, he reminded the authorities had constituted a breach of their harem laws, the villa being occupied by the women of the household!

There was a great tempest in the town and the ever

glowing embers of religious fanaticism were fanned by agitators into menacing flames.

Vidal despatched his secretary to Malta to wire to Washington a full account of the gross indignities to which the United States of America had been subjected.

The vexatious question as to the status of Tripoli was thus forced into the open. We had tacitly acknowledged that that country had become a part of the Ottoman Empire but we had never waived any rights under the old treaties entered into with Tripoli in the days of her independence. Without taking up this Vidal complaint through the regular diplomatic channels, the State Department caused orders to be issued to the *Congress* to proceed to Tripoli and to the *Hartford,* on her way home, to follow. Horace Maynard, our Minister at the Porte, was left embarrassingly uninformed.

There seems to have been some confusion as to the tenor of the orders sent to Captain English. Later, when the subject was threshed out in correspondence between Secretary of State Fish and the Sultan's envoy Aristarchi Bey and between Mr. Maynard and the authorities in Constantinople, it was averred by the State Department that the *Congress* had been instructed to investigate and report. This, however, was not the understanding of the Captain. To his surprise, no such rational course was outlined in the despatch he received and instead he was to enter Tripoli and, to use Evans' words, "exact ample reparation."

Between the citadel on the one side and the row of ancient forts on the other, steamed the *Congress*. There were the minarets and cupolas of the mosques composing the sky line of the city. In the foreground was the old Roman marble arch.

Nearby lay the wreck of the *Philadelphia*. Even though they were not to learn the absurd details of the Vidal incident until their arrival, the officers of the *Congress* were well aware that this was no glorious mission to terminate the bloody tribute levied by a piratical potentate. What if the *vali* should be adamant and those crenellated *enceinte* walls flash out defiant destruction to the unarmoured *Congress?*

Captain English lowered away his gig.

"Stand by the oars!", "Shove off!", "Out oars!", "Give way together!" and he was on the delicate errand, while heterogeneous throngs dropped their daily tasks and rushed to the waterfront to watch the hostile arrival and babble wild gossip in the dialects of three continents.

The Captain was greeted by derogatory shouts and threats of personal injury, which gave the United States a real grievance (for which the *vali* duly expressed his regrets).

As for the occurrence at the grand vizier's villa, the *pasha* protested that the only impropriety intended or committed had been on the part of Vidal himself in the course of his alleged self-protection. Captain English explained that under his orders the facts were immaterial and that, regardless of what might be his own views, only an apology by the *pasha* could avert serious trouble. The latter, furious at Vidal, repeated that the Sultan kept a scimitar brightly sharpened for the necks of subordinates who disgrace the Porte by offering apologies without cause. He manned the batteries and Captain English delivered his ultimatum. Unless within four hours the *vali* agreed to apologize and comply with various other demands, the *Congress* would open fire. So far as the relative strength of the ship and the shore fortifications were concerned, Captain English might almost as well have had a canoe armed with bows and arrows. Nevertheless, he went about the business of preparing for action, with thorough gravity. The ship was swung around so that her full broadside bore on the town. Then all hands crowded the seaward rail and let forth a lusty cheer. Standing in at this crucial moment, the Stars and Stripes streaming from her gaff, was the gallant old *Hart-*

ford, looking as self-confident as before Mobile, despite her years. She dropped her hook near the *Congress* and quickly cleared for action. The *pasha,* said Evans, probably thought "that the entire American navy was coming."

The situation now became extremely tense. The European inhabitants trembled for their lives as there loomed up the hideous menace of a massacre. To the Mohammedans, Americans and Europeans were all infidels of one indistinguishable group and the animosity toward Vidal's countrymen extended to all of the other Christians in the town. The British, French and Italian Consuls addressed an urgent note to Captain English pleading with him to moderate the terms of his ultimatum and this he did so far as his construction of the Department's orders permitted. The last minutes before the expiration of the four hours were terrifying ones to the foreign inhabitants. Armed boats from the Congress and the Hartford were ominously taking soundings in the inner harbour. The preparations on the decks were plainly visible from the quays and waterfront windows. There was significant activity in the rigging. The superannuated ships might be sunk but they obviously intended to play their rôles unmindful of the probabilities. As the time shortened, the *vali* did some rapid reflecting. Then, almost at the last minute, he sent word of his submission. The ceremony of apology was to take place at noon the following day. Peace was restored. Tripoli returned to normal.

The next morning, the *pasha,* in full dress uniform, drove in state to the American Consulate, where the gloating Mr. Vidal was awaiting the moment of his triumph, flanked by the naval officers. The *pasha* was a good sport. Having decided to submit, he did it with the best and most dignified Oriental grace. Bowing to the offended party, whom he personally loathed, he humbly offered his apology and, among other customary protestations of extravagant self-abasement, declared that he ate dirt. This, however, did not satisfy the Consul who, Evans said, "demanded that the dirt should be actually eaten"! Captain English ordered his fellow countryman to "pipe down" and, thanking the *pasha,* announced the proceedings at an end.

Mr. Vidal slunk aboard the *Congress* and, the net result of the affair being his departure from Tripoli, perhaps the *vali* thought that it was well worth the vocal soil-swallowing.

There remained considerable parleying for the diplomats over the reopened question of Washington's relations with Tripoli. The incident itself, however, was closed. It had scarcely added to the prestige of any party concerned excepting the officers of the American ultimatum squadron, who had exhibited the intrepidity and good sense expected of them. They did not exult over the achievement. "Those of us who knew the real facts in the case," wrote Evans in retrospect, "were not very proud of the whole performance."

On September twenty-fifth, the *Daily Levant Herald,* Constantinople's only English newspaper, published a fair editorial on the crisis. While at least impliedly praising Captain English and his men, it characterized the proceedings as "rowdy" to a degree that they were confident would shock the Washington authorities when they learned the details. Secretary Fish, however, was quite vague in his comments and he avowed ignorance of the naval performance that had ensued from his directions; but he was satisfied with the outcome and never admitted any doubt as to the technical justification for Vidal's attitude.

Indulging in even the most casual speculation, one shudders at the contemplation of what might have happened. Had the Hartford not arrived or had the *vali* stuck to his guns on the harbour emplacements, Captain English would have been obliged to open fire. Before being able to discharge her second salvo, the *Congress* almost certainly would have been splintered by the fusillade from shore and her remains deposited near those of the Philadelphia. Captain English, Lieutenant Commander Evans and the entire ship's company might have perished without even a fighting chance, and war precipitated between two nations that had no genuine quarrel with each other.

"What mighty contests rise from trivial things. . . . "

The incident taught Evans what he had long suspected, that the State Department was not infallible, especially in its *ex parte* decisions, and that the great American indoor game of poker has its outdoor uses. He had seen Captain English play a good hand and Evans was to remember this in another emergency when the full responsibility rested upon his shoulders, seventeen years later.

The *Congress* stood out of Tripoli with esteem for the *vali's* dignified behaviour and contempt for the personage now aboard who had caused the disturbance. The latter was disembarked without undue honours.

The seascape of the Mediterranean was a cheering sight after the cramped and hostile horizons of the harbour. The program was Italy and then another winter on the Riviera, a pleasing prospect. The Department, however, had formulated other plans which were learned at Villefranche. The base there was to be abandoned. The naval colony would consequently be uprooted. The ships were ordered to diverse places, the *Congress* to home waters. Another cruise was drawing to a close.

Crossing the Gulf of Lyons there were gales of farewell. At the Rock, Evans once more spliced the main brace with his many *confrères* in Her Majesty's service. Then the course was set for Port Royal via Madeira and St. Thomas, the track he had followed three years earlier in the *Shenandoah*. The *Congress* reached her destination in midwinter.

There were several weeks of squadron drills in home waters. The old ships were put through all their paces. What delighted Evans most during this period was the continued success of his oarsmen. In an exciting five mile race against the crack cutter of the *Brooklyn*, which had hitherto won all the honours, the crew of the *Congress* sprinted at the finish and maintained its coach's prestige.

This was the era of circuses and Exhibitions. The latter were the high points of popular entertainment and each outdid the best previous efforts. When Philadelphia planned one to commemorate the one hundredth anniversary of the birth of the nation, the entire country coöperated toward ensuring the success of the project on the grandest scale to date. For years the Fair was in course of preparation and now in the Spring of '76 the elaborate construction in Fairmount Park was nearing completion. Immense buildings had been erected to house the displays collected from all over the world. The official opening was scheduled for May tenth and not only Philadelphia but many other cities declared the occasion a public holiday. The newspapers gave over their entire front pages to the World's Centennial Exhibition. Crowds poured into Philadelphia from every direction and there were visitors from many foreign countries.

The Navy was represented by an exhibit in the grounds and by the *Congress,* moored in the river.

The great day dawned in Pennsylvania's finest May style. It was clear and bright and the sun shone warmly. As the forenoon advanced, it became very hot. There was, of course, to be a parade, as imposing a one as the managers could arrange. It formed on Broad Street at eight o'clock in the morning. Between the local Keystone Battery and the Third Regiment of the State National Guard, there fell in the landing party of the *Congress,* commanded by the Executive Officer. The bluejackets, in excellent physical condition after their long hardening cruise, made the uniformed civilians ahead of and behind them appear amateurish. The sailors were not professional paraders but they were professional sea fighters and they marched in the swinging cadence characteristic of military mariners, their wide trousers smartly wrapped in leggings and their bayoneted muskets over their shoulders.

The unpaved streets were covered by a thick layer of mud and the marchers soon looked as though this were a forced cross country movement rather than a dress parade. The wretched conditions under foot and the increasingly high temperature made the tramping most uncomfortable. At Twenty-second Street, the residence of George W. Childs, editor of the *Public Ledger,* was reached and here President and Mrs. Grant joined their escorting columns. The procession pounded its long and tedious way to the Exhibition Grounds. Crowds in numbers that were record breaking pushed through the gates, probably a couple of hundred thousand persons being at the Main Building when the presidential party arrived. Among the other celebrities, Emperor Dom Pedro of Brazil and his Empress received the most attention.

As General Grant approached, the throngs were milling about in excited confusion. Several individuals had been prostrated by the heat and the crush. The President was not only failing of recognition but finding it impossible to force a pathway to the platform. The police were helpless. A regiment of Boston cadets bravely charged the unruly mob and was thrown back in disorder, glad to keep its feet. At this point, Bob Evans saw what was transpiring. He snapped out the command and led his sailors on the run into the tossing sea of humanity. The effect was immediate. They made a gangway for the President. Bayard Taylor, watching the proceedings from a perch atop the roof of the Main Building, wrote that ". . . a company of armed seamen from the *Congress* formed a wall on the opposite side. After that there was peace until the close."

There was a notable program. Richard Wagner had composed a march for the occasion and John Greenleaf Whittier a hymn. The Exhibition was formally dedicated by an address by the President, who was in the last of his eight summers in that office.

The ceremonies were at last over. Evans, no more enamoured of soldiering than ever and even less so of policing, led a weary lot of sailors back to the ship that evening.

Until July the *Congress* lay off Philadelphia, one of the sights of the Fair. While here she was visited by the Board of Inspection, which in its report paid glowing tribute to Captain English and Lieutenant Commander Evans, commending these two officers and stating that "the whole organization and condition is as near perfection as our system will admit."

In midsummer the old veteran of the deep was taken to Portsmouth, New Hampshire. At this place, where he had helped fit out the *Piscataqua*, Evans now assisted in placing the *Congress* out of commission.

7

COMMAND

~~~~~~

THERE were now several weeks of long overdue leave and some work at the Department in connection with signalling. Out of the latter sprang an invention of Evans' perfected in conjunction with Lieutenant Maxwell Wood. It was a lamp for visual communication at sea at night and between vessels too far apart to read each other's flag hoists or semaphores. The device, which was patented and used by the Navy for some time, may be regarded as one of the forerunners of the shutter-searchlight whose long range flashes upon clouds may be decoded at night far beyond the horizon.

Before the Christmas holidays of 1878, came sea orders.

Years later Evans pronounced his next cruise "the pleasantest duty that has fallen to me in peace times during my naval career." There was much more to enchant him than the relative novelty of captaincy. For two years he combined blue water sailing—and literally sailing under unaided canvas—with the fun of teaching boys that vanishing art.

To-day's mighty aircraft carrier *Saratoga* bears a name famous in naval annals. She is the fifth of the line. Her grandmother, the third *Saratoga,* bore no resemblance to this electrically propelled floating hangar. A sloop of under a thousand tons, she could not boast half the length of a modern destroyer but her beam was relatively broad and she had the imposing square stern of her type. Launched eighteen years before the Civil War, with a record of distinguished service against African slavers and the Confederacy, she had been turned over to the Naval Academy as a practise and gunnery ship.

Evans was now directed to fit her out for the training of naval apprentices, lads in their teens aspiring to enter the enlisted ranks of the service. The sloop was brought up the Potomac and put into seaworthy shape at the Washington Yard, under the supervision of the new skipper. A crew of novitiates was gathered from the vicinity. Under the young "old man" with the limp and the smile, the assurance of a veteran and the enthusiasm of a youth, the *Saratoga* finally stood down the river with as green a lot of deckhands as ever were introduced to yardarms and marlinspikes. They proved to be apt pupils.

Vicariously Evans relived the strenuous days at Newport when his own legs had been sound and had scampered with alacrity at the orders shouted in the unforgettable voice of Stephen Luce.

The adaptability of the boys, the familiar smell and feel of the sea, the thrill of the first command all delighted Bob Evans.

Along the coast, out to Bermuda and back, across to the Madeiras and return cruised the *Saratoga*.. The landlubbers developed into able-bodied seamen. After each long voyage a new complement was signed up and the process of indoctrination repeated. This involved patience and hard work but Evans found it highly gratifying by virtue of the successful results. Throughout his life he preached the doctrine that the efficiency of any navy depended first upon personnel and only secondly upon matériel. In his farewell speech as an active officer, at San Francisco, he stressed this conviction. During the two years as captain—teacher of the *Saratoga* he delivered to the service many dozen competent sailors who were as essential to its excellence of condition as were the officers graduated at Annapolis. Later Evans was to devote himself with deep interest to the im-

Courtesy U. S. Navy Department

U. S. S. SARATOGA

provement of steel and to ship fabrication generally. The work with the raw humanity was even more to his liking.

After the summer cruising of 1879, an extended period of overhaul at Washington provided Evans with another welcome winter at home.

His confidence in the ability of these tyros to handle the ship in any wind and weather was increasing with each new group. In the spring he ventured into the Mediterranean. The sloop poked her nose into Funchal, Lisbon, Gibraltar, Tangier, Villefranche, Naples.

Evans enjoyed the return to old haunts and the sight of familiar English faces at the Rock and in the Mediterranean Fleet. Many new friendships were formed. There were hunts and drinks in gay company on the European and African shores. The ship's schedule permitted unhurried visits wherever her anchor dropped. Joining with these foreign officers in their own sports and recreation mellowed relationships that no end of mere dry conversation could have dragged out of the casual class.

One of Evans' favourite companions out there was the subsequently famous Hedworth Lambton, then Flag Lieutenant on the staff of Sir Beauchamp Seymour, Commander-in-Chief. Years later at Valparaiso, when Evans was alone in hostile surroundings, it was a delight to meet Lambton again.

On the long legs of the voyages, Evans perfected his mastery of seamanship and his knack of handling men under all conditions.

Whenever possible, he combined some incidental service with the *Saratoga's* chief mission of training personnel. In coöperation with the Navy's hydrographers he ran lines of transatlantic soundings; in coöperation with the Smithsonian Institute the ship gathered a valuable collection of deep sea fishes; and these secondary pursuits lent added purpose to the trip.

On the whole, however, the extended stretches of sailing

made up an uneventful period of Evans's life which yielded satisfying contentment in the company of young men and the sea, with little to distinguish one pleasant day from another.

When, towards the end of November 1880, he completed two years of command of the *Saratoga* and was relieved by Harry Taylor, Evans knew that his brother-in-law could anticipate with confidence a professionally profitable and an enjoyable tour of duty.

The third *Saratoga* eventually became the *Public Marine Schoolship* at Philadelphia and functioned as such until within a year of Evans's own retirement. Often, in these later years, when at the Philadelphia Yard on various errands, he must have looked fondly at his last ship without an engine.

8

ON THE BEACH

~~~~~~

THE enjoyable *Saratoga* cruise was followed by about nine years ashore during which Evans had varied occupations, acquired much experience that was subsequently to prove of great value and made many significant acquaintanceships among civilians. His most important work was in connection with the design and construction of the so-called New Navy in steel, which later he was to help successfully fight to distinction in the crucial test, the only real test, of action against an enemy.

His very first assignment pointed to metallurgy. As equipment officer of the Washington Navy Yard, he was obliged to concern himself with the manufacture of chain cables and gun forgings. This was an altogether new field for him and one to which he brought no theoretical training. It proved enormously interesting. His alert mind readily acquired the zeal of the scientific pathfinder and was soon enthusiastically absorbed in the experiments being made at the Yard for the welding of steel. Refusing to be blocked in his efforts by the handicap of lack of a technicological education any more than Pasteur was disheartened by his limitations of training, Evans soon caught up with the relatively meagre knowledge of steel which then existed.

With his knack and good fortune of always being on hand and ready for the unforeseeable opportunity, Evans' activity in steel processes coincided with the need by the Navy for expert opinion upon just that subject. European navies, clear of the wooden age, were quickly jumping over iron to steel. Our own ships were becoming more ridiculously inadequate each year. The naval nadir of the post-Civil War decline was reached in the Hayes Administration.

President Garfield placed at the head of the Navy Department W. H. Hunt, a secretary who realized the perilous state of unpreparedness into which the country had been permitted to drift. He appointed a Naval Advisory Board to report upon the needs of the service and, when the macabre delusions of a lunatic placed Vice-President Arthur in the White House, Hunt, retained as Secretary, won for the new President the credit of laying the foundation of the rehabilitation of the Navy.

The Advisory Board was a hard-working, intensely earnest group, presided over by Rear Admiral John Rodgers and including Evans among its membership. This gave him his great opportunity to put forward his views not only as to the importance of rebuilding the Navy, with which all of his colleagues were in accord, but also as to the importance of rebuilding it of steel and of steel only, a point upon which there was prolonged controversy. Italian tests had demonstrated pretty conclusively the superiority of steel over iron and, when Evans offered his all-steel resolution, it was warmly supported by the other line officers on the Board. Opposition, however, developed from the representatives of the Construction Corps, who knew the difficulties in the way of steel manufacture, in which this country was then notably behind Europe. Evans promptly turned their argument into a point in favour of steel, contending that a steel naval program would give the domestic steel industry a tremendous impetus. He stoutly claimed that the American foundries could duplicate the performances of those abroad if the prospects of profit were sufficiently alluring. Although the constructors filed a minority report, which to-day sounds absurd in the light of the

subsequent outstanding steel supremacy attained by the
great companies of Pennsylvania, Evans carried with him
the majority of the Board, which recommended that eighteen of the proposed new ships be of steel. Congress made
its own investigation into the merits of steel and came to the
conclusion that it was the proper metal for the naval units of
the future. Evans always took pride in the part he played
in hastening the day of the steel Navy and in the consequent
fostering of the American industry. His very lack of
expert training had proved an asset. Where those better
versed in the difficulties had been discouraged, he bluntly
ploughed ahead with the determination that a refusal to
recognize the obstacles would overcome them. It was not
an intellectual attitude but an effective one. Evans adhered
to it during all his work with steel. He never accepted the
second rate and brushed aside the pleas of "can't."

The political machinery functioned with exasperating
sluggishness and the steel ships took a long time reaching
the water but the doctrine of steel had been established.

After a couple of years at the Washington Yard, at the
end of which Evans had acquired a familiarity with steel
manufacture remarkable for one not an engineer, he was
again ordered to the lighthouse service, as inspector of the
district that embraces the region between the head of Chesapeake Bay and Beaufort, North Carolina. This practise
of wasting a skilled naval line officer upon such assignments
has fortunately been discontinued. In those days it was
made tolerable by the paucity of ships. The Commander
undertook the tasks of paymaster, supply officer and general
administrative chief of this district.

It was not in him to be the slave of routine. Evans
was never a worshipper at the shrine of things as they
are. He proceeded to apply his native intelligence and his
executive experience to his new position. This was, of
course, contrary to all of the rules. The lighthouse service

was the political plum orchard that bordered the continent and was deemed the exclusive property of the patronage dispensers. Evans began to straighten out matters under his jurisdiction just as he would have taken in hand a disordered ship of which he was given command. Politicians meant nothing to him. Warnings as to what happens to those who trespass upon these preserves of the vote-controlling potentates brought from him only a profane expression of indifference and contempt.

His seagoing political naiveté was shocked by the discovery that the lighthouse keepers were obliged to pay out of their small salaries a regular tribute to the appointing powers, in the form of a party contribution. This was a practise that prevailed generally in almost all of the lower strata of public employment during those dark days before the Civil Service reform. Evans could ignore nothing of that sort and certainly could not countenance such a system of extortion since he knew of its operation among his own subordinates. Characteristically, he told his keepers to stop meeting the levies. This was withholding the fuel from the political machines. It was heresy, treason, outrageous interference!

Evans had declared war upon the politicians and they were furiously ready for the hostilities. A pretext for his punishment soon would be found. Not even a superficially sound one was awaited. When the refractory inspector refused to rubber-stamp his approval upon the nomination as keeper, of a delegate to a party convention, who was patently unfit for the position, the Secretary of the Navy yielded to the clamour of the politicians and detached Evans on waiting orders "without asking a word of explanation."

The injustice and discourtesy and humiliation of this disgraceful performance naturally infuriated the honourable officer who had devoted his life to the service he loved only to be reminded in such a crude way that the entire uniformed hierarchy is subordinate to the political party that is in office. The Secretary who lays the sordid paw of political manipulation upon the professional organization he temporarily directs, does a vile act which the service can not and the public should not forgive. William E. Chandler was the Secretary who removed Evans and the latter never condoned the mistreatment. It is fair to assume that Evans was deeply hurt not only by the personal inconvenience and financial loss he sustained but even more by the rank unfairness of the action and its sinister implications. One thing he refused to do was pull any political wire to seek redress. In his scorn of such tactics, his conduct and his principles were congruent.

The Secretary being away from the Department, Evans applied for and obtained a year's leave with permission to go abroad. He realized that he would be left idle on the beach as long as Chandler remained in office and thought that he might as well take his family to Europe and enjoy the enforced vacation. It probably would be the last opportunity to spend a prolonged period with the children while they were growing up. Europe was less expensive and offered attractive recreational and educational facilities. Mrs. Evans had the baggage packed and the family was excitedly counting the days to the departure when a telegram came from the Department revoking the leave and again placing the Commander on waiting orders. Secretary Chandler had returned to his desk. In his *Log,* Evans comments: ". . . I had felt the sting of insects before in my life, and did not consider them of much importance." The cancellation of the leave was a confession of Chandler's malice.

Evans did have to await Chandler's retirement before the country would call again for his services. Fortunately from this standpoint, the election of 1884 produced a change of administration so there was not so long to wait. Chandler was a rugged New Englander, who remained active in Republican affairs to the end of his long life. Evans maintained a healthy hatred of him that never flagged. When

Rear Admiral he did not permit this enmity to prevent the appointment to his staff of Chandler's son, now a retired Rear Admiral himself, but Evans invariably left the ship whenever his aide expected a visit from his father.

His profession being temporarily closed to him and Europe being forbidden, the only practicable alternative to idleness at home was civilian employment. The steel work at Washington proved to be an asset. Evans was engaged by the Baltimore and Ohio Railroad Company to inspect at Pittsburgh the material for the new bridge at Havre-de-Grace.

Most of the railroad bridges built up to that time had been constructed of iron. This great new crossing of the Susquehanna River at its broad mouth was to be made of steel. It was for this reason an important engineering project. There was considerable uncertainty as to the ability of the Carnegie Steel Company, which had the contract for this first Bessemer steel bridge in this country, to properly roll and fabricate the metal. Evans was exacting in his requirements and would pass only such material as seemed to him absolutely flawless. The railroad engineers soon knew that any shipments approved by Evans were all right and the mills learned that nothing but the best would satisfy him. Andrew Carnegie was the active head of his company at that time and developed a deep respect for the self-taught naval metallurgist who could show the company's engineers a great many things about steel. Evans liked and admired Carnegie and the two men always remained friends.

Probably on no other election day of his life did Robley Evans await the announcement of the result as eagerly as on that November day in 1884 when the Republican Party, weakened by internal dissensions and the excesses of its long dominance of the national government, went down to defeat under James G. Blaine as the result of Grover Cleveland's carrying his own State of New York by a perilously few votes. Evans went along with his outside work through the winter, confident that the termination of Chandler's tenure of office would restore him to the good graces of the Department. President Cleveland appointed to his Cabinet as head of the Navy, William C. Whitney, whom Evans called the "prince of secretaries." Probably almost any one relieving Chandler would have appeared great to him, but there is no doubt that Whitney earned the high regard of the service and left behind him a record of substantial achievement. One day in the spring of 1885, not long after the Cleveland inauguration, the new Secretary sent for Commander Evans and he was welcomed back into the fold. Incidentally, this interview was his first opportunity to ascertain from an authoritative source the nature of his alleged offences and to state his version of the affair. He was restored to his former lighthouse post with the assurance that his side of any future controversy would be heard and that politics was not to run rampant in the service.

By this time, the New Navy was a lusty infant. The gunboat *Dolphin* had been completed and the cruisers *Atlanta, Boston* and *Chicago* were under construction. Congress now authorized the building of two additional cruisers, the *Newark* and *Charleston,* and the gunboats *Yorktown* and *Petrel*.

Secretary Whitney sensibly made use of Evans' knowledge of steel which had been so advantageously utilized by the Baltimore and Ohio Railroad. The Commander was detached from his lighthouse duties, this time under the most pleasant auspices, and made chief steel inspector of the new ships. His office was in Washington but he travelled about, to the mills and to the shipyards, wherever the situation indicated that his presence was most necessary.

Evans had proclaimed the feasibility of constructing steel ships and was only too ready to seize the opportunity of proving it. The specifications were exacting and the inspector insisted upon a meticulous compliance. Several of the rolling mills protested that the Commander was demanding the impossible but he answered all such remonstrances with unreasoning denials and persuaded the Department to back him up. "I knew, of course," said Evans, "that pot metal was cheaper than steel, and that our people would go on making pot metal until we forced them to do something better."

Carnegie used to relate the exasperation of his superintendent at the Commander's relentless scrutiny. The superintendent was a German whose thrifty habits survived his acquisition of wealth. The old fellow, William Borntraeger, was quite a character in the steel industry and is still remembered by many who saw him working around among the men, always smoking his one-cent Wheeling tobies. As quoted by Carnegie, the old fellow pushed into the former's office one day, complained bitterly about Evans' severity as an inspector and fairly shouted his greatest grievance: ". . . he gomes in and smokes my cigars and then he goes and contems my iron. What does you tinks of a man like dat?"

The benefit of the high requirements thus imposed accrued to both the Navy and the American steel industry. Before long, these standards were taken for granted.

Evans became known in steel circles and was recognized as an authority upon ship plates. There was an interview with him in *Iron Age* for June sixteenth, 1887, and it was republished in the *Proceedings of the United States Naval Institute* for June of that year.

A vacancy occurred in the naval secretaryship of the Lighthouse Board and Evans accepted the offer of appointment. The steel inspection had reached the point where it was routine and could be adequately continued by the subordinates he had indoctrinated with his standards and methods. The many years of service in one capacity or another in the lighthouse corps had suggested improvements to Evans which he was glad to be in a position to urge. Foremost, of course, was the constant passion for divorcing lighthouse keeping from political servility. He tried to engender a greater self-respect among the men and a pride in their attention to duty. Turning instinctively to the methods used aboard ship, he put the keepers into uniforms and stressed the cleanliness of the stations. The greatest achievement of his régime was the installation of electrically lighted buoys along the channel leading into New York Harbour. This was an epoch-making stride forward in the field of piloting aids. Buoys fitted with fixed and occulting gas lights had been in use for some years but this illumination of the New York Channel was the first system of the kind in the world.

In the latter part of Secretary Whitney's Administration he was encountering the most stubborn kind of bureaucratic inertia in his creditable efforts to hasten the completion of the two capital ships to be constructed by the Government in its own yards. One was to be built at Brooklyn and somehow the Secretary had not been able even to have the keel laid. He had seen Bob Evans in action as an executive who got things done. He discussed with him the vexatious delays and asked the Commander's assistance. It was a matter that required a driving energy and an inspiring personality on the spot, to cut through the red tape and put the project into motion. Evans planned to spend two days a week at this exhortation task in New York and to attend to his Lighthouse Board duties on the remaining four days of the working week. He was geared up to the rhythm of modern American business. It was a full program but he carried it out. The complications at the Brooklyn Yard that seemed to hopelessly block any progress toward starting the new warship, yielded before Evans' onslaught. He smiled, patted on the back, encouraged, berated and swore. He did not solve the problems that beset

the constructors; he ignored them. If they persisted in
intruding themselves, he pounded them into submission by
brute force. Instead of the tedious correspondence between
the Yard officials and the Department bureaus, his weekly
commuting afforded a rapid communication by the more
satisfactory means of personal conference. The keel was
placed in the blocks. As the frame grew and the plans
were revised, the armoured vessel began to take on the
aspect of a battleship. Bob Evans was the cheer leader of
the ill-fated *Maine*.

The fortunes of politics swung back to the Republicans
at the next presidential election. Cleveland's victory in 1884
could not be repeated. Benjamin Harrison, a far less colourful and far less natural leader than Blaine, succeeded where
the latter had failed. "The prince of secretaries" was
doomed to supersedure and Evans wondered what would
happen to him upon the restoration to power of Chandler's
party. As a matter of fact, the New Hampshire statesman-
politician was to spend the balance of his active public life
in the United States Senate and it was under the Harrison
Administration that Evans was to achieve celebrity and
become an international figure. All this was hidden in
the near future. For the moment, the Commander merely
knew that he was exhausted by the double duty he had been
cheerfully performing and that of all things he dreaded
most any fresh subjection to politically inspired abuse. He
applied for a year's leave of absence while the applying
was good. This was granted. Evans could not remain
long a gentleman of leisure. A little rest restored his vitality
and he had neither the temperament nor the financial means
to enjoy an extended release from work.

He negotiated with the company organized to construct
the proposed isthmian canal through Nicaragua and almost
engaged in that enterprise but the parties failed to come to
an agreement. The Manufacturing Investment Company

Courtesy U. S. Navy Department

U. S. S. *YORKTOWN*

of New York, headed by ex-Secretary Whitney, engaged him to travel through northern New England to select a site for a plant to manufacture wood fibre under a new process. This was a new field and absorbed Evans's interest by its novelty and the immensity of its industrial possibilities. The company for which he acted was seeking water power near available forests of spruce, as this was the wood that it planned to use. He eventually supervised the erection of the plant but it was in Wisconsin, not Maine. Many months of hard work in freezing weather brought their reward when at last the whole vast plant was in successful operation.

During this period, between the trip to Maine and the commencement of the Wisconsin project, there was a curious interruption. For no good reason that was perceptible, the Commander's leave was again cancelled. He began to fear that he was indeed the plaything of Republican Secretaries and this was not dispelled by the inspection of the vessel to which he had suddenly been ordered. She was an unseaworthy old steamer named the *Ossipee,* which had been rotting away at the Norfolk Yard and was pronounced by the officers there as unfit for service. For some inscrutable reason, the Department had selected this aged hulk with neglected machinery to transport to Hayti our Minister and his family.

Evans examined the ship and concealed his disgust. He was not fazed. The wind would carry him to Port au Prince and he "would drift back with the Gulf Stream."

A suspicious newspaper reporter, however, conceived the ingenious notion that Evans had deliberately disabled the *Ossipee* to avoid making the trip and this absurd libel was actually printed. The news value of the canard, the detail which gave it a sensational twist, lay in the person of the Minister. He was Frederick Douglass, the famous mulatto orator and journalist, whose mother had been a slave and father a white man. He had escaped from slavery to become a leading abolitionist in New England and was now prominent in Republican circles. It was entirely fitting that such a man be selected as our diplomatic emissary to the negro Republic of Hayti. Evans was unjustly accused of a disinclination to carry this coloured dignitary as a passenger. "I had known Mr. Douglass all my life," he said, "and entertained the highest respect for him." This, however, was immaterial. A naval captain is hardly in a position to censor accredited representatives of the country whom he is ordered to take aboard. To scotch all rumours, Evans wired the Department that he was ready to get under way, sailing if he could not steam, and that he "had no feeling as to the cargo" he might be ordered to carry, "be it ammunition, ministers, dynamite, or mules."

The Department reconsidered the matter and decided to send the Minister in a ship more certain of remaining afloat. The *Ossipee* was permitted to relapse into its atrophic decadence and Evans resumed his civilian employment.

9

"FIGHTING BOB"

~~~~~~

WHEN, at the end of the summer of 1891, Evans was given command of the gunboat *Yorktown,* neither the Department nor he had the slightest intimation that this duty would prove to be the most important in the service during the ensuing year. Surely the ship herself could have given no such hint. Relatively new and a unit of the White Squadron, she was not very potent even for those days. In view of the effective use her new skipper was about to make of her, it is interesting to note that she was unarmoured, displaced only seventeen hundred and forty tons and cost less than half a million dollars; little more than a yacht, upon which was mounted a main battery of six six-inch guns.

At first her duties harmonized with her mild appearance. In company with the rest of the squadron, the *Yorktown* cruised along the New England coast and provided a free side show at various ports where fairs were in progress. After watching the horse races and seeing cattle exhibits, the crowds poured over the decks of the ships and the officers, as always, took it in kindly, submissive spirit, knowing that some strenuous holy-stoning and a week at sea would restore cleanliness and discipline. It proved fortunate that the *Yorktown's* crew had this interlude of suspended routine and extensive recreation on the beach, as there lay ahead long months of arduous sea duty and exasperating weeks in foreign harbours without liberty.

While the White Squadron was thus lending its exotic and martial glamour to the county fairs, there was developing in Washington a situation which might make it necessary for the Government to shake its naval fist in the face of Chile. The State Department was creating an international impasse which only its sister Department could dispel. The *Yorktown* spent about ten vigorous days at the Brooklyn Yard scrubbing off the mud of her recent visitors and fitting herself for a prolonged cruise and possible hostilities. The flood lights burned all night and on October eighth Commander Evans stood out for Valparaiso with orders to report to the admiral commanding the Pacific Station. Storm signals were flying at Sandy Hook but these had to be disregarded because of the storm signals that he well knew were flashing over the cables from Minister Egan to Secretary of State Blaine, the big power of the Harrison Administration.

Wars constitute the histories of nations but war scares soon bury themselves in the forgotten tombs of pedantic diplomatic tomes. It will be seen how the United States came literally within a stone's throw (at Commander Evans' gig) of a conflict that would have radically affected the future of the western hemisphere. After thirty years the facts seem clear enough although the motives consciously and unconsciously actuating the President and the Secretary of State may remain forever in doubt.

Towards the end of his first term of office, President Cleveland had called a Pan-American conference at Washington presided over during the next administration by Blaine and featured by the same extravagant and probably sincere orations of mutual love and affection and amicable intention that are familiar to subsequent generations. South America was in a state of general unrest; the Chile-Peruvian War had ended only recently; Brazil was dispensing with its Emperor; the Argentine was in ferment; the atmosphere of *Nostromo* pervaded the continent. Conditions resembled those of 1930.

In time honoured fashion, the particular elements that were disturbing Chile proclaimed their respective devotion to the cause of law and order. The country, although actually ruled by a small landed aristocracy, had all the forms of a republic including a perfectly complete written constitution, adopted in 1833, in the most approved American style. President Balmaceda was a liberal whose progressive ideas were ahead of the times and earned the hostility of the reactionary property owners and clergy who dominated the nation. While it was really for his liberalism that the President had fallen into disfavour in high places, the alleged basis for the opposition was his method of carrying it out. He was charged with corruption and nepotism, and probably was none too scrupulous, even according to the standards of that time and locale. Reminiscent of the Stanton removal, which had provided the pretext for the impeachment of President Johnson, one of the questions upon which the Chilean factions joined issue was the power of the president to retain in office a cabinet that had been officially censured by Congress. The Constitution, supplying a deficiency of ours, which, of course, makes no mention of a cabinet at all, expressly gave to the president the power both of appointment and removal, but it had become the custom for a cabinet to retire in European parliamentary fashion when formally censured by the legislators. The oligarchy opposed to the President was in control of Congress.

President Balmaceda had sponsored an ambitious program of military preparedness and public works. His enemies accused him of improprieties in the expenditure of the large sums appropriated. The influential clergy brought pressure to bear against the President for his continued efforts to further separate the church and state. The reactionary forces saw in the President a dangerous radical

whose power must be curbed. Bitterness became intense.
The President could not form a ministry that had both his
own confidence and that of Congress, so one was appointed
in harmony with the former's views. Knowing that this
ministry would be censured at the very first opportunity,
the President omitted to summon an extraordinary session
of Congress to deal with the budget for the coming year.
A financial crisis threatened the government as 1890 passed
into 1891. Balmaceda tried to escape from the dilemma by
arbitrarily decreeing that the 1890 budget should be adopted
for 1891. This he had no colour of authority to do and on
this point the opposition had a clear case against him. He
was accused of being a tyrannical usurper of extra-constitu-
tional power.

The ranking officers of the Chilean Navy were by caste
sympathetic to the Congressionalists and on the night of
January sixth, 1891, some of the leaders of that faction,
including the vice president of the Senate and the president
of the Chamber of Deputies, boarded the fleet at Valparaiso
and in the name of Congress, proclaimed an insurrection
against the Balmaceda Administration. Civil war followed.
The President had the Army; the insurgents the Navy;
and, in a country thinly extended along a coast and dependent upon the water for its means of intercommunication,
sea power was bound to prevail. Soon gaining the upper
hand by means of the navy, the revolutionists demanded
foreign recognition for their *de facto* government. Washington naturally and properly refused to be rushed into
what might turn out to be a premature recognition; it politely announced that it would await further developments.
Woodrow Wilson was not the first of our chief magistrates
to survey the southern horizon with the policy of watchful
waiting. To cynical Nordic eyes it looked like the ordinary
Latin American struggle between the Ins and the Outs. As
a matter of fact, Chile is the one country of South America
which has been conspicuously free from such internal con-

flicts. Until recently it boasted of never having had a revolution, the struggles of 1891 being dignified in its history by the name of Civil War.

Pending recognition, the rules of international law had to be rigidly enforced by the United States and, when the ship *Itata* slipped out of a California port, a floating arsenal counted upon to equip the newly raised Congressionalist Army, she was pursued all the way to Chile, overtaken and brought back, all with a strict punctillo beyond justifiable criticism. The anti-Balmacedists were, nevertheless, very much incensed at this disappointing collapse of their arrangements and more than ever resented the continued withholding of our recognition, which had now proved so costly in a tangible way. The people of Valparaiso, which had been captured by the revolutionists and was the hot-bed of that faction, extended their animosity to include the Yankees among its objects. When insurgent forces attempted a clandestine landing at Quintero and were fired upon by a reception committee of the Balmacedists, a rumour gained ready credence in Valparaiso that Admiral Brown of the United States Navy, then in Chilean waters, had learned the secret plan and communicated it to the enemy. This rumour was denied and certainly was false but any wild anti-American accusation would have been hailed as an established charge. When Admiral Brown finally steamed away, it was generally believed that the then missing Balmaceda was aboard. Only his subsequent suicide in the Argentine legation at Santiago convinced the insurgents that he had not escaped on the American flagship. As the Civil War ended in a complete triumph for the Congressionalists, they turned their attention from their local enemies to the alleged but absolutely non-existent hostility of the United States. This was due in part to the mistaken impression that Patrick Egan, our Minister to Chile, a little Irishman who owed his appointment to political expediency but made up in character what he lacked in diplomatic attainments, was partisan to the presidential faction. The chief grievance against him was that he harboured in the legation at Santiago several of the distinguished Chileans, hunted down by the insurgents. When, despite the death of Balmaceda and the collapse of his faction, Egan continued to protect these fugitives, the Congressionalists whipped themselves into a frenzy of hatred against the United States, which pressed for an outlet.

The outlet came a week after the *Yorktown* had taken her departure and about when she was coaling ship at St. Thomas as rapidly as her energetic captain could do so.

The new cruiser *Baltimore,* later to distinguish herself in the Battle of Manila Bay and commanded by Captain Winfield Scott Schley, who was to figure prominently at Santiago de Cuba, was showing the American flag during these hectic days in the harbour of Valparaiso. On the afternoon of October sixteenth a liberty party of about one hundred and fifteen petty officers and men lay aft on the quarter-deck, passed inspection and shoved off in the running boats, arriving at about one thirty in the city, where the men scattered in small groups to spend their money and amuse themselves. Also abroad on the streets were large numbers of discharged longshoremen and sailors from the insurgent transports. Two of the American bluejackets, Talbot and Riggin, were strolling along about six o'clock, over four hours after having hit the beach, when a Chilean gratuitously spat in Talbot's face and was duly knocked down for his pains. The insult had been unprovoked and, as the question of sobriety became so prominent in the subsequent parleys, it may as well be stated here that, remarkable to relate, Talbot and Riggin and all of their shipmates who became involved were absolutely sober, despite Commander Evans' incredulity when he was so informed. A howling crowd of the native flotsam previously referred to collected so promptly when Talbot hit his expectorating host as to indicate a preconceived stratagem. The two sailors endeavoured to escape from the mob and jumped into a street car, which was surrounded. The scene was like that at a jail besieged by a blood thirsty lynching party and, when the conductor began to fear for the safety of his other passengers (and possibly for his own), he delivered up the desired victims, in striking contrast to the persistent refusal of the doughty Egan to surrender his refugees to an equally brutal throng in the capital. As the lads alighted, stones flew and Riggin went down, badly hurt and apparently dying. Others of the *Baltimore's* liberty party heard the excitement and rushed to the scene, where they too were assaulted. The sailors were out-numbered about ten to one, were unarmed and were attacked with knives, stones and clubs. The speed of the mob in assembling was not matched by that of the local authorities. The police station was three minutes' walk distant from the place where the fight started and the *Intendencia*, a military garrison, was not much further away, but it took the police and soldiers over half an hour to arrive. When the majesty of the law finally did put in its appearance, the American bluejackets saw to their horror that it was to reënforce the mob! Reliable eye witnesses later testified that the prostrate Riggin was finished by a soldier's bullet.

A check-up of the liberty party aboard ship disclosed that eighteen men had been stabbed or beaten. One had received eighteen knife wounds. And every wound of every man was in the back, which, as Evans noted upon his arrival, "tells its own tale." The entire Chilean casualty list was one man wounded. Somehow one death in an affray of that kind is more dramatic than countless injuries, and an American seaman had lost his life and another, mortally wounded, died a few days later. It was a wonder that the riot had not terminated as a wholesale massacre of the unarmed bluejackets.

True enough, the mob had been the scum of the water-

front and many reputable Chileans had intervened to stop
the fighting and save the bluejackets, but there were two
facts which lent to the affair a sinister international aspect.
First, the attack had been against the American uniform as
such and because of hostility to acts and omissions of the
American Government.   Second, the local authorities had
by their conduct manifested an official tolerance toward if
not an active support of the gangsters.

On New Year's Eve of that year, while the *Yorktown*
was riding at her anchor off Valparaiso amid the greatest
tension of the crisis, Captain Evans wrote in his journal,
regarding a rumour then current: "When the United States
is willing to submit the question of the murder of her sailors
in uniform to arbitration, I must look for other employment—the navy won't any longer suit me.   They can arbi-
trate 'till the cows come home about the people in the legation at Santiago, but if they ever hint at such a thing about
the *Baltimore's* men, I think the voice of the American
people will be heard in no uncertain tones."

Secretary Blaine awaited no such voice.   He demanded
an apology and reparation.   The President stoutly backed
him up.   The Chileans were at first disposed to brazen it
out and a sharp interchange of communications between the
governments burnt up the cables during the following weeks.

Of course, the judicial machinery in Valparaiso began
to move with respect to the riot, but it squeaked badly.
Adding insult to injury, thirty-six bluejackets had been arrested.   They were quickly released.   A few of the rowdies
also had been gathered in and some were, after a relatively
long time, convicted in the police court.

Fortunately for his good temper, Captain Evans missed
most of the spectacle of this administration of justice.   The
Yorktown anchored two miles from the Valparaiso landing
at the end of November, fifty-one days from New York,
eager to see what was what.   There had been few stops

after St. Thomas and those only to take on coal. The little *Yorktown* had buffeted heavy weather and found it particularly hard steaming after making the memorable passage through the Straits of Magellan, but she arrived in fit shape for what is usually euphemistically referred to as "any eventuality."

Evans, like almost all other human beings, whether or not aesthetically inclined, was deeply impressed by scenic splendours. The fewest can give any partially adequate expression to the admiration inspired at such times. "Grand" is as satisfactory an adjective as any other. Evans applied it to the beauty of the Windward Islands and superlatively to the magnificence of the glacial mountains near the Straits. That he stood upon the bridge thrilled by the wonders of the towering Andes that hemmed in the tortuous channel, we can not doubt. The next time he was to behold them would be after many years, with the gold of exalted rank upon his uniform, fame and glory upon his brow and rheumatism racking his limbs into uselessness, leading a great fleet in formation as safely between the hazards to navigation as in this season of his prime he brought the *Yorktown.*

The new Chilean cruiser *Errazuriz* gave added spice to the voyage. While at Montevideo, Evans received many cables from the Department regarding her and, when he learned that she was undergoing repairs at Buenos Aires, lost no time cogitating upon the ethics thereof but sent one of his officers in plain clothes across La Plata "to have a look at her." The latter proved to be an excellent sleuth, managing to get aboard the *Errazuriz* and not be ejected until he had learned enough to enable his "old man" to confidently wire the Department that he "could do her up with the *Yorktown* in thirty minutes." The news now indicated probable war and at any moment. A Chilean gunboat put in her appearance at Montevideo before the *Yorktown* left and Evans considered it more than likely that the *Errazuriz,* upon learning of his departure, would endeavour to outrace the *Yorktown* to Valparaiso. Perhaps the wish was father to the thought. Characteristically, he yearned for a chance to let his gunners prove their accuracy and rapidity of fire against this real adversary. "I wish we could have a scrap with the *Errazuriz*," he confided to his journal as the ship took shelter inside Cape Virgin in the Straits to await the absolutely necessary daylight, "for I feel confident that we could take her into camp in forty-five minutes by the watch, notwithstanding all her new French rapid-fire guns. . . ." His glasses scanned the reaches of the channels but the *Errazuriz* was never sighted *en route*. Even if she had been, however, the order to open fire would have had to await positive news of war. In those pre-radio days, the uncertainty aboard the warships at sea, as to whether or not an impending declaration had actually been made, added to the perils of such crises. The *Yorktown* had no means of ascertaining the state of affairs as she steamed north along the west coast of the continent. She put in for coal not far from Coronel, off which port Von Spee was to destroy Cradock's squadron in 1914 a few weeks before being vanquished in turn by Sir Doveton Sturdee at the Falkland Islands. No word of war here. On up the Pacific now, with no possible news short of Valparaiso, the *Yorktown* pressed ahead. Days might make no difference; minutes might count decisively; there was no way to find out.

The Valparaiso harbour entrance was sighted the next afternoon. Now they would know! The shore batteries would tell the story. Tensely the ship steamed within range. No firing. There could be no war yet. Inside the harbour, there lay at anchor the fleet of the prospective enemy and the familiar *Baltimore*, as peaceful looking as if in the Hudson River. Well, for whatever was going to happen, Evans was in time.

When Commander Evans finally came over the side of the *Baltimore* at Valparaiso to pay his official call upon

Captain Schley as Senior Officer Present, he found the latter engaged in the protracted correspondence with the local authorities that to the direct-acting Robley D. seemed preposterously fatuous. For Winfield Scott Schley, a serious man with a long and honourable service record but of an altogether different temperament, he seems never to have had a high esteem, and the calm interchange of objectively poised communications between ship and shore was exasperating to him. In his *Sailor's Log,* written many years later, Evans said: "He was in the midst of a correspondence with the *intendente,* conducted in the most perfect Castilian, to show, or prove, that his men were all perfectly sober when they were assaulted on shore. I did not agree with him in this, for in the first place I doubted the fact, and in the second it was not an issue worth discussing. His men were probably drunk on shore, properly drunk; they went ashore, many of them, for the purpose of getting drunk, which they did on Chilean rum paid for with good United States money. When in this condition they were more entitled to protection than if they had been sober."

Evans was contemptuous of Schley's having been drawn into an irrelevant controversy that had been injected into the discussions to obscure the real issue. He would in effect have interposed a demurrer to the drunkenness charge (admitting it for sake of argument, what of it?) and have converted it into a point for his own case. To the spirited Virginian of more than one stand-up fight, enraged at those cowardly stabs in the backs of the defenceless bluejackets, there seemed

> ". . . . . a tongue
> In every wound of Caesar, that should move
> The stones of Rome to rise and mutiny."

To dignify the cowardly brutality by the kind of note-writing then in progress seemed to Evans unworthy of an American naval officer. Dining in the cabin of the *Balti-*

more that night, he found it difficult to conceal his disgust. Once back aboard his own ship, however, further effort at self-restraint was abandoned. The young watch officer on duty, now a distinguished Admiral on the retired list, distinctly recalls the return of the gig that night and pacing up and down the quarter-deck with his irate Captain from whom poured a crackling drumfire of profane vituperation. His wrath thereby soothed, Old Gimpy went below, less excited but with his disapprobation of Schley's attitude undiminished. Perhaps it was there and then that he formed the conviction of his senior's pusillanimity, which, legend has it, he so dramatically denounced in a spontaneous outburst, immediately after the Battle of Santiago, because of the *Brooklyn's* turn, away from the enemy. Evans mistook poor judgment and a lack of instinctive boldness, for cowardice.

The usual formalities in the way of paying and receiving calls were complied with and both Evans and the Chileans, possible enemies to-morrow, were careful to give no basis for offence until their respective State Departments saw fit to declare the quarrel officially picked. Evans misjudged the situation in one respect, which was natural enough under the circumstances. He believed the widespread anti-American feeling to be the result rather than the cause of the *Baltimore* assault. This mistake may have been fortunate in checking any vent to his indignation. Feeling that the *Baltimore* was the *bete noir,* it was reasonable to suppose that the proper deportment of other United States men-of-war might restore local good will. His conception of such proper deportment was an admixture of tact and firmness, with emphasis on the firmness.

Inshore lay most of the Chilean Navy, such as it was, nine vessels in wretched condition, but seething with the hatred of the most intransigeant Congressionalists for the United States, and feverishly putting themselves in shipshape for war. Less than two weeks after Commander Evans' arrival, the *Baltimore* departed for the north, leaving the *Yorktown* to hold our first line of defence unaided. As the *Baltimore* stood out past the *Yorktown,* the crew of the latter gave a lusty cheer. Without another American flag in the harbour and surrounded by Chilean warships and coast defence batteries, Valparaiso seemed far from home. A flash from the *Yorktown's* batteries and the war would have been irrevocably declared by the resultant Chilean salvos, however wildly aimed or awkwardly fired. The Captain's patience was dangerously tested and upon several occasions almost yielded, but the Yankee-baiters soon learned that to scratch the yacht-like *Yorktown* would be to arouse a Bob Evans and they let well enough alone.

The allusion to the scratch is no mere figure of speech nor the adaptation of an old adage. One day the Chilean torpedo boats dashed about the harbour and plunged directly toward the *Yorktown,* putting the helm over only at the last minute and averting a collision by a narrow margin, in one instance by less than six feet. The Captain sounded general quarters and gave orders that "if one of them even scratched the paint on the *Yorktown,* to blow the boat out of the water and kill every man in her, so that there could be no question of an accidental collision." Later he saw the officer in charge of the so-called drills and told him that he certainly must have great confidence in the steering gear of his torpedo boats but that, if this confidence ever should prove to have been misplaced and one of the boats struck the *Yorktown,* the latter would "blow the bottom out" of the torpedo craft. The Chilean replied that the water in the harbour belonged to his Government and Evans retorted that the *Yorktown* and her paint belonged to his. This stopped the offensive character of the drills.

Valparaiso celebrated New Year's Eve with uproarious gusto. As midnight approached, the city appeared from the decks of the *Yorktown* a maze of polychromatic, danc-

ing lights. The Chilean warships contributed to the festivities by flashing searchlights and discharging rockets and, as
a night-splitting climax of the pandemonium, firing twenty-
one gun salutes. As the flames leaped out of the invisible
muzzles and the hills echoed the reports, the rockets began
to sparkle in lower trajectories and were observed to be war
rockets, one of which almost struck the American gunboat.
The Captain was taking no chances of having any such hit
explained as accidental; up the flagstaff went the largest
available ensign; out broke the searchlights; and the entire
harbour beheld the *Yorktown* bright as day, the illuminated
Stars and Stripes defying insult and—to remove any possible
prospect of non-resistance—the gun crews, in the spot light,
at their stations. The rockets sought other directions.

The *Errazuriz* finally stood in one night and swept the
bay with her beacons, as if trying to locate something, until
the beams straddled the *Yorktown* and rested there, as if
having found the object of their search, awakening some of
the sailors sleeping near port-holes suddenly illuminated.
The demonstration was discourteous and, under the circumstances, unmistakably hostile. Promptly the men "showed
a leg" from their hammocks, hit the deck and fell in on the
topside, singing the *Star Spangled Banner*.

Throughout the trying weeks at Valparaiso, the crew
never put foot ashore, and the long cruise south, followed by
the tense inactivity in close confinement on a vessel two-
thirds the length of a modern destroyer, was an exacting test
of the ship's morale, which it met and passed gallantly. To
have sent bluejackets ashore would have been to court a
second *Baltimore* affair. Under normal circumstances, Evans
always was willing to trust his men to take care of themselves and had no fear of the consequences. Here he knew
that circumstances were anything but normal. He probably
figured that a small group might have been massacred and that
a large liberty party might have caught the ship with an embarrassing shortage of hands in an emergency. The officers

went ashore in the afternoons. Evans frequently visited the city and made a trip to the capital and metropolis of Santiago, beautifully pocketed in the Andes, which had been systematically sacked in cold blood with a remorseless diabolism that made the atrocities of our Civil War seem tame in comparison.

There he saw Minister Egan and his equally plucky wife sheltering, under the aegis of the eagle *del Norte*, the terrified refugees who scarcely dared peer through the shutters at the murderous spies constantly surrounding the legation. To Evans the pathetic group presented an object lesson in the gratitude of republics. He was particularly moved by the sight of the aged ex-Minister of War and General of the Army, who had devoted a lifetime to Chile, separated by only the walls of the building from certain assassination.

The fearless spokesman of Washington, standing on the very periphery of its sphere of prestige, grasped eagerly at the symbol of its might which lay at anchor in Valparaiso under the dashing command of a temperament no less conciliatory than his own, where a principle was believed to be at stake. Egan consulted Evans but the latter, with all due friendliness and no timidity about assuming responsibility, which was an old bedfellow, refrained from interference with the diplomatic fencing. No one should later scorn him as a sea-lawyer meddler. The State Departments of the two countries were rapidly enough preparing the way for their respective navies to settle the score. Secretary Montt had set forth Chile's position as to the *Baltimore* tragedy in a cable that was utterly unacceptable. There was a vast amount of eloquent deploring and no admission of national responsibility. One note led to another and, as January wore on, the situation approached a crisis. Among other things, Montt accused the American naval officers of having sent their Government false reports. It seemed that there would have to be an ultimatum and then—submission or force. Secretary Blaine was getting in deeper and deeper. Europe cynically mocked at our professed Pan-American pacifism and laughed at our depleted Navy. Many Americans could see nothing more nor less to Harrison's firm stand than a cheap political manœuvre in anticipation of the coming presidential campaign; but the majority of the articulate public echoed his demand for a Chilean apology and compensation. When the new Government implied that Egan was no longer *persona grata* at Santiago, the United States as a whole enthusiastically applauded his support by Washington.

A false move on the part of Chile and the door to a peaceful solution would have been slammed shut. On the night of January sixth, the anniversary of the revolutionary outbreak, Captain Evans was warned by a drunken stranger that his ship was to be sunk or captured in a surprise attack. Had any such treachery been attempted, the reaction at home would have been the same as it was to be a few years later, when the streets of the States rang to the cry: "Remember the *Maine!*"

An incident regarded by the President as grave indeed was the stoning of Evans' gig as it lay at the landing and the menacing mutterings of the guilty throng of hoodlums as he limped along and stepped into the boat. Difficult it was for him to turn the other cheek but, when the occasion required it, he could do even that.

As hounds baying at a treed animal lose patience and seek to bring the prey to earth, the celebrity scalp-hunters about the American legation barked defiance at those very time honoured doctrines of international law which Chile herself had invoked most vociferously when the shoe was on the other foot, at the time of the recent revolution in Peru. More prudent counsels among the insurgents finally prevailed, however, and it was arranged that the refugees would be transferred from the asylum of the legation to the asylum of the *Yorktown* via the protected route of *salvo conducto*.

Once aboard the gunboat, these excited passengers, including other refugees from the Spanish legation, ironically

shielded from their fellow countrymen by the prospective
national enemy, constituted a nerve-racking cargo. An
item not to be overlooked in contemplating the monetary
rewards of American naval service is that Commander
Evans' anxiety was concerned not alone with the dangers
and physical discomfort inherent in the situation but also
with the enormous mess bills that this enforced hospitality
would entail.

They might scoff in London at his problems, but Evans
could occasionally dine aboard H.M.S. *Warspite* with Admiral Hotham, assured that the latter watched the volatile
performance of the hour with the sympathetic understanding
of a cordial professional colleague. Hotham and Evans
were to see much of each other in many waters and their
camaraderie was to actually thrive on the contiguous boundary of their countries' delicately delineated treaty rights.
The British Captain was none other than Evans's old friend
in the Mediterranean, Hedworth Lambton.

The arrival on the *Yorktown* of the last refugees was
ceremonial in the extreme, with the fanfare of boatswain's
pipes, side-boys, gun salutes and the impressive escort of the
Spanish and Italian Ministers. The first group, however,
came alongside at daybreak in the *Yorktown's* steam launch,
which had picked it up at a rendezvous in accordance with
the arrangements of Mr. Egan, who placed safety first and
Latin dignity not at all. "My heart sank into my boots when
I saw the women," said Evans, "but fortunately they went
on shore afterward. . . . " The chivalry that bestowed
immunity upon the ladies greatly facilitated the operations
of South American revolutions.

His cabin crowded (the refugees had been threatened
with rifle fire if they appeared above decks), his galley taxed,
his responsibilities multiplied, Captain Evans at last hauled
up his anchor from the mud of Valparaiso harbour and got
under way for Callao, with a relief that can readily be
imagined and that was shared by all hands. Friendly Ad-

miral Hotham, on Evans's farewell call, pointed to the smoking stacks of four of the Chilean warships and mentioned the report that the *Yorktown* and her still terrorized guests would be followed.   Evans impressed upon the Admiral, for the purpose of having it reach Chilean ears, that, although the sea was open to mankind, if his wake were tracked by any Chilean craft, he would regard such shadowing as an insult to his flag.   The *Yorktown* may have looked none too potent but her visit had sufficed to make the natives realize that she flew a battleship-size ensign and was commanded by an officer who knew how to defend it.

In the cities and villages of the United States, the war spirit was being aroused.   National pride and jingoism joined in a chorus of righteous indignation and there was the anticipation of an exciting drama in a conveniently remote theatre.   Volunteers organized, martial music played, orators thundered.   The New York *Herald* did as much deploring on the editorial page as had Secretary Montt in his foolhardy missive of bravado, but more conspicuously displayed were articles estimating the relative naval and military strength of the prospective belligerents, maps illustrating possible landing of expeditionary forces at the feet of the Andes and drawings of the prominent leaders, including Commander Evans.   There was a palpable omission of censorship and the disposition of our few and not very powerful warships was broadcast to the world.   The Chilean crisis had been for some time the big news topic and Evans a familiar hero.   Finally Secretary Blaine delivered an ultimatum.   When no reply arrived, President Harrison, on January twenty-fifth sent to the Capitol a special message, which brilliantly, forcefully and, therefore, from a somewhat partisan standpoint recited the chain of events, outlined the official correspondence and asked Congress "for such action as may be deemed appropriate."   It was a war message and Congress was ready for it.   Extras carried its substance far and wide. The nation was thrilled as it had not been for many a year. The dissenters to the Harrison-Blaine ultimatum were shouted down in the general chorus of approval although, as soon as the crisis was safely passed, their voices became audible once more. At the moment, war seemed inevitable and each edition of the press made this more certain. There was a spurious story that Egan had been assassinated and many other wild rumours in addition to the true news of the affronts to the Minister and Captain Evans, which had been set forth in detail in the President's message.

The anti-Administration and anti-ultimatum *Herald's* headline on January twenty-sixth was: "All Ready For War." This was typical. Across the Atlantic, the Europeans took the outbreak of hostilities for granted. The London *Chronicle* said: "Mr. Harrison's declaration that America does not covet territory ought not to be taken as a pledge, but rather as an ingenious device to allay suspicions not wholly groundless." But the London *Standard* admitted that even if naughty we were not dangerous: " . . . if the mere contemplation of hostilities brings home to the minds of the American people the inadequacy of their armaments something will have been achieved." Right they were. The "something . . . achieved" turned out to be preparedness for the break with Spain when it occurred six short years later—short in the time necessary to authorize, plan, construct, shake-down and properly train a warship. The immediate effect was to stimulate contributions in New York for the silver service to be presented to the new cruiser of that name, then nearing completion, which was destined to have a distinguished career and to be Evans' next command after the *Yorktown*.

While Congress was listening to the reading of the stirring message, the clerks at the State Department were busily engaged in the prosaic task of decoding a long despatch from Santiago which, when finally laid on the desk at the White House, turned out to be a last-minute reprieve from war. Pereira, the new Chilean Minister of Foreign Affairs, ate Montt's words. Without sacrificing either his country's or his Government's dignity, he repudiated the special pleading as to the *Baltimore* outrage and offered to make amends, so far as that could be done. Gold was deposited for the families of the slain sailors, and Commander Evans, fortunately, did not, in chagrin at any arbitration, have to "seek other employment." Minister Egan was acknowledged to be in the good graces of the Government to which he was accredited. The war bubble had been pricked. Chile soon retired from the front pages.

The *Yorktown* received the news and, after some much needed rest and recreation in Peru, where the skipper and his crew enjoyed the sights of Lima and its mountainous environs, the homeward-bound pennant was two-blocked and the course set for San Francisco. A batch of mail reached the ship while she was still at Callao and the Captain, after reading the newspapers, asked his journal: "Why should they call me 'Fighting Bob'?" Why, indeed! He had thought himself the very master of self-control and proponent of pacifism. Upon any number of occasions, by just relaxing this grip upon his natural impulse, he could have lighted the war fuse or, more properly, failed to extinguish it when lighted by others, and of this he was fully aware. "Looking back at it now, I am glad I did just what I did, and in the way I did it. . . . In the discharge of my duty I gave the Chileans a fine chance to fight if they wanted to, and the odds were enough in their favour—nine ships to one. But they backed water every time. . . . "

And "I am glad also that I got away from Valparaiso just when I did, for I am sure that if we had been there when the President's ultimatum came I should have had to open on them, the feeling was so intense."

It may fairly be wondered how glad he really was.

In any event, the new sobriquet, bestowed by the head-lines and quickly adopted by the people, was to be his for ever after, on the beach. In the service he remained Old Gimpy and it is by that name that his surviving shipmates speak of him to-day.

The *Yorktown* reached San Francisco in April and received the welcome she richly deserved. Commander Evans was now a national figure and hailed on the streets, even in mufti, as Fighting Bob. If there was no powerful fleet to cheer, there was a hero.

The return journey up the coast had been without any unusual incident. One of the officers contracted typhoid and, fresh milk being prescribed as essential, Evans recalled an experience of his younger days and put into Acapulco for a goat, which proved to be a less troublesome passenger than a refugee.

This was not the first time that Evans had been a ship-mate of a goat. Back in the old days aboard the *Shenandoah* he had had an unforgettable intimacy with one, which he vividly describes in his *Log*.

"The paymaster was very ill at this time and growing worse. Many of us, who knew him well, thought the best thing he could do would be to die—the best for all hands, particularly the wife. The captain, at the instigation of the doctor, purchased a goat, in order that the patient might have the advantage of fresh milk on the passage over. We left Madeira early in the morning, and at eleven o'clock that night the orderly turned me out, saying the captain wanted to see me on deck. I was at a loss to know what he could possibly want with me at that hour, but, supposing it to be something of importance, hurried into my clothes and reported to him on the quarter-deck, when the following conversation took place: 'Evans, you know the paymaster is very ill, and may die?' 'Yes, sir; I hope he will.' 'Well, he surely will unless he can have some goat's milk. I have sent for you to ask if you won't milk the goat for us. I know you can do it. So far we have not succeeded in getting a drop of milk from the beast, though she seems to have plenty.' To this proposition I was naturally disposed to make a sharp reply, but, having a great regard for the captain, I only said, 'I was not aware, sir, that it was any part of the navigator's duty to milk a goat.' 'Of course not, Evans, of course not; I ask you to do it as a matter of humanity, and to oblige me.'

"That, of course, settled the question, and down I went to tackle Mrs. Goat. I found her in a very excited state of mind apparently, having butted out the captain's steward and a marine orderly who had attempted to relieve her of her milk. One of them had tried to hold her while the other went for the milk. I remembered how the darkies in my young days had treated a cow under the same conditions, and procuring some warm water and exercising a little patience in the premises, soon relieved her of the milk, which was evidently giving her pain. This I sent to the cabin, and went back to my sleep. At breakfast in the morning the whole mess knew what had taken place, and I was, of course, the subject of no end of chaff."

The *Warspite* was lying there and, although the *York-town* remained in port only two hours, Evans managed to shake hands with his friend Hotham, who sent the sick officer the rarest gem of the tropics: a cake of ice, the only one in Acapulco. The patient fought gamely, to his skipper's admiration, and, with the latter's care, reached Mare Island alive and later recovered.

In the wardroom was a young officer destined to go far in naval fame and on the heights of applied ingenuity. Already he had many important inventions to his credit and was so pregnant with more that he had seriously considered forsaking his naval career, before the *Yorktown* sailed from New York. Competent at his duties of watch and division officer, he was, nevertheless, often yearning for the facilities of the laboratory as he did his trick on the bridge. The particular device that occupied his thoughts during this cruise was one that his shipmates, including his distinguished Captain, regarded as "of no value on board ship": the telescope sight, which very soon thereafter revolutionized naval gunnery and has for years been used by every navy in the world. Lieutenant Bradley A. Fiske was engaged in the uphill struggle of all pioneers. When he reached Valparaiso, he was gratified to learn that the current number of *Revista de Marina,* the Chilean naval magazine, had published an article about his range-finder which was to be installed in their new battleship *Captain Prat,* then under construction in France. One had been tested on the *Baltimore,* and Fiske eagerly went aboard to ascertain the results, which had been favourable.

Now he wanted to demonstrate the soundness of the principle of his telescope sight and, on the cruise north, after the regular target practise, Evans grudgingly complied with the orders of the Bureau of Ordnance to try it. The old sea dog of the sailing era had little patience with these new gadgets although he did invent a loading apparatus at one time. When, because of a faulty adjustment of the sight, the shots fell short of the target, the Captain and the Executive Officer passed hasty adverse judgment, which the former embodied in a report to the Department. The report was filed away and the telescope sight survived, for Fiske's faith in it was only shaken and not shattered and he overcame the obstacles and proceeded to perfect other valuable instruments, as well as to round out a brilliant career of active service.

Such are the pranks of memory that when Evans discussed telescope sights in the days of his retirement from active service, he completely forgot the incident on the *Yorktown,* despite other tests, remarkably and indisputably successful, made by the ship at Unalaska the following September.

"A telescope sight," he wrote in a magazine article in 1909, "had been invented years before by Lieutenant Bradley

A. Fiske but for some reason it had not found favour in the service."

"For some reason!"

If Fiske's tour of duty in the *Yorktown* under Captain Evans was not a good mother of invention, it created necessities that bred the staunchest seamanship.   The officers and men who steamed the twenty-eight thousand miles that the log showed between October '91 and October '92 had been to sea sure enough.   As the ship lay in dry-dock at Mare Island, the most stormy part of these long stretches was still to come.

From Captain to mess attendant, all hands revelled in the joys of liberty among friends.   It was the hey-day of San Francisco's Barbary Coast.   The men rated a spree and it is fair to assume that they had it.

10

READING BETWEEN THE LINES

ON April twenty-fourth, the Admiral commanding at Mare Island told Evans that the Department had inquired when the *Yorktown* could be made ready for sea, to which the junior replied that he had been ready for sea ever since he had arrived! By such spirit was builded the tradition that so impressed the British Admiral Bayly, commanding at Queenstown, when in 1917 Lieutenant Commander Taussig brought in the first squadron of American destroyers to augment the allied forces and, upon being asked how much time he required after the arduous transatlantic trip before commencing active duty, answered like Fighting Bob: "We're ready now, sir."

Evans was taken at his word. Orders promptly came to proceed to Port Townsend on Puget Sound and prepare for sealing duty in the Bering Sea. At first this seemed merely like glorified revenue cutter service but it quickly presented itself as the most important assignment in the Navy. Evans was to command a fleet of six vessels—an admiral's job, as he said himself. To navigate the then uncharted channels and passages between the islands along the northern shore required ships of shallow draft, and the battery of a gunboat was as effective against an outlaw sealer as that of a division of battleships. The vital factor was the command of the expedition and the Department knew that Evans was the man for the job. After six tempestuous months in the dirtiest weather on any of the seven seas, this choice was abundantly vindicated.

The conservation of the fur-bearing seal was a matter that had vexed all of the nations bordering on the North Pacific. In 1892, when the *Yorktown* was sent to the rescue, time was pressing; a few more years of greedy slaughter and there would have been no animals left to protect. Evans realized this fully because he had himself lived to see the almost complete extermination of the buffalo, which had roamed the prairies in apparently unlimited numbers when he had journeyed to Utah as a lad. At that time, any suggestion of the possibility of there being no more bison at large in the United States in thirty years than elephants or tigers would have aroused ridicule. The young Evans and his companions of the covered wagon had slain the big animals for their tongues alone or even as a whim. Thousands had been shot wantonly from train windows when the first railroads were pushed West. The fate of the buffalo thus having fallen within his own experience, Evans faced his new task with the stimulating conviction that it was worth while.

The fur-bearing seals of the North Pacific were known even before the discovery of the Pribilof Islands at about the close of our Revolutionary War. They were, in fact, mentioned in the notes of the German naturalist Steller, who accompanied Vitus Bering on his horizon-lifting explorations in 1741 for Peter the Great, when the leader left his name and his body in the straits that he found divided the continents. Because of their economic value and the solicitude of nations for their preservation, an amazingly complete knowledge of the life and habits of these animals has been acquired and recorded by experts. The vanity of the ladies has sent thousands of hunters, officials and students into the Arctic and might easily have provoked armed conflict. The curse of these gentle, defenceless mammals of the sea is, of course, their black or dark brown fur which, when dyed, has found a demand that persists above and beyond the waves of vogue. There are two principal herds in the North Pacific which do not intermingle: the larger one based on the Pribilof Islands and the smaller on the Commander Islands. During the decade preceding Evans' patrol, the Pribilof seals were variously estimated to number from two to five million, the Commander seals about half that, but by 1896 the numbers dwindled to a seventh. After we acquired Alaska, the Pribilof Islands became ours; the Commander Islands remained Russian.

These seals are as much the creatures of unvarying routine as are the people whose civilizations their hides adorn. In May of any year, an observer on a promontory of one of the five bleak Pribilof Islands would sight the vanguard of the season's males, heading in from their winter cruise to the south, as punctual to schedule as human commuters. The favoured breeding grounds are boulder-strewn beaches or rocky slopes near the shore. The unit of rookery life is the family group or harem, each bull collecting as many cows as he can control, this number ranging from one to a hundred or more, in this respect reminding Evans of the Mormon families he had seen as a lad in Salt Lake City. Males too young for wedlock or unequal to the competition for spouses or having no susceptibility to the allurements of domestic life, haul out of the water to rest on beaches near but distinct from the breeding grounds, a habit which, as presently will be explained, facilitates discriminate hunting that is consistent with conservation of the species. The early arrivals at the rookeries select their places and the colony enlarges until, in the traditional bridal month of June, the cows, which are strikingly smaller than the bulls, begin to reach the seraglios. Each family has its own recognized place and woe betide the intruder. The height of the mating season is mid-July, when there is apt to be at least half of the herd on the foreshores. The community then gradually thins out until, in the early autumn of those latitudes, there is not a seal in sight. Within a day or two of her arrival at the rookeries, each cow gives birth to one jet black pup weighing about ten pounds. A week later the former is served by her bull, after which she goes to sea to feed, returning to nourish her pup at gradually lengthening intervals throughout the summer, during which the pups have to shift for themselves. They learn to swim during their second month and accompany the herd when it departs. If the mother is killed at sea and hence fails to return with food, the pup starves. The bulls fast at the breeding grounds until in about August they return to the water for good. During the annual cruise, which extends to nearly the tropics, the herd keeps pretty well together and seeks its food, chiefly certain kinds of fish, in deep water, usually at about the hundred fathom curve, which is well off the coasts.

The early nineteenth century sealing was mostly confined to the animals' insular resorts. A straggler was occasionally spotted inshore of the herd by some observant Indian on Vancouver Island, who would paddle out in his canoe and catch the laggard, but these instances were so rare as to be negligible in effect.

During the period of Russian sovereignty over both sides of the North Pacific, seal-hunting was a monopoly enjoyed by one trading company, which moderately contented itself with about seventy-five thousand skins a year in accordance with an intelligent system based on the polygamous habits of the herd, whereby the breeding females and their pups were safeguarded and the killing confined to the superfluous males. The latter, as has been referred to, identified themselves by segregating in bachelor quarters, were surrounded by the hunters at night, rounded up in groups of a couple of thousand more or less and driven to the killing grounds further inland, where the three year olders were marked for sacrifice and clubbed, the rest being permitted to lollop

back to the beach and escape. So long as the catch was confined to this sane system, the herd needed to have no fear
for its future. The best pelts thus were obtained without
jeopardizing the species. What threatened it with extermination—and speedy extermination—was the deep sea killing that became active in the seventies. Sailboats from
Asia, Canada and the Pacific ports of the United States
began to assail the herd while on its long annual migration,
during which it never put flipper on land. The Russian
company's monopoly had, upon the sale of Alaska in 1867,
so far as the Pribilof Islands were concerned, passed into the
hands of the Alaska Commercial Company, whose operations were carried on in the same rational way as had been
its predecessor's.

The outlaw depredations were, however, making drastic inroads upon the herds, not alone because of the
quantities speared and shot at sea but because this kind
of hunting was necessarily a catch as catch can affair, without restriction as to age, sex or the future. Nothing mattered except the glossy skins for the current market. The
slaughter on the high Pacific and up into the Alaskan
passages was ruthless and enormous and, worst of all,
promiscuous. A revolting feature was that a majority of
the animals killed sank before their bodies could be retrieved. By 1879 these exterminators were each winter
tracking the herds on their northward swim and following
in their wake. When the *Yorktown* was refitting in Puget
Sound, there were over a hundred vessels used for this purpose (Evans fixed the number at about one hundred and
ten but this was probably an underestimate by a dozen)
and each of them carried five to twenty small boats for the
hunting crews. Some flew the American and some the English flag and the ownership was by no means always the
same nationality as the registry but the entire fleet was
banded together into a sort of pelagic poaching association.
The work was dangerous and strenuous and highly re-

munerative, the danger having been due to the mutual dis-
loyalties of the gangs, who often left boatloads adrift, and
not to any sporting opposition on the part of the quarry as,
for example, was the case in whaling. There is no saga of
the seal comparable to *Moby Dick* because the avaricious
crews that sneaked off the West Coast bore more resemblance
to modern rum runners than to the hardy Nantucketers who,
generation after generation, made careers of circumnavigat-
ing the globe to eke out a bare livelihood from the conquest
of the leviathan which could and everlastingly did hit back.
Fighting Bob infused some excitement into the Bering
fisheries during the summer of '92, however, and it soon
became too much for the outlaws' peace of mind.

This was the period between the ratification of the Anglo-
American arbitration treaty and the sittings of the tribunal
appointed pursuant thereto, which was to and eventually did
decide certain questions of international law that were raised
by the so-called Bering Sea controversy. While the *Yorktown* was riding out the Chilean storm at Valparaiso, Secretary Blaine was also asserting our claims regarding the
regulation of sealing. Queerly enough, these claims were
based upon Czarist ukases against which we had joined with
Great Britain in filing protest. In the course of the diplomatic parleys, we had abandoned some of the more pre-
posterous pretensions of the Russian monarchs to virtual
proprietorship of the North Pacific, which alleged rights we
said Secretary Seward had purchased as a sort of bonus
along with Alaska, but Washington continued to insist upon
having fallen heir to the benefits attributable to the ukase
of 1821 whereby foreign vessels had been forbidden to approach within a hundred Italian miles of the coasts of
Russian America. The diplomatic correspondence on both
sides was resourceful in argument and the issue became
complicated by a tangle of old treaties and their meanings,
and general doctrines of the law of nations and their application.

The discussions fell into two parts: the factual and the legal. The United States abhorred the immorality of the butchery and denounced the eventual destruction of the species involved in pelagic sealing. Great Britain replied that this noble and far-seeing attitude was all very well for Russia, which could take its annual quota of skins on its Commander Islands, and for us with the Pribilof Islands within our sovereignty, but asked what the Canadians were to do upon whose shores no herd maintained its rookeries.

The legal justification for the American attempt to suppress oceanic assaults upon the Pribilof seals was declared to be dual: the *mare clausum* absurdity, later giving way to the exclusive jurisdiction theory just mentioned; and the more tenable argument that seals had some of the characteristics of domestic animals in which a property interest might vest, as in horses or cattle, which would enable the United States, as the owner, to extend to them its protecting arm wherever (even on the high seas) they might be found.

Pending the adjudication of the controversy by the illustrious arbitrators, the two governments had adopted a temporary *modus vivendi* whereby their two navies would coöperate to drive the pelt pirates out of northern waters. To Evans delight, his British colleague was none other than Admiral Hotham. The former set about the business with his unflagging vigour. Notices to keep out of the forbidden zones, signed by both commanding officers, were served upon the sealing vessels. Then, not much after the northern sweep of the Pribilof herd, the *Yorktown* emerged from the picturesque Straits of San Juan de Fuca and cut across the corner of the Pacific to the Aleutian Islands where, at the God-forsaken outpost of Unalaska, she established her base of operations. As the skipper and his navigating officer pored over the available charts, they found few aids to navigation in those waters. A more naturally hazardous stretch probably does not exist in the world than off the

Alaskan coast, which for the most part can be approached only through narrow passages between innumerable islands, with submerged reefs on all sides and thick fog a frequent condition. The difficulties exist even to-day with the elaborate modern geodetic surveys, some having been made by air, and the generous allotment of lighthouses and buoys, and the modern depth finding devices and the radio compass. In 1892, there was little more reliable information to be obtained about some portions of the Alaskan coast than could Commander Frost gather in Japan when leading the destroyer detachment to the Kuriles in 1924 to await the around-the-world Army fliers and was told in all earnest that the surest means of keeping off the rocks would be by listening for the bark of the sea lions through the inevitable mist! The Klondike had not yet revealed its glittering magnets that would in a few years draw thousands up the Inner Passage to Skagway and awaken the United States to a consciousness of its new northwestern empire, previously regarded as a good short sale. Many a cargo of gold still rests on the bottom of those fjord-like passages as the evidence of their treacherous rocks and currents. In Evans' days up there, one necessary method of holding the narrow middle channel of a mountain bordered strait on a thick night was to keep blowing the whistle and noting any difference in elapsed time between the return of the echoes from the two sides. Out on the wide seas, these problems of navigation were overshadowed by those of seamanship. Day after day, night after night, there was heavy weather that put to shame the wildest tempests that the ship had encountered off the notorious south shore of Chile. Once every officer and every man jack aboard that salty seasoned craft was seasick, surely an achievement of which any ocean might be proud. If there weren't snow storms there was opaque fog and if the atmosphere was clear there was green water coming over the forecastle, and often the gunboat tossed mercilessly, the victim of every evil outburst known to the elements.   The dampness raised havoc with the Captain's wounded legs and caused him intermittent suffering throughout the summer.

During such weather as rendered them visible and there were some bright pellucid days, the Alaskan mainland presented an awe inspiring spectacle of titanic snow-topped peaks with green glaciers in the shoulders between, each frozen river melting into a magnificent torrent that roared straight down into the sea, or, in the case of those glaciers in more remote ranges, into the valleys unseen.   The grandeur was of the same sort and degree as that of the Andes that a few months earlier had so stirred Evans in the Straits of Magellan and along the Chilean coast.

As a recreation centre, the town of Unalaska on the island of that name had little to offer.   There was a polyglot population of about three hundred and a billiard table in the fur company's office.   Admiral Fiske never forgot a game he played there with the Captain.   The then Lieutenant's cue ball, after hitting the first ball, jumped onto the rail of the table, ran along to the other end of the table, fell back on the table and hit the second ball, for a perfect shot,   The skipper laughed "until he was almost sick."   The other diversions were hunting and fishing, the salmon still running in a profusion that glutted the mouths of the rivers.

Up and down the Bering Sea and between the islands of the archipelagos steamed the ships of the American squadron on separate patrols.   There were few sealers sighted because for the most part they had no desire to be caught by Fighting Bob in a red-handed violation of his written warning.   The *Yorktown* visited the Pribilof Islands to see at their homes the objects of such international solicitude. The Captain and those of his officers who were not on duty crawled along a cliff above the rookeries and, lying flat on their stomachs, peeped over the edge to behold what Evans described as "certainly one of the most interesting sights of my rather varied experience."   The beach, as far as the eye could see, was covered by countless thousands of seals in their family groups, carrying on their general domestic affairs not unlike the human inhabitants of vast urban communities, even to the point of kissing and fighting one another and howling in as seemingly purposeless a fashion as traders on a stock exchange.

Looking about the northern seas for trouble—and that was his mission—Evans evolved a plan. The Canadian sealers had been each summer in the habit of meeting a steamer at some appointed rendezvous, secret and remote, where the skins were transhipped and sent to a British Columbian port and supplies taken aboard the fleet. This was illegal if within Alaskan territorial waters and, in any event, undesirable. Even if he found the steamer on the high seas, Evans intended to seize her. The first difficulty he had to overcome was information from the Intelligence Bureau, which went to a great deal of nosing about in its dark and mysterious fashion and then, in the most secret cipher, notified Evans that the rendezvous would be at a latitude and longitude that turned out to be about as near to the point as Newfoundland is to Ireland and named the wrong steamer as the one to expect. Next, the commander of the detachment had to resign himself to the possibility that, even though successful, if the seizure took place outside Alaskan waters he might have to be sacrificed as the scapegoat on the altar of international hypocrisy—but this deterred him not at all.

He later said: "I read plainly between the lines of my orders that the Washington authorities considered it of vital importance that she should be captured, and I made up my mind to get her legally if I could, illegally if I must. If I took her at sea, the Department could disavow my act and punish me; but in the meantime my mission in the North would be accomplished and sealing broken up, at least for that year. The schooners would have to go back

to Victoria for provisions, and it would then be too late for
them to return to Bering Sea and do any real harm."

The Department knew to whom it was sending instructions. How many officers could have understood as well
as he how to read "between the lines"?

Evans was well aware of the futility of trying to catch
his game by mere patrol. In the World War, the German
U-boats easily evaded the enemy so long as they were hunted
by that fatuous method. Their doom was sealed by Admiral Sims' persuading the allied naval forces to adopt the
convoy system: to ambush the submarines where they would
naturally strike rather than merely to scour the whole zone
for periscope feathers. Evans knew that, if the British
sealing craft were watched, he would sooner or later catch
his steamer. In the meanwhile the *Yorktown* and the rest
of the force seized several vessels violating the sealing laws
and/or the *modus vivendi* and sent them into Sitka under
arrest. In his journal the Commander said: " . . . we are
raising considerable of a row, I am afraid, but we are stopping sealing in the Bering Sea, which is what I was sent up
here to do."

The trap for the supply ship was carefully set and one
day the alert ship *Corwin,* carrying out Commander Evans'
orders, sprang it at Port Etches. There she came upon
about thirty of the Canadian sealing craft blithely ex-
changing ship stores for contraband skins with a steamer
called the *Coquitlan.* The seizure was made before the
astonished poachers could realize what had happened; and
the game was in the bag, with its thirty thousand skins
which, Evans dryly commented, "will help the Government to pay damages if the arbitration goes against us."

The Bering Sea was not being molested that summer.
Up and down the coast, from fishing hamlet to trading out-

post, sped fantastic legends of the fire-breathing demon who would toast sealers alive. Fighting Bob became the dictator of the northern seas. In all manner of things he was consulted. Upon one coaling visit to Unalaska he was appealed to by the skipper of a mutinous crew, which had demanded nothing more extreme than coffee at nine A.M. Evans summoned the gang, asked them why they had not requested five o'clock tea each afternoon and then curtly told them that, if they didn't promptly turn to, he would put them in double irons "where the dogs wouldn't bite them," one of his favourite expressions. Of course, he had no authority whatsoever to interfere in the matter but the strikers resumed work.

In harbour, out again, over the stormy Bering, "very unlike the White Squadron picnic" was the routine and, although the tension in Chile might have been more trying, off Valparaiso there had been at least the heartening "possibility of a fight every day to make the time pass." If, however, the sealers afforded little need for a sharp look-out, the elements did their best to supply the deficiency. It was nothing unusual for the *Yorktown* to buffet its way through one of those sounds with a gale blowing in one direction and a raging tide setting in the opposite. Well named was the *Yorktown;* after a village insignificant in itself but representing so much. Her half dozen six-inch guns that fearlessly had stood eye to eye opposite the concentrated batteries of the Chilean Navy could not intimidate the surf-washed crags or the unrhythmic billows of these crazy waters. Only expert seamanship, twenty-four hour a day navigation and eternal vigilance could and did bring the ship safely back after each patrol. The wonder was that the American squadron logged over sixty thousand miles since leaving Port Townsend without scraping a bottom, not that one day Admiral Hotham found his flagship high on the rocks. This latter catastrophe was not only plain bad luck but seemed an ill reward for a sense of humour that

could and did chuckle at his friend Evans' coup in the
Coquitlan affair.

The return trip to San Francisco in October epitomized
the weather of the entire summer; there was snow, hail,
rain and finally wind that blew with hurricane force causing the ship to heave to for a day and a night while the
harassed skipper, his legs aching mercilessly, clung to the
stanchions on the bridge soaked to the skin. The Golden
Gate was a welcome sight.

The crew lustily chanted a song that had been inspired
by their recent experiences, part of which ran as follows:

> "Just think of all our dreary tracks
> To shield the jaunty seal skin sacks,
> To have Old England laugh in glee
> While Yankees guard the Bering Sea.
>
> For ne'er can sailor salty be
> Until he sails the Bering Sea
> And views Alaska's dreary shore
> And fills himself with Arctic lore.
>
> Columbus and Balboa too,
> With Nelson form a salty crew,
> But they are fresh to you and me
> They never sailed the Bering Sea.
>
> So when you boast of fiercest gale,
> That every ocean you did sail,
> You can not salty sailor be
> Until you cruise the Bering Sea." *

Evans wrote a lengthy report upon the sealing situation, which was exhaustive and important but not as
preëminent in the literature of that subject as he supposed.
His misgivings throughout those arduous months in the

* Quoted by permission from *The Book of Navy Songs* collected by
the Trident Society of the Naval Academy and published by Doubleday,
Page & Company in 1926.

Bering Sea as to the official response with which his efforts would meet turned out to be baseless. For once Washington was properly appreciative. The Secretary vouchsafed Departmental approval of no mere perfunctory degree and the President in his message to Congress commended Evans and his work. Twice mentioned in presidential messages, for entirely distinct services, was his record in 1892. The man in the White House and the man on the street recognized that, although Robley D. Evans did not yet wear the fourth gold stripe of a captain and was only forty-eight years old, he was the most picturesque figure in the Navy. Admiral Luce was the beloved dean of the Outfit and the works of Captain Mahan were being read in many maritime languages, but, for every person who knew of these scholars, a thousand were familiar with the exploits of Fighting Bob.

The laudations poured upon Evans were even more subjective than objective. After all, Evans did not and could not exterminate the exterminators or solve the sealing problem. The arbitrators met augustly in Paris. For the United States there sat Justice Harlan of the Supreme Court, "the great dissenter," and Senator Morgan; Great Britain was represented by one of the foremost English jurists and an eminent Canadian; and there were three distinguished neutrals. The advocates were of equally high standing. Quite correctly, the decision was in favour of the British. (When the damages were subsequently assessed they amounted to less than the value of the skins Evans had seized with the *Coquitlan.*) The ponderous doctrines of international law having been duly expounded, the practical question as to how to preserve the fur-seal became more urgent than ever and, in accordance with pre-arrangement, the commission shoved aside its buckram case books and got to work devising a system for conserving the species by joint action of the governments interested. This system did not function satisfactorily. Every succeeding president had the problem called sharply to his attention. By 1910 the Pribilof herd had been cut down to about a hundred and thirty thousand; the end was in sight. Had nothing drastic and effective been done, the once plentiful animals by now would have become museum rarities. Evans lived to see the North Pacific Sealing Convention concluded in 1911 between the United States, Great Britain, Japan and Russia, whereby for the first time the way was cleared for effective conservation and economic use of the Pribilof seals. Pelagic hunting is practically prohibited in the Pacific north of the thirtieth parallel of north latitude, below which the herd does not swim, and an adequate force patrols this zone. The Pribilof Islands are guarded against raiders. Only the Government may kill and then only in accordance with the results of an analytical census taken the preceding year. The skins are auctioned at St. Louis and the proceeds divided seventy percent to our Government and the balance equally between the Canadian and the Japanese. In this way the number of the Pribilof seals has been increased to nearly a million and before long should attain its original size. The vagaries of administration under the revolutionary régime have prevented the Russians from obtaining anything like as satisfactory results with its Commander Island herd, similarly safeguarded.

Evans' campaign of 1892 was very important. It arrested the slaughter by clearing the Bering of sealers and it crystallized several phases of the problem. Instead of the Navy having sustained any loss of dignity by reason of performing duties usually assigned to the Coast Guard, Evans actually added to the prestige of his service by the dashing manner in which his squadron carried out its mission, in one of those periodical troughs of American naval history when every iota of inspiration had to be as tenderly nurtured as a pup on the Pribilof beach. Evans was helping to pilot the Navy onto the crest.

11

THRESHOLD SEAS

~~~~~~

U PON reaching Washington, Evans again was ordered to the Lighthouse Board, this time as naval secretary. It was then that he and Grover Cleveland formed a lasting friendship, the President along with members of his Cabinet often accompanying Evans on short inspection trips in lighthouse steamers.

The commanding officer of every ship of the Navy being called its captain, the title was a familiar one to Evans long before he actually attained that rank in 1893. Thoroughly rested from the stress and strain of the memorable months in the *Yorktown,* he was naturally eager, after nearly two years of duty on the Lighthouse Board, to return to his now natural element the sea. Home life and the jolly associations of the beach were most delightful interludes but Evans was not the man to find contentment very long in any such tame existence as supervising coastal lamp-lighters. With the four stripes on his sleeve and the new eagles on his collar, he looked forward to a captain's cruise that would not prove an anti-climax to the experiences encountered while a commander. He was to escape disappointment by no narrow margin.

The roster of active ships showed few that were really first-class and, until more of the New Navy slid off the ways, an attractive command seldom would be available. The previous summer there had been commissioned the *New York,* our first armoured cruiser, a fast eight-inch gun ship

costing the then large sum of nearly three million dollars
and embodying the latest construction principles for vessels
of that type. A vacancy occurring in her cabin, the Secretary of the Navy turned her over to Captain Evans, who
rejoiced upon reading his orders. He bade his many friends
au revoir, leaving for the very last his companion of so many
recent week-ends, Grover Cleveland, to whom he paid a final
visit at Gray Gables. The President was loathe to say good-
bye and postponed the moment of doing so by accompanying
his friend from the Buzzards Bay Summer White House to
New York and seeing him safely aboard his new command.

Here Evans relieved Captain Jack Philip, his lifelong
friend. A few days later, he added to his uniform the gold
aiguilettes of Chief of Staff to Admiral Meade, commander
of the North Atlantic Squadron, whose flag flew on the *New
York*. The Admiral, noted for his ability and character but
not for his good temper, reminded Evans that the relationship of an admiral and flag captain was always a difficult
one and frequently marred by fighting. "Well, Admiral,"
said Evans, "you can count on me to do my part."

As a matter of fact, Meade and Evans worked together
amicably and with great mutual respect. The Admiral was
skilled at his profession and had in abundance that quality
which Evans always placed above all others in the requirements of a naval officer—courage. The constant surveillance of an admiral and the carrying of a staff organization
as extra passengers independent of the organization of the
ship's company, the attributes of flag captaincy, are often
irksome, but Evans' happy relationship with Meade left no
room for friction. The squadron included the two brand
new protected cruisers *Columbia* and *Minneapolis*, authorized after and even more modern than the *New York*, and
those twins, also in the infancy of their long and distinguished careers, the *Cincinnati* and *Raleigh*.

Admiral Meade was bending every effort toward preparedness for the war against Spain, which he knew was

inevitable despite the honeyed assurances of noninterference
emitted by the State Department after every crisis in Cuba.
The Admiral and the Captain sat many an evening over their
cigars, in the flag quarters of the *New York,* speculating
upon the length of time that must elapse before the sympathy
of the entire American people for their oppressed neighbours would burst through all governmental restraints and
let the Navy complete the eviction of Spain from the western
hemisphere. Each mail contained newspaper articles of
fresh uprisings in Cuba, more cruel suppressions by Governor Weyler and his assistant despots, filibustering expeditions from Florida or the Gulf States, governmental
explanations and increased tension between Madrid and
Washington. To Meade and Evans these conditions pointed
only one way and they wanted to go there direct, having no
stomach for the circumambulations of statesmen. The Administration, however, had heavy responsibilities. The
Cuban problem was by no means the only Caribbean worry.
The old dispute as to the boundary between British Guiana
and Venezuela was rapidly being subordinated to the much
more important controversy between the United States and
Great Britain as to our right under the Monroe Doctrine to
insist that the boundary question be submitted to arbitration.
President Cleveland probably will be remembered longest
for his courageous stand in maintaining that territorial
aggrandizement was not altered in substance by being called
a boundary dispute. He jeopardized peace by pressing the
point but it was one vital to American interests. He won
out and the Monroe Doctrine emerged triumphant from its
severest test, with the added prestige of its acceptance by the
British Empire. During this winter, however, the friction
between London and Washington was increasing and was
aggravated by difficulties in Nicaragua. Besides these
British complications, the Government realized that the New
Navy was not nearly ready in sufficient force to give us a
comfortable superiority to Spanish sea power.

EVANS AS A CAPTAIN

As things turned out, it is perhaps just as well that the explosion of the *Maine* and the resultant explosion of long-controlled popular indignation did not occur in 1894 and that the Secretary of the Navy ordered the outspokenly pro-Cuban Admiral and his no less reserved Chief of Staff to remain out of Cuban harbours.

These two officers used their time sharpening the sword in their hands for the hour that they both knew could not be far off, when the nation would draw it from the scabbard. The squadron steamed in column and in line and deployed in every formation known to the *General Signal Book*. The orders were given by flag hoist, semaphore and searchlight, the latter being developed for the first time for long distance daytime communications. The ships with torpedo tubes practised firing them at moving targets and maximum ranges. The crews were called day after day and often aroused at night to general quarters, collision quarters and all of the other ship and gun drills. By midwinter the squadron was in fighting trim. Press reports indicated that at any moment it might have need for this acme of efficiency. On the north coast of South America, on the Mosquito Coast of Central America, most malignantly on the largest of the West Indies, there were centres of trouble. Secretary of State Gresham was finding his exalted office no sinecure and Evans' genial friend in the White House was losing many a night's sleep worrying over the issues that he was valiantly striving to confine to nonviolent adjustment. Beyond all comparison, this was Grover Cleveland's most exacting year in office. The North Atlantic Squadron was kept within hail of the danger spots. Evans once more was sailing off the Spanish Main, among the islands whose beauty had won his eye when rushing the *Yorktown* to Chile. With the *Cincinnati* and *Raleigh*, the *New York* touched at Martinique, St. Lucia and Barbados. As the ships cruised about in these beautifully tinted waters, pale green around the islands and

deep blue outside of the coral reefs, the forecastles sang to
a rollicking tune:

> "Away, away with sword and drum,
> Here we come, full of rum,
> Looking for some one to put on the bum,
> The Armoured Cruiser Squadron."

At St. Lucia no salute was fired as the British had no
saluting guns there at the time and were frankly unwilling
to disclose the position of their concealed batteries!   A
lengthy visit was paid to Bridgetown, Barbados, where
Washington's Birthday was celebrated in fitting fashion by
boat races and general festivities, as well as by the full dress
ship prescribed by the Regulations.   The community was
entertained by the *New York* at what the English there referred to as an "on board."   The itinerary was affording
much interest and recreation to the officers and men, who
had plenty of work during the almost constant manœuvres
while under way and enjoyed playing tourist.   The flagship
and *Cincinnati* steamed over to St. Thomas.   These two
ships had with them for testing purposes, the only two specimens of a new device, called the stadimeter, invented by
Bradley Fiske.   When the height of the mast of a ship was
known and the instrument adjusted accordingly, the distance of that ship from the observer would be recorded.
Fiske was inspired to develop the stadimeter by the desire to
supplement the rangefinder by an instrument that could perform its function if the latter delicate optical instrument
became damaged during action.   The stadimeter, however,
was tried out by Admiral Meade as an aid in keeping station
during squadron manœuvres.   It proved valuable for this
purpose and the report was excellent.   It is now in a handy
place on the bridge of every warship and the fleet relies upon
it to a considerable extent in maintaining the prescribed
distance from the guide during formation cruising.

Early March found the *New York* and the sisterships *Cincinnati* and *Raleigh* swinging at their anchorages five miles from the waterfront of Port-of-Spain on the orchid, parrot, asphalt island of Trinidad. H.M.S. *Buzzard* was also in the harbour.

One afternoon the city closed its shops and declared a holiday so that every inhabitant might attend the gala sporting event at the cricket grounds, where the All Trinidad eleven was playing an English team. Those on duty aboard the ships suddenly perceived an uncommonly thick column of smoke rising from the very heart of the business section of the town. The strong trade wind was blowing as usual from the eastward and the officers of the deck, through their glasses, could see it waft the smoke over the wooden structures along the closely built up streets. Now tongues of flame were visible. Instantly the Admiral was informed and, with a rapidity that showed the result of the daily drills, the fire and rescue parties were ready to shove off with their rescue, fire, relief and gun-cotton details. While the general alarms were still sounding through the ships and the boatswains were piping "Away fire and rescue party!" the assembly call on the bugle brought the marines to their stations, ready to disembark. For the near-by Captain of the Royal Navy the situation presented no problem but Admiral Meade knew that, despite the spreading of the fire, he could not land organized American forces on British soil solely upon his own initiative. He must await a request. To Evans this appeared the height of absurdity. The city was burning; it had inadequate fire fighting facilities; the squadron, whose presence seemed almost providential, alone might check the destruction; what mattered international usage? He made no secret of his impatience, as he chafed under the Admiral's restraint. Hitherto the latter had been a man of action; Evans wondered whether he had been suddenly transmogrified into a diplomat. Whoever heard of awaiting an engraved invitation to help extinguish a fire? The smoke cloud expanded and the sparks scattered in showers. Old Gimpy paced the quarter-deck in disgust. Was this the Navy or a school of etiquette? Lives might be at stake. Was humanity to await the bidding of political sovereignty? Could there be a mind so distorted as to see in a small relief corps a hostile expeditionary force? Evans was to learn, when himself an admiral, that there could be. A decade later, when his first aid to the Jamaica earthquake sufferers was so unbelievably misunderstood by an ungracious Governor, he appreciated the sagacity that prompted Admiral Meade's delay. At the moment, however, the delay almost over-taxed the Captain's self-control. The fire was raging and the landing parties were straining at the leash. For the Admiral, the suspense was no easier. The responsibility was on his shoulders and the most difficult task just then was to do nothing.

Tensely the summons for help was awaited and it was not nearly as long in coming as it seemed to all hands in the squadron. The moment it was received and the Admiral thus felt enabled to give the word, the boats hastened across the harbour to the city under the command of the *New York's* Executive Officer. Even in response to the appeal for help, the Admiral had hesitated to adopt his Chief of Staff's suggestion that the marines be armed to prevent looting and to facilitate the work of the ship's fire brigades but finally told the latter to use his own judgment. Fortunately for Port-of-Spain, Evans was as ready as always to accept responsibility and the loaded rifles carried by the soldiers of the sea were exceedingly useful symbols in protecting the burning areas. Evans knew that there were always some renegades who would seize such an occasion to plunder.

The fire had started in a store and to this day the origin has not been determined. Many believed it to have been incendiary. When the fire and rescue parties reached the scene and made their way through the crowds of helpless and in some instances mischievous spectators, recalling with terror the stories of the complete destruction of the city by the Great Fire many years before, the ridiculous local fire brigade with its one small hand-engine was not even retarding the spread of the conflagration. The naval officers realized at once that, if the city was to be saved, they would have to check the progress of the fire by creating barriers to leeward that the flames could not ignite as they were crackling from house to house. Not a minute could be lost. It was necessary to take drastic measures and immediately. The marines cleared the adjacent streets and the gun-cotton details proceeded to destroy rows of dry wooden buildings that were the next marked victims of the advancing fire. The citizens, chased out of danger, heard the blasts of the explosives as these structures were ruthlessly razed. The wind drove the flames toward the cleared spaces and, instead of finding more food for their insatiable appetites, they found their progress halted by lack of fuel. The plan was successful. The city was saved. During the burning fight the sailors did their work with characteristic indifference to the difficulties or dangers, of both of which there were plenty. When at about ten thirty that night the fire was completely under control and the destruction, although grave, restricted to the two most important business blocks, the marines turned over to the local authorities the further protection against looting and then all hands ashore returned to the ships, from where the fire had at its height been a magnificently tragic spectacle.

The townspeople were profoundly grateful to the American Squadron. The Port-of-Spain *Gazette,* the leading newspaper of Trindad, declared that the sailors had cut down the losses to one-tenth of what otherwise they would have been, and Governor Sir Frederick Napier Broome wrote Admiral Meade a letter expressing heartfelt appreciation of the efficiency and bravery of the bluejackets and marines. The squadron had every reason to feel gratified at its day's work. The Chief of Staff was proud of his men.

This feat of rescue was not generally known in the United States for some time. While the Navy was saving one British possession, the people at home were reading about the crisis involving the boundary of another on the Venezuelan mainland near-by. There were also accounts of the *Allianca* affair, which further aggravated our détente with Spain, of the mysterious disappearance of her warship *Reina Regente,* and of the readiness for sea of Dewey's future flagship the *Olympia.* The inside columns of the papers contained frequent references to the coming celebration of the opening of the Kaiser Wilhelm Canal at Kiel.

Upon the return of the *New York* to home waters, Admiral Meade, pursuant to his own request, hauled down his flag and passed into retirement at what seemed to his Chief of Staff the prime of usefulness. A lifetime of preparation had led to the hoisting of the flag and for how brief a period it flew!

12

POMP AND DIPLOMACY

WALKING arm in arm through the rose gardens of Kilverstone during a week-end in the summer of 1910, Lord Fisher was discussing the German situation with his house guest Sir Maurice Hankey, later the Secretary of the British War Cabinet. He was speaking without pretence of any judicial moderation but in his usual dogmatic manner that brooked no questioning. "War will come," he asserted, "and in 1914." To indicate that this was not based upon any such abstruse logic as Henry Adam's similar prognostication and that it was not a wild shot of prophecy in the dark, the Admiral explained that, as far back as the launching of the *Dreadnought,* he had ordered a group of experts to ascertain how long it would require to enlarge the Kiel Canal sufficiently to accommodate the new German battle fleet that would inevitably be laid down and that the estimate had set the date of completion as 1914. This great undertaking involved the construction of locks larger than those at Panama, the enormous deepening and widening of the channel and the elevation of the bridges. The task was finished in June 1914; the ultimatum of Austria to Serbia was delivered in July; and the only comment one may make is that the Canal was enlarged and the war did break out, both in precise punctuality to Lord Fisher's time-table. When reminded of these forecasts after the events, he declared that "they really weren't predictions; they were certainties."

Commander Carlyon Bellairs of the Royal Navy and a Member of Parliament, J. Ellis Barker and many other students of the subject concurred in the view that peace was assured only until the High Seas Fleet could make the Baltic-North Sea transit without going through the Skaggerak and Cattegat. In any event the Canal played a prominent part in international contemplations.

It was there also that Robley Evans first beheld European diplomacy and intrigue in all their fantastic glory. In June 1895 he attended the formal opening of the Canal and learned that there were more currents and cross currents in those waters than appeared on any chart or than the most adept pilot could safely navigate. Little did he dream, however, that in their deep and shifting courses they would reach the coasts of his own country with as direct an effect as has the Gulf Stream upon the climate of Ireland.

A glance at the map of Denmark will suffice to make obvious the importance of a direct waterway across the base of the peninsula from the North Sea to the Baltic. Such a route, avoiding the perilous passages among the Scandinavian islands in which many a skilfully handled vessel had met disaster, was a great boon to commerce and, entirely within German territory and the protection of her coastal batteries, an interior line of inestimable strategic value in the event of war on both fronts. For five hundred years there had been a canal which, although shallow and tortuous, had been of substantial service to the mariners of the Hanseatic League. In 1784 the large Eider Canal was opened and the cross-cut improved but the many locks were serious obstacles and only small craft could pass through. Bismarck conceived the idea of a modern ship canal as an important item of his program of industrial, commercial and military development after the establishment of the Empire. The estimated cost, however, was so great that many of those in the high Imperial counsels thought that it was out of all proportion to the benefits that could possibly be derived. Von Moltke threw all of his prestige against the project. Why, he argued, dig a titanic ditch so that a possible divided fleet can be united, when it will be cheaper to build two fleets, thus giving as much naval strength in either sea as with the canal and always having at least the chance of being able to swing one around Denmark? The Iron Chancellor, however, was not to be balked in the completion of that colossal manœuvre, begun by the acquisition of Schleswig-Holstein and carried forward by the coup of Heligoland. A route was surveyed and the engineers given eight years to finish the construction of the new canal, between Kiel Bay on the Baltic and the mouth of the Elbe River opposite Cuxhaven, the port of Hamburg, on the west, deep and wide enough to take care of Germany's then largest warships and as straight as practicable. At the end of the alloted period, Kaiser Wilhem II announced to the world that he was ready to celebrate the formal opening and invited the participation of the other powers. It was to be an impressive nineteenth century revival of the pageantry and peace festival of the Field of the Cloth of Gold. The ceremonial phase was carried off with a magnificence that surpassed all prior efforts in that line but the prospective love feast, as will be seen, left much to be desired by the ambitious young Emperor, who should have known that the moment was not altogether propitious for a demonstration of unalloyed mutual affection among the European powers. Bismarck, from the seclusion of his country estate and with the empirical sagacity of his eighty years, watched the false moves with a malignant satisfaction but no joy.

The French people were at this time laying a wreath on the Strassburg Monument whenever the name of Germany was mentioned. Pasteur felt constrained to accept a medal from the Kaiser only in secrecy lest his countrymen turn against him. "Ravanche" was in full bloom and there was plenty in the despatches from Madagascar, Egypt and Turkey to vex the patriots as they read their June papers outside the Parisian cafés. Only in the Far East was the prospect encouraging. Even there, it was noted with French alarm, a German man-of-war was injecting herself into the Formosan revolution and anxiety was felt that the Chinese loan might not be consummated without German participation. All depended upon Russia. The ultra-western Republic beckoned coyly to the latest of the Romanoffs. Bismarck aptly called it "coquetry."

The French voters, unversed in the arts and manners of nations, which are not very different from those of well-bred individuals, could not reconcile the loathing for Germany with an apparently cordial participation in the opening of a canal whose chief significance seemed, paradoxically, to connect French and Russian waters in a way that would keep French and Russian navies apart. On June eleventh a young socialist deputy, Millerand by name, who was starting vigorously down the political boulevards to the Elysee Palace, interpellated the Government in the Chamber about this seeming inconsistency and inquired whether or not it reflected a change of policy. Foreign Minister Hanotaux arose, somewhat shy as always, raised his *pince nez* and answered less abruptly than usual, in the negative. France merely was being polite; sending a squadron was an empty gesture. The Chamber was thrown into excited debate. Ex-Premier Goblet called a spade a spade: the Kiel affair wounded the sentiment of France; was there a Russian alliance or not? Premier Ribot sensed the sympathetic reception to that speech and the danger of a complete evasion on the part of the Government. France had united her interests with those of Russia, he admitted, for the preservation of the peace of Europe, an already familiar phrase that no statesman seems ashamed to use. A vote of confidence was passed but the crisis by no means. All through the festivities at Kiel, the Opposition plagued the Government

for its refusal to decline the Kaiser's invitation, and there
was hardly a citizen who did not resent every salute fired by
the French squadron to the Imperial Standard. The fact
of the Russian alliance was forced into the open, although,
even after France was brazenly proclaiming it by denying
that no *written* alliance had been entered into, Russia made
every effort to minimize the significance and scope of the
entente. Japan had been coerced out of Korea and generally
subdued for the time being, and Russia did not need Gallic
support as much as she wanted to avoid Teutonic enmity.

Premier Ribot was in a dilemma. He compromised by
sending Admiral Manard with a squadron but giving him no
fireworks to take along.

Captain Evans, on the other hand, was racing the *Columbia* across the North Atlantic, more worried about the
fireworks he carried on the *New York's* decks than he had
ever been about his powder or shells. He was as much
relieved to see those fireworks eventually go up in smoke
for the edification of the Kaiser as he had been to disembark
the Chilean refugees from the *Yorktown.* The United
States, with a beneficent inability to foresee the events of
1917, entered wholeheartedly into the celebration plans. The
country was proud of its New Navy, even if most of it was
still under construction. Because of the Caribbean disturbances, the Department at first thought that it would send
only the *San Francisco,* flagship of the European Squadron,
and the *Marblehead,* a gunboat with a sufficiently light
draught to carry the American flag in the parade through the
Canal, but there seemed to be a public demand for a repre-
sentation less incongruous to our status as a nation. Later
Captain Evans' *New York* was ordered to attend the opening
and also the *Columbia,* two new cruisers that would do credit
to any navy. Altogether, when the program got under way,
one hundred and sixteen men-of-war lay at anchor in Kiel
Harbour, so it was fortunate for American prestige that this

squadron of four made up in smartness what it lacked in numbers. As a matter of fact, we did not have a single capital ship there—among the twenty battleships present—for the excellent reason that the Navy did not possess any. The battleships which were to prove the nucleus of our naval strength against Spain in the near future were building but not yet commissioned.

Evans steered as direct a great circle course to Southampton as the icebergs permitted and he gave the *Columbia's* vaunted triple screws a merry chase across. It was foggy on and off so that Evans had no means of knowing whether the *Columbia* was ahead or behind. Entering Southampton harbour, he scanned the vessels present, saw the *San Francisco,* flying Admiral Kirkland's flag, the *Marblehead* and the *Alliance*—but no *Columbia!* How Old Gimpy must have chuckled, forgetting in his jubilation the agony his refractory legs had caused him most of the trip, probably because of the dampness.

British maritime circles were less interested just then in our cruisers than in the maiden voyage of the new American liner *St. Louis,* which threatened possible transatlantic competition. At Southampton, Evans already felt the holiday atmosphere of the Kiel festivities. Two Italian warships stood in *en route,* he learned that Queen Victoria was sending as her personal representative the present King, then Duke of York, and that Mr. Gladstone was venturing forth from Hawarden to attend the ceremonies in his eighty-sixth year.

Running up to London, Evans was naïvely astonished at the warmth of his reception. Many old friends entertained him and new acquaintances invited him to accept their hospitality and, as he expressed it, "made as much fuss" over him as if he "were named Mahan." The importance of the latter's writings had been more quickly appreciated in England than at home. Whereas the Department had a couple of years before obstinately refused his request for additional

shore duty in order to continue his epoch making writings
and had wasted his unique genius upon the command of
the *Chicago,* then flagship of the European Squadron,
which many other officers would have been equally qualified
to undertake, the British from the Queen down had lionized
him, both Oxford and Cambridge had conferred honorary
degrees upon him and he was everywhere hailed as the
greatest naval philosopher of modern times. The Kaiser
had exclaimed "I am just now, not reading but devouring
Captain Mahan's book; and am trying to learn it by
heart . . . " and placed a German translation on each of
his ships. An American naval officer was teaching the old
world the oldest principles of sea power.

The name Fighting Bob Evans, much to its owner's
astonishment, was also familiar to those sea-conscious
islanders, who had been stirred by the tales of his exploits
and had heard of his remarkable personality. In Royal
Navy circles he was cheerfully admired as an officer worthy
of their own service, and into the clubs and homes that succeeded in capturing him for luncheons and dinners he
brought a fresh salt breeze that fulfilled the most romantic
expectations. He found London exciting and took in all
of the usual points of interest and the gossip and the political chatter, the latter concerned with the imminent collapse of Lord Rosebery's Ministry.

The voyage was soon resumed. One June morning, as
day was breaking over the Channel, the early fishermen
were stirred by a race between two white cruisers flying the
Stars and Stripes. Through a rising mist, other men of
war, neither British nor American, were picked up ahead
and gradually overtaken, which were identified as the Spanish squadron Kiel bound. Evidently not wishing to exchange salutes on account of the Cuban tension, the Spaniards hauled down their ensigns and slunk off in the fog. It
was Evans' first glimpse of the *Infanta Maria Teresa* which,
three short years later, he was to repay for this snub by

shooting to pieces off a tropic shore. For the present, he admired her trim lines and jet black sleekness against which her brass fittings stood out in gleaming brightness, and he laughed good-humouredly at the pettiness of the discourtesy and the foretaste of the harmony that was to prevail at the assemblage. So even the United States was to feel a cold shoulder in the diplomatic mêlée.

Without a pilot he steered his ship through the devious channels under the beautiful Swedish mountains that in the June of those high latitudes knew scarcely an hour of darkness each night and found his way safely into the awkward harbour of Copenhagen. All naval routes led to Kiel and, as the *New York* entered the neck of the bottle where they converged, new flags were sighted every little while. Copenhagen was used as a dressing room where the warships did their final primping for the grand entry. There Admiral Kirkland shifted his flag from the *San Francisco* to the more imposing *New York,* whose facilities for entertainment were far superior, and these two vessels, along with the *Columbia,* polished up their brass and made certain that the white hulls, yellow superstructures and the interiors from bow to stern were immaculate. For Copenhagen, these ablutions of so many squadrons may have been interesting indeed but the occasion was as much suggestive of her decline as a great seaport as it was suggestive of Kiel's inauguration. In frantic efforts to prevent what she could of the diversion of traffic, Copenhagen declared herself a free port, placed in the channels additional aids to navigation and constructed modern docks, but it was too late; but at least that city had a part in the present performance.

The refurbishing complete, Admiral Kirkland in the *New York* led the American squadron through the Little Belt to the entrance of Kiel Bay, where the formalities commenced with an exchange of salutes with the batteries on shore. A German torpedo boat came out to meet the visitors and put aboard the flagship an officer to explain the detailed arrangements perfected under the exacting supervision of the Kaiser himself, who was rapidly earning a reputation as a lavish stage director.

The *New York, San Francisco* and *Columbia* found their numbered buoys ready for them, each with an American flag mounted on the top and a telephone wire with shore connection, the latter an impressive convenience for those days. The Imperial Navy was spread out in double column and the crews manned the rigging and cheered as the ships from the new world gracefully slid along and picked up their moorings with a finesse that proved their right to be in this exalted naval gathering. Our officers would not have admitted it to themselves but until the Spanish War they felt the need of showing their professional brethren of other navies that ours was first rate in quality, however small in size. At Kiel all of the fleets were self-consciously straining every effort to make a favourable impression and indeed any move aboard a ship made it the cynosure of every marine glass in the harbour. Compliments flew and criticisms were noted.

When Evans arrived, the air was thick with holiday gaiety and anxiety lest any untoward feature of weather, diplomacy or slip-up in the program mar the elaborate party. As the Kaiser delivered an oration on an especially and expensively constructed island in the Alster at Hamburg, lightning flashed ominously in the distance but the storm did not break. Mr. Gladstone graciously responded to a toast at a dinner held on his ship in the harbour near-by, assuring the world that the fraternal feeling between Great Britain and Germany would continue for long generations. The Czar in one breath bestowed upon President Faure the Order of St. Andrew and in another admonished his sailors to manifest no partialities at Kiel. Bismarck regretfully declined to attend the ceremonies because of his health and the Kaiser showered fresh honours upon the Count's detested enemy Dr. von Boetticher, as the alleged sponsor of the Canal.

Even the waterway itself added to the complications. The final work had been done in great haste under Imperial pressure, so that the dredging was not complete, and now the little *Kaiseradler,* on a trial passage, ran aground in the Canal. Just as Berlin was broadcasting the absurdity of there being any Franco-Russian alliance, the two fleets of those nations, having met off the Danish coast, probably by design of Admiral Manard and to the embarrassment of the Grand Duke, made a dramatic joint entry into Kiel Bay. In its exultation at that news, Paris forgot its indignation at the extra mess allowance given to the wardrooms for entertaining the hated hosts.

Kiel was during that June week the focal point of the world. Evans kept his eyes and ears wide open and had a thoroughly good time. Among the hundreds of foreign officers present were many old friends and acquaintances and he made new ones.

Besides the apparently unending rows of warships of every nation and of every type and of every period of design, stretching down the Bay as far as the eye could see, there was a myriad of yachts showing the colours of every club of the North Sea and Baltic ports. In the town of Kiel, darting about the harbour in all manner of running boats, and across the Canal at Hamburg, were uniforms of every conceivable rank and station of the maritime world. The opening of the Canal was decidedly a naval party. The Kaiser had indeed mastered his Mahan. He was launching Germany upon both of her seas. So obviously sound did this naval policy seem to Evans and so straightforward was the manner of its presentation, that his first impression of the young ruler was that in him the German Empire had a sovereign who knew his business.

It must in all fairness be emphasized that every word and every act of William II during these ceremonies was aggressively pacific. He did everything humanly possible,

consistent with his frankly expressed program to establish
Germany as a first-class maritime power, to foster an atmosphere of good will among the heterogeneous visitors.
It was not the subsequently famous "*Deutschland ueber
alles*" but "*Ich stelle den Frieden ueber alles.*"

To eliminate the necessity of official calls, which would
have taken up the entire time of every ranking officer, the
Kaiser invited all of the flag and commanding officers to
breakfast aboard one of the German battleships and had
each one drop his card in the mail bag of each of the other
guests, very much like the modern clearing house system of
banks. Thus all of the naval dignitaries had met and none
of the proprieties was sacrificed.

The crews presented a more difficult problem. It would
not have added to the harmony of the occasion were the
Turks to have assaulted the French sailors or the French
to have boisterously wined the Russians or the Germans to
have come to blows with any of their visitors, so liberty
parties were discreetly scheduled with a view to the international alignments of the hour.

The mechanism functioned smoothly. Even the diffi-
cultly-placed Admiral Manard was to some degree won over
by the marked cordiality of the Emperor and the Empress.
After all, the Germans had achieved their ends as to France;
they had no possible grievance against their recently vanquished foe and with characteristic Teutonic inability to
comprehend the opposing point of view, they failed to understand why the French should not forget Versailles of
1871. The Kaiser thought he was being gracious when he
tactlessly let it be known that he might honour the Paris
Exposition of 1900 with his Imperial presence.

About the harbour ran the dozens of boats of every
maritime power, to and from the big ships and the landing.
Everything was festive. The stage had been magnificently
set. At last on June nineteenth the curtain was to rise on
the first act. This was the Burgomaster's banquet on the

artificial island in the Alster, previously mentioned. It was a gala spectacle, with all of the music, fireworks, crowds of people and other properties of such events, culminating in the Kaiser's outdoor address of peace on earth. The following day the Canal was opened by the international ship parade. In the van, breaking the thread across the western entrance, came the Imperial yacht *Hohenzollern,* with the Emperor on the upper bridge in the full dress uniform of an admiral. Originally, it had been hoped to have the largest visiting warships make the transit. Fortunately, this was not attempted as the channel proved none too large for the craft in the parade as it was. The United States, in accordance with the plans, was represented by the *Marblehead,* which lived to do her bit in the war against Germany twenty-two years later. For the occasion, she flew Admiral Kirkland's flag and carried many of the officers of the *New York, San Francisco* and *Columbia,* including Captain Evans, who resented the fact that we had sent such a "baby admiral" that the *Marblehead* had to take a position near the end of the procession, formed in order of rank. He doubtless was satisfied, however, to be a mere passenger that day, as the task of keeping station and remaining in the channel was an exacting one. When several ships ahead touched bottom and a traffic snarl resulted, the *Marblehead* found herself in difficulties, which were complicated by a strong wind abeam. With almost instant resourcefulness, lines were run out to the windward shore, but they proved unequal to the blow and had to be cast off. Despite every effort to manœuvre the ship of her predicament, with the Canal blocked ahead and astern, the *Marblehead* grounded on the leeward side, but she slid off again when the congestion cleared away. The *Hohenzollern,* meanwhile, was emerging through the eastern locks into Kiel Bay and there receiving the salutes of the arrayed squadrons.

A banquet to a thousand guests was given with every

pomp in a mammoth ship erected for the purpose on land and thereafter the warships vied with one another in searchlight and firework displays that must have been spectacular indeed across the water. Evans saw the last of his volatile cargo set off without an accident and with the desired stupendous effect. There were great pyrotechnic pictures of President Cleveland and the Kaiser as the grand climax. The French ships were conspicuously dark and quiet amid all of the noisy festivity in the Bay; it must have reminded Evans of the *Yorktown's* New Year's Eve at Valparaiso. Admiral Manard was not supplied with any very ingenious excuse; all he could say was that the fleet had to leave during the night to be in home waters on the anniversary of the death of President Carnot. Evans stood close to the Emperor and the French Admiral as they had their strained but scrupulously polite conversation at the banquet hall, during which the former seemed entirely at ease but the latter quite the opposite. This was Evans' first presentation to the Kaiser, who impressed him enormously and favourably and with whose family he was to have friendly contact the rest of his life. It has often been observed that, superficially at least, the Kaiser and Theodore Roosevelt bore a marked resemblance to each other, and one thing that they did have in common was a profound admiration for Fighting Bob. They both recognized in him the born sea fighter and leader of men.

During the night, the French and Russian squadrons slipped their moorings and stood out of the Bay into the freer air of the Baltic, but the manner of their departure was not calculated to enliven the rest of the Kaiser's program. On June twenty-first he dedicated the mighty undertaking and delivered another internationally soothing speech, rebuking the Bismarck organs for their anti-French expressions. "In the memory of Emperor William the Great," he finally pronounced, "I christen this Canal the Kaiser Wilhelm Canal, in the name of God, in honour of the Emperor

William I, for the weal of Germany and the welfare of
nations"; and in the corner-stone he placed a document saying ". . . All seafaring people may share in the advantages its use procures. May it be a work of peace! . . ."

Then came an inspection of the fleets by the Kaiser,
steaming up and down the rows of vessels in the *Hohenzollern.* The *New York* was swinging at her anchorage off
the Naval Academy and, for the review, Captain Evans entertained the daughter of Secretary of the Navy Herbert
and a party of her friends.

The officers were all professionally interested in the
rival ships present and took advantage of the opportunity
to note as many of their improvements as they could ferret
out without arousing suspicion or being positively rude.
Pride in display and natural cordiality competed against
patriotic prudence. By the time the various ships stood out,
it is reasonable to infer that they had been gently ravished
of many of their structural and instrumental secrets. Three
times the Russians examined the *Columbia* from truck to
keel, and our entire squadron was closely scrutinized by
visitors from every other fleet. The *New York,* as the
flagship, was the object of great general interest and won
universal praise as a smart ship, but the newer and more
advanced *Columbia* excited even more professional curiosity.

On the twenty-fourth, she was honoured by a call by the
great German Super-Admiral himself. The crew manned
the rails, fired the salute of twenty-one guns and received
the royal visitor on the quarter-deck with that utmost ceremony reserved for sovereigns and presidents. Evans was
seeing European court functions and personages at close
range and in action. He was a simple man and lived a
simple life, and for those very reasons distinguished between
the pomp and circumstance on the one hand and its personages on the other. He admired no man just because of

his trappings but neither did any petty overemphasis of caste or station obscure from him human worth beneath the regalia. It was at Kiel that he met Prince Henry of Prussia, the Kaiser's brother and an officer of the Imperial Navy, without knowing who he was. With him and his charming consort the Princess Irene ensued a friendship which substantially contributed, nearly a decade later, to the success of the Prince's visit to the United States, when Evans occupied a position in his own country no less distinguished than the Prince's in Germany. For the Kaiser, he had by this time acquired a high personal regard that failed to penetrate the virile manner to a perception of those basic weaknesses which brought disaster in their train. Evans accepted him at face value, a patriotic, peace loving, intelligent and energetic executive, with a striking personality and a thorough indoctrination in the importance of sea power.

A few days after the Kaiser's reception on the *New York,* he was the guest of honour at a dinner given by Evans in her cabin, when the handsome silver service presented by the people of that city was taken from its glass case and placed before a king. The Kaiser had by this time heard a great deal about Captain Evans from Prince Henry, who was also present, and he made a point of cultivating his own acquaintance with the colourful American. After the cigars, no pains were spared by the skipper in showing the Emperor the intricacies of the cruiser. The latter inquired as to the speed with which the water-tight compartments could be closed, and was told two minutes, at which Wilhelm shook his head dubiously and frankly expressed incredulity. Evans stepped to the nearest voice tube and, as the distinguished visitor stood transfixed in astonishment at such a readiness to support by a test the accuracy of a casually questioned estimate, Evans broke the stillness of two A. M. in the harbour by sounding general quarters and brusquely saying: "Please time this, your Majesty." The royal watch was taken in hand and ticked off the carefully counted seconds of elapsed time as the men piled out of their hammocks and quietly ran to their stations. In one minute and a half by the Kaiser's chronometer the ship was ready for action and water-tight integrity established. The *Columbia*, startled by the commotion and wondering what was happening, broke out a searchlight, which disclosed the Imperial Standard at the *New York's* mainmast. The Kaiser never again manifested scepticism of any statement Evans made. The former followed with friendly interest his host's subsequent career until its very end. In writing a longhand letter to President Roosevelt from Corfu in 1908, the Kaiser referred to the cruise of the United States fleet around South America and said: "Admiral Evans has again proved his fine qualities as seaman and leader. . . ." The significant word was "again."

An analytical treatise has been written of the last of the Hohenzollern dynasty, attributing his personality and behaviour to the mutual interaction of his vanity and his withered arm. One who delights in that kind of psychological probing might indulge in a study of contrasts between this erratic potentate and his American friend, who for half a century so heroically carried off his much more crippling and painful defect of limb.

The public at home was awakening to the fact that the New American Navy was being discovered by Europe at the Kiel show. Although far down the list (we ranked seventh), we were once more beginning to take our place as a maritime power.

Before leaving, the *New York* held a public reception aboard and, despite the fact that by that time the glamour of visiting a foreign man-of-war must have been somewhat dimmed for the populace by the wealth of opportunities, a vast throng clambered up the gangways and percolated into every recess of the cruiser.

The American squadron seemed like a haven of friendly

refuge from the diplomatic entanglements of the European powers. Except for the Spaniards, who were not much in evidence, all of the officials could step aboard the deck of any of Admiral Kirkland's ships and feel clear of the tension that pervaded almost all of the other craft.

Captain Evans was always particularly proud of his boat crews and encouraged racing at every opportunity, so that he considered it the greatest mark of his esteem to name the *New York's* fastest boat the *Victoria Louisa* for the Kaiser's only daughter. Whether or not the All-Highest fully appreciated the honour bestowed upon his two year old child, he was most gracious in accepting it for her and sensed the cordiality of the intention. This good old American hale-fellow-well-met geniality was a welcome note in the finale of discords with which the Kiel ceremonies came to a close. The more radical Berlin newspapers decried the eight million dollar expense and they were in a position to know how lavish had been the largess because, shrewd press agent that he was, the Kaiser had seen to it that the journalists were given favoured attention and the best vintage champagne at every event. Nicholas felt called upon to express his royal displeasure at the French fleet's misbehaviour, but this came rather tardily and without carrying much conviction. The *Sardegna*, Italy's flagship, went aground in the Great Belt on her way home. Hamburg felt that, with her guests out of the front door she could speak out plainly about the extravagance of having created that Alsterinsel to gratify the Emperor's whim. In France, the chorus of disapprobation about the Kiel participation sang out afresh, and the Kaiser, exasperated at the perversity of chancelleries and fate in withholding coöperation in his pacific enterprise, lost his temper and decreed a celebration of the twenty-fifth anniversary of Sedan that would be ostentatious and exclusively German. As the last ships departed from the scene of the festivities and the new Canal came into use, the deep voice of Bismarck spoke out with injured wrath at the upstart monarch's insolent treatment of him who had fathered the entire project. He had sat by while the sugar-coated pleasantries were passed around. He had heard von Boetticher receive all the credit and Baron Marschall von Bieberstein, who had no more to do with the Kaiser Wilhelm Canal than with the Panama Canal, have forced upon him the Imperial gratitude. The Count was in no mood for gracious insincerities and had snubbed his fellow veteran Mr. Gladstone's overture for an interview. Bismarck's personal vanity needed no artificial respiration. The diplomatic manœuvring, however, was his particular forte and in this he could not bear to see his own creature Reich so vulnerable to the obvious intrigue of its neighbours. He continually ridiculed the boastful French implications of a Russian alliance but he feared the worst. Angry and irreconcilable, he ordered his son-in-law to resign his post as Minister to The Hague.

The War of 1914 was exactly one generation ahead and Captain Evans was returning to New York with the latter's namesake, across stubborn summer seas, satisfied that *with the necessary matériel,* our Navy would be ready to hold its own against the best of the old world, whenever national interests would tear us out of our detached seclusion. In other words, all that the Navy needed was ships; it still had the *esprit de corps* and smartness of the days of Farragut and Porter.

13

BATTLESHIP NO. 1

~~~~~~

A̲T the end of July, the flag quarters were made ready for the third admiral during the period of Evans' command, "a rare experience for any captain, and one I imagine few captains would ever care to have." Admiral Bunce hoisted his colours at the main and the *New York* became flagship of the North Atlantic Squadron.

There ensued several weeks of intensive fleet manœuvres which were featured by hard work for all hands. The torpedo was coming into its own. During the Chilean Civil War it had been successfully employed to sink the battleship *Blanco Encalada* and the European navies were using it in their manœuvres. Obviously, this new weapon was to revolutionize naval tactics. Some authorities, like the one-idea aircraft overenthusiasts of a later date, insisted that it spelled the doom of the capital ship and the same arguments were used almost word for word in the one case as in the other. The French were convinced by this plausible theorizing, so compatible with their budget difficulties, and their navy became second rate. The British, on the other hand, while making full offensive use of the torpedo, devoted equal energy to developing a defence against it. Their naval supremacy was not to be shaken by a new weapon. The torpedo boat inspired the torpedo boat destroyer and the perfection of the secondary rapid-fire batteries on the big ships. The smoke screen and the blister and additional protective devices were for the more remote future.

As a matter of fact, this new under water projectile was to play an insignificant part in the war against Spain, which was now clearly in the cards, but Admiral Bunce drilled his squadron in firing and eluding the automobile torpedo and in the handling of the queer little torpedo boats of those experimental days.

The three modern battleships authorized by Congress in 1890 and preceded by only the *Texas* and the *Maine*, were at last nearing completion. So that all sections of the country would be represented, they had been christened the *Massachusetts, Oregon* and *Indiana*. The last of the trio was at the most advanced stage of construction and lay in the Delaware River, ready to be delivered by Cramp's Shipyard to her naval complement for final fitting out. The captaincy of the *Indiana* would, of course, be the outstanding command in the service. There were a number of officers of the rank of captain well qualified for the post. The problem of the Department was to see that, while the eyes of the maritime world were focussed upon the early trials and while Congress was observing the preliminary tests, she should be in the hands of the most capable skipper of them all.

Orders finally were issued and, with little or no hesitancy, they were addressed to Captain Robley D. Evans. So well did he acquit himself at this important duty that later, when on the brink of war a newer and even more formidable battleship, the *Iowa*, needed a commander to lead her into action, the same officer was entrusted with the responsibility. Well, surgeons of the Norfolk Naval Hospital, for condemned limbs the old legs seemed to be doing nicely! Old Gimpy was coming along; coming along in the van.

The *Indiana* was a fighting monster, every ton of her, and she looked the part with her stub nose, hunched-up superstructure of heavy steel and squat pair of smokestacks.

In turrets fore and aft were her four thirteen-inch breech-loading rifles, along the sides were her eight eight-inch batteries and her dozen broadside six-inch rapid fire guns. Compared to a post-Jutland superdreadnought she was only a little more than half as long, about a third in displacement and horse-power, and but a fraction as costly. Among her contemporaries, however, she was without a peer, with the possible exception of the units of the *Royal Sovereign* class in the British Navy.

Evans was thrilled with his new ship. True, there were no genuine masts or yardarms, no rigging in the proper sense and not a scrap of canvas, aside from the crew's sea bags and hammocks and the collision mat. There was nothing except the sea and the compass to remind one of the old marlinspike days. But there were compensations. This was the floating fortress that so excited Rudyard Kipling when he breakfasted aboard her one morning with her Captain, who inspired the famous ballad, penned by the poet in a set of his works presented to his host. She was a complicated mass of machinery, armour plating, guns and all manner of devices, to become familiar with which required considerable close study on Evans' part. He was fascinated by the concentrated power, by the flexibility of the awkward looking leviathan, by the ingeniously devised economy of space whereby every wire and every fitting had its particular groove and niche. Like a mechanically-minded boy with his first watch, he mastered the function of every screw and every cog.

Evans became impatient to take this immense gun platform to sea and pit her against the elements, which his career had taught him to respect. "So long as a ship is afloat," said Grand Admiral von Tirpitz, "it retains a certain fighting value . . ." and only so long; a truism often under-emphasized by the paper strategists and parlour constructors. Evans wondered how seaworthy this ponderous steel hulk would prove to be.

For two months of the autumn, the naval officers and crew whipped their battleship into shape, as she lay at her wharf at the foot of Philadelphia. The skipper was ill much of the time but he personally supervised every detail of the completion of the ship. Then she was pronounced ready to cast off. Bob Evans felt her powerful engines and rudder respond to his commands, as he skilfully guided her into the bay and out into the Atlantic. This was a craft! Let Neptune dip his trident!

The ship called at Newport and hoisted aboard the giant cigar shaped projectiles for her torpedo tubes. Then, after the briefest of shakedown cruises, the Inspection Board, presided over by Commodore Dewey, took its trip in the *Indiana* and marvelled at her prowess. We were, after all the heartbreaking years of Congressional torpor, building a Navy of ships for the Navy of men. Perhaps Spain would not find us totally unprepared. The Board was deeply impressed by the inherent possibilities of these new battleships and the excellent state of efficiency to which Captain Evans had in so short a time brought the *Indiana*.

Later in the winter he embraced opportunities to test her ability and stamina in heavy weather. In a hurricane off Cape Hatteras, Evans "kept her going at full speed and drove her hard into the seas." The forecastle buried itself in green water until the forward main gun turret was all seas under and those on the upper bridge were drenched in heavy spray, but the vessel always came blithely out of the waves and shook off their pounding, without causing the slightest uneasiness to the expert sailor in cómmand. The mustang of the deep felt the hand and spurs of the master, and she rode out the storm in thoroughbred fashion. Having satisfied himself that the *Indiana* could stand any amount of sea, Evans "slowed her down to good steerage way, when she was as dry as a cork and looked like a small island surrounded by seething white breakers." Later in the season, she struck an even more severe storm off the Virginia coast

ement, the war against Spain had been held off during his

and showed that, if properly induced, she could rear and buck with the best of them but be relied upon to keep her feet.

Getting her in and out of the Port Royal dry-dock presented problems as new as the ship and Evans had to almost jump her over the shallow bar at the very instant of high tide. The Department learned that shore facilities must keep pace with the increasing size of the ships. After several narrowly averted disasters, the *Indiana* with her bottom cleaned was safely brought back to sea, but only the skipper's expert seamanship had made this possible.

At Hampton Roads came another real test of a different sort. The *New York* was lying there, and the *Indiana's* untried cutter, *Uncle Sam,* challenged the *Victoria Louisa* to a race. Without Evans, the star oarsmen of Kiel were not quite as strong; against him, they were outrowed.

After a year—the crucial year of service in the new battleship—Evans was returned to duty on the beach, again with the Lighthouse Board, but this time as a full-fledged member.

To his surprise and it must be admitted his disappointment, the war against Spain had been held off during his tour of duty afloat. Feeling as sure of its imminence as of anything in the uncertain realm of the future, he naturally wanted to be in it on the first line.

Once, while in Washington at a short conference with President Cleveland and the Assistant Secretary, a report was brought in of another critical incident in the long series of Cuban complications. The President shook his head anxiously and Evans is said to have blurted forth without reserve: "The *Indiana* is the finest fighting machine afloat. If you will say the word, I will go down to Cuba and with her alone will undertake to clean out the entire Spanish fleet."

Evans was never in his life more serious or earnest.

The Chief Executive smiled approvingly but reminded his good friend of the prime obligation of the Government to preserve the peace as long as it could possibly be done consistent with national self-respect. The sailor gave the statesman a quizzical look implying that such a point had long since been reached. For what must we delay? The answer, of course, was beyond the range of perception of any mere mortal. We must wait until we can remember the *Maine*.

The Captain soon took his leave. A clerk in an antechamber thought that Old Gimpy was limping more than usual and scowling with unaccustomed disgust, as he pounded his way along. He was muttering and some of the words were audible: ". . . if they would only give me a chance in Cuba with the *Indiana,* no language but Spanish would be heard for the next five years in hell!" From this soliloquy in undertone spread another story to adorn the growing legend of Fighting Bob.

When he relinquished command of his great battleship, he feared that it was to be his lot, after the long career of preparation, to sit remotely on the beach while Spain was driven out of the western hemisphere. The tour of duty on the Lighthouse Board at least kept him at the hub. In Washington he resumed old companionships and was in the inner circles of official activity. For about a year he remained at this post, and this period of Evans' life is notable chiefly for two signal achievements: the settlement of the line and staff controversy by the so-called Evans Board, and the establishment of his friendship with Theodore Roosevelt. The two are somewhat interrelated, as Roosevelt presided over the Board.

This dynamic young man had come down from New York with the restoration to power of the Republicans, when William McKinley succeeded Evans' friend Grover Cleveland in the White House. As Assistant Secretary of the Navy under John D. Long, he had an official status which, with his entrée into the *sanctum sanctorum* of Washington's social élite and his ample private means, opened to him every house in the capital and made him, as Henry Adams has observed, "equally at home in them all." Into what this philosopher-historian has characterized as "the dead-water of the *fin-de-siècle*," the boisterous aristocratic politician plunged with both feet, and, in the exuberance of his spirit, splashed the sedate reactionaries, who were dying with the century. Everything interested him and he either interested, entertained or amused everybody—or did all three. He had studied and written about the Navy, and he knew the gospel that Mahan was spreading. As Assistant Secretary, he was bending every effort—and he was a gifted executive—toward whipping the Navy into proper condition for the coming fray, which he, too, saw was inevitable. Naturally, two such similar personalities as his and Bob Evans' could not fail to establish a warm relationship. They saw eye to eye and spoke the same language. Evans was Roosevelt's idea of a dashing naval leader, and, in the Assistant Secretary, the sailor recognized one who was more than a dressed up political office holder —one who understood the service in which he rated a seventeen gun salute. It was worth while discussing Department affairs with this man; he listened intelligently and, most remarkable of all, he accomplished things. Cabinets, Congressional Committees, pacifists were mere obstacles that gave more zest to his labours. Here was a civilian chief after Evans' own heart.

The friendship was a boon to the nation. It endured throughout their joint lives and thus during Roosevelt's tenure of the presidency. It made itself felt for the betterment of the service they both loved.

The first concrete benefit to the Navy was the termination of the old line and staff feud. In the days of sail there were in the wardrooms only the line officers and the medical doctors and paymasters, with an occasional chaplain. These staff officers knew their place and kept it. They were well aware of the fact that their function was merely auxiliary and hence dispensable. While they performed duties that were important in their way, they were not of a military nature and, after all, a man-of-war's mission is to move and fight. Upon the introduction of steam and the advent of engineers, the trouble began. If these new officers, recruited at first from civil life, did not directly fight the ship, they did move her and they refused to be relegated to the non-combatant class of surgeons, auditors and preachers. There had been a growing jealousy between the old line corps and these new kings of the vessel's underworld. When it came to pay and to other matters involving legislation, both pulled political wires but, at this game of landsmen, the line was conspicuously inept. Being indoctrinated from their youth with the concept that a naval officer worthy of his commission does not demean himself by resorting to political influence for individual ends, they were slow to employ it as a group. The engineers were hampered by no such tradition and they lobbied vigorously, before that word was in common usage.

There were petty squabbles and more serious disputes. The line and staff differed at every point of impact: pay, rank, prerogatives, authority, uniform, insignia and so forth. The would-be palliatives adopted by the various secretaries accomplished nothing. The breach widened. No one in authority had seemed intelligent and courageous enough to face the problem squarely and to attempt a permanent solution, until Roosevelt came along. He feared nothing, much less ugly facts. On the contrary, he rather relished the excitement of a suppressed controversy thrown into the open.

Secretary Long duly appointed a board to sift the vexatious question. Roosevelt presided but Evans was the ranking uniformed officer and it has always been referred to by his name. The designation of Evans caused general misgivings among the staff partisans. Not only was he a line officer but he was known as a line officer of the old school, which had decided views to the effect that a staff officer aboard ship should be seen but not too frequently heard. Upon various occasions he had sharply rebuked engineers who, in his opinion, had overstepped the bounds of their departmental authority. The staff almost abandoned hope as to the outcome of the proceedings.

The Board held hearings. With Roosevelt and Evans in attendance, there was a drive to cut straight to the heart of the issue. The object of attaining a satisfactory adjustment was never lost sight of in a maze of testimony.

Finally the report was rendered and in due course made public. Its contents were astounding to all concerned, line and staff alike. Not only adopting the pleas of the staff but going beyond what the latter had asked, the Board recommended that the distinctions between the two corps be lessened and, so far as the engineering officers were concerned, abolished. The latter were to be incorporated with the line, wear line uniforms and, so far as possible, perform line duties. The denizens of the fire rooms came above decks to gasp in delighted astonishment. The line grumbled but soon learned to see the wisdom of the amalgamation. The recommendations of the Evans Board were duly enacted into law in the Naval Personnel bill. When feeling was still rife, Evans said: "The scheme of amalgamation embodied in that bill was first proposed by me, and I wish to assume the responsibility which attached to my act."

The credit should also be his.

14

THE "UNTOWARD INCIDENT"

DURING the campaign of 1896, the issues that absorbed popular attention were domestic. Bryan, who in 1925 would turn loose his oratorical powers against evolution, was now inveighing against the monetary laws and urging the voters to arise in their economic omniscience and place him upon a silver dais. Mark Hanna, however, saw to it in his quiet way that the country became "normally Republican," and William McKinley was inaugurated our fourth war president. The war was not far off.

Soon after entering the White House, the President realized that despite the campaign, his heaviest responsibilities involved not domestic affairs but foreign. He began to ponder over those vexatious problems which Cleveland had on March fourth so cheerfully forsaken for his fishing rod. The Secretary of State, old Senator John Sherman, selected with particular care the Minister to Spain. General Stewart L. Woodford sailed in midsummer. On Monday September thirteenth, at the Miramar Palace at San Sebastian, on the shores of the Bay of Biscay, he presented his credentials to the Queen Regent. Five days later he had his first official interview with the Duke de Tetuan, Minister of Foreign Affairs. There was a great deal to discuss and, within the bounds of the most courtly diplomatic parlance, there was some straightforward Yankee talk. In the interval between the genuflexions to Her Majesty and the business conference with her suave Minister, General Woodford had made the acquaintance of the British Ambassador, to whom he expressed the hope that their conversation would be reported to Lord Salisbury and his Cabinet. The General had put in his first week at the summer capital very satisfactorily, and the chancellories of Europe became aware of the fact that the Cuban situation was at last being forced to a crisis.

Ever since Simon Bolivar had in 1805 sworn his oath on the Aventine Hill at Rome, the signs had pointed to the recession of Spain from the western world. What the South American peoples had done for themselves, the Cubans seemed unable to achieve without aid. Destiny had long been asking the United States to lend a helping hand and there was every reason why this appeal should fall upon sympathetic ears.

It is all very well for the logicians to press their analogies of miseries ignored elsewhere and often. No, we were not crusading for the elimination of sin from the universe. A pedestrian run over by a vehicle before one's eyes demands and obtains more ready solicitude than a thousand distant Asiatics hungering in flooded rice fields. Fortunately for our sanity, the imagination has its narrow limits. Only ninety miles of Gulf Stream blue separated Cuba from us. Indeed Columbus, who discovered it, died believing it a part of the continent. It lay at our very door step, as McKinley said.

The voices of sentiment and of interest were heard as part of one loud persuasive appeal. That we should not have heeded either had its tone lacked the reënforcement of the other, it is open to cynics to aver.

Certainly we needed the cane sugar of the island upon which we depended for ninety percent of our large consumption. Certainly the natural market for our products was alluring, and indeed Cuba is to-day a great American customer. Certainly the vast property interests of Ameri-

cans, who had invested what President Cleveland had estimated as from thirty to fifty millions of dollars in the
island, demanded protection. Certainly the United States
was obeying the prime instinct of self-preservation when at
last she sought to extirpate the excellent breeding grounds
of yellow fever and other loathsome disease bacilli, that
Spain maintained so near to our border that no quarantine
barriers could exclude the waves of deadly contagion.

Granted that our Government was motivated by all of
those considerations and still the story has not been told
by half. The people, influenced by and then in turn influ-
encing the press, were advancing more rapidly than their
Government toward interference with Spain's dominion,
largely because of their fellow feeling for neighbours struggling against mediaeval despotism of a nature so cruel and
relentless that submission was convincingly shown to be out
of the question.

The fundamental sources of Cuba's discontent had always been economic. Spain still believed that colonies existed solely for the enrichment of the mother country. She
had imposed undue trade restrictions, arbitrary methods of
taxation and a régime of official debauchery that stupidly
failed to share any of the spoils with native grafters. Political change was sought chiefly as a hope of bettering
economic conditions rather than as an end in itself. The
people as a whole and individually craved prosperity. They
held the sugar bowl of the world and some of the finest
tobacco; they yearned for the rewards of industrial wealth.

The Ten Years' Civil War had at both ends overlapped
the Grant Administrations and had nauseated the Americans by the horrors of its barbarities. Spain had claimed
that the uprising had been caused by a few irresponsible
agitators in the eastern provinces and that the Cubans, on
the whole, had remained loyal to the crown. Nevertheless,
a decade of bloody suppressions had been necessary to re-
ëstablish even the appearance of quiescence. In 1877 and

1878 certain measures of colonial administrative reform had been grudgingly granted by Madrid. The Spaniards also insisted that, if only the United States would enforce the laws against exporting arms to the insurgents, all would be serene on the Pearl of the Antilles. We had assigned a large part of the Navy to the distasteful task of thwarting these filibustering expeditions, but to stop the flow of munitions to Cuba was as difficult as stopping the flow of liquor to-day across the Canadian boundary. The illicit cargoes could slip out of any harbour from Maine to Texas, and could enter any of the fifty harbours of Cuba or even be landed on a stretch of beach along the island's extensive coast.

Despite the suspicion that Cuba's internal disturbances had not subsided as completely as Spain would have had the world believe, foreign capital, chiefly American, had been induced to attempt the work of reconstruction. There was plenty to be done along these lines to keep Cuba abreast of nineteenth century development, especially after the mangling that the country had undergone during the long conflict.

The more, however, that an outsider in the eighties saw of conditions there, the less substantial did the alleged peace appear to be. The period was, in fact, only an interlude for the recovery of sufficient strength to maintain a fresh outbreak. This was realized by Americans familiar with the situation. Their heavy investments looked precarious. It required seventeen years to raise another generation of spirited Cubans, liberty loving not because of cherishing abstract principles of political independence but because of feeling upon their backs the economic lash of the oppressor. Cuba could see prosperity around her but did not share it. Spain's worst administrators, and they were wretched indeed, seemed to be reserved for infliction upon Cuba, where they enriched themselves in a corrupt orgy of greedy exploitation, without doing anything whatsoever of benefit to the colony. These rapacious parasites rotated in office as though upon a political merry-go-round. Almost every passenger ship disembarked its quota of new tormentors, who would abuse, steal and then make way for the next fortune-hunting rascals.

The new trouble started in 1895. As upon the former occasion, it was local in origin, broke out in Oriente, and received its first support from the lower classes, who understood little of what was transpiring but knew the pinch of hunger under the existing régime. This time, however, the movement spread with great rapidity from Cape Maisè on the extreme East to Cape San Antonio on the extreme West. The reactionary tobacco raising districts of Pinar del Rio and Havana Province fell into line. The revolt percolated upwards from one social stratum to another. Spain was thrown upon the defensive and aroused to a final effort of furious resistance. A policy of absolute ruthlessness was adopted, which only the madness of desperation could have sanctioned. The world was shocked by the inhumanity of this latest campaign of subjugation, which seemed to devise new outrages as the old ones failed to accomplish the object of suppression. The United States could not ignore the frightful atrocities. Constitutional guarantees were suspended in Cuba and such meagre civil liberties as had been permitted to exist were abrogated.

The property of foreigners became jeopardized and then destroyed; their lives endangered and then lost; there was one complaint after the other to our State Department. Spain argued and explained and regretted, but did nothing. She could do nothing. She was utterly imcompetent to handle the situation and was lucky to be able to retain a foothold on her refractory colony, much less restore order. The island was in passionate revolt. Spain poured men and treasure into the enterprise and, by virtue of her control of the sea, the routes from the Spanish ports to Havana and Santiago were open to her transports.

There came a deadlock that made clear the futility of the struggle. The cities and military fortifications were safe from the insurgent's conquest but the latter swarmed over the open country in forces too powerful for the Spanish garrisons to scatter. The rebels destroyed sugar centrals, houses, everything of value, rather than have them fall into Spanish hands, and the Spaniards countered with a terrorizing campaign of devastation that also applied the torch to whatever they could not use. Cuba was being irreparably ravaged and would soon be for ever lost to both Spain and her own inhabitants.

"The policy which obviously attempts to make Cuba worthless to the Cubans, should they prevail," wrote Secretary Sherman to the new Minister, "must inevitably make the island equally worthless to Spain in the event of reconquest, whether it be regained as a subject possession or endowed with a reasonable measure of self-administration."

The capital and effort that had been contributed by Americans and other foreigners after the truce of 1878 had been lost in the general débâcle.

"Weighing all these facts carefully," the Secretary went on to say, "and without prejudice, in the judgment of the President the time has come for this Government to soberly consider and clearly decide the nature and methods of its duty both to its neighbours and itself."

The United States tendered her good offices to help effect a mutually honourable adjustment. These, however, Spain declined with thanks. No one can blame her for that. We were hardly disinterested, and no terms acceptable to both sides could possibly have been devised. Cuba was resolved that once and for all the hated red and yellow ensign should be hauled down from Morro Castle. If Spain were

to grant independence, there would remain nothing to
settle.

The British Ambassador had listened sympathetically
to General Woodford's recital and asked what the United
States proposed doing. The latter replied that "some means
must be found" to solve the problem before Congress met in
December. To the Duke, the recital was followed by an
equally vague and most polite ultimatum, implying that unless Spain herself established peace, we would do so by
intervention.

When the Russian Ambassador at Madrid asked General
Woodford about the situation, he gave a full history of the
Cuban problem and could not refrain from reminding his
colleague of Spain's unfriendliness during our own Civil
War, which contrasted with the Czar's gesture of cordiality
in sending his squadron to New York, and of the open
blockade running between the Confederate ports and Havana. The mills of the Gods . . .

The colonial policy of Spain was an accurate reflection
of the irresponsible political depravity at Madrid. Cuba
suffered not only from the intristic hardships imposed upon
her but almost as severely from the dread uncertainty as
to what would be perpetrated next and who would be the
new Governor to-morrow. In addition to all this, Spain had
in those days the tragic genius of performing her occasional
worthy acts at exactly the most unpropitious moment.

The enormous Spanish Army in Cuba floundered about
ineffectively. General Gomez was, toward the close of '95,
sweeping the revolution to the very gates of Havana.
Avoiding engagements with large bodies of troops, he waged
a very successful guerilla warfare. General Campos, the
Governor, was then superseded by Spain's ace in the hole,
her last bloody trump card, Valeriano Weyler, "the
Butcher." Even among the Spanish colonial administrators
of the nineteenth century, this energetic and dehumanized

despot had found no difficulty in making himself conspicuous throughout the Empire. In that company of slaughterers, the sobriquet "Butcher" had been reserved for him, and his right thereto has never been questioned. His bloody trail had led from the Canaries to the Balearics, from the Philippines to the Basque provinces, and the sun never set upon the cemeteries that marked the uprisings he had suppressed. He was the supreme insurgent matador of the Imperial arena and one of the most honoured celebrities of Madrid. It was gruesomely fitting that he give the remorseless campaign in Cuba the last turn of the screw, because that was where, as a promising young warrior in the Ten Years' War, he had learned the niceties of Spanish colonial rule.

With the advent of '96, General Weyler became Governor of Cuba upon a platform of uncompromising severity. The inhabitants shuddered as he reached Havana. The garrote and the firing squads had been busy under previous administrations. What new instruments of torture would this arch tyrant be able to devise to maintain his prestige for unequalled cruelty? Surely, he would bring some new method of intimidation stamped with the imprint of his own personality. In this terrified expectation, the people of Cuba were not to be disappointed. Weyler promptly promised the islanders that he would employ measures of inexorable repression calculated to crush the revolt, even if all Cuba had to be crushed in the process. The diabolical system of concentration stockades was thereupon introduced. It was fully worthy of the great Butcher and indeed enhanced his reputation to such an extent that it probably will stand in history as the crowning achievement of his long career, that ended in October 1930 at the age of ninety-one.

Into these outdoor detention camps were herded the noncombatants of the district, men, women and children, called *reconcentrados,* where they could lend no assistance to the revolution. There was scant food and no protection against disease. The conditions were unhygienic in the extreme and, as the rural population was chased into these filthy stockades under penalty of death, the suffering became intense. True, the revolutionists had themselves initiated certain modified forms of concentration for self-protection and had themselves laid waste some of the rural properties. Weyler, however, proceeded to carry both types of operation to the very limit.

President McKinley, referring to the *reconcentrados,* said that this "was not civilized warfare; it was extermination. The only peace it could beget was that of the wilderness and the grave."

Not only were the citizens of the United States obliged to hear the screams of anguish and watch the reckless shedding of Cuban blood and the denuding of the island of all tangible improvements, but humanity impelled them to send thousands of dollars worth of food, medicines and other relief supplies to the unfortunate *reconcentrados,* confined under conditions that in this country are unlawful in the penning of cattle.

Then, in August, an obscure anarchist, lurking in the shadows at the baths of Santa Agueda across the Atlantic, altered the entire nature of the Imperial policy. When Antonio Canovas del Castillo, Premier and unquestionably the leading Spanish statesman of the era, was suddenly cut down, his régime of no concessions to the colonies, no reforms and no surrender fell with him. At the time, he was vigorously engaged in forwarding to Weyler all possible support, including an army of two hundred thousand men. Had the hand of the assassin been stayed, it is barely possible that the Cuban revolt might have been suppressed and American intervention avoided, despite the sanguinary price that would have been paid for peace.

The Queen Regent had no alternative to handing over the Ministry to Praxades Sagasta, the Liberal leader who

From painting by W. A. Rogers in Harper's Pictorial History of the Spanish-American War

GUERILLAS DRIVING PACIFICOS INTO ONE OF THE
STATIONS OF CONCENTRATION ESTABLISHED
BY GENERAL WEYLER

had preceded Canovas in office. His policy had always been one of relative moderation and now, when it was too late, he tried to retrace the Government's steps in the direction opposite to that taken by Canovas. America's outraged protests against the Butcher were honoured by his recall and the appointment in his place of General Ramon Blanco, who promptly tried to undo the worst of Weyler's work. It was, however, of little immediate benefit to the uprooted *reconcentrados* to be released with no homes or labour to which to return and too weak or ill to get there.

Sagasta announced autonomy for Cuba and Porto Rico, and followed this by other dispensations. In each instance, however, certain powers were reserved to the central authority, and the time for half-way measures had long since passed. In 1895 these concessions might have ended and would certainly have postponed the revolution, but now General Gomez and his colleagues were in a position to demand all or nothing.

Fifty years earlier, Spain had rebuffed our overtures toward purchasing Cuba. Again the proposition was broached, tactfully and unofficially. She still declined to consider an amicable sale. In this respect, no progress had been made since the Ostend Manifesto of 1854.

Feeling in both Spain and the United States was growing bitter. Spain resented our constant interference in her affairs and attributed to it the great difficulties under which she was labouring. Naturally enough, the most selfish motives were imputed to us, and Spain was by no means alone in believing that we were aggravating the situation in order to seize her West Indies possessions for our own national aggrandizement.

All Europe was sceptical as to the sincerity of American protestations of sympathy for the oppressed Cubans. The hardened old cynics of the foreign offices could see no distinction between what we were doing and the game that they themselves had been playing in Asia and Africa. The British were making ready to absorb the Transvaal and the Orange Free State into the Union of South Africa. Germany was, at Tsingtao, driving her wedge into the Far East. Russia and Japan were drifting toward the clash of arms not far beyond the turn of the century. France was avidly eyeing Africa. The teachings of the Darwinites and the post-Darwinites were much in vogue. The world of affairs believed it was witnessing just one more encounter in the struggle for survival among the big nations. Probably no foreign country recognized in our activities anything but a step toward imperialism. That within five years Cuba could, by our efforts, not only be rid of Spain but achieve her independence, was beyond the credulity of Europe. Such a prognostication would have been—and was—scorned as the visionary dream of an idealist who mistook the earth for Utopia, or as the palaver of modern conquerors. Let it be conceded that Cuba's subsequent sovereignty was qualified by the Platt Amendment and that the United States was to derive special economic advantages from the relationship; nevertheless, Cuba was to attain a degree of independence which could be greater only by being absolute.

As Spain in the autumn of '97 relaxed her severities, Washington renewed the hope for a solution of the problem without war. The temper of the American people, however, had by now been aroused to a pitch that rendered the situation a very delicate one. President McKinley was honestly striving, under greater difficulties, to continue Cleveland's policy of pacific restraint. The influential banking and industrial and commercial powers with vested capital in Cuba clamoured for intervention, and a large element of the press stirred up the sensibilities of the people. It was of vital importance that the atmosphere should be kept clear. Secretary Sherman expressed to General Woodford the Government's daily fear lest "some untoward in-

cident . . . abruptly supervene to inflame mutual passions
beyond control. . . . "

The "untoward incident" was to "supervene" very
shortly and was to be of a nature that no American could
have anticipated. In its all-engrossing grasp upon public
attention, it was to eclipse the concern about Cuba.

Conceding that the United States Government could not
have ignored the Cuban situation, there was one course it
might have adopted midway between such affirmative passivity and armed intervention. By recognizing the state of
belligerency that had in fact existed on the island for a long
time and for which recognition there was abundant war-
rant in international law, Washington would have enabled
the insurgents to equip themselves openly in the United
States and, by such means, possibly to win their country's
independence. The difficulty with such a policy would have
been the slowness of its effect. With the control of the sea
in Spain's hands, it might have taken Cuba many years to
expel the Spanish troops from the strongly fortified cities.
Little would have been left of Cuba by that time. Furthermore, such a policy would have been a cowardly straddle
between candid hostility to Spain and a weak disregard of
a neighbour's plight.

If Cuba was to be launched into the family of nations,
the method actually employed was probably the least objec-
tionable. Even many Spaniards, particularly those of the
dominant military classes, felt that, if Cuba must be lost, to
lose it in war would be the most honourable way. *Noblesse
oblige* has its Castilian construction not always perspicuous
to the American observer.

The "untoward incident" was to strike close to Evans.
What a fate awaited his *Maine,* the ship whose construction
he had commuted from Washington to Brooklyn to super-
vise!

The Sagasta-Blanco régime constituted the lull before

the storm. To celebrate the restoration of the modicum
of Spanish-American good feeling between the two Governments, it was arranged that the old custom of friendly naval
visits would be revived. The Spanish cruiser *Vizcaya* was
ordered to New York and, in exchange, a battleship was to
visit Havana. In accordance with plans formulated in con-
cert with the Spanish authorities, the *Maine* arrived off
Morro Castle on January twenty-fifth, 1898. A Spanish
pilot conducted her into the harbour and she was duly assigned to one of the man-of-war berths. The commanding
officer was Captain Charles D. Sigsbee, who, it will be remembered, had been at the Academy with Bob Evans.

There were thousands lining the Malecon and the
harbour front as the American battleship slowly steamed
through the narrow entrance and picked up her buoy. The
roofs of the white buildings were covered with people. As
the salutatory cannonading lent ceremony to the arrival,
the Spaniards for the most part did not dare to hiss, and
the Cubans did not dare to cheer.

The national salute was returned by the Fortress of
Cabanas on the Morro side. The *Alfonso XII* replied to
the guns fired for her flag officer, Rear Admiral Manterola.
This cruiseless cruiser swung at her buoy, with boiler tubes
so rusted that for a year she had not been able to turn over
her engines. The appropriation for her refit had been
voted but, like so many other Spanish naval expenditures,
there had been many a slip 'twixt the Cortes and the ship.

The official visits were notable chiefly for the variety of
the Spanish officers' uniforms. Havana seemed overflow-
ing with polychromatic army officers, addressed by every
conceivable title of military and civil rank. The best troops
were reserved for parades along the Prado. Less in evidence were the long columns of overseas recruits, young and
untrained, who disappeared into the provinces, where they
died of guerilla bullets or the assorted fevers, or whence they
dragged themselves back to the congested and unsanitary

Havana hospitals, to moan of the unspeakable miseries of the campaign, with its one meal a day in a trough and its exasperatingly fatuous direction.

The officers of the *Maine* found the surface atmosphere so hostile to the United States that they ventured on the beach in civilian garb only. Then, when they penetrated the thin tinselled layer of superficial gaiety and met the influential Cubans of the capital, they were warned that Spanish treachery rendered the place extremely unsafe for an American warship.

The authorities were seeking to divert the attention of the inhabitants from the revolution. Among other devices, they imported Spain's champion matador, who gave exhibitions of his skill across the harbour not far from the laurel grove in which the Cuban insurgents were disciplined by firing squads. The ferry loads of spectators going to and from the bull fights became more openly inimical as the *Maine* lingered, and mustered up sufficient courage to shout derisive epithets across the water as they passed by.

Governor General Blanco returned from a trip to the East which, it was commonly gossiped, he had taken in a fruitless effort to buy off the insurgent leaders. Captain Sigsbee called upon him. The return call was omitted.

Neither the hosts nor the guests were enjoying the *Maine's* visit. A rumour aboard that she would soon depart for the Mardi Gras at New Orleans led all hands to hope for such orders, but they never came. In the meantime the other foreign men-of-war stood out. The French flagship *Dubordieu* left for the Mardi Gras; so did the German ships; only the American vessel was not going to the party of her own countrymen, it seemed. Sunday, February thirteenth, found her pretty much alone among the Spaniards in the crowded harbour. That day a crude drawing was found on the blank side of a building in the city, depicting the explosion of a battleship—the writing on the wall. A scurrilous circular inciting violence against the Americans was thrust into Sigsbee's hand in the city.

The "untoward incident" occurred on Tuesday the fifteenth. Exactly what it was or the cause, no American knew and no American knows. The mystery of the *Maine* will probably never be solved. The mosaic of impressions pieced together the following morning has not been altered in any substantial detail during the many years of subsequent investigation and speculation.

The story has often been told. The explosion that shattered the darkness and the quiet and first threw most of the ship high in the air and then sent all of her to the bottom, went off when most of those aboard had turned in to sleep. A few officers were writing letters. The routine of the first watch was well under way. Long since, the orderly had entered the cabin.

"The Officer of the Deck reports eight o'clock, sir."

"Make it so."

The evening reports had been presented as usual. The quarter watch, used instead of merely the ordinary anchor watch, had been mustered, and the extra sentries and gun watches, unobtrusively maintained as a prudent precaution during this friendly little visit, had been stationed. The magazines were all locked and the keys hung in the Captain's cabin.

Up forward, in the starboard gangway, an accordian was pumping out a tune to which some sailors, scantily clad because of the hot sultry night, were dancing. At the other end of the ship, a gunner's mate was perched on the after turret, strumming upon an old mandolin. The smooth waters were softly lapping against the sides of the battleship, which occasionally felt the wash of a passing boat. The hail and answer would each time ring out and the boat recede into the darkness. The lights of Havana and of the many other craft at their moorings sparkled. The tropical heavens were overcast.

When, at nine ten, "Lights out" was sounded, the bugler little knew that he was blowing his own taps. In half an hour he was dead.

Captain Sigsbee was seated at his table. He had just completed a technical report on torpedo tubes for Assistant Secretary Roosevelt, and was writing a letter to his wife.

At nine forty came the end.

The explosion was more than a deafening noise, a blinding flash that reached the sky, a devastating disintegration of that world. It was an experience that crashed into the core of every soul aboard the *Maine* or near her. It left those who survived, utterably unable to describe what had happened, for ever different from what they had been before. All was over in a moment. The immediate impressions were varied and confused. To some passengers lounging in steamer chairs on the deck of the *City of Washington,* a Ward liner lying near-by, it looked as though the *Maine* had been caught in the freshly opened crater of a new submarine volcano. The officers were shocked not only by the violence of the ship's explosion but also by the unexpectedness of the assault, for such it seemed to be. Several of them believed, to their horrified amazement, that the shore batteries and the *Alfonso XII* had suddenly opened fire upon the *Maine.* Before they could reach the topside, they knew that the ship was lost. In the testimony at the subsequent hearings, there was a division of opinion as to whether there had been one or two explosions.

The forecastle took the brunt of the upheaval and was blown to bits. The crew's quarters were there. Dozens of the men were blasted from their hammocks into fragments; dozens were hurled into space and fell, burnt and dazed, into the harbour, where they sank; dozens were instantly transmuted to a death and burial in the sunken wrenched compartments where they had been sleeping. The after portion of the ship, covered with débris and torn by the explosion, was for a short while left above water, its interior collapsing and gradually following the forward section to the slimy bottom of the harbour.

The cabin, wardroom country and steerage (junior officer's quarters) being aft, all but two of the officers escaped destruction. Regaining their bearings with miraculous rapidity and with the calmness of accustomed authority, they supervised such rescue work as was possible. The discipline of the few surviving members of the crew was perfect. No one heeded the grave peril of further explosions in the magazines.

The boats of the *City of Washington* and of the Spanish cruiser were around the wreck, aiding those in the water or clinging desperately to the sinking hull. Captain Sigsbee, bereft and heartbroken, maintained his nobility of sober leadership until the very end. The poop was slipping into the water. Even when nothing more could possibly be done for ship or men, the tragic group of officers was standing by until their *Maine,* which they would never forsake, was involuntarily taking her leave of them. The last moment was at hand; the stern was about to take its final plunge.

Lieutenant Commander Wainwright, the executive officer, saw that the boats containing the surviving bluejackets would not pull off without the senior officers. Seeing no move by the Captain, he tried to be matter of fact and cleared his throat.

"Captain, we had better leave her."

Sigsbee was choking with grief. Of all moments, however, this was not one for what might seem like mock heroics.

"Get into the boats, gentlemen."

There was the clatter of shoes on thwarts, of looms in oarlocks. A protrusion of steel wreckage, crowned by the mainmast, emerged from the surface of the water. The *Maine* was gone.

Of her complement of three hundred and eighty-three, all but about a hundred had departed with her.

She rested in twisted decay on the oozy bottom of

Havana Harbour, but her spirit would soon sweep the Spaniards from the sea.   Throughout the world rang the news
of the destruction.   Wherever a commission pennant floated
from the masthead of an American warship, vows were solemnly sworn that the lost comrade would be avenged.   On
the seventeenth, the *Olympia* stood into Hong Kong, and
Commodore Dewey was shocked to read a cable from the
Department: *"Maine* destroyed at Havana February 15th,
by accident. . . . "

By accident! Hardly an American believed that, and yet,
in compliance with the request in Sigsbee's famous despatch
the very night of the disaster, the Government was suspend-
ing judgment pending the findings of the Court of Inquiry.
This appeal for fair play to the Spaniards, despite his conviction that his ship had been the victim of treacherous foul
play, justly earned renown for the *Maine's* Captain.

Three distinguished officers, headed by Captain Sampson, set about the gruesome post-mortem task, disregarding
the obstacles by which the Spanish authorities stupidly endeavoured to surround the investigation, thereby adding to
the suspicion.   The integrity of this Court was beyond question.   It has been characterized by a noted Briton, who dis-
agrees with its conclusions, as having been composed of
officers "who would not be swayed by national bias."

It was considered by all concerned a reasonable presumption that, if the explosion had been internal, it had been
accidental; if external, deliberate and hostile.   All visitors
to the ship at Havana had been carefully guarded by an
assigned "guide."

There was no doubt that the forward magazines had
blown up.   The great question was and is whether they had
been set off by spontaneous combustion in any magazine or
in any coal bunker aboard, or as the result of an explosion
outside of the vessel, either by submarine mine or submarine
torpedo.

American public opinion, hardly held in leash pending

the inquiry, burst forth in unrestrained fury when the report of the Court was announced. It had found that a mine had been exploded beneath the *Maine* at about frame eighteen. That a Spanish Court, whose procedure invited little confidence, rendered a contrary opinion, impressed no one. Many neutrals, however, while accepting the verdict of the American Court, were disposed to attribute the deed to Cuban insurgents or debased Americans desiring intervention at any price, rather than to Spaniards. The American Court expressed its inability to establish the guilt.

In 1911 the wreck was raised by means of cofferdams and another eminent American group sought the answer to the riddle. The Vreeland Board consisted of the Admiral whose name it bears, the officers who later became Admiral Hughes, Chief of Naval Operations, and Admiral Strauss, who laid the North Sea Mine Barrage in the World War, Chief Naval Constructor Watt and Colonel Black of the Army Engineer Corps. These experts, working leisurely in harmonious surroundings and removed from the hysteria of the days following the disaster, made an exhaustive study. The verdict was unchanged. The lengthy and thorough report ended with the finding that "the injuries to the bottom of the *Maine,* above described, were caused by the explosion of a charge of a low form of explosive exterior to the ship between frames 28 and 31, strake B, port side."

The points that are still urged in support of the theory of spontaneous combustion are forceful. First of all, the close watch maintained, particularly as to approaching boats, was so alert that the undetected laying of a mine after the *Maine* arrived at Havana would have been a difficult feat. (It would not, however, have been an impossible one.) Secondly, in all the years following the disaster, not one clue of any treachery has come to light, and such a plot would have involved at least several persons, probably a dozen. Thirdly, the ordnance experts who warned of the dangers of self-ignition in magazines have been all too well confirmed in their fears by several subsequent catastrophes unmistakably due to that cause, in the British, French, Italian, Japanese and Brazilian navies. In the case of many of these explosions, the ammunition had been properly manufactured and carefully stowed aboard ship in magazines whose temperature was under constant surveillance, thus disposing of the American contention that the cautious attention to the *Maine's* powder and shells precluded the possibility of spontaneous combustion. Fourthly, no trace of a mine was ever found in the soft mud. Fifthly, the other vessels in the harbour noticed no such upheaval of water as usually accompanies a submarine explosion, and no dead fish were seen in the harbour the following morning, although the basin is notoriously unwashed by the tides. (On this fish question the experts differed sharply as they did on many of the other points.) Lastly, it seems incredible that, under all of the circumstances then existing, any of Spain's partisans could have been blind to the folly of thus blasting the diminishing patience of the American people.

The contrary hypothesis, however, lends itself to as convincing argument. As for the placing of the mine, it may have been done prior to the *Maine's* arrival, with advance knowledge of the buoy to which she was to be assigned. The battleship rode head to wind in Havana Harbour, and it is a sinister coincidence that, for the very first time since her mooring, she pointed, on the fateful night, to the northward. Furthermore, as has been indicated, the unspeakable atrocity of blowing to pieces a visiting warship was actually hinted at in advance by the friendly Cubans, who had become bitterly versed in the tricks of the Don. The Spaniards at Havana, aside from the officials directly in charge, almost openly exulted at the calamitous ending of the Yankee battle-wagon. Then, too, the bending of the plates of the bottom was concave, and, although the two American Boards named different frames as the place of impact, both were unanimous in pronouncing the explosion external. Not a single

one of these conscientious experts dissented or even registered a doubt. As to the matter of imprudence, reference
often has been made to Spanish publications of the period
minimizing the prowess of the American Navy. Such
articles might have led uninformed fanatics to suppose that
the destruction of the *Maine,* mistakenly assumed by many
in Havana to be our finest battleship, would have turned the
scales of relative naval strength in favour of Spain. Some
of the populace even believed the *Maine* to be our only large
warship.

The possibility of a torpedo having been the cause was
entertained but, for many reasons, adjudged very remote.

(Although the subject is hardly one for jest, and no disrespectful levity is intended, it may not be out of place at this
late date to add that one of the survivors of the *Maine* suggested that the explosion might have been attributable to
Captain Sigsbee's choice of a gift to General Parrado in
reciprocity of the latter's presentation of a case of fine
sherry. The Captain had no typically American object at
hand suitable for the purpose and sent his orderly to the
Spanish General, whose knowledge of the English language
and of oceanography was extremely limited, with a carefully wrapped autographed copy of the donor's scholarly
treatise entitled *Deep Sea Sounding and Dredging.*

The grim certainty to which the United States awoke on
the morning of February sixteenth was that the *Maine* had
prematurely passed on into the shades of memory and that
more than two-thirds of her complement had been sent to
their deaths—more casualties, by a wide margin, than were
to be sustained by the American Navy in all of the engagements and battles of the ensuing war.

When the news broke, Evans was at the Carnival at New
Orleans. So we had to await such a cause! He resolved to
be discreet and did manage to repress the expression of his

THE "UNTOWARD INCIDENT" 241

opinions and sentiments. There was not a scintilla of doubt in his mind as to the nature of the explosion and, had he been Admiral Sicard, he later admitted, he would have acted with less restraint. "If he had gone into Havana the morning after the disaster with his whole fleet and said to General Blanco that he had come to find out why these American officers and men, the guests of Spain, had been foully murdered, it would, in my opinion, have produced immediate results and saved much time." Upon reaching Washington, he bluntly told Secretary Long that such would have been his action had he been in Sicard's place.

"In that event," said Long, "you would have been promptly recalled and reprimanded."

"Undoubtedly," smiled Evans, "but the people would probably have hailed me as the next President!"

His gauge of public sentiment was accurate. Nothing was further from his ambitions, however, than a civilian career, and we may be sure that, had there been an Evans-for-president boom, he would not have fallen into the trap as did the politically naïve Dewey.

The *Vizcaya* was *en route* to New York, and certainly her officers and men must have felt extremely uncomfortable when they arrived there and heard what had happened to the ship whose visit they were repaying. Nevertheless, they were shown every courtesy, and their safety and that of their ship were thoroughly guarded by the American authorities. Some days later, the *Vizcaya* saw at Havana what was left of the *Maine* above water: a tangled mass of wreckage, marked by day and night as an obstruction to navigation. Ahead of the *Vizcaya* lay but a few weeks of continued existence.

The Governments were actively engaged in what they were pleased to call trying to preserve the peace. Evans had long been convinced that the only peace Cuba would ever know would follow a war of the United States against Spain. He regarded these last energetic efforts of the statesmen and diplomats as the prescribed finale of a drama whose termination was familiar to all in advance. There would be meetings and despatches and pacific gestures, but the curtain would fall upon the declaration of war, which was plainly written in the script. It was the only rational end to the plot that had been unravelled from the opening scene of Spain's discovery of the new world.

What availed the terms, conditions, words? To Evans it seemed a waste of time to read them. They were like the answer of the convicted criminal to that hopeless question: "Have you anything to say as to why sentence should not be pronounced?"

The outcome was to Evans a foregone conclusion.

The external explosion explanation being accepted in the United States, the disaster of mid-February accelerated the culmination of the crises in two ways: by its effect upon public emotion and by its demonstration of Spain's inability to safeguard lives and property in Cuba. "You can't or you won't."

There was, of course, much diplomatic ado in the Spanish Legation, in the State Department and across the street in the White House, but the important negotiations took place in Madrid, after the American Court of Inquiry pointed its finger at Spain. President McKinley harboured an assertive conscience which required him to expend every possible effort toward continued peace even though he must have gradually come to realize that the effort was futile. This conscience demanded a record in history of resistance to the very last against the growing clamour for war. Its exactions were duly met, and no one can deny that the President was led into strife by his country, rather than the reverse. In General Woodford, his conscience had a loyal ally. Had the widening differences between the nations been susceptible of diplomatic adjustment, our Minister would have saved the peace. He enjoyed the confidence of the Queen Regent's Liberal

Government and dealt with it as a friend, frankly if firmly, valuing every concession and constantly invoking the aid of the eminent conscience at headquarters to postpone the abandonment of amicable treaty.

At all hours of the day and night, and at various places, public and private, official and residential, he discussed the delicate and interrelated issues with the new Foreign Minister. The General's Spanish being rather limited in its fluency, the Minister of the Colonies often attended as interpreter, and toward the end Sagasta threw the weight of his prestige into the conferences. The Premier protested that his pursuit of liberal policies in Cuba, accorded scant appreciation in the United States, went as far as and possibly further than Spanish opinion would permit. Judging by the newspapers and popular demonstrations, this was true. Sagasta was reviled for alleged truckling to the Yankee pigs. Yet his conciliatory concessions were not enough. Spain gave ground always a little too late and, by the time a position had been yielded, the pressure of American opinion demanded more. The latter was kept at a high pitch. So-called Big Business, excepting the interests directly concerned with Cuban investments, manifested the usual reactionary opposition to war, but the man in the street was drifting toward it with each trip to the news-stand.

The papers were filled with tales of Cuban atrocities. Senator Proctor of Vermont, Dewey's friend, returned from a tour of the island with a first hand report of conditions that shocked the nation. Statistics were inexorably against the suave assurances of Sagasta. Even his moderation had left a bloody trail. For example, there had been about 1,600,000 inhabitants of Cuba in January 1895. Spain since then had dumped 200,000 soldiers upon the colony, and now, in the spring of 1898, the total of the populace plus the remnants of the Spanish expeditionary force was hardly 1,200,000. That could not be explained away in softest Castilian.

The time was approaching for American insistence. The

leisurely manner of proceeding with official business in Madrid was taxing the patience of even the conscience-in-chief. The policy of delaying and deferring, in the pursuit of which the Spanish Ministers displayed the masterly skill bred of generations of training, was reaching the exhaustion of its resources. Finally General Woodford was obliged to deliver, in the most courteous manner, what amounted to an ultimatum. The reconcentration order must be absolutely revoked and Spain must consent to an armistice over the summer. Sagasta evaded and argued and manœuvred for time. He was always willing to meet American demands—in a modified form; and, under scrutiny, the proposed modification in form was always perceived to be a modification in substance. This conversation took place at the Premier's office. The Spaniards listened and then pleaded for time. (Give them enough time, they always reasoned, and they'd need nothing more.) A friendly request for a short delay is a difficult one to refuse in the course of any negotiation. Sagasta promised a definite reply within three days.

The American Minister, repeating that he had no secrets from his Spanish friends even with his own Government, whose attitude was as open as the fresh air, seated himself at Sagasta's desk and drafted a cable direct to the President, which he read aloud to his conferees. It urged awaiting the promised answer and expressed the sender's confidence that the parleys in Madrid would soon achieve a solution of the difficulties "honourable to Spain and satisfactory to the United States and just to Cuba."

The delay was granted but its accomplishment was nil. At this eleventh hour, nothing short of Spain's voluntary and complete relinquishment of Cuba to the Cubans could have stemmed the tide toward war. This the pride of the hidalgo forbade.

The Pope attempted mediation. The neutral powers spoke touchingly of the blessings of eternal peace. Their accredited representatives in Washington addressed a joint note, urging upon the conscience a peaceful solution—coals to Newcastle. These institutional consciences had to go through the motions, however barren of promise. The maintenance of official international peace was traditionally to be exalted, regardless of the greater human suffering it might involve in a conflict not dignified by the status of recognized belligerency. The tradition was honoured. The consciences, domestic and foreign, were respected. The President acknowledged the joint note with a gracious, non-committal reply, and the procession of events resumed its forward march.

Spain finally indicated a willingness to grant a truce and the reconcentration decrees were repealed. She was again clutching at the chance that had passed. Still behind the train of actuality, she was constantly slipping further back, despite her sincere efforts to go ahead. American demands seemed the unapproachable limit. At this late date, she at least should have manifested a willingness to agree upon some method for the future control of Cuba. Not only did she omit to do this but she let it be known that the full extent of her utmost concessions had been reached. Did her Intelligence Service not read the American papers? Was the mobilization of our fleet ignored?

The attitude of Spain was probably immaterial at this time. On April eleventh, the President submitted the entire situation, including the affair of the *Maine,* to Congress, and reluctantly advocated intervention in Cuba. Congress responded with alacrity. Its joint resolution went beyond the President's recommendation and demanded the withdrawal of Spain from Cuba. With conscience appeased, McKinley affixed his signature and Spain had the unhappy choice of submission within three days or recourse to arms. She severed diplomatic relations and General Woodford, weary and resigned to the inevitable, departed for Paris. He had done his worthy best.

The American people were enthusiastically united. North and South, Government and citizenry, stood together, ready for the occasion. It had been perfectly timed, not by design but by the advance of circumstance. The nation rolled up its sleeves and set to work with a zest upon the expulsion of Spain and the cleansing of Cuba. The war was the exciting termination of a rather dull era.

On the twenty-second of April, the President issued his proclamation of blockade of the Cuban ports, the following day he called for volunteer troops, and on the twenty-fifth, at his behest, Congress exercised its exclusive constitutional prerogative to declare war, which it said had existed since the twenty-first.

As late as March, Robley Evans had been chafing on the beach, hoping for the assignment to one of the merchant ships that, in the event of hostilities, would be converted into a cruiser. The regular berths in the Navy were, of course, filled. He, nevertheless, resolved that the fray should find him on the firing line. This was the prime of his life. The years of experience in all parts of the world, the decades of training for just such an emergency, were awaiting the call to active service afloat. When war became imminent, Secretary Long and Assistant Secretary Roosevelt speeded up preparations. Their foresight during the period of incumbency was counting for the country now. Taking advantage of Evans' presence in Washington on and off during the early part of the year, these civilian executives consulted him frequently. He stressed the importance of Key West as a base of operations and the weaknesses he had observed there ever since the *Virginius* crisis, which defects had never been remedied. His warning was heeded and the proper steps taken.

The Department carefully pondered the paramount question of fleet command. Imperfections in supreme leadership that can be overlooked during peace may be fatal to the

nation in war. All considerations of personal sensibilities
must, in the crisis of hostilities, be subordinated to the ruthless elevation over the heads of his colleagues of the man
deemed most capable of executing the naval mission. Whenever this elementary principle has been disregarded, the
penalty has been severe.

In the nature of things, the most eminent officer can not
be kept in continual command throughout peace times but,
once the fleet strips for action and is on a war footing, that
man must be summoned to his proper station.

Nelson was sent from the amorous ease of his estate at
Merton, graced by Lady Hamilton, to hoist his flag on the
Victory and assume the Mediterranean command that was
to achieve Trafalgar.

A century later, the same Admiralty did not hesitate,
upon the British entry into the World War, to appoint its
secretly long chosen leader Commander-in-Chief, in relief
of a senior and close friend whom he respected and loved.
Admiral Jellicoe has said that "the idea of taking over his
command at *the* moment of his life naturally caused me feelings of the greatest pain." The sincerity of that statement
is not open to question. When, two years thereafter, his
three great decisions at Jutland proved that he was over-
cautious, he found himself superseded by the dashing Beatty.

Secretary Long knew that Admiral Sicard's health was
not so robust as to be able to meet the rigorous exactions
of war duty. The latter was condemned by a medical survey.
The outstanding officer for the responsibility of command
was sought. The final choice won the approval of the entire
service. It fell upon Captain Sampson, who then commanded our greatest battleship, the *Iowa*.

Evans happened to be in the Secretary's room when the
order was dictated. He naturally approved of the designation, despite an indefinable mental reservation as to Sampson
that he had confided to some of his friends in the service during intimate chats. There was no question in Evans' mind

as to Sampson's ability and character; in fact, Sampson seemed without blemish or weakness. His long career had been a succession of preëminent achievements. There were no mistakes or indiscretions. It seemed to Bob Evans that Sampson was almost too perfect, that the inevitable Achilles' heel must exist, and that it might become evident in a moment of crisis. Evans' judgment pronounced Sampson the ideal leader for the occasion; an instinctive premonition whispered that Sampson might fall down at the big moment. In 1892 Evans remarked in confidence to an intimate friend: "If Sampson ever is subjected to a great strain he will weaken." The premonition and not Sampson fell down. Evans was among the most enthusiastic of his superior's admirers, when the latter's brilliant war record had become history.

Then came one of the thrills of Evans' life, as great as it was unexpected. Mr. Long turned to him and said: "Now, Captain, I have a surprise for you." The Secretary smiled as he spoke. Bob Evans was all eyes and ears. "I am going to order you to relieve Sampson in command of the *Iowa*. How soon can you start?"

How soon? The *Iowa!* Afloat, the battle fleet, the finest unit!

Now, at once, yesterday!

The conductor of the next train south punched the ticket of a happy warrior in civilian dress. It was worth the years of suffering from those miserable legs to bring them to this climax. Mightier even than the *Indiana, Iowa,* monarch of the western seas, lay in those waters off Key West, out beyond the old whistling buoy and within sight of that towering lamp-post familiar to all American sailors, the Sand Key Light, where the pale green of the shoals merges into the deep blue of the Gulf Stream. A smoking launch was puffing its eager way out from the harbour. It came alongside the *Iowa*. Officers and men watched the energetic new skipper clamber up the gangway. A thrill of proud expectancy shot through the ship.   Hail to Old Gimpy!

Back in the days of the *Virginius* crisis, when Bob Evans had relieved Sampson as Executive Officer of the *Congress,* he had found an excellent ship; now, upon taking over the *Iowa* and again stepping into the shoes of this able officer, he found this modern craft equally smart in every respect.   The *Iowa* and Fighting Bob were ripe and ready for each other and for any enemy.

15

WAR

~~~~~~

T HE *Iowa* was an improved *Indiana,* larger, faster and steadier. Defects in design noted in the earlier class, by Evans and others, had been eliminated. Her guns, slightly smaller in calibre (twelve and four inch) embodied the latest improvements and constituted a more effective battery. The newer ship, however, lacked the appearance of pugnacious stolidity that earned for the *Oregon,* one of the *Indiana's* sister-ships, the title of *Bulldog of the Navy.* This was chiefly due to the ungainly height of the *Iowa's* thin smoke stacks. In general, however, the two battleships were sufficiently alike for the first skipper of the *Indiana* to feel entirely at home in his new command. Few, if any, of his contemporaries of the old school had had as practical training for the modern steam driven steel warships as Captain Evans. There was the poise of self-confidence in the sure manner with which he assumed his new responsibilities.

He was now two years past fifty, still in robust general health and robust physique except, of course, for those chronically painful legs to which he pitilessly refused to extend any special privileges. Every inch the vigorous, competent, hearty sea fighter, he was old enough to carry the salt encrusted by years of spray and young enough to match in mental agility and bodily stamina his most dashing subordinates. Robley Evans was a respected and popular officer, within the service, and one of its leaders most widely and favourably known by the people of the country. The deck hands and the men of the "black gang," who nourished the furnaces, boasted in their letters home that they were stripping ship for action under Fighting Bob. The wardroom officers were equally proud of the fact that the *Iowa* was to face the foe under Old Gimpy.

The ship was a part of the North Atlantic Squadron, with headquarters in the open sea off Key West. Sampson drilled his force day and night during the last weeks of the ebbing peace. He brought it to the point of highest battle efficiency. The tales of Spanish naval might did not alarm him, nor did those of Spanish naval decadence lull him into a sense of security. He determined that his squadron should be ready to do its very best, regardless of the strength or weakness of the enemy. He realized that theoretical comparisons of power are often rudely jarred by the concussion of gunfire.

Not having been tested in modern warfare, the navies of the United States and Spain were uncertain in quality. Neither possessed in any sense of the term a battle fleet, an organization of homogeneous capital ships with proportionate auxiliaries, trained to manœuvre and fight as a unit. Spain, in fact, had no battleships except the old *Pelayo,* which was not fit for service at the outbreak of the war, but she owned more modern cruisers and gunboats than did we. Her pride was centred in the armoured cruiser squadron under Cervera. On the basis of statistics, the American Navy with its five battleships, two armoured cruisers, *New York* and *Brooklyn,* and the lesser craft, seemed superior, but by no margin that could not have been wiped out by talent and good fortune. Spain had a larger supposedly trained personnel.

As soon as war threatened seriously, the Navy Department used funds appropriated by Congress to augment its list of combatant vessels. Yachts were converted and the foreign market scoured, the latter yielding to us the *New*

Orleans. Madrid remained languid. The naval authorities were afraid to reveal the true state of decrepitude, and those directing the affairs of state were ignorant of the impotent sea force at their beck. The summer was to confirm Nelson's laconic comment that "the Dons may make fine ships— they cannot, however, make men." This had no reference to the individual bravery of Spanish officers and sailors, which was of the finest, but to their joint skill in fighting the ships at their disposal. No outsider was to learn until much later to what degree deterioration had been permitted to corrode their navy.

Secretary Long wisely followed the example set by Secretary Welles at the outbreak of the Civil War in creating a substitute for a Naval War Staff. During most of the campaign his Naval War Board was composed of Rear Admiral Sicard, Captain Crowninshield and the sage of strategists, Captain Mahan, recalled from retirement to this paramount duty, a fitting climax to his life work. They set about their problems of estimating the strength, disposition and probable intention of the enemy, and of formulating our naval plans. The Spanish strength was accepted at full paper value. The disposition was known. Admiral Montojo had his Asiatic Fleet in the Philippines, and the remaining ships were divided between home ports and the Cape Verde Islands, where, in Portuguese territorial waters, Admiral Cervera was assembling his fast cruiser squadron. The probable intention was open to the Board's expert inference.

Our forces had been gradually assembled at Hong Kong and at Atlantic ports of the United States. All of the fighting ships not assigned to Commodore Dewey should have been concentrated in the North Atlantic Squadron, but concessions to public ignorance and timidity resulted in a dispersion of our very limited combatant vessels that might have proved costly. Old maids along the New England and Middle Atlantic coast had nightmares of a horrible invasion by Cervera's roving sailors and demanded the comforting presence of American warships that they could see and touch. The Department, in defiance of all sound strategy, felt obliged to station various squadrons along the seaboard, notably the Flying Squadron at Hampton Roads under Commodore Schley, senior on the list to Sampson but subordinate in assignment, and Commodore Howell's squadron further north. Such valuable units as the *Brooklyn, Massachusetts, Texas, Columbia,* and *Minneapolis* were diverted to the pacification of popular alarm, instead of remaining with the force at Key West to constitute an overwhelming fleet that would enhance the chances of eventual success. The Flying Squadron was the badge of democracy, the sop to the quaking laymen whose knowledge of strategy was derived solely from their terror of a sudden attack by Cervera.

Secretary Long has written that "the campaign adopted by the Navy Department had two main objectives,—the absolute crushing of the Spanish squadron in Philippine waters and the control of the sea in the Atlantic Ocean." The natural zone of operations to set about the seizure of control in the Atlantic was, of course, the West Indies. We had resorted to arms to liberate Cuba, and the first step was to cut off Spain's access and communication to her colony, hence the blockade.

During the tense *ante-bellum* period, Sampson conferred almost daily with Chadwick, his Flag-Captain, Captain Taylor of the *Indiana* and Captain Evans. Their discussions of tactics naturally involved questions of strategy, upon which they found themselves in entire agreement. A sharp conflict of opinion soon arose, however, between these four officers on the scene, on the one hand, and the more remote minds at Washington on the other. Sampson and his captains wanted to seize Havana immediately upon the declaration of war. The Department had two valid reasons for forbidding this. First, there were powerful land batteries guarding the Cuban capital which might cripple the squadron before it had met the Spanish naval forces. Secondly, the Army was not nearly prepared to hold Havana if the Navy took it. Evans was particularly disappointed at the Departmental veto because Sampson's battle orders, already issued against the eventuality of war, provided that the *Iowa* was to lead the assaulting column upon Havana. He considered the decision in favour of a close blockade of Havana and against its bombardment, as an erroneous one, and he adhered to this view in after years.

"I have always thought that we could have captured or destroyed Havana two days after the declaration of war, and it is my belief that this of itself would have ended the struggle in a very short time, and that Cervera's fleet would not have crossed the Atlantic. I make this statement with a full knowledge of what we had to encounter and after close study of the situation, which afterward changed very rapidly and was entirely different when General Blanco had strongly fortified the entrance."

Writing of the work of the Naval War Board, Mahan stated the objections to this plan: "It was clearly recognized that war cannot be made without running risks; but it was also held, unwaveringly, that no merely possible success justified risk, unless it gave a fair promise of diminishing the enemy's naval force, and so of deciding the control of the sea, upon which the issue of the war depended."

It would, however, have been remarkable had Evans not sponsored the bold stroke, especially as he would have been one of those to bear the responsibility of delivering it.

The preparations, long and arduous, which in Evans' case may be said to have started with his entry into the Academy, at last, on April twenty-first, gave way to the event. The warrior captains sat around Sampson's table in the cabin of the *New York,* waiting into the night for word that the frock coated pacifists had turned on hostilities. A torpedo boat raced out through the darkness from Key

From Harper's Pictorial History of the Spanish-American War

REAR ADMIRAL SAMPSON (STILL WEARING HIS CAP-
TAIN'S UNIFORM) AND FLAG CAPTAIN CHADWICK

West with a despatch from the President. "The expected,"
said Evans, "had happened this time at least."

The statesmen had made war. It was now the function
of the Army and Navy to make peace.

All was ready in the North Atlantic Squadron. At one
bell of the morning watch, it weighed anchor and steamed
through the dawn, ninety miles across the Gulf Stream
towards the hills of Cuba. In the van rode the *New York,*
followed in column by the *Iowa, Indiana,* the old monitor
Amphitrite, the *Cincinnati* and the converted yacht *Mayflower,* later the darling of the presidents, and, in a second
column, five other gunboats. The war was on. Within
three hours, its first shot was fired as the *Nashville* stood
out of formation and captured a Spanish merchant ship.

To accord with his duties, Sampson had just been given
the rank of Acting Rear Admiral and his new flag was for
the first time hoisted at the main truck of the *New York,*
to the delight of the entire squadron. Evans, just abaft the
flagship, signalled a request for permission to fire a gun
salute. He was met with the code flag signifying a reply
in the negative, but the modest Sampson was not to escape
as easily as that. The smiling friend on the bridge of the
Iowa sheered his battleship out of column to port, increased
speed and, when nearly abeam of the *New York,* led his men
in a hearty cheer for their former Captain, who was now the
"old man" to the whole fleet. It was a spontaneous demonstration that deeply impressed all who witnessed it. In a
few minutes the *Iowa* was back at her station, the blockading
force continuing its march towards the objective without
further incident. The squadron was an assortment of craft
utterly lacking in any semblance of homogeneity. The flagship was the fastest vessel of the lot and, when a suspicious
looking craft was sighted to the eastward, the Admiral felt
obliged to himself undertake the pursuit, which after a hot
chase resulted in the seizure of a valuable prize.

As he withdrew from the formation, flying the hoist

"Disregard movements of commander-in-chief," and rapidly disappeared down the current of the Gulf Stream, the guide flag broke at the fore of the *Iowa,* signifying that upon Captain Evans had devolved the responsibilities of Senior Officer Present. He remained in charge until the return of the *New York* early the following day and he thus supervised the establishment of the blockade of Havana and the conduct of the first day's and night's activities.

In view of the Departmental plans, the only circumstance under which Evans might attack the batteries was their firing upon the ships, and he eagerly hoped that the garrisons would show that much spirit.

"We had orders not to bring on an engagement, but I did not consider that this order would apply in case the Spaniards fired on us." (Just try to imagine Bob Evans passively submitting to a fusillade!) "When the *Iowa* was about five miles from the Morro Castle, I made signal, 'Head of columns right!' and, as the signal went up, I saw the flash of a gun on shore, and then others, until five had been fired. I gave the order to stand by to fire, and cautioned those about me to watch carefully for the splash of a shot; but, unfortunately, none came; they were only signal guns to announce our arrival."

The hope of a bombardment was quashed by the defender's nonresistance. Disgustedly, Evans resumed the more prosaic business of disposing of his blockading force to shut the harbour. The nights were exciting enough until it became pretty clear that no torpedo attacks were to be launched by the enemy under cover of darkness. After a day or two, the patrol settled down to a matter of routine, but the sea itself hardly settled down at all. The ground swells rocked and shook the vessels twenty-four hours a day.

There lay ahead of the *Iowa* many weeks of such duty, exacting and monotonous, tense and exhausting, on both coasts of the island. The task of constantly watching through rain and shine, light and dark, without having an opportunity to strike at the enemy, kept the crews under a strain. They could see the Spaniards at Havana strengthening their fortifications and increasing the difficulties of reducing the city, the work going on almost under the squadron's nose and without molestation.

Once a couple of Spanish torpedo boats darted out of the harbour, evidently in an effort to run the blockade. They soon found escape barred, and turned right about in their wakes and retraced their course toward the old shelter. Evans tried to cut off their return and got within range, just as the little craft slipped into the narrow channel past the Morro. ". . . I could no doubt have reached them with my heavy guns, but they were not of much consequence, and I did not fancy the idea of sending a shell into the mass of women and children on shore."

Sampson had by the end of April established a blockade of all of the northern seaports of Cuba having railroad connection. As Mahan expressed it, the importance of the blockade "lay in its twofold tendency to exhaust the enemy's army in Cuba, and to force his navy to come to the relief."

16

TIDINGS FROM AFAR

A̲S the *Iowa* pitched and rolled in the ground swells off Havana, there came to her via the despatch boats from Key West the exciting news of the Battle of Manila Bay. Evans had heard, of course, that Dewey with his six small warships and some auxiliaries had cleared Hong Kong upon the outbreak of war. On May first came the disquieting announcement of the Spanish Governor of the Philippines, who controlled the cable, that an indecisive and mutually costly engagement had been fought, in the midst of which the American Squadron had been driven off. Thus the emotional way had been paved for the true report when, three days later, it broke through like the sun after a squall. The facts seemed too good to be credible. The wires carrying the message electrified the nation and thrilled to the very heights of exultation the naval forces arduously maintaining the Cuban blockade. Their comrades in the Far East had annihilated the Spanish Fleet without sustaining the loss of a single American life or vessel. The neutral flotillas in the Orient could scarcely believe it; the world was aroused to respectful attention, and the effect upon the morale of the combatant peoples was great beyond the possibility of exaggeration. American prestige had received an incalculable impetus. The war had been begun under dramatically glowing auspices.

Evans was particularly proud and happy because many of the victorious officers and men had served with and under

him. It all had a profound personal meaning. Several of
the captains were Brethren of the Brood. Well had they
applied the seamanship of Luce and the gunnery of the
Rodgers, mellowed by the experience of thirty-five years,
side by side with him in the service. The decades of drills,
manœuvres, planning and concentrated reflection, that peace
time Congressional indifference had been unable to dis-
courage, scored at the critical hour. What had been achieved
in those distant waters would be repeated, Evans felt confident, in the more important theatre of operations. Fighting
Bob's martial ardour was stimulated by the exploit in the
East; hardly could he await the sight of Cervera's smoke.

Slowly the details of Manila filtered through. As each
item of news arrived, it found in Evans' memory some close
association with his own friendships and travels. The great
bay, almost landlocked, with its narrow gap to the sea
further narrowed by a belt of islands across the entrance,
was familiar to him. He visualized the picturesque metropolis at the head of the expanse of water, bewildered at the
sudden twist of history.

When affairs in the other hemisphere brought war to
its remote inhabitants, they were positively assured that no
hostile force could break into the bay, with its strong liminal
defences, but that, should such an unlikely misfortune occur, the intruder would find himself in a basin of death, helpless before the batteries that studded the city's waterfront
and the eleven men-of-war that flew the protecting colours
of Spain. The Governor issued a fiery *pronunciomento*:
"A squadron manned by foreigners, possessing neither in-
struction nor discipline, is preparing to come to this archipelago with the ruffianly intention of robbing us of all that
means life, honour and liberty. . . . Vain designs! Ridiculous boastings! . . . The aggressors shall not profane the
tombs of your fathers, they shall not gratify their lustful
passions at the cost of your wives' and daughters' honour, or
appropriate the property your industry has accumulated as a

provision for your old age . . . let us fight with the conviction that victory will crown our efforts. . . . "

The Spaniards responded bravely but the sanguine fore-
cast of late April was, on the very first day of May, mocked
by the unheeding realities. Dawn disclosed to the startled
Europeans and Asiatics of Manila that the impossible had
commenced to happen: plainly visible from the windows was
the American Squadron, calmly sweeping through the "impenetrable" bay. Their harbour had been raped—what next?
At dusk that evening, the amazed populace crowded in serried ranks at the water's edge, listening to the band aboard
the *Olympia* satisfying its "lustful passions" by a rendition
of *La Paloma,* while the setting sun, behind Cavite across
the water, shone upon the Stars and Stripes flying over the
fortress, and upon the smouldering wreck of the Spanish
Fleet.

When, at daybreak, the Commodore had led his column
past the city and finally espied the enemy in an extended
arc, in the shallow water before Cavite to the West, and gave
his famous command to the flag-captain: "You may fire
when you are ready, Gridley," the battle was already all but
won. From then on, it was a relentless exhibition of tactical
efficiency against tactical inefficiency, the unarmoured American ships ignoring the inaccurately aimed shore fire and
overwhelming the heroic but unfit enemy with salvo after
salvo, delivered with the unhurried rhythm of target practice. Marching and countermarching, Dewey pressed closer
each time, creeping further inshore, toward Montojo's collapsing line, upon each of the five death-dealing American
parades. Several hours of furious fighting ensued until eyes
smarted with smoke and ears buzzed with the uproar. The
sound and spectacle of the battle itself, with its crashing and
flaming devastation and its strenuous intensity was, however, no more unforgettable to the American participants
than the preceding night when Dewey, after taking counsel
with his captains and with his hallowed memories of Far-

ragut, decided that he, too, would "damn the torpedoes." He would back his estimate of Spanish military and naval ineptitude against the vaunted impregnability of Manila Bay. Even the friendly British had thought that any attempt to force the entrance would meet with disastrous failure. Both channels were flanked with batteries that could have blown the thinly protected cruisers and gunboats to sudden destruction. The old *Immorality,* as the bluejackets called Admiral Chichester's flagship *Immortalite,* lay at Hong Kong when Dewey's heterogeneous flotilla stood out. The British, waving a cordial adieu, feared that if the American Commodore was foolhardy enough to stick his head into Boca Grande, the great mouth, or Boca Chica, the small mouth, the two channels to Manila Bay, his head would be bitten off, and that their parting cheers really meant good-bye.

To Bob Evans, that distant column that crossed the China Sea was not a mere list of names of ships and men; it was a group of well-known craft, with their respective communities of colleagues, many of whose faces and mannerisms were as familiar to him as those of the men in the *Iowa.* The *Olympia,* in the van, he hardly knew, but her officers he did and well. Then the *Baltimore,* the *Raleigh,* the *Boston,* the *Concord* and the *Petrel*: each with her intimate connotations. Bradley Fiske, checking the ranges of each salvo of the battle with his stadimeter, was perched on an improvised platform aloft, on the foremast of the *Petrel,* called the *Little Battleship* because of her valuable work inshore, where the larger ships drawing more water could not venture. Every bridge, every engine-room, almost every gun station had its old ship-mate. It was almost as if Evans had been the only one of the old crowd missing; that is, until he thought of the great majority with him on the Atlantic. Their turn would come.

Gazing at the palm fringed coast of Cuba, the Captain was reminded that the shore line of the Philippines was not so dissimilar in appearance. His imagination followed

Dewey's approach to Luzon the morning before the great day. Evans understood why the landfall had been at the mouth of Subig Bay, thirty miles from Manila Bay. Sound strategy dictated that there the Spanish Squadron establish its base and position. Admiral Montojo had indeed taken his force (or as much of it as was mobile) to Subig, but, finding that the guns long before sent to constitute the main shore batteries had not been mounted, and remembering that the water was of a depth unsafe for nonswimmers (" . . . ships and men would have sunk, causing great loss of life," he later said), the Spanish commander returned to the shoal off Cavite. There, relying upon the protection of the fortresses at the entrance to the bay to exclude the enemy, and upon those directly behind and alongside of him, as a secondary defence, he awaited the worst, which was not long in coming. His calculations conceded a hopeless preponderance of strength to the Americans, which proved to be correct, not upon any standard of measuring matériel but in the skill with which it was employed. The Spaniards were fully aware of the poor condition of their ships and the inability of their crews to fight them. The Americans suspected but they could not afford to rely upon the lack by the enemy personnel of every military and naval qualification except courage. On paper the American Squadron was only slightly superior and, in a battle within easy range of the Manila, Cavite and adjacent shore batteries, it was woefully inferior. Unfortunately for the Spaniards, the engagement was not decided on paper.

Dewey sent some of his ships to reconnoitre Subig, and Evans could fully appreciate that, in the former's own words, he "waited very anxiously for their signal." When it came, reporting the bay devoid of warships, the Commodore turned to Robley's old Academy-mate Lamberton, acting as Chief of Staff: "Now we have them."

The plans had been so clearly and completely communicated to the captains that, when they repaired aboard the

Olympia outside Subig for the final conference, there remained practically nothing to be said. Evans could picture them, old friends all, leaving for their respective ships, saluting the serenely quiet Commodore as they stepped onto the gangway. Course was set to reach the entrance to Manila Bay about midnight. The tropical night set in. A storm suddenly swept the squadron and passed off, leaving a new moon occulting behind fast moving clouds, that in daytime would have been white and puffy. The crews were at general quarters. Only a faint, carefully screened taffrail light showed on each stern to guide the ship behind.

Evans knew the perils that lay ahead. There was a gambler's choice between the two heavily fortified, reputedly mined, narrow channels. Dewey had selected Boca Grande, the passage between the towering island of Corregidor on the left and the rocks called El Fraile on the right. Without a pilot, with all navigation lights ashore extinguished, without the use of his searchlights, directly over the area sown with explosives and within point blank range of large calibre guns on solid emplacements, the *Olympia* felt her steady way, leading the squadron toward its possible destruction before even sighting a Spanish ship. Dewey knew, however, that mine-laying was a highly technical art, that a shore battery is no more effective than those who serve it and that the British charts were reliable. A few minutes, just at the witching hour, would tell the whole story. The *Maine* had entered Havana Harbour as a friend and been blasted asunder. Perhaps the Asiatic Squadron, entering Boca Grande as an avowed foe, might with poetic justice live to emerge intact.

Ahead loomed the bulky mass of Corregidor. Dewey was again the youth in the steam frigate *Mississippi,* forcing her way up the river of that name behind the indomitable Farragut. It seemed but yesterday—and now the full responsibility was his. He clearly recalled how, on the night of the Battle of Port Hudson, the Confederate fire had been precipitated by a signal rocket. Now—in the blackness to landward—there suddenly leaped high—a signal rocket! Farragut had held his course; so did Dewey. The *Mississippi* had been lost. What awaited the *Olympia?*

There was no sound but the gurgle of water along the sides of the ships. The column was standing in. Lighthouses were, as expected, indistinguishable parts of the darkness. The men in the chains sang out the depths, as they heaved the lead. The *Olympia* now found the channel and clung to its invisible thread, her comrades following in perfect formation. Now the islands on both sides were abeam. Any second a submarine explosion or a cannonading from the shore might sweep the American Navy from the Asiatic seas. The big guns had been placed upon those forbidding sentinel islands to frustrate just such invading expeditions. The flagship was squarely between them. No sound. These were the crucial minutes. Dewey often had remarked that during the fiercest hour of Port Hudson he had lived five years. Entering Boca Grande seemed a decade.

All hands were alert. Despite the navigational hazards, the squadron was now steaming at full speed, to leave behind as soon as possible the zone of greatest military danger. Fast, silent, ghostly, the silhouettes stole past the menacing batteries. Flash! A tongue of flame on El Fraile and a loud report. A shell whistled between the *Petrel* and the *Raleigh*. The four rear ships blazed back an angry answer. Three times El Fraile fired and missed, as the squadron pressed ahead. Then the surroundings relapsed into their former stillness and darkness. The mystery of the feeble resistance offered by the guardians of the gate remains hidden in the inscrutable Spanish temperament. The exchange of shots had at least served to break the terrific tension in the squadron, which now realized that Corregidor and El Fraile had dropped away astern, and that the smooth water that stretched out in all directions was at last Manila Bay.

The faint glow on the northeastern horizon, that fixed the exact location of the city, was now the helmsman's guide. As the *Olympia* drew nearer, and the light of the returning sun illumined the Philippine capital, the Commodore could see that the enemy fleet was not there. He veered around toward Cavite, about five miles from Manila, and there he beheld his objective. From the battery on Sangley Point to the battery Las Pinas, the Spanish ships were anchored in battle array like the French at Aboukir. Out broke the American battle flags. Gridley was ready. Spain's colonial tenure in the Orient was at an end.

When the day's task had been well done, each of the American captains thought that his own ship's unscathed survival of the desperate fighting, without loss of a man, was nothing short of a latter day miracle, and he dreaded the reports of the others. When they all convened on the flagship, the joy of sharing such astounding good fortune was naturally ineffable.

Dewey had mightily risked and mightily won. By Evans, the greatest gratification was derived from the splendid performance of his comrades in blue, especially his intimate contemporaries. The Navy had not failed.

The nation had not been over-generous in the ships it had built for the contingency that, at Manila Bay, became a vital occasion, but the Navy had made them fulfill their mission, had made them do so by sheer efficiency of personnel, and had made the task actually seem easy.

17

BLIND MAN'S BUFF

~~~~~~

ON April twenty-ninth, Admiral Cervera left the Cape Verde Islands. When intelligence of this promptly reached the Department, there was anxious speculation as to his destination. The reasonable possibilities could be reduced to four: a home base, a northern American port, the West Indies, and the interception of the *Oregon* on her cruise around South America from the Pacific.

The best guess seemed the West Indies, the theatre of general operations and the locale of the colony over whose affairs the war was being waged. After the long transatlantic passage there would be need of fuel and probably repairs. The logical place to coal and refit would be the fortified harbour of San Juan on the other large Spanish island of Porto Rico, which lay directly on the route to Cuba.

The Army was not nearly ready for joint operations in Cuba and there seemed no valid reason why the North Atlantic Squadron should not act upon this most probable intention of the enemy and try to surprise him at anchor in San Juan harbour. The suggestion was wired from Washington to Admiral Sampson and promptly adopted. The flagship was then at Key West.

The *Iowa* had hurried across the Florida Straits the previous day, coaled ship from tossing lighters near Sand Key in record time, and resumed her station off Havana. This

business of refueling was the greatest problem of the blockade. Evans said that "coaling off Havana was impossible
owing to the heavy trade-wind sea and practically the same
conditions held at Key West for vessels which could not
enter the harbour. Yet we coaled the ships somehow, and
without unnecessary delay."

The glasses on the *Iowa's* bridge discerned in the distance the approaching flagship, steaming along the blockading line. From her forward yardarm flew the signal,
addressed to the *Iowa, Indiana* and *Detroit,* to stand to the
eastward at eleven knots. Anything that broke the monotony of the blockade was welcome. The *New York* disappeared and soon the three units named were proceeding
in obedience to the order. That night they reached an appointed rendezvous off the Cruz del Padre Light, near
Cardenas on the north coast of Cuba, and were met by the
New York, the old monitors *Terror* and *Amphitrite,* the
torpedo boat *Porter* and the *Montgomery.* The Porto
Rican expedition was under way.

Evans said that "Admiral Sampson had every reason to
believe that he would find Admiral Cervera's ships in the
harbour of San Juan, so preparations were accordingly
made to destroy them." The first problem was getting
there, a distance of well over a thousand miles. The monitors could neither carry enough coal to make the voyage nor
be refueled at sea, so there was no alternative to towing
them. The *New York* took one and the *Iowa* the other.
They had never been broken to a leash and, as line after line
parted, none seemed strong enough to hold. At best, the
Spanish Squadron was rated faster than the American.
Now the tortoise was setting forth to catch the hare, and
the former had a ball and chain tied to its feet, a chain
whose links repeatedly broke and had to be repaired.

W. A. M. Goode, the correspondent for the Associated
Press aboard the *New York,* was in the Admiral's cabin
one of these nights when on the deck above "there was a

report like the firing of a 4-inch gun. . . . The flagship shook as if she had been jerked out of water. Before the deck steadied there was another loud report." The press man thought an enemy was being engaged, but the Admiral seemed only disgusted. "In a tone of resignation" he simply said "I'm afraid she's gone," and started up the companionway.

"Who's gone, sir?" asked the bewildered layman.

"The *Terror.*"

Sure enough, the monitor again had carried away both towing hawsers.

Evans had his troubles with the *Amphitrite,* which also tore free a couple of times and had to be reattached, under the most difficult conditions. Later, in a naval preface to a large pictorial volume on the war ("The Story of the War of 1898" by W. Nephew King), he was able to register a protest against the composition of the squadron, in terms of extreme moderation but, at the time, he left to his chief over on the flagship the "tone of resignation" and indulged in a salvo of profanity that must have brought blushes to the cheeks of Poseidon's wife, as she saw and heard her intractable namesake being lashed to Fighting Bob's sea chariot.

Had the clumsy monitors been left at Hampton Roads to reassure the civilians and the Flying Squadron been available to Sampson, the situation would have been very different. (As a matter of fact, events were rapidly shaping themselves to liberate Schley for the zone of action.)

To add to the squadron's delays, the *Indiana* sustained two engineering breakdowns and, as the result of one of them, was once lost for a few hours.

At Cape Haytien there was a message from Washington that was more baffling than helpful. It gave no information as to Cervera's whereabouts but implied that his force was substantially stronger than previously understood and, in fact, than turned out to be the case. The despatch, one important word of which was garbled in transmission, cautioned Sampson not to jeopardize the battle effectiveness of his squadron in an attack on land batteries until Cervera had been disposed of. The sea must first be subjugated; then the land. What had applied to the proposed bombardment of Havana, applied *a fortiori* to San Juan.

There were also at Cape Haytien press reports of a remarkable nature, to the effect that the much sought black flotilla had been sighted off Martinique; remarkable because of the coincidence that Cervera was then steaming straight for that island but was still so far to the eastward of it that he could not possibly have been seen and reported in those pre-aeroplane, pre-radio days. Some one had accepted a guess as an observation and the guess happened to be correct.

With the unanimous approval of his cabinet of captains, Sampson held on toward Porto Rico. He finally brought his ponderous armada, more of a floating fortress than an automobile fleet, off the coast near the entrance to San Juan. The approach was set for the following morning, May twelfth. The plan called for the stoutest unit to take the van. This was the *Iowa*. The Admiral, wishing to be among the first to get into action, temporarily shifted his flag to Captain Evans' battleship.

The program for the assault required an early start. At three thirty of the mid-watch the column moved toward San Juan. It was pitch dark. The lights of the city blinked over the horizon ahead. The *Detroit* scouted in advance. Following her came the heavy artillery: the *Iowa, Indiana, New York, Amphitrite* and *Terror,* the monitors now under their own steam, and the *Montgomery* brought up the rear.

Dawn extinguished the lights ashore and revealed the hills of Porto Rico, stretching beyond the promontory in the foreground capped by the Morro Castle that was invariably found at the gateway to every Spanish-American harbour. Was Cervera inside? All eyes were straining at the entrance. Stealthily the squadron moved closer until within easy range of the shore batteries. The land with its detail was now plainly visible and everything was inert, a suitable subject for a painting entitled "Spanish colony at dawn." An observer described the scene as "one of the most entirely peaceful panoramas that ever beautified a May morning." There was not a sign of life.

The first manœuvre was executed to perfection. Lieutenant Jungen of the *Maine* challenged fate a second time. Commanding a tug, he towed a rowboat to the ten fathom curve and there anchored it as a marker. This exploit was performed in such proximity to the forts that the odds were against its success and overwhelmingly against the survival of those to whom it had been entrusted. Jungen located the spot, anchored his boat-buoy and returned in safety. Not a shot had been fired at him.

The *Detroit* and *Montgomery* took station on the wings close inshore, to head off any torpedo boats that might spring from the harbour. The *Porter* was detailed to similar duty and assigned to a position erroneously supposed to be beyond train of the coastal guns. Before the day was over she presented the spectacle of a naval monument surrounded by fountains of splashing shells.

Onward swept the column. The interior of the harbour was now in plain view and it disclosed not a trace of Cervera's squadron. The monitors had been towed all those days and the enemy was either late or unorthodox in his tactics. In any event, he was not as obligingly present as had been Montojo at Manila Bay. To say the least, it was keenly disappointing. The guns fairly itched for action and would have to be placated by fire of some sort. Any plausible pretext would suffice.

"To give our men practise and season them a bit for what was to come, Admiral Sampson decided to bombard the batteries," explained Evans, who at the time stood beside him on the bridge of the *Iowa*. Up went the battle flags: three

huge ensigns on each ship. To keep his mainmast clear for
one of these plumes of combat, Evans had improvised a
halliard on the after smoke stack from which unusual place
now flew the Admiral's flag.

When about a mile from the Morro, with the Admiral's
permission, Evans crisply ordered the bugler at his elbow
to sound "Commence firing!" As an orchestra dramatically
strikes the first note of a symphony in obedience to the
maestro's baton, the outstretched starboard guns spat flame,
and the ship heeled over with the recoil of the first salvo.
The ear-splitting roar was echoed down the line as one ship
after the other opened her broadside. Dust and dirt were
thrown up in clouds along the fortifications, and geysers
of foaming water marked the "shorts." Evans observed the
shells striking "in and about the batteries" and believed them
to be causing substantial damage. A subsequent check-up
with post-war data indicates, however, that the firing was
inaccurate and the ammunition none too dependable. Many
shells failed to explode.

It was at least five minutes before the garrison returned
the reveille salute, five minutes of concentrated firing by the
heavy artillery of the ship's turrets and the rapidly reloaded
secondary batteries. Just when the squadron was wondering if the Spaniards were going to rely upon a defence of
nonresistance, there came a salvo from ashore, then another
and finally a fusillade from all the batteries on the hills. The
chief target among the attacking ships seemed to be the
thinly protected *Detroit,* which was vigorously blazing
away with her own five-inchers from under the shadow of
the Morro.

"She was simply magnificent," said Evans, "a veritable
spitfire. After we had passed over the firing line the second
time she was signalled to change her position and draw off
somewhat, but" (Captain) "Dayton took a long time to
answer the signal, and withdrew with great reluctance. We
were much relieved when he signalled that he had escaped

without injury. If I had had the power I would have changed the name of the *Detroit* that morning; I would have painted '*Gamecock*' on her stern and kept it there as long as she remained afloat."

On the second run past the batteries, the latter at last began to find the range of the attacking column and make matters pretty hot. They were soon straddling the targets and Evans declared "it was the best shooting I saw the Spanish artillery do during the war." The *Iowa* was struck three times and the *New York* once. A seaman on the latter was killed and several men on both ships were hit by splinters. One shell nearly cost the country dear. It burst near the bridge of the temporary flagship and barely missed the Admiral, Captain Evans and several of the staff officers. The loss of any of these leaders would have been an excessive price to pay for the day's questionable gains.

The third run past the shore batteries found them much weaker. The rally was evidently over. Rightly or wrongly, it was now felt in the fleet that San Juan could be taken without having to overcome much further resistance. A breathing spell seemed fully warranted and the Admiral withdrew his forces to seaward for rest, refreshment and reflection. The engagement had lasted three hours, longer than any other sustained naval fight in Atlantic waters during the entire war.

As the *Iowa* led the column out of range, the sun was high, and it was very hot above decks. Mess gear was laid and the crews sent to breakfast. Sampson and Evans went below to the latter's cabin, washed up and had a bite to eat. The Admiral was inclined to follow Dewey's example and return for a post-prandial finish to the morning's work, momentarily overlooking the important distinction that Dewey had confined his efforts to destroying the enemy fleet, not attempting to take Manila the first day without troops to invest it.

Evans perceived that any further expenditure of time

and effort, fuel and ammunition, against San Juan would be an unjustifiable deviation from the main objective. Sink Cervera first! Let nothing interfere with that. Had a single Spanish man-of-war shown herself at San Juan, nothing could have persuaded Fighting Bob to withdraw until the enemy had been destroyed, but the vacant harbour had offered no opposing naval force to attack. Any minute the elusive cruisers might appear. Cervera's flagship might be sighted by a look-out while the Admiral was deliberating. Evans argued that, for that occasion, bound to be met sooner or later, their strength must be husbanded. The Department had so ordered and sound strategy so demanded. Sampson had advanced a thousand miles from his base to attack not San Juan but Cervera. The bombardment, the Captain reminded his senior, had been for the morale of the men, to season by fire those unaccustomed to performing their functions to the accompaniment of screaming projectiles overhead and an occasional hit aboard. That purpose had been served. The squadron's proper movement now was a return to Key West to maintain fitness for the hour with Cervera. With him out of the way, the sea would be safe for any and all further operations; with him haunting every horizon, the slightest diversion was hazardous. "The fleet in being" must be destroyed. Ever the Captain reverted to the central theme: sink Cervera first. Evans was sound in his view. One wonders only whether the bombardment had been justified at all and what would have been said of its prudence had one of our valuable capital ships been shattered under an accidentally accurate series of salvos.

Fortunately, Sampson's was an approachable mind and Robley Evans enjoyed its respect. The Admiral listened. Finding no answer to the Captain's objections, the former yielded to them. To quote his report, he "reluctantly gave up the project against San Juan and stood westward for Havana." Once more the *New York* carried his flag and the Porto Rican expedition was being ended.

The Spaniards hailed the withdrawal as a successful repulse. They were welcome to whatever meagre comfort they could extract from the train of events.

Fast scouts, mostly converted passenger liners commanded by naval officers, had been watching for Cervera along carefully designated patrols. Sampson hoped to receive before very long some positive information as to the enemy's whereabouts. More than coal, food or shells he needed information, that element without which all his activity was left to the guidance of guess-work.

The arduous and tedious water trek of the previous week was repeated in the reverse direction, with trained eyes in the military platforms aloft scanning the horizons for friend and foe.

The following day the American hospital ship *Solace,* out of Key West, brought the astounding news that Cervera's squadron had returned to Cadiz, Spain. A despatch boat from St. Thomas corroborated this report and yet its tenor did not seem credible. Sampson could not bring himself to accept its correctness. All of the preliminary factors and intelligence pointed to the unlikelihood of the cruiser squadron having been recalled to home waters. The report, seemingly confirmed, could not be ignored, but Sampson shrewdly refused to act upon it. If indeed the Spaniards had run back to Cadiz, the North Atlantic Squadron could return to Porto Rico and finish its job there but, pending absolute assurance of the fact, the Admiral chose to doubt the accuracy of the report. He resolved to garner every scrap of available information.

The *Porter* was sent in to a cable station on the San Domingo coast and brought back a valuable bit. It was, in fact, the first real intelligence Sampson had been able to obtain since Cervera had cleared the Cape Verde Islands. It rang true because it fitted in with the general probabili-

ties. The Department had wired that on May fourteenth
the Spanish ships had been off Curacoa.

This tremendously important message was delivered to
Sampson when the *Porter* came alongside at three thirty in
the morning of the fifteenth. It was almost up-to-the-hour
news. The useful torpedo boat was rushed ahead to Cape
Haytien and the flagship followed, leaving Captain Evans
in command of the slow-moving main body. The monitors
were as balky as ever, and towing them back, under the
pressure of Cervera's established proximity, was a nerve-
racking feat of seamanship. They were mill-stones about
the battleship's necks. The *Monitor* as a type came into
glory when the patriarch of the line fought the *Merrimac,*
and it proved its uselessness for modern warfare upon this
memorable cruise to Porto Rico. For several days the
queer organization buffeted its way to the westward. Finally, during the evening of the eighteenth, to the intense
relief of her skipper, the *Iowa* anchored off Key West not
far from the *New York.* Near-by were other bulky craft,
which Evans soon recognized as the Flying Squadron, down
from Hampton Roads. That was news. Under the glare
of cargo lights, Schley's vessels were busily coaling ship.

Learning that Evans had *en route* sustained a painful
injury to his shoulder, Admiral Sampson ignored the prerogative of seniority, called away his barge and hastened
over to the *Iowa.* The two men had been apart but three
days and they had, nevertheless, much to tell each other.

Evans met the Admiral at the head of the gangway,
with his right arm strapped in bandages to his side. He reported the return trip as officially uneventful. There had
been a brush with two small Spanish gunboats off the Cuban coast, which the *Montgomery,* neither towed nor towing, chased up a shallow inlet. The rest of the cruise had
been coloured and flavoured by the monitors, which were
even indirectly responsible for the Captain's injury.

The Admiral had sent a torpedo boat under Commander Kimball to intercept the *Iowa* with important orders. She was to turn over her monitor to the *Montgomery* and steam to Key West at full speed. The monitor had to deliver a parting shot.

Doubtless Evans related the incident to Sampson in much the same language he later used in his *Sailor's Log:*

"I cast off the *Amphitrite,* signalled the *Montgomery* to take her in tow, and Captain Taylor to assume command of the squadron, and went below to my cabin with Kimball to read the despatches which he had in his hand.

"We seated ourselves at the cabin table and I was deeply interested in Cervera's movements, when I heard a startled voice exclaim, 'Look-out, captain!' I threw my head to one side to see what I was to look out for, when there was a tremendous crash and I was aware that I was hurt and more or less dazed. My first impression was that one of the Spanish gunboats had sneaked up on us and put a shell into my cabin. I had been thinking all the afternoon what a fine chance it would be for them that night; but when I was really conscious I saw that that was not the trouble. My cabin was full of men, all staring at me, their eyes fairly sticking out of their heads. They thought I was killed, and wanted to see the last of the 'old man.' I was soon aware that one of the doctors was feeling and twisting my right arm and that my right shoulder was in pretty bad shape. Through it all I was very sorry for Kimball, who, I thought, was surely killed, and I was greatly relieved when I heard his voice, which sounded a mile away.

"The accident was soon explained. The men were running in the steel hawser, which we had been using to tow the monitor, and it had picked up the steel battle hatch, weighing something over four hundred pounds, which was lying on deck ready to be put on the cabin hatch when needed. The line had carried it along until it came directly over the hatch under which I was sitting, when it slipped off, came down edge first, and caught me on the shoulder instead of the head. The man who called to me to look out held on to it in his effort to stop it, and came down with it. My shoulder was badly mashed and dis-

located, but the excellent medical men soon wiped the blood
off, reduced the dislocation, bandaged my arm to my side, and
turned me in with a stiff glass of grog under my belt."

Evans made light of his mishap. He might have troublesome legs and only one good arm, but his head and voice
were functioning and they would suffice to lead the *Iowa.*

The Admiral, for his part, explained that at Cape Haytien had come a batch of messages from Washington conveying the first really complete information. Cervera had
indeed been at Curacoa on the fourteenth, with his four
cruisers and two torpedo boats. A third torpedo boat had
put into Martinique for repairs. The Flying Squadron, no
longer needed as a sedative to northern nerves, had been
promptly ordered to the centre of naval activities and had
reached Key West the previous midnight. As Evans had
observed, it was taking aboard fuel and was to get under
way the next morning to cover the south coast of Cuba,
while Sampson's squadron would lie off Havana on the
north coast. The Navy was at last concentrating its forces
to achieve the prime mission of meeting and defeating
Cervera. Sampson had at his disposal virtually all of the
ships not with Dewey at Manila. Besides his flagship the
Brooklyn, Schley's south coast detachment, still called the
Flying Squadron, consisted of the *Massachusetts, Texas*
and *Scorpion,* and, Sampson now informed Evans, was to
be reënforced by the *Iowa.* That explained the summons
delivered by Commander Kimball.

It can not be supposed that Bob Evans was exactly delighted at this shift from Sampson to Schley, but it was all
part of the game and personalities were to be disregarded
as completely as crushed shoulders.

Already the *Iowa* was coaling from lighters and taking
aboard large quantities of fodder for the guns and the men
behind them. The round trip towing party to San Juan,
the bombardment there and the extra duties of war routine

had taxed the stamina of the crew, but it good-naturedly and vigorously turned to with whip and shovel. All night they hoisted and stowed, all the following day and, with one hour's rest, all the second night. The weather had roughened up and the lighters tossed about on the surface of the open seaway, where the harbourless battleships were obliged to base. All hands were exhausted, literally exhausted, when daylight of the second day found them still at work. It seemed as though all of the coal, shells and baked beans in the world must have been taken aboard, but there were more to come. Preparations were made for a long blockade on the south coast, far from supplies. Officers and men toiled steadily. The guns and engines of the *Iowa* faded into memory and the ship seemed an insatiable maw, devouring faster than shovels could fly. Late in the forenoon came blessed relief. The boatswains passed the word to discontinue. There had been a signal from the Admiral: "You must go now, cast off lighters, show yourself off Havana before sundown, and then proceed with all possible despatch to Cienfuegos and report to Commodore Schley."

In ten minutes the *Iowa* was under way, "decks piled waist-high with boxes of provisions and ammunition, while the whole ship was black with coal dust, and the officers and men looked like a gang of chimney-sweeps."

Late that afternoon the sentries in Havana's Morro espied the premier American battleship back on the blockading line. As soon as darkness concealed his movements, the Captain started at full cruising speed to the westward, to double Cape Antonio and swing around through the Yucatan Channel to the south coast of Cuba.

Evans was not aware, and even the Department had received only an unconfirmed rumour of the fact, that early the previous morning Admiral Cervera had dropped the anchors of his ships inside the long, narrow, tortuous harbour of Santiago de Cuba. Such knowledge, of course, would have greatly simplified matters for the Navy, by eliminating the anxious days of reconnaissance that followed.

If Sampson suffered from inadequate information, Cervera must be said to have been cast adrift in the Atlantic utterly devoid of any and of the means of obtaining any. The Americans had at least a well organized system of naval intelligence, and displayed reasonable imagination in communicating to Sampson whatever of interest reached the Department. The Spaniards, however, were as deficient in their news gathering facilities as in the other elements of sea power, and it must ever be remembered that, as Mahan tersely expressed it, "Communications dominate war."

In contemplating Cervera's cruise from St. Vincent, which terminated at Santiago, that gallant Admiral's fists must be regarded as padded by defective ordnance and poor gunnery, his feet bound by collapsing machinery, and his eyes blindfolded by complete ignorance, both as to the disposition of the enemy and the colonial facilities in the West Indies. The part played during the war by Almirante Pascual Cervera y Topete was that of a martyr to the ineptitude of a demoralized State. He was ordered to make bricks without straw and, if he failed to perform miracles, he failed with a bravery and a grace that Spain would like to believe accorded with her finest naval traditions, and that really transcended them. To the Latins, who particularly delight in the gesture of a glorious defeat, Cervera must for ever remain a hero. His rôle was of a mood whose poetic grandeur would have been dimmed by any ending other than a tragic one. Santiago was for him a glorious defeat gloriously arrived at.

Cervera's career in the service had been brilliant in achievement and radiated with integrity of character. He was a Spanish officer and gentleman of the old school, that school which has always been old and honoured. Ignoring the succession of politically debased ministries, whose vacillating policies, if any, the armed forces were maintained to execute, Cervera was one of those patriots who served the sovereign and trusted to Providence to lead the civilian blatherskites at the capital along a similar course when the national safety was involved. Although but one year older than Sampson, the rhythm of his life had slowed down to a more stately tempo of easeful moderation of activity. It was the Iberian manner of attaining the dignified ripeness that precedes the rather early old age. The war found him gently slipping into the psychology of retirement, but his unquestionable courage, his professional competence and his personal popularity were drafted to lend prestige to the Government and the cause. When given command of the vaunted cruiser squadron, he felt himself condemned to a hopelessly thankless sacrifice, but he was not the man to shirk. In a letter to the Minister of Marine, about a month after the explosion of the *Maine,* he pitifully opened his heart: " . . . when peoples are disorganized, their governments . . . are disorganized too. When, as the natural consequence, disaster follows, they do not look for the true causes but raise the cry of 'treason' and search for some unhappy victim who expiates the faults which were not his. For these reasons I hesitated exceedingly before accepting my command, but having accepted it I will face all the consequences which it involves, and as I have said I will do my duty."

From that time on, almost all of the Admiral's suggestions were over-ridden and his squadron's matériel needs neglected. In the first place, he pleaded for concentration, but the naval authorities sinned against this basic commandment of strategy even more outrageously than did the Americans in establishing the Flying Squadron. Madrid tried to make two forces out of units not powerful enough in toto to adequately constitute one. Admiral Camara was given a weak squadron whose chief performance during the war was to pay double toll through the Suez Canal, on a fatuous sally toward the Philippines and a prudent retreat.

Early in April, as war was rapidly approaching, Admiral Cervera sailed his flagship the *Infanta Maria Teresa,* the *Cristobal Colon,* three new and three old torpedo boats, for the Canary Islands, and thence to St. Vincent in the Cape Verde group. Here he was joined by the *Vizcaya,* returned from New York and Havana, and the *Oquendo,* also from Havana. The *Colon* was a new armoured cruiser of Italian construction, well protected and supposed to mount two ten-inch rifles in addition to a strong secondary battery of rapid-fire guns. The ten-inchers, however, had not been ready, and she had been obliged to proceed without them. The *Teresa, Vizcaya* and *Oquendo* were Spanish built sisterships about eight years of age, each carrying two eleven-inch guns as a main battery and ten 5.5-inch rapid-fire guns. They were not much smaller in displacement than the light cruisers of our present *Omaha* class. This quartet of cruisers was credited with a speed of twenty knots, very fast for those days, but the *Vizcaya* in particular was slowed down by need of docking. The *Furor, Pluton* and *Terror* were up-to-date Clyde torpedo boats, somewhat exaggeratedly called destroyers. These seven ships constituted Cervera's available force.

Not troubling to inform the Admiral that war had been declared, the Marine Ministry notified him that a conference at Madrid had decided to hurl him at the American fleet. He was simply to proceed to the West Indies while the Government decided upon his mission there. On April twenty-ninth he set out under what a British naval authority has characterized as these "mad orders." The three destroyers had to be towed. Into the wastes of the Atlantic he disappeared, arousing in the United States the consternation already noted, and his unknown course was slightly to the southward of due west.

While the abortive San Juan towing tour of the Amer-

icans was under way, Cervera was slowly crossing from the
Cape Verde Islands to the Windward group of the West
Indies.   He did not know where he would find fuel or what
his squadron could even hope to accomplish so far from a
base and reinforcements.   Had the grey bearded gentleman
on the bridge of the *Teresa* been aware of the anxiety he
then was causing in diverse American bosoms, he might
have felt some confidence in his vague mission and at least
would have enjoyed some malicious satisfaction.   Wildly
reported off Nova Scotia, Maine and Key West, he labor-
iously dragged his torpedo boats straight for Martinique.

Just then Bob Evans' classmate Charlie Clark was yearning for more powerful optical instruments and a wider
range of vision, to pick up the celebrated enemy squadron,
should it seek to arrest his *Oregon's* circumnavigation of
South America.   This sister of the *Indiana* and *Massachusetts* had been at Puget Sound when the *Maine* blew up.
Her bottom had been partially scraped by divers, and on
March sixth, as a part of the Department's assembly of
forces, she had started on her fifteen thousand mile journey
to join the North Atlantic Squadron, a journey that emphasized the imperative necessity of an isthmian canal.

First the *Oregon* had gone to San Francisco, where Captain Clark had assumed command.   Then, with a full supply
of ammunition, she had stood south to Callao, then pushed
on to Valparaiso, where she had met the *Marietta,* and then,
as war broke out, had pierced the Straits of Magellan, where
a Spanish torpedo boat at Montevideo might with more enterprise have tried to ambush the big battleship in one of the
narrow passages of the Straits.   Captain Clark had known
that at any port he might learn that a state of war existed,
and he had governed himself accordingly.   The gun crews
had slept at their stations, lights had been screened, and all
possible pressure had been put upon the engines.   At Rio
he had been informed that the war was on and Cervera

had sailed the previous day from St. Vincent. The *Oregon* and the Spanish squadron were now steaming on converging courses, toward Barbados and Martinique, respectively, two islands less than one hundred miles apart, but neither knew the position or course of the other.

Clark was prepared to put up a stiff fight if he met Cervera; indeed he lacked the speed to escape had he been so inclined. He had mapped out his tactics and almost hoped that the faster enemy would seek and find him, despite the latter's preponderance of strength. Clark was confident that, even if the *Oregon* were vanquished, she would be able to exact a price from Cervera that would render him no longer a menace on the seas. Cervera did not indulge his imagination in hypothetical engagements with the *Oregon* for the reason that his Government had neglected to inform him that this powerful unit had made any unusual move from its remote base.

The whole United States, tensely aware of the *Oregon's* dash around the continents, was relieved and overjoyed when, on May twenty-fourth, the signal station off Jupiter Inlet, Florida, saw the ship loom into view, ask by signal the whereabouts of the fleet and then hurry to Key West.

Admiral Cervera, thinking no more of the *Oregon* than of shelling Boston, slowly advanced toward the West, his attention absorbed by tow lines and other problems of seamanship.

On the morning of May twelfth, while at San Juan the *Iowa* was leading the attacking column toward the harbour entrance, the Spanish Squadron expected to be found there was nearing the island of Martinique. French sympathy with Spain had been almost openly proclaimed throughout the period of the Cuban crisis, and Cervera naturally selected a French port rather than a British at which to make his landfall. To disclose his whereabouts was an unfortunate necessity. His bunkers were empty and besides, like

Sampson, he had to obtain information. Accordingly, one of the torpedo boats had been sent ahead to Fort de France, and she poked her little nose into the harbour on the eleventh. There was no coal but too much information. Great events had been taking place while the fleet had been in transit. War finally had been declared and the Philippine Squadron at Manila Bay destroyed. The approaches to the Caribbean were patrolled by fast American scouts, ready to report Cervera's arrival to the North Atlantic Squadron, now off San Juan. Cuba was blockaded north and south, but the harbour of Santiago not yet guarded.

As though the tragic mood had pervaded the cables also, a despatch authorizing Cervera to return to Spain if he saw no chance of operating successfully in the West Indies, never reached him.

Santiago, this batch of information told him, was thus the one Cuban or Porto Rican port he might be able to enter without a battle, and he felt obliged to try. From Martinique it was twice as far to Santiago as to Curacoa, where the Government had promised to send a collier. His fuel would barely take him to Santiago and an erroneous report led him to believe that his bunkers could not be refilled there, so the Admiral resolved to seek the collier at Curacoa and then attempt to slip across the Caribbean to Santiago. The boilers of the destroyer *Terror* had become useless and this vessel had to be left behind.

It would have been remarkable had the Marine Ministry succeeded in having the collier at Curacoa as arranged; it would have been out of line with the general blundering. No such exception is to be recorded. The collier was not there. From the Dutch authorities, the Spaniards received a frigid reception. Two ships only were admitted to the port of Willemstad, and the duration of their stay and the quantity of coal they might purchase were strictly limited.

It was now the fifteenth and, it will be recalled, Sampson, returning from San Juan, received at Cape Haytien the news of Cervera's presence at Curacoa. The Atlantic naval zone was narrowing as the mists of misinformation began to rise.

Schley was steaming to the southward with his Flying Squadron, from Hampton Roads to Key West, as Cervera made his dash to the northward, eluding the American scouts. On the morning of the nineteenth, when the Flying Squadron was standing out of Key West for the south coast of Cuba, when the *Iowa* was frantically coaling to follow Schley, and when the *Oregon* was not far to the eastward on the last leg of her great cruise, the garrison of the Morro at the mouth of Santiago Bay cheered the arrival of the long awaited Spanish fleet.

The ships felt their way up the difficult channel to the city, and the emotion was profound as they, at weary last, settled in the refuge of a Spanish port and the loyalists ashore saw the emblems of the motherland's maritime might. The cheers were lusty while they lasted, but soon they subsided into an anxious gloom. The Spaniards in Cuba learned to their disappointment that this was not the vanguard but the whole of the expeditionary 'naval force. Admiral Cervera, on the other hand, found to his dismay that the city needed succour from him and was in no position to restore his ships and men to fighting condition. Instead of the city and the squadron finding in each other their salvation, there was one more heavy burden upon each.

18

"INCOMPREHENSIBLE"

~~~~~~

THE radiant morning of May twenty-second found the *Iowa* plunging to the eastward across the Gulf of Cazones. At about noon she sighted the Flying Squadron off Cienfuegos, and she spent the following nine days, until Sampson joined forces at Santiago on June first, as a part of Schley's detachment. These days were to prove the most critical of that officer's career, and critical in almost equal degree to the cause. They spanned the last and most anxious period of the search for Cervera.

Practically all of the secondary and much of the primary material relating to these nine days are coloured by the misnamed Sampson-Schley Controversy after the war. What should have been narrative, consciously or unconsciously, became argument and rebuttal. Evans deeply deplored the "washing of Navy linen in public" but, when he undertook the transcription of the events in question, he found it impossible to ignore the Controversy, and it can not be spared reference here.

Within the service there was no Controversy. Schley's claim to what he called "the guerdon of victory" for Santiago was taken no more seriously by his colleagues than his far-fetched analogy of Nelson's credit for the Nile. Sir John Jervis had been many days sailing from Aboukir Bay, whereas Sampson had been within signal distance of at least some of his engaged ships. The latter characteristically refrained from taking any part in the discussions, which were a distasteful sequel to a difficult task well done, so the Controversy had no legitimate title to his name.

"My sympathies," said Evans, "were well known to be on the side of Admiral Sampson, for I made no effort to conceal them . . . " but he was equally outspoken in denunciation of the "personal and vicious" attacks upon Schley. The affair at Valparaiso remained fresh in the memory of the captain of the *Yorktown*. While he expected little of Schley in '98 and was not disappointed, his sense of fair play revolted at the boorish criticism by the press and public of professional conduct beyond the scope of their lay appraisal.

To properly understand the manœuvres of those nine days, one must penetrate the Controversy to the facts. The Battle of Santiago was more than a month ahead. Had it not been fought, had it not been indisputably won, had Sampson not happened to be temporarily out of the blockading ring and in the direction opposite to that taken by the fleeing Spaniards, there would have been no Controversy. There was glory enough for all, and had Schley been a man of as great and generous a nature as Sampson, he graciously would have joined his brother officers and the authorities in according to the Admiral the plaudits for having devised the successful operations. Schley should have found distinction enough for any hero in the honours that were undeniably his, as Senior Officer Present during the major portion of the engagement. His pretensions to the laurels of Sampson in addition to his own, inspired acrimonious attacks against himself, that went to outrageously baseless extremes and eventually compelled him, in self-defense, to request an official inquiry. Three years after the war, there was held a most unedifying post-mortem, possessing only such dignity as were lent to the proceedings by the eminence of the members of the Court, presided over by Admiral Dewey.

Despite popular misconception, partly predicated upon

an irrelevant passage in Dewey's minority (but not dissenting) opinion, this Court did not and was not authorized to settle or attempt to settle the Controversy or any issue of relative achievement or title to credit. It was concerned exclusively with the conduct of Commodore Schley, first, during the battle, and second, during those last nine days of May, which throughout the Controversy had constituted the basis for many adverse criticisms of Schley's direction of the Flying Squadron.

The findings of the Court as to the conduct of Schley in the battle itself, will be referred to in their proper place. The more important findings, those on the second subject of inquiry, attributed to Schley grievous errors of omission and commission in the quest for Cervera at Cienfuegos and Santiago.

These errors were perpetrated while the *Iowa* was with the Flying Squadron. Evans was obliged to mutely stand by and watch these exasperating blunders, unable to do anything to prevent or rectify them. He chafed under the constant delays, when time was of the essence, but the aloof, austere Schley was not in the habit of confiding in his subordinates, so aboard the *Iowa* it was assumed that the mysterious moves and halts of the squadron had some rational basis in information securely locked in the bosom of the Commodore.

A dispassionate review of the facts serves to confirm the soundness of the Court's conclusions. Schley was ably represented by counsel and given full opportunity to present his evidence and explanations. He did so again in his elaborate apologia entitled *Forty-Five Years Under The Flag,* an appeal from the Court of Inquiry to the court of public opinion. The efforts to exculpate the Commodore were not, and after all these sobering years are not, convincing.

It must, however, be conceded that, as President Roosevelt declared in his statement approving the opinion of the

Court, the Department and Admiral Sampson had been at fault in condoning during the war conduct which they later characterized as "reprehensible." The Admiral's delicacy, throughout the Cuban campaign, in asserting the authority of supreme command over a life-long senior on the list bespeaks the former's fineness of feeling, but it was not conducive to the most effective joint operations. Furthermore, several of the orders with which Schley did not comply were lacking in that explicit phraseology which is the first rule of military communication. Schley was no Evans to "read between the lines" or err on the side of over-zealous pursuit of the naval objective. His instructions should have been drafted in terms that were as free from ambiguity as the English language and the secret codes permitted. The hastily dictated letters and cables that were destined to be construed and explained, long after their transmission, by groups of ingenious advocates alien to the service and remote from the occasion, do not stand the test of analysis. Expressions of Sampson's opinions or tactfully tendered suggestions were not mandates to Schley as, for instance, they would have been to Evans.

Schley had a mind apart, whose reactions were often at variance with those of his colleagues, and he was Sampson's senior on the Navy list. Under the doctrine of those days, the Department asked a great deal of both Sampson and Schley when it placed the junior in supreme command and the senior second. This inversion ran counter to the life-long training of the two men. Why this burden was imposed is not clear. Once Sampson had been selected for the prime responsibility, the command of the Flying Squadron, inevitably bound to serve directly under him before the war was over, should have been bestowed upon the best available junior. Had there been a senior so conspicuously the best choice, it is likely that he would have received Sampson's position. The Department's assignments would have been warranted only had Sampson been the outstanding officer for the command-in-chief, which he was, and Schley not Sampson's peer but nevertheless the outstanding officer for second place, which it can not be pretended was the case. Schley was a gentleman born and bred, and an officer with a long and honourable record, who had, however, exhibited no unique talent to meet the exacting demands of the emergency at the head of the Flying Squadron. His was not the spirit to gracefully accept the subordination of his Commodore's pennant to the flag of one who was a Captain, temporarily vested with the stars of a Rear Admiral. Had the Department merely failed to relieve him of the command upon the outbreak of war and promotion of Sampson, it would have been open to less just criticism than it merited for having deliberately gone out of its way to transfer him from shore duty to the newly formed Flying Squadron. Perhaps it was too much to expect that Schley would be so gratified at this signal honour that he would disregard the fact that his only superior afloat had been junior to him throughout their careers. This Schley was not able to do, although he honestly tried. There seemed to him no valid reason for the reversal of their relative positions. The irrepressible consciousness of this twist in the hierarchy, so trivial to the outsider and so important to the wearer of the cloth, rankled throughout the campaign. If he was qualified for second place, he kept wondering, what blemish did the Department perceive in his character or record that pronounced him unfit for first?

Without the Battle of Santiago, Schley would have nursed his grievance in silence and made the most to the world of his second-highest station. The taste of personal triumph, however, in the engagement, whet his appetite for the full measure of acclaim he had seen accorded to Dewey. Sampson's distance from the harbour that Sunday morning doubtless seemed to Schley a providential righting of a Departmental injustice. Where Sampson was nobly self-effacing, Schley grasped thirstily for the first draught from the hero's bowl. His nettled vanity was easily provoked by frustration, followed by newspaper calumnies and a slanderous history book, into an unbecoming championship of his own claims and of his own record.

The log-books were dusted off and memories refreshed. Every move of the Flying Squadron was scrutinized anew, and mistakes that otherwise would have been cheerfully left hidden behind the clouds of triumphant gunpowder at Santiago, were exhumed and displayed to the vulgar gaze of the contemporary world and posterity. The decisions of a moment were debated for years. The crisis of the Controversy was reached when, in the Congressional war honour promotions, Schley was recommended by President McKinley for an advance, but less than Sampson's, and to an extent that would place the latter ahead of Schley on the permanent list. By pressing for more, Schley's influential Maryland supporters accomplished nothing for their candidate, but they marred the tribute properly due Sampson, and advertised the disappointing performance of the Flying Squadron during those nine days before June first.

How ironic was that title Flying Squadron! It was a queer one in the first instance for a force including ponderous battleships. The performance of the squadron was to almost parody flight.

Having left Key West a full day and more before the *Iowa*, Evans was, upon his arrival at Cienfuegos, astonished to learn that it had beaten him by a scant six hours. In a chapter contributed to correspondent Goode's book, Evans laconically wrote that " . . . it was surmised that they had met with thick weather off Cape San Antonio, and thus been forced to slow or make a wide detour. It now appears that they made a wide detour." This was the closest Evans would approach the publication of any unfriendly comment as to Schley's leadership, when there seemed nothing for the service to gain by so doing.

"After saluting the Commodore," he said, "the *Iowa* became one of the Flying Squadron, and proceeded to drift leisurely with it off and on, Micawber-like, waiting for something—we hoped the Spanish squadron—to turn up."

At Cienfuegos, Evans surveyed with profound admiration the scene of one of the most daring feats in all American naval history, that had been performed quietly and successfully a fortnight earlier. The heroes had been Lieutenant C. M. Winslow, nephew of the Captain of the *Kearsarge* when she sank the *Alabama*, Lieutenant Edwin A. Anderson, later Admiral, and a handful of volunteers from the *Marblehead* and *Nashville*. In small open boats, they had in broad daylight proceeded over the shoal water and, within a couple of hundred feet of the Spanish-infested shore, calmly grappled for the three cables leading to Santiago, and had located, raised and cut them. This task had involved nearly three hours of exposure to the small arms fire of a thousand enemy soldiers, carefully sharpshooting from behind breastworks in the dense brush fringing the beach. Hits had been made, of course, but the victims, regardless of how painfully struck, had managed to maintain absolute silence so that their unhurt comrades could continue the operation. These boats had held their positions until every cable had been severed. Never was Congressional reward more valiantly won than by Winslow and Anderson, who were advanced five numbers each in the wartime promotions. The casualties in the boats had represented the first naval blood drawn by Spain in the war.

Schley was not resourceful in ascertaining that Cervera was not within the concealed harbour of Cienfuegos, when the Department was sending report after report that the enemy almost certainly was at Santiago. Instead of blind man's buff, the game in the Caribbean had now been changed to hide and seek. What was required was no Micawber but a man of vigorous action. Not only did Schley exasperate the authorities at Washington and Admiral Sampson, by his dallying off Cienfuegos, but he tried the patience of his subordinates in the squadron, who felt sure that they were blockading an empty harbor.

Sampson had computed the minimum stop of Cervera at Santiago as five days, based upon the probable tasks that could not be postponed and upon a conservative estimate of the harbour facilities. Any time thereafter, the Spaniards might emerge into the open sea and once more disappear. The five days would expire on the twenty-fourth, and no amount of Sampson's persuasion, always avoiding the peremptory tone, seemed able to drive over Schley to the entrance of Santiago within that time.

Impugning the reliability of the information by which the Department and Sampson were being guided, Schley himself had been misled by various false indicia into an intellectual doubt that Cienfuegos was not unoccupied by the enemy fleet. It remained for the Captain of the *Marblehead,* acting upon his own initiative, to establish communication with insurgents on the beach through Lieutenant Anderson and conclusively prove, even to the satisfaction of Schley, that the disobliging Cervera was not hiding behind the screening hills of Cienfuegos.

This was the twenty-fourth, when Cervera's estimated repairs and refueling might be completed, and when the Department and the *New York* confidently relied upon the Flying Squadron barring any attempted departure from Santiago Bay. Cervera's failure to venture forth was Schley's good luck. A little more enemy haste, and the ambitious Commodore doubtless would have faced a Court Martial, convened with the ominous mandate ending "the United States being then at war," instead of a Court of Inquiry desirous of letting the mantle of victorious peace, so far as honourably possible, cloak the foibles of war.

The Flying Squadron was now a. w. o. l. at Santiago. It would be supposed that, immediately upon the realization that Cienfuegos Bay was empty of Spanish warships, the

Flying Squadron would have spread its wings for Santiago, but even now, while those responsible for American naval strategy were counting the minutes, the squadron proceeded as though it had days to spare. The business of getting under way was not hurried, and speed was set at the low rate necessary to enable the yacht *Eagle,* of little combatant use, to maintain station. The dangerous interval during which Cervera might sally forth without interference was thus further enlarged, but the crowning blunder was committed when the mountainous coast of Santiago came at last into distant view.

On this twenty-sixth day of May, Schley executed a remarkable manœuvre and sent an announcement thereof to Washington that plunged the Government into what the Secretary of the Navy later described as "the darkest day of the war." The despatch was delivered to him at an Army review, and he handed it to President McKinley, whose "face fell." The Flying Squadron was—its own commander said so—flying home! The sentry post had been abandoned! The excuse was flimsy. Secretary Long read and re-read the strange words from the front: " . . . Impossible to remain off Santiago in present state of coal account of the squadron. . . . It is to be regretted that the department's orders cannot be obeyed, earnestly as we have all striven to that end. I am forced to return to Key West, via Yucatan Passage, for coal."

The President and his Naval Secretary looked at each other in dismay. While the volunteer troops paraded before them and the bands played, these two civilian chieftains knew that the first line of defence had opened a gap at the pivotal point.

"It was incomprehensible—," wrote Long in retrospect, "the first flinching of the campaign." He later admitted that the Department was open to just censure for not having forthwith removed Schley from his command and ordered an inquiry. Sampson's only possible delinquency throughout the war was his leniency at this juncture toward Schley, said Long, who, be it remembered, was responsible for the embarrassing relationship of these two officers: " . . . it was taken for granted that the commander-in-chief, Sampson, who was near at hand, would take proper action, which, had he been senior in service, he would probably have done, and not doing which he too failed to do his duty."

Long's words were overly bitter toward Schley and must also be read as the partisan statement of one of the chief protagonists of the Controversy. Schley, who never should have been designated in the first place, should now have been replaced in command of the Flying Squadron, not as a punishment or rebuke to him, but because of lack of confidence that he was the man best qualified for the position. After all, Schley had not attained the command by any affirmative effort on his own part. Like many another unfortunate in history, his mediocrity, adequate under normal conditions, was pitilessly exposed by the effort to thrust greatness upon him.

Evans had coaled under "impossible" difficulties in the Florida Straits, and Schley was himself to learn that this trick could be performed right where he then was.

The most damning fact was that immediate refueling was not imperative at all. At the Court of Inquiry in 1901, it was developed that, when Schley abandoned his station for lack of coal, his vessels had sufficient in their bunkers to remain on blockade duty—the *Brooklyn* for twenty-six days, the *Iowa* sixteen, the *Massachusetts* twenty, the *Texas* ten, the *Marblehead* five and the *Vixen* twenty-three—and then be able to steam to Gonaives, Hayti or Cape Cruz, in either of which sheltered places they could have replenished their supply from the collier in company. Perhaps Schley dreaded an engagement with his ship's engines fighting on empty stomachs, but he had quite a margin of safety, and surely it would have been preferable to risk Cervera's superior speed than to leave the seas clear for him.

If this retrograde movement, then regarded as the renegade movement, from Santiago, was "incomprehensible" to those at Washington, it was nothing short of amazing to the captains on the scene. Just as land was dimly discerned and some American scouts off the harbour entrance identified, Evans saw the Ardois signal lights flashing from the *Brooklyn*. That it was the expected command to close the fortifications and attack, he took for granted. The red and white lights spelled out the message. Its import was not what Evans anticipated—quite the contrary. It was staggering, incredible-"incomprehensible."

"Destination Key West as soon as collier is ready via south side Cuba and Yucatan Channel. Speed nine knots."

Retreat! Retreat without repulse! Retreat without even attack! Impossible!

The *Iowa* happened to be within hail of the *Texas*. Evans shouted through his megaphone to Captain Philip:

"Say, Jack, what the devil does it mean?"

"Beats me," boomed back the answer, and then: "What do you think, Bob?"

"Damned if I know anything," growled Evans, "except that I'm the most disgusted man afloat."

To those on the bridge of the *Iowa*, there seemed only one possible explanation for this *volte face* at the moment of arrival: that Cervera had escaped during the Micawber dawdling off Cienfuegos and was to be pursued to the westward. Evans hoped that this would turn out to be the case—that the bow of the *Iowa* would be kept pointed at the enemy—but he feared that it would not. Schley, as usual, kept his own counsel, and it is interesting to speculate upon the rich flow of profanity that would have gushed from the lips of Old Gimpy had he read the cable about having to steam around Cuba to coal ship.

The disabled collier referred to in the Ardois signal was the *Merrimac*, which had to be taken in tow, causing a delay that was fortunate in holding the squadron in the vicinity of the enemy who, of course, was inside Santiago. The weather moderated and the *Merrimac* was able to limp along under her own power. Jack Philip then unwittingly ridiculed his senior's despatch by coaling the *Texas* right then and there. The situation was changing, and with it Schley's point of view. As more urgent directions to blockade Santiago were delivered by overtaking scouts, the Commodore's military vision cleared. The man never lacked physical courage. Back toward Santiago steamed the Flying Squadron.

The reversal of course to the eastward, rendering the previous withdrawal more perplexing than ever, was construed by Evans to be the result of news that Cervera's flight had been in that direction, probably through the Windward Passage to San Juan or Havana. This hypothesis was exploded when, in the late afternoon of the twenty-eighth, the squadron, upon again sighting Santiago, lay to for the night. Then, after all, Cervera must indeed be there and have been there all along! At least the *Iowa* was now facing him.

PRELUDE

~~~~~~

F ROM the City of Santiago, the harbour appears to be a landlocked basin. From the sea, the mouth of the harbour appears to be a shallow indentation. The tides ebb and flow through a narrow, twisting slit in the coastal range that from either end is almost a hidden passage. No matter at what angle one gazes towards it from afar, the background is always the same tropical green as the precipitous slopes of the foreshore. Large vessels can navigate the channel only with perfect piloting free from the slightest miscalculation of current or dimension.

The morning following his second arrival, Commodore Schley led the Flying Squadron in a sweep past this slender aperture in the hills. As each ship in the column crossed the line of vision running into this apparent *cul-de-sac*, she could catch a fleeting glimpse of the harbour entrance. The *Brooklyn* in the van gave no sign of observing anything unusual. Nevertheless, as the bridge of the *Iowa* was coming abeam of the gap, glasses were tensely poised to peer into its depths. With a shock of delighted astonishment, Bob Evans beheld the break in the cliffs reveal, as by the drawing of a curtain across a V-shaped proscenium, a long, low craft moored at the first bend of the channel. By her peculiar rig of single mast between twin smoke stacks, she was instantly recognized as the *Cristobal Colon!* So the flagship had treated that as unworthy of announcement! Could she have missed the *Colon?* Evans signalled word to the *Brooklyn,* and the exciting report elicited only the cryptic hoist: "I understand." Maybe Schley did, but Evans did not. Now, as the second joint of the finger-shaped entrance opened into view, the *Iowa* saw the flagship *Maria Teresa,* lying as serenely as at Kiel, and, protruding above the elevation of foliage at the turn, the masts of a third enemy cruiser. Cervera in full force! At last!

Upon sighting the enemy, the *Iowa* went to general quarters, anticipating from second to second the Commodore's order to engage. The *Brooklyn's* halliards, however, two-blocked no such flag message, and her guns remained mute. Were we at war with Spain or not?

In much less time than it takes to recite the event, the verdant scenery shifted back across the harbour entrance and again screened it from the *Iowa.* The act was over. The squadron neither halted in its course nor countermarched, but steamed ahead, apparently oblivious of the presence of the Spaniards. Evans felt that he was learning new tricks. It had been his naïve notion that, when a long sought enemy is sighted by an adequate force, fire is opened. Was this a naval review for the diversion of the Morro garrison? There remained nothing to do but ruefully secure his unused batteries. The bugle sounded and the crew wondered.

To even the inscrutable Commodore, at least seeing was believing, and he rushed off Captain Sigsbee, ex-*Maine,* now commanding the fast scout *St. Paul,* to Hayti, to cable to the Department and to Sampson what they all but positively knew as to the whereabouts of the Spanish fleet.

(The evidence of Cervera's entire fleet being at Santiago was still circumstantial, although convincing. It was confirmed by the statements of Cuban insurgents who had seen the flotilla from the hill-tops. On June seventeenth, however, Lieutenant Victor Blue, later Admiral, dissipated the technical doubt by travelling through the jungle on a donkey in the full regalia of his rank and, from a lofty promontory overlooking the bay, counting off the Spanish vessels with his own eyes.)

The commanding officers present were summoned aboard the *Brooklyn*, where, according to Schley's account, "The fact of the enemy's presence was announced, the form of blockade was explained, the method of attack, if the Spanish fleet should attempt a sortie, was declared." There was no conference in any real sense—just a proclamation.

The Flying Squadron was to patrol back and forth across the entrance. "One of the commanding officers," said Schley, "asked if the purpose was to dash into the entrance if the enemy attempted to escape. He learned, with some emphasis, that such was the purpose and order." The emphasis, to administer a rebuke for a stupid question, was misplaced. In view of the omission to attack the *Colon* that morning, the question had been a proper one. The logic of the policy to penetrate the harbour fortifications if the enemy first emerged and then retreated, but not otherwise, is no clearer to-day than it was to the perplexed captain.

The Court of Inquiry in 1901 adjudged that the Commodore "should have endeavoured to capture or destroy the Spanish vessels at anchor near the entrance of Santiago Harbour on May 29th and 30th" and that "He did not do the utmost with the force under his command to capture or destroy the *Colon* and other vessels of the enemy which he attacked on May 31st."

This latter finding referred to an abortive execution two days later of what Evans had assumed would have been the almost instinctively ordered plan when the *Colon* was first sighted on May twenty-ninth. On the thirty-first, the *Brooklyn* and *Texas* were left out of range coaling. Flying his broad pennant on the *Massachusetts,* Schley led the *New Orleans,* fresh from the foreign market and hasty organization, and the *Iowa* toward the entrance.

From drawing by Charles Graham in Harper's Pictorial History of the Spanish-American War

BIRD'S-EYE VIEW OF SANTIAGO DURING BLOCKADE

The Department's injuction against exposing the ships to the fire of shore batteries had expressly and naturally qualified this restraint by excepting operations against enemy naval craft, whose destruction, as the prime objective, justified such risk. Schley proceeded to ignore the exception and obey the rule. The range he prescribed was too great to be effective, and, not content with this precaution, the distance from the forts actually maintained by the temporary flagship in guiding the column was in excess of that prescribed range. As the American ships approached, two guns of the Socapa battery left of the entrance and two of the Morro east of the entrance showed their flaming tongues and, during the brief periods in which the units of the column were successively passing the harbour mouth, the *Colon* exercised her batteries. Evans kept increasing the range of his sights as each run's salvos fell short. The opposing forces did practically no damage to each other. They barked noisily across a safe interspace.

"Not a projectile struck the *Colon*," lamented Evans, "and the *Iowa* found herself with strained elevating gear, caused by high-angle fire."

The opinion of the Court of Inquiry justified the exasperation of the *Iowa's* skipper at the ineffectual manner in which his fighting leviathan had been employed. Her guns had been designed to hit, not to splash.

To Evans, one of the most interesting lessons of the bombardment was the demonstration of the incalculable value of smokeless powder, which the British-built *New Orleans* used in her six-inch rapid-fire guns. He later remarked that "the cloud effects produced by the *Massachusetts* were very beautiful, but the rattle of the *New Orleans'* battery was very businesslike." It was obvious that the old kind of firing charge would soon be as obsolete as the muzzle-loading gun.

The nine days with the Flying Squadron had not improved Old Gimpy's temper. We can imagine the smile that was induced by the Officer of the Deck's report, on the morning of June first, that the *New York* was standing in from the eastward. She was there to stay, and, as Admiral Sampson assumed supreme command of the situation, Bob Evans knew that "the beginning of the end was in sight."

A conference aboard the *New* York was attended by Schley and the captains. Sampson was gratified at the extent to which Evans' shoulder had healed. Charlie Clark was there. In the undemonstrative manner of those sailors, they gave him a hero's welcome. They appreciated the magnitude of his achievement in having brought the *Oregon* around South America to the Santiago blockading line, fit and ready for action, and the degree of his audacity in having determined to alone face and fight the Spanish fleet if courses crossed. Many of the officers and men were seeing the *Bulldog* for the first time. Sister-ship of the *Indiana* and *Massachusetts,* but with a distinctive rig conspicuous to the trained naval eye, she looked the powerful reënforcement that she was. And one more gallant captain drew up his chair to the conference table.

Santiago was now, of course, the strategic centre of the war. If Cervera's fleet could be conclusively denied the sea, the campaign would be as good as won. The natural impulse of every naval officer was to force the entrance and settle with the enemy fleet in its own private pond. This was the line of least emotional resistance. It must ever stand to Sampson's credit that he did not yield thereto, and to the Department's credit that it backed him up.

The imposing fortifications, contemplated alone, deterred Sampson no more than had the shore batteries deterred Farragut or Dewey. This single winding channel was in fact mined, and it was positively known by the Americans to be mined. So narrow was its navigable lane that the explosion of an American ship, which Sampson would have risked, would have meant the blockading of the ingress of the others. An attempt to force the entrance would have been inexcusable folly. With our diplomatic horizon darkened by clouds more ominous than those precipitating the Spanish storm, such a stroke would have been a reckless disregard of the national welfare.

Sampson resolved to turn to his own advantage those very physical attributes of Santiago that seemed to thwart his progress. He would bar Cervera's exit rather than his own entry, and by means of a dispensable noncombatant vessel rather than with one of our few capital fighting ships. He would sink a collier in the passage. Then, if the Army would arrive and do its part ashore and seize the batteries, the channel could be cleared of the collier's wreckage and of Spanish mines, safely admitting the American fleet to the inner basin for the death fight with the transatlantic squadron. This was sound strategy, contemplating aggressive tactics that were not foolhardy.

No time was lost in initiating the program. With Sampson's arrival, a feeling of confidence pervaded the fleet.

The very first change instituted by the new régime was the substitution of the circular close blockade for Schley's remote patrol. This close blockade was maintained until, over a month later, Cervera vainly tried to break through it. With the tightening of the blockade and the stiffening of the morale, came the conviction to all hands that Micawber tactics had been relegated to limbo. Washington and the nation at large were likewise inspirited. Answering an official query suggested by Schley's "incomprehensible" message, Sampson declared that he could maintain the blockade "indefinitely." That was more like the Navy.

The next move was the sinking of the *Merrimac* inside the entrance.

Lieutenant Commander Richmond P. Hobson of the Construction Corps had initiated the plan, worked out the details and won from the Admiral the honour of commanding the suicide mission. With him were to go seven enlisted men. They were to be carefully selected for their respective tasks.

When the call for volunteers reached the *Iowa,* Captain Evans directed Lieutenant Commander Rodgers, his Executive Officer, to explain to the ship's company at quarters the grim nature of the business on hand.

"Bring me the names of those who volunteer."

The bugle sounded and in a few minutes Rodgers again entered the cabin—but without a list.

"There have volunteered, sir, *every* officer and man aboard!"

Evans proudly signalled this to the Admiral and inquired how many men were wanted from his ship. The answer was that only one seaman could be used. The problem "was how to select one man out of six hundred good ones."

Memory must have evoked that far off day when Acting Ensign Evans was one of the young volunteers chosen for the sacrifice to the prestige of the service and for the inspiration of the Army. Times, he must now have reflected, had changed the appearance of the American fleet but not its character. Who spoke of iron ships and wooden men?

For once in his career, Evans shunned responsibility, but he met it half way. Rodgers and he would each select a candidate and leave to the toss of a coin the final and fatal designation. Rodgers named J. E. Murphy, as fine a seaman as trod the Navy's decks. There was in the ship's company one McLean, who had been an outstanding sailor on the memorable cruise of the *Yorktown,* and whom Evans had been pleased to find in the *Iowa,* wearing the uniform of a petty officer. The Captain nominated his old shipmate.

The two men were summoned. In the eyes of their comrades, they had received the accolade. McLean, regretting only that his skipper had not reserved to himself the absolute choice, turned to Murphy and offered him fifty dollars for his chance. It was refused.

Evans spoke: "I am sentencing one of you fellows to death. Do you understand?"

"Yes, sir."

"Do you still want to go?"

"Yes, sir."

A coin flipped in the air and clanged upon the cabin table. Murphy won.

McLean blurted out that he had one hundred and fifty dollars in the world and begged Murphy to take it for his place in the *Merrimac,* but to Murphy that place was priceless. We have Evans's word for it that McLean left the cabin vainly trying to conceal the tears that "were streaming out of his eyes because he had lost a chance to have his head shot off."

From her point of vantage directly opposite the harbour entrance, the *Iowa,* alone of the ships constituting the barrier arc, had a view of the macabre fireworks that greeted the *Merrimac* upon her last mission. Evans watched the dismantled collier, with a belt of torpedoes strung around her sides, slip off during the dark night of June second. Before daylight was otherwise evident, the silhouette of the condemned ship became faintly visible beneath the Morro, creeping into the enemy's maw. From the other decks, the *Merrimac* passed out of sight behind the capes, but those following her death march from the pivotal *Iowa* could discern the receding shape moving up the channel towards Punta Gorda at the first bend, as calmly as though she were bringing fuel to Cervera, but without displaying a light.

Suddenly the outraged forts burst into indignant protest at the brazen intrusion. The notch between the hills was filled with fire, smoke and reverberating noise. Down from Socapa and the Morro crashed salvos of deadly pyrotechnics, and the defenceless ghost-ship was simultaneously subjected to rapid fire assaults from ahead and abeam.

To Evans, the *Merrimac* looked like a tiny black shadow engulfed in the exploding furnace of Satan. This rôle of helpless bystander was too much for his nerves—nerves which nothing but such harrowing inactivity could unsettle. Unable to lift a finger to aid those eight brave men diving into an open crematory, he turned aside from the spectacle and limped into the privacy of his cabin, not to attempt sleep but to sit in the quiet with his pipe and his thoughts: thoughts, we can presume to guess, of the toss of the coin on the table in front of him, of his own landing with sound legs and sound youth beneath the guns of Fort Fisher, and of those old sea-dogs who had vainly awaited Somer's return from the harbour of Tripoli. Evans could expect for Hobson no more merciful fate than had claimed Somers.

The quiet Sampson had been less pessimistic. Most of the cable-cutters had escaped alive at Cienfuegos. Keenly feeling the awful responsibility of his having despatched the *Merrimac,* he clung to a belief that there was a chance— one slim chance—that not all of the little party would perish. To fortify that one slim chance, he ordered Naval Cadet Powell to lie west of the harbour entrance in the *New York's* launch—an assignment comparable in hazard to Hobson's. Powell and his volunteer crew lingered at their post until, the echoes of the cannonading died away, the fumes of the powder cleared the channel, and day disclosed the stack and masts of the sunken collier inside the bay. Finally the little launch was seen, pitching and rolling back towards the flag-ship, constantly under heavy Spanish fire, the cynosure of friendly glasses. Anxiously the cockpit was brought into focus, but not a glimpse could be caught of Hobson or any of his men. They were not in the launch. Powell reported that he had been unable to espy any sign of life near the wreck. Such a disregard of his own danger had he displayed that it was almost a miracle that the launch had not been shot to pieces.

The hearts of all in the fleet were heavy, especially when it was realized that the sacrifice of the *Merrimac's* party had been futile. The wreck did not seriously obstruct the channel. For what little impediment she offered, the Admiral was determined that the *Merrimac* should remain just where and as she lay. He ordered the *Iowa* to approach the entrance and prevent any interference with this resolution.

Evans showed his contempt for the shore batteries by bringing his battleship near enough to gain a distinct view of the wreck. The scene appeared to him to be quite as lifeless as it had to those in the rescue launch. While engaged in this scrutiny, Evans saw a white speck moving in the extreme background. He soon identified it as a launch, conspicuous for its white awning, coming down the upper reaches. Straight for the wreck it headed. Evans intently watched its every move. Rodgers, alongside on the bridge, suspected that dynamite was being affixed and advised opening fire. This seemed reasonable, but something intuitively restrained the Captain from giving the order. As Evans and Rodgers stood there, the launch withdrew whence it had come, and disappeared. No explosion followed. All was as still as before.

That afternoon, when Hobson had for hours been believed to be one with the gallant Somers, there came puffing out of the harbour toward the *New York,* flying a flag of truce, a Spanish launch. Over the side of the flagship climbed Captain Bustamente, Admiral Cervera's Chief of Staff, with one of the most thrilling messages ever delivered to an American admiral.

Hobson and all of his men were safe and sound! Cervera himself, in the launch which Evans had fortunately refrained from sinking, had picked them up from the water, clinging to their raft near the wreck. So deeply touched by the

bravery of these men had been the Spanish Admiral, that he
had ignored nationality and warfare in the generous reception accorded to them. Captain Bustamente was sent not
only to convey the news of the rescue but to arrange for the
prompt exchange of the prisoners and to bring them their
clothing.

This was Admiral Cervera's first contact with the
American Navy, and his is to this day a name honoured in
its annals. When, a few weeks later, he became a prisoner
of war, first in Captain Evans's ship and then at Annapolis,
every effort was put forward to express by deed the gratitude of the service for the kindness of this officer and gentleman towards the survivors of the *Merrimac*.

Exactly one month before the battle, Captain Bustamente
and Admiral Sampson sat chatting together upon the
quarter-deck of the *New York*. Their mutual respect and
personal good will typified the international camaraderie
that exists among the naval officers of the world, professional colleagues all. The Navy believed that whatever
treachery had destroyed the *Maine* had not emanated from
the Spanish Navy, and deplored the fact that the Spanish
Navy would have to bear the brunt of the revenge exacted
by the muzzles of the American warships. As Sampson
and Bustamente conversed on this tropical summer afternoon, peace and friendship seemed to dominate the atmosphere. Far from the causes of Spanish-American embroilments had run the careers of these two officers, and in their
possible achievements lay the sole prospect of peace. Sampson, for decades the mild leader of strong men, talked face
to face with Cervera's distinguished emissary, the foremost
torpedo expert of the Spanish service and a handsome man
of aristocratic bearing, who was to perish of wounds in the
land defence of Santiago, before the fatal sortie of his fleet.

The *Merrimac's* protruding masts and funnel remained
a symbol of American daring, but the wreck was of no

tangible significance. The channel, such as it had been, was still open. Close blockading had to remain the order of the day and of the night—unremitting, tense, inexorable, regardless of weather or circumstance. Cervera could choose the hour, and so Sampson had to make certain that no time chosen would be the right time. He was ever concentrating upon the moment of Cervera's dash. Be it daylight or dark, rain or clear, rough or smooth, "up sun" or "down sun," that moment must find the American squadrons as ready as if it had been agreed upon in advance, ready not just to defeat or cripple but to annihilate the European who challenged our control of the threshold seas. Sampson had the superior forces and knew that the utmost was expected of them. Every move was pre-arranged against every contingency reasonably to be anticipated, and one writer has declared that "the battle could have been fought with Sampson dead or living, with Sampson a thousand miles or only one mile from the harbour." His blockade and battle orders that were worked out in careful detail left little to the imagination of his captains—and yet almost everything to their initiative.

Nothing in naval warfare sounds easier to a layman and is more difficult in execution than the maintenance of an effective blockade "indefinitely." Here off Santiago the sea behaved and misbehaved, the wind rose and fell and veered with unpredictable caprice, the ground swells rolled up from the depths of the Caribbean and tangled themselves in the tideways and tidal currents along the shore; and, during every minute of every watch, the American fleet had to keep exact station. These floating fortresses had to dig themselves into watery emplacements, ever ready to leap forward into action. Minutes would count vitally when— if and when—the Spaniards emerged. Hours, days, weeks must be toiled through without relaxation, to avoid the possible loss of a single one of those precious minutes.

The ships were organized into two divisions, led, of

course, by the *New York* and *Brooklyn,* respectively. The
Iowa was happily in the *New York's* group. She was always the keystone of the arch, lying directly opposite the
harbour entrance, so that, no matter in which direction he
might flee, Cervera would be unable to elude Fighting Bob
and our premier battleship.

The blockade was indeed close. At first the radius of
the arc was six miles; later it was reduced to four. A
sortie under cloak of darkness was what Sampson dreaded
most, and, instead of withdrawing his capital ships at night
to frustrate torpedo attack, he actually moved them nearer
the entrance and the hill-crowning forts. The reputedly
swift black squadron might conceivably steal down the hidden channel some moonless night with lights out and rush
east or west against the inky cliffs, either escaping or jumping into a lead that would be difficult or impossible for the
lumbering American battleships to overcome. Of the
eventual destruction of the Spanish fleet, Sampson entertained no doubts, but he was disinclined to accord the opportunity for any glorious Castilian swan song in the form of
the bombardment of an Atlantic seaport. Cervera had
chosen Santiago; that was where Sampson now intended him
to fight or submit.

This possible night crisis demanded the Admiral's most
resourceful counter-measures. He made one of his great,
aggressive decisions when he issued the famous searchlight
order. At Jutland, Admiral Jellicoe withdrew his superior
fleet during the night because of his dread of German torpedo attack. Sampson weighed this risk, realized its gravity,
and assumed it. Each night, the *Iowa, Oregon* and *Massachusetts* took turns lying within two short miles of the
formidable Morro, and, by their powerful searchlights,
making the narrow channel as bright as Broadway. So
effective was this illumination that Cervera abandoned all
further thought of selecting the night for his venture. The
broad sunlight was less inimical to his purpose than those

glaring beams that stripped every vestige of surprise from any move in the lower reaches of the bay and rendered it impossible to steer a vessel into their blinding brilliance.

These bold tactics of Sampson were in courageous defiance of the orthodox doctrine of the period, and, naturally, were to Evans' fancy because of their sheer audacity. He was proud to be the first captain to perform the searchlight duty. The light had to steadily flood the channel, and yet never disclose the intervening American picket-boats. This required the most precise training of the lamps and was no easy task on a heaving ocean. It demanded a nicety suited to the placidity of a duck-pond, and no one has ever accused the open Caribbean, upon which Schley said he could not coal ship, of simulating a duck-pond. Yet the duty was performed as directed.

In speaking of it later, Evans called it "the hardest work" he ever performed.

"Imagine," he graphically challenged, "a black, dark night, not a light anywhere to be seen, except the searchlight beam of the ship in position, ugly cross-currents and frequently a heavy swell to contend with, two auxiliaries inshore of you, one on either side of the searchlight beam, inshore of them three picket-boats close under the enemy's battery, and, inshore of them still, rapid-fire guns and Mausers without end, ready to open on the first American thing made visible by an unsteady hand at your searchlight. To run in and take this position, and not to disclose the position of any of your friends, was the work we had to do every night, and there we had to stay, holding our position, frequently within one hundred yards of the beach, for three hours every night for thiry-five nights."

For a month this vigil endured. Admiral Sampson and his staff held the blockading line under constant observation. Any ship out of position or headed other than toward the entrance received by flag hoist or blinker a rebuke that promptly eliminated the discrepancy between the fact and the diagram. That arc of steel was required to stand intact and without a blemish. It was always Admiral's inspection. The *Iowa's* only break in the monotonous grind was one trip to refuel at Guantanamo. This large, protected bay to the eastward had been seized by the Navy as a coaling depot, and is to this day, by virtue of a lease from the Cuban Government, one of the main bases of the American fleet. The strain of this month was severe. For Evans and the other captains there was no rest.

On June sixth, Sampson delivered a bombardment of the forts. As at San Juan, his purpose was chiefly to feel out the defences and test the morale of both his own bluejackets and the Spanish garrisons. Evans was eager to give his men as much experience under fire as possible, especially as he was assimilating in his complement a number of reserves who had not heard the whistle of shells at Porto Rico.

The *Iowa* steamed at one end of the two columns and had some valuable target practise. The manœuvring of the attacking ships, however, did not run smoothly at the outset but it improved as the exercise continued. Little damage was done to the fortifications although to the garrisons the fire was a terrible ordeal, which they felt certain surpassed in horror the greatest previous naval bombardments in history. When the *Iowa* resumed her station in the reformed blockading line, every man jack aboard felt himself a salty sea fighter.

The long June tropical days lazily followed one another in torrid succession, and, by the languor of their mood, mocked the strenuous activity aboard the American ships. Cervera made no move. Perhaps he would never emerge. To the men who maintained it, the blockade seemed to have lasted for years—and in an era before the earth cooled. It became the exacting normality. All hands yearned for a release from the tension. The obvious means was by the awaited fight. Formerly they had wondered when; now they began to wonder if.

Sampson's plan of using troops to seize the terrain back of the channel, scour the latter, and file through with his ships, directed the attention of the Navy toward the activities of the Army's expeditionary force, which the former had escorted to and disembarked at Siboney, east of Santiago. Infantry, dismounted cavalry, engineers, artillery, regulars, militia and volunteers; white and black; thousands of these fellows had been ferried around from Tampa. Woolen uniforms, foul canned food and loose organization at the concentration camps had imposed burdens not properly a part of soldiering. They were as eager to see action as was the Navy, and they welcomed the feel of Cuba underfoot. Slowly they crawled through the dense brush and climbed the coastal range. Magnificently they fought the bloody battles of El Caney and San Juan Hill, making their own heroes and paying dearly for every mile taken. It was a roasting advance under fatiguing exotic conditions but, by the end of June, Santiago lay almost within General Shafter's grasp. He, however, was unaware of the weakness of the enemy and was almost persuaded by his own difficulties to retire to a stronger position, as retreating is usually called. A man in the sixties, of enormous bulk, accustomed to a temperate climate, he found it impossible to readjust himself to the maddening heat and the unwholesome jungle of the rainy season. The achievements of the Army had been due to the highly skilled excellence of the regulars and the intrepid aggressiveness of the volunteers rather than to any distinction of supreme leadership. We suffered the inevitable penalty for having had no campaign plans or Army Staff. Only the fortunate absence of more determined opposition saved from exposure the War Department's ineptitude and wretched unpreparedness—an exposure that would have been far less of a reflection upon the Department itself than upon the members of Congress and their constituents.

Theodore Roosevelt, serving under General Shafter with the Rough Riders, declared that "The two striking facts in the war with Spain were the preparedness of the navy and the unpreparedness of the army."

The heroic task of the soldiers in Cuba was rendered even more onerous and dangerous than necessary by the outrageous lack of foresight on the part of the Army in having despatched them to the midsummer tropics, equipped in a manner suitable to a Redskin campaign on the North-west plains, and without any intelligent provision for the maintenance of sanitary field conditions. In marked and damning contrast, the Navy had landed its force at Guantanamo so well prepared to cope with the guerilla war-fare and equally hostile and more insidious disease germs, that, at the conclusion of the successful operation, every man returned alive to his ship and a scant two per cent had been wounded or ill.

Sampson was doing everything within his power to coöperate with the sister service ashore, but the latter failed to keep him properly informed of developments and dis-coveries, as well as in other respects. The joint operations were not effectively handled by the Army, which had had no training along those lines, whereas the Navy was not only incomparably more efficient generally but was accus-tomed to working with landing parties.

While Sampson was anxiously awaiting the reduction of the fortifications and the sweeping of the channel, Shafter began to lose his singleness of purpose, an almost fatal weakness in any military commander. As though it were a bright and original idea, he suggested and then urged that the fleet be ordered to smash its way into the harbour through the uncleared channel and thus open the city to the Army! He seemed to forget the reason for his expedition,

and why he was at Santiago rather than at Havana or elsewhere, and why he had been sent down before the end of the
rainy season, when the malignant fevers were rife. Had it
been prudent for Sampson to crash the entrance, he would
have done so long before the soldiers arrived, and had the
attempt been successful, the Army would have been required only as Dewey needed its aid, to occupy Manila after
the enemy fleet had been sunk.

Shafter's mission, to aid in the destruction of Cervera's
fleet by the capture of the gateway forts and the opening of
the channel to the fleet, was somehow lost sight of by the
General in the mazes of the bewildering thickets. He sent
his troops inland, and hurled them against the Spanish
block-houses and entrenchments, that dominated the high
ground back of the city. The frightful casualties, for which
he had not been emotionally prepared, seemed to prey upon
his mind, as the leaden tropical climate weighed down his
spirits and impaired his health. With a record as distinguished as Cervera's, he was equally unable to respond
to the demands of this strenuous duty at his time of life.

The heavy losses were not bringing the American fleet
one inch nearer to the Spanish, and that was what irked.
The channel was still clogged with its mines, and the guard-
ian forts stood undemolished. The city itself, furthermore,
which by some unaccountable mutation in Shafter's mind
had suddenly become his objective, showed no signs of falling. As many of the junior Army officers pointed out had
been the case in all Spanish military history, the enemy
offered little resistance until behind some works but, once
there, held as at Saragossa. Down through the jungle
trails to the low land near the beach, where headquarters had
been established, came the depressing trains of wounded and
tallies of dead. Shafter, himself ill, had little stomach for
this sanguinary business and was "seriously considering"
having his advance skirmish lines fall back from the subur-
ban heights, nearer to his base. The younger officers pro-

tested, and the Department discouraged any such withdrawal, in terms that in effect constituted a flat veto of the suggestion.

Shafter then turned in desperation to the Navy and once more besought Sampson to batter his way through the narrows. The Admiral was a model of patience. He was most eager to be helpful and was characteristically tolerant of the cracking of the General's nerves beneath the tenebrous gloom of the death-filled forest. It occurred to him to follow the example of Admiral Porter at Fort Fisher and inspire the faltering Army leader by naval coöperation *ashore,* in the Army's own element. He would land his marines to assault the west cape and seize the Socapa battery, if only Shafter would return to the main objective and vigorously attack the Morro side of the entrance. This was not theoretically efficient, as the marines were integral parts of the ship's complements and would be needed in any naval engagement, but Shafter's drooping morale made the plan practical.

To formulate the details of this proposed joint operation on land, Sampson considered it imperative to confer with Shafter. He sent Captain Chadwick of the *New York,* Chief of Staff, to Siboney on July second to arrange the meeting for the following morning. The General was by this time physically unable to board a ship or even travel the few miles to the beach at Siboney, so the Admiral was to call at Army headquarters. Loath as was the latter to leave the blockading line for even the few hours necessary to make this trip, he realized the importance—the paramount importance—of seeing Shafter face to face and diplomatically pointing the Army at the proper objective with the requisite vigour of command.

Events were obviously moving toward the climax, but Cervera alone knew how rapidly. His black ships were white elephants at Santiago, despite the guns and men landed to aid the soldiers in the defence of the beleaguered city. The food their crews ate was naturally begrudged by the starving inhabitants, and, most of all, their presence was resented because it had attracted the American expeditionary force and occasioned the tight blockade. The squadron, for whose arrival in May the loyal elements of the populace had prayed, was now regarded by all as a pestilential breeder of woe, whose departure would be more than welcome.

Cervera and his captains knew that a sortie was thoroughly inadvisable. It would involve the recall of the landing parties and thus hasten the collapse of the city. It offered little promise of escape to any of the ships, and even escape meant only refuge in another harbour, where the Santiago situation would be duplicated and the agony merely prolonged. Cervera volunteered to sally forth under any other officer named to supersede him, regardless of rank, but he firmly refused to accept the responsibility for the "hecatomb." In letters distinguished by lucidity and grace, he stated the reasons. The authorities, however, did not want to understand. They preferred a wild gamble and a dramatic harikiri of the fleet to a colourless surrender.

At his own request, Captain-General Blanco at Havana was placed in supreme control of naval as well as military forces in Cuba, and Cervera passed under his command. Blanco was an army man and chose to minimize the technical as well as the tactical objections to the sortie. That many rounds of the ammunition were defective, that the foul bottom of the *Viscaya* reduced her speed considerably, that the *Colon* lacked her main battery, that the *Oquendo's* and *Teresa's* rapid-fire guns were partially unserviceable, made as little impression upon him as did the scant likelihood of the blockade being penetrable.

As conditions at Santiago became more acute, Blanco's hesitation to overrule Cervera was being gradually mastered by the former's inclination. At this critical juncture in the formulation of his decision, there came the unexpected approval by a naval expert of the plan Blanco wanted to believe feasible.

The Germans were almost openly sympathetic to the Spanish cause, and the Captain of their cruiser *Geier,* snooping along the Cuban coast to prove the illegality of our blockade and now at Havana, gave freely if not wisely of his counsel to the Captain-General. The German officer boasted that, in Cervera's place, he would dauntlessly steam out of the harbour and break through the American squadron to safety. In fact, this side-line hero had several schemes for accomplishing this feat by day or by night.

These were honeyed words. Cervera was politely but positively ordered to leave Santiago. At daybreak of July second he so informed his captains. The valiant Bustamente was dying of his wounds in a Santiago hospital, and Captain Concas of the *Maria Teresa* assumed the additional duties of Chief of Staff. The landing parties were recalled from the trenches, and four o'clock that afternoon was set as the zero hour. The men from the *Vizcaya,* however, did not return until just about that time and were completely exhausted by their soldiering, so the departure was postponed until the following morning.

During the day, Admiral Sampson terrified the city by unleashing another bombardment in aid of Shafter's offensive, that disclosed the ominous fact that the unseen ships could pulverize the buildings of Santiago at will.

Evans was now becoming convinced that the enemy would not come out. He correctly appraised Cervera's judgment, but he was not aware that that judgment no longer guided the Spanish fleet. That night he watched the burning of the block-houses on the hill crests around the city, presaging its fall. The sunset over the sea to the west and these fires on the summits to the north made a striking panorama.

The tropical air was unmoved by any breeze. Flags

drooped and smoke ascended in perpendicular lines. The *Iowa* had the first searchlight duty and, as she closed in to perform it, the Officer of the Deck pointed out to the Captain six columns of smoke against the darkening sky behind Socapa. The latter frankly admitted that he did not regard this as indicative of any unusual activity of the Spanish warships—they often moved about the inner basin. His quartermaster, however, was of a different mind. Venturing no unsolicited comment, he quietly plucked three code flags from the bag, and he bent on a halliard, ready to hoist, the signal "Enemy ships coming out." The flags remained so all night and saved a few of the decisive seconds when the great occasion finally arrived.

The last searchlight watch that night was the *Massachusetts'* and, when at daybreak she extinguished her lamps and receded from her station, it was to stand eastward toward Guantanamo for coal. One of her boats on picket duty was left behind and came alongside of the *Iowa*. It was in charge of Naval Cadet Franck Taylor Evans and, after a snatch of sleep, he breakfasted in the *Iowa's* cabin with his father.

During the night the Spaniards without detection removed the mines from the channel.

July third was a perfect tropical day with a faint haze at dawn that soon gave way to high visibility and sharp horizons. At about seven o'clock, Captain Concas crept down the bay in a small gunboat and reconnoitred the entrance. He carefully noted the bearings and distances of the American ships and the absence of the powerful *Massachusetts*. The blockading wall to the eastward was forbiddingly solid, but between the *Texas* to the southwestward and the western shore there were only the *Brooklyn*, well out, and the little yacht *Vixen*.

Upon the return of Captain Concas all was ready. The flagship would dash at the *Brooklyn*, the rest of the flotilla would endeavour to escape between that mêlée and the coast to the westward, and as many as possible seek to reach Havana or Cienfuegos.

In single column, of course, and at four times the usual cruising intervals, Cervera led forth his fleet. One by one they entered the tortuous channel and gingerly felt their way through its intricacy, first the *Maria Teresa,* then the *Vizcaya, Colon* and *Oquendo,* followed by the destroyers, *Pluton* and *Furor.* From the *Teresa's* first appearance until the clearing of the last unit there elapsed twelve minutes.

As the flagship made the forty-five degree turn at Diamond Bank and, with battle flags flying majestically, steamed through the portal formed by the Morro and Socapa, the order was given to open fire. There was a flourish on the bugles and the forward turret rendered the overture. American shells were already showering about the vessel, and overhead the Spanish fortresses were roaring their support. The battle was on.

Captain Concas turned to his revered Admiral and said: "Poor Spain."

The latter, speechless, made a gesture of submission to higher authority.

Then they settled down to the desperate task at hand.

On this particular morning, the blockading line, in its usual arc from east to west, consisted of the yacht *Gloucester* nearest the eastern shore, about three miles from the entrance, then the *Indiana, New York, Oregon, Iowa* due south of the entrance, *Texas, Brooklyn* and *Vixen* near the western shore. At eight fifty the *New York* flew the signal: "Disregard movements of Commander-in-Chief" and hauled off to the eastward to fulfill Admiral Sampson's appointment with General Shafter. The *Indiana* edged over toward the place thus left vacant, to equalize the gaps between ships.

As for a month past, the fleet was all eyes on the entrance. The Brethren of the Brood were faithfully on guard. What a stake Mrs. Evans had in that line! Her beloved Bob at the pivotal post in the ace of our battleships, her brother Harry commanding the mighty *Indiana*, and her only son aboard his father's ship!

Bob Evans knew his comrades. Besides Harry Taylor there were Jack Philip in the *Texas* on his port hand and Charlie Clark in the *Oregon* on his starboard. It was almost like that Annapolis night in *Old Ironsides*, when these same fellows had stood ready to fire on Ben Butler's ferry-boat.

Admiral Cervera estimated the American preponderance of strength at three or more to one. He reckoned with tons and calibres. They spelled defeat. The columns of statistics said nothing of the Brood. That spelled annihilation.

20

THE BATTLE OF SANTIAGO

To her everlasting regret, the *Massachusetts* was far beyond the horizon, and the *New York* was nearing Siboney but within signal distance, when, at nine thirty-one, while he was proudly watching Taylor struggle with a he-man's cigar after breakfast, there burst upon Bob Evans the climax of his career.

He was awaiting word that the crew was drawn up for captain's inspection, when the ship resounded with the alarm of general quarters and vibrated with the scattering of six hundred pairs of feet.

No sooner had the black nose of the *Maria Teresa* exposed itself in the green depths of the harbour than the crouching *Iowa* sprang into action. The bent-on signal flags leaped to the yardarm, full-speed ahead was rung up to the engine-room, battle stations were sounded, all at the same instant. Sailors, too hurried for the wrungs of ladders, dropped into compartments below, and others seemed to soar aloft, all stripping to the waist as they dashed, and violating the dead-silence rule of general quarters by spontaneously shouting a welcome to the enemy. The long tension of the blockade had been broken.

"Papa," exclaimed Taylor, "the Spaniards must be coming out!"

Papa seemed to have been bolted from his chair up the cabin hatchway. Ordering Taylor to the division corresponding to his own in the *Massachusetts,* he reached the

bridge as the alert Officer of the Deck was firing the first
shot of the Battle of Santiago.

Off to the left, Jack Philip's *Texas* was excitedly getting
way upon her, and off to the right, the *Bulldog* and Harry
Taylor's *Indiana* were moving forward, but Evans' eyes
were fixed upon the fast-stepping *Infanta,* clearing the entrance and rounding the shoals, with guns flaming and
looking her noblest in fresh black paint, shining brightwork
and resplendent battle flags of red and gold.

It was to be a captain's fight, each ship doing her part
to carry out Sampson's plan, as distinguished from an
action by a fleet operating as a unit.

Admiral Sampson's written instructions had been: "If
the enemy tries to escape, the ships must close and engage
as soon as possible, and endeavour to sink his vessels or
force them to run ashore in the channel."

How Evans prayed for speed! The big-waisted battleship was slipping ahead, but all too ponderously. The engines were straining to overcome the inertia of rest and,
with every revolution of the crank-shafts, accelerating her
advance. It had been impossible for the fleet, so far from
a coaling depot, to maintain throughout the long blockade
a constant full head of steam. Irretrievable minutes would
now unavoidably be lost before the heavy wagon could be
rolled along at even her present maximum gait, which was
far from a cruiser's gallop. The cylinder heads had not
been removed for six months. In addition, the bottom was
covered by a luxuriant forest of barnacles that had accumulated in the warm waters during the seventeen months
since the *Iowa* had last seen a dock and that now retarded
her like a sea-anchor. The impatient skipper yearned for
superhuman strength to pick up this floating Olympus and
throw it at Cervera's head, the while his batteries were fling-
ing at the enemy through the diminishing space their modern bolts of Jupiter. Down below decks in the insufferable
heat, the black gang was stoking coal with the fervour of

fanatics and dripping rivers of sweat. In the turrets and magazines, the half-naked gun crews and ammunition teams were functioning with a dynamic fury.

The *Iowa* was now hurling herself directly at the enemy flagship, with a bone in her teeth, her own salvos drowning the deafening roar of those from the other ships of both flags and from the overhanging fortresses on the shore. She was the projected embodiment of Fighting Bob rampant.

Santiago Bay was at last disgorging its indigestible pills of attempted relief and, as the six of them were spewed forth from the narrows, explosives ruled supreme. The *Teresa* in the van, clear of the shallow bank, veered to the westward, firing at the unaccountably receding *Brooklyn,* which was taking her subsequently famous queer turn to starboard *away* from the enemy, and at the disconcertingly approaching *Iowa,* and scored hits on both. Clouds of powder filled the air. Through one of the rifts, Evans perceived the other three Spanish cruisers also dashing into the open arena of the Caribbean "like mad bulls" and, in accordance with their plan, hugging the shore more closely than was the leader. The Spaniards' salvos were being discharged "with mechanical rapidity," but the more deliberate American fire was under better control.

There is a credible yarn that Bob Evans had made a wager with Captain Higginson of the absent *Massachusetts* as to which of them would first ram one of these enemy warships in the event of a sortie. Certain it is that the former, all too conscious of his limitations of speed, which would count him out of a running fight, had soberly resolved to use the *Iowa's* weight and strength while the usage was possible. In execution of this preconceived plan, he jumped into the conning tower and took personal charge of the wheel. First, he vowed, he would try to ram, then to torpedo and then to make the most of his heavy shells, although, of course, the batteries were blazing away all the time with every gun that could be brought to bear.

The *Iowa's* inferiority of speed was offset by Fighting Bob's fearless pugnacity as, with his orders snapped into the quartermaster's ear, he squinted through the slits in the conning tower between banks of powder smoke and held his course straight towards the enemy's.

"I kept the *Maria Teresa* open on my starboard bow, so that the guns could have a chance at her, until it became evident that I could not ram her or even get within torpedo range, when I swung off to port, gave her the full benefit of my starboard broadside, and then swung back quickly and headed across the bows of the second ship, hoping to be able to reach her with my ram. . . . I soon found that the *Vizcaya* would also pass ahead of me, and that I could not reach her with ram or torpedo. I accordingly swung to port, gave her my broadside, and, as she passed at nineteen hundred yards, put my helm to port and headed in again to try for the next ship."

Perhaps there flashed through Evans' mind that sentence in Nelson's battle memorandum at Trafalgar:

". . . no Captain can do very wrong if he places his ship alongside that of an enemy."

Despite their impairments, however, these three swift cruisers were not to be intercepted by the lumbering battleship on their flank. The *Colon,* like her two predecessors, eluded the *Iowa's* itching ram, and Evans appreciated the futility of trying to reach the *Oquendo,* last of the quartet, and the probability that to attempt such a manœuvre would draw him out of range. Reluctantly he reconciled himself to a gunnery duel. There was the compensating satisfaction in now feeling warranted in entrusting the steering to a subordinate and thus being able to command his *Iowa* from the unconfined freedom of the open bridge. In peace-times he enunciated the dictum that "every battleship should be fought from her conning tower," but in the heat of the combat he refused to be pent up within its crowded protection.

The head-on thrusts had now brought the *Iowa* nearest of all of the American ships to the enemy column. Her broadside straddled the passing vessels and, although the percentage of direct hits was not high, according to later-day standards, the big guns were making themselves felt. "The sides of the cruisers," noted Evans, "were just thick enough to explode our common shells with the most disastrous effect to the gun's crews of the Spanish ships." Adequate armor belting had been sacrificed by the constructors of the cruisers for added speed.

As the *Iowa* drew closer to the *Maria Teresa*, the former's giant twelve-inchers not only smashed into the latter's vital organs but also interfered with her return fire. In his official report, Captain Clark of the *Oregon* commented upon this important work of the *Iowa* at that crucial stage of the battle: "For a short time there was an almost continuous flight of projectiles over this ship, but when our line was fairly engaged, and the *Iowa* had made a swift advance as if to ram or close, the enemy's fire became defective in train as well as in range."

Structural defects in a man-of-war have a catastrophic habit of manifesting themselves in battle. As, at Jutland, the thinly protected handling rooms and magazines caused the loss of the *Indefatigable* and *Queen Mary* within a few minutes of each other, so at Santiago the wooden upper decks, lacking steel reënforcement, of the three Spanish-built sister ships doomed them to destruction. The *Colon* alone was fairly well safeguarded and, having also the highest actual speed when the real test came, was the longest to survive under the American barrage. The decks of each of the others quickly caught fire and there was no way to prolong the combatant lives of the ships. The *New York's* hand-carved woodwork, which had won great praise at Kiel, and all the other timber products in the American fleet, had been ruthlessly cut out and jettisoned when, upon the outbreak of hostilities, the ships had stripped for action. All but a very few boats apiece had been discarded by the ships at Key West so that they could do no harm by splintering or burning. Everything inflammable, excepting only articles of absolute military necessity, was taboo. Unfortunately for the Spaniards, the decks of the cruisers could not be chopped away from under their feet, and there was nothing to do but curse the landlubber designers. That provided no fire-proofing.

As the *Colon* raced by, she smacked the *Iowa* twice in rapid succession, almost offering ironic proof, because of where the shells struck, of the soundness of the Captain's theory that his place was behind thick armour. "The first shell she fired at us, through a rent in the smoke, struck on the starboard side a little forward of the bridge, about four feet above the water line, passed through the cellulose belt, and exploded on the berth deck, demolishing the dispensary, breaking almost every medicine bottle in it, and doing great damage otherwise. The smells that came up in consequence of this explosion were variegated and intense, a mixture of medicine and mellinite." The second shell did not explode but "made an ugly, jagged hole, eighteen inches long and eight inches wide, through which the water poured with great rapidity."

The leak was plugged up and each hit only stung the *Iowa* into increased frenzy of attack. Several times more she was struck, and once a fire was started in the berth deck but quickly extinguished. In his official report, Sampson declared that, while the *Brooklyn* had been struck more often than any of the other American ships, the greatest material injury had been done to the *Iowa*. This was not enough, however, to interfere with her battle effectiveness. If ever

there was a hard-hitting, hard-fighting man-of-war, it was
the embattled *Iowa* at this stage of the engagement.

Now, as the *Colon* pulled ahead, Evans concentrated his
crushing broadsides on the *Oquendo*, which was also under
the fire of several of the other American ships and bravely
taking terrific punishment. Once Evans thought she was
sinking and about to haul down her flag, "but she pluckily
held on her course" and "fairly smothered" the *Iowa* "with
a shower of shells and machine-gun shots."

The fighting was now at its hottest, at point-blank range,
and for twenty long minutes and until the fate of the
Teresa and *Oquendo* was sealed, the *Iowa* was in the thick-
est of it. It was during this period that she fired most of
the twelve hundred and seventy-three shots that constituted
her day's total. The recoil of one discharge was followed
as quickly as humanly possible by the loading and accurate
firing of the next. This was the time when the endless
drilling scored. And below, feeding the ravenous furnaces,
the shovels fairly flew as the hull shook with the rhythmic
salvos.

Cervera's pessimism was being vindicated. His best
plan was proving inadequate. The attempt to squeeze the
Vizcaya, Colon and *Oquendo* between the *Brooklyn* and the
shore was not meeting with success. Employing a rough
analogy to football, the Spanish flagship was supposed to
act as "interference" and "take out" the *Brooklyn*. The
American left-end—the light *Vixen*—was to be "sucked in"
or overcome by sheer momentum. (As a matter of fact,
she deliberately took station seaward of the American battleships.) There would be no secondary defence to worry
about, and the martyred *Teresa* had hoped to see her three
comrades escaping through the gap to the westward, leaving the slower American pursuers astern. The play broke
down, however, before it was fairly started, because the
stocky forward defence line charged it off its feet. Possibly
the decisive factor in the upset was the uncalculated thrust

of the *Iowa* which, while failing to throw any adversary by ramming, spilled the formation and demoralized the attack, as Captain Clark recognized. The *Brooklyn*, furthermore, overcoming the handicap of her "incomprehensible" turn away from the Spaniards, soon swung into effective action at high speed, and, with the powerful aid of the *Oregon*, forced the *Vizcaya* and then the *Colon* out of bounds, after the *Teresa* and *Oquendo* had been eliminated.

The *Maria Teresa*, first out of the harbour and longest under bombardment, for a while presenting herself as the sole Spanish target, was the earliest unit to succumb. Runing toward the westerly American ships to execute her assignment as "interference" for the rest of the squadron, she came under that barrage from the *Oregon, Iowa* and *Texas* that made the very sky seem to rain shot and shell. Many of the explosions aboard ignited portions of the deck and, when a projectile from the *Iowa* severed the fire main, the flames took possession of the ship. She was soon a pyre. Six and a half miles and forty-five minutes of the freedom of the seas proved to be her allotment. Frantically she dove through the surf to avoid sinking in deep water, and she beached what was left of her. Cervera's nightmare of a "hecatomb" had quickly become a reality.

A thousand yards further along, the equally distraught *Oquendo* also tried in her death struggle to turn amphibian. Half of the proud cruiser squadron had now been disposed of.

During the final hot engagement with the *Oquendo*, Evans was shocked to behold a young midshipman improving an interlude in his duties by standing on the roof of the forward turret, with machine gun bullets whizzing about him, calmly focussing a camera on the enemy cruiser. The skipper for a second was dumbfounded at this exhibition of recklessness, but his very admiration for the lad's intrepidity increased his indignation at such unnecessary exposure. "I think he got his snapshot," said the Captain

later, with a twinkle in his eye, "and he will probably remember for many years to come the few words I addressed
to him." We can safely guess that the photographer recognized in the "old man" a master of the art of terse admoni-
tion, and felt just a bit proud of being rebuked by Fighting
Bob himself for recklessness under fire.

Coming abeam of these wrecks, Evans discerned a white
flag fluttering feebly above the Spanish flagship, and he
signalled the surrender to his comrades so that they could
devote their undivided attention to the fast fleeing *Vizcaya*
and *Colon*. The *Vizcaya* soon followed her sister-ships on
the shore, leaving afloat only the *Colon*, desperately breaking to the westward with the *Brooklyn, Texas* and *Bulldog*
barking on her port quarter.

The *Oregon* was ploughing through the water at a
speed that showed complete disrespect for her rated maximum. Wildly she overtook the *Iowa* and *Texas* and now
had the presumption to steam neck and neck with the fleet-
footed *Brooklyn,* just as if she possessed the celerity of a
cruiser, with the battery and armour plating of a battleship.
The *Bulldog* was sinking her relentless jaws into the stern
of the *Colon* and could not be shaken off. Observers,
American and Spanish alike, were amazed at this spectacle
of the impossible. The *Colon,* on the other hand, was unable to extract from the engines her contract speed or even
continue at her initial rate, and the deficiency was proving
fatal as ominous splashes ahead announced the coming
within range of the pursuing Americans. Evans was drop-
ing back in the chase, but he correctly gauged the situation
and felt no anxiety as to the possible escape of the *Colon*.
His one regret was the *Iowa's* inability to be in at the death.

Cervera had directed the destroyers to take station inshore of the cruisers, on the latter's disengaged beam, and
make off as well as they could. The *Pluton* and *Furor*,
however, had not been able to get very far from the harbour entrance, one running on the rocks and the other

being sunk. To the gallant *Gloucester* (the converted Morgan yacht *Corsair*) must go the chief credit for this portion of the victory. Utterly unprotected, she lay at the mouth of the narrows as the cruisers emerged, waiting for her particular prey. When they appeared, she lunged at the more powerfully armed torpedo boats with a fusillade that swept them off their balance. Her Captain was Lieutenant Commander Wainwright, formerly Executive Officer of the *Maine*. The *Gloucester* was solidly supported by the *Indiana*, which had been unable to get up speed quickly enough to cross over from her station at the eastern end of the blockading line to the westward track of the Spanish cruisers. While Evans was engaging the *Teresa* and *Oquendo* with his main battery, he was effectively employing his rapid-fire guns against the Spanish destroyers and hastening their demolition. The *Iowa* was firing projectiles from every muzzle that would bear.

"In the heat of the action," said Evans, "several men were blown away from the 6-pounders by the blasts from the 12-inch gun. They were back at their stations in a moment, and several were blown away a second time. . . ."

Evans was still in the conning tower when, through a peep-hole, he saw the Spanish destroyers gasping their last. Above the din of the cannonading came the familiar voice of a boatswain's mate on the superstructure deck: "Now boys, mind them torpedo boats; give 'em hell for the *Maine!*" and the clear interjection of the division officer: "Steady, there; don't waste your ammunition!" The *Furor* and *Pluton* obviously were done for, and further firing at them might have resulted only in striking the *Gloucester*.

Evans was now opposite the grounded *Viscaya*, eighteen miles west of Santiago, and he realized that, with the *Colon* a smudge of smoke on the horizon, his work of destruction was done. Thereupon he plunged with unabated energy into the hazardous task of rescuing as many Spaniards as possible from the exploding wreck and the waters around it. The *Iowa's* men below decks, grimy and sweaty and forgetting their exhaustion in the exhilaration of the battle, whose progress had been dramatically shouted down the hatchways, much as it would be broadcast by radio to-day, clambered aloft for a breath of air and a glimpse of the spectacle. Out of the stuffy turrets squirmed the cramped gun crews. All hands responded nobly to the Captain's orders to lower away the few boats and save the survivors of the *Vizcaya*. His report of the battle was concluded with a memorable paragraph inspired by this incident: "I cannot express my admiration for my magnificent crew. So long as the enemy showed his flag they fought like American seamen; but when the flag came down they were as gentle and tender as American women."

At about this hour (eleven thirty) the *New York* came steaming along inshore under forced draught, and her position in the wake of the *Colon* was a guarantee that the lone surviving enemy ship could neither safely double on her course nor escape by a sudden dash to the southeast. Evans knew what his old cruiser could do in the way of speed, when properly aroused.

He was standing at the stern of the *Iowa* as the *New York* passed between her and the *Vizcaya*. Those of his officers and crew not engaged in the rescue work were massed over turret-tops, superstructures and decks white with saltpetre from the guns, the men hardly recognizable after their morning's work as the spotless complement of Sunday quarters. When they espied Admiral Sampson on the bridge of the flagship, they emitted a thunderous roar, reminiscent of that April day when the fleet left Key West. Then it had been a cheer of encouragement and support to their former skipper, just elevated to supreme command; now it was the ecstatic tribute for the job well done. The

Admiral was as serene in victory as he had been at the outset of the campaign.

When the din subsided Captain Chadwick reached for his megaphone and, on behalf of the Commander-in-Chief, inquired as to the *Iowa's* casualties. "Not a man hurt," called back Captain Evans. The astonishment of those aboard the *New York* may be imagined. They could hardly believe their ears, after what their eyes had seen.

The Admiral was deeply impressed by the rescue operations, which he later characterized as "the occasion of some of the most daring and gallant conduct of the day." The nature of the difficulties involved, he reported to the Department: "The ships were burning fore and aft, their guns and reserve ammunition were exploding and it was not known at what moment the fire would reach the main magazines. In addition to this a heavy surf was running just inside the Spanish ships. But no risk deterred our officers and men until their work of humanity was complete."

Sampson sped on after the *Colon* and ordered the *Iowa,* as he had the *Indiana,* to resume her blockading station, taking no chances of any additional ships sneaking out of Santiago. Aside from the decrepit *Reina Mercedes* and a few other inconsequential craft, there happened to be no more that could come out, but this precaution on Sampson's part was in line with his unflagging thoroughness.

The *Colon* ran forty-eight miles from the Morro before her strength was spent and her spirit of defiance broken. Not nearly so badly damaged as had been her comrades, their destruction and the baying of the American hounds at her tail broke her morale, and she too took refuge in the shoals that all her life she had been vigilant to avoid. The *Brooklyn, Oregon, Texas* and *New York* were there at the finish and took off her crew. Less than four hours, the duration of a watch at sea, had elapsed since the *Infanta Marie Teresa* had first been sighted by the *Iowa.*

The *Brooklyn* reported the death of a petty officer and one injury. These were, in fact, the only casualties in the fleet. The miracle of Manila Bay had been almost duplicated. The Spaniards lost about six hundred men out of some two thousand engaged, and only the skilful and heroic efforts of the Americans prevented much longer lists of missing.

Before returning to Santiago, Evans completed his work of human salvage in and about the *Viscaya*. Deeply moved by the pathos of the situation, he quite forgot for the time being the glory of his own arms. That he had brilliantly met the crisis of his half century of life was a small matter in the face of the tragedy being enacted before him, as the dead and wounded "were tenderly lifted over the side and handled by the men who, half an hour before, were anxious to kill them all."

This was a day of superlatives in Evans' life. Probably the nadir of atrocity in the wide reaches of his experience was plumbed by what he saw around the *Viscaya*. That proud greyhound of the deep, which recently had represented her nation at *New York,* was pouring her complement over the shattered decks and through the bursting sides into the débris-filled water below. The *Iowa's* boats were hauling over their gunwales every survivor they could pluck from the inferno. Some of Evans' bluejackets actually carried their rescue work onto the burning ship herself. While the Americans were thus saving Spanish lives at the risk of their own, a rattle of musketry was heard from the beach. Cuban insurgents had slunk through the brush and were shooting at the many Spaniards who had taken refuge upon a sand-bar between the *Viscaya* and the shore. It was an exhibition of revolting brutality that shocked the saltiest of the *Iowa's* tars. Were these people worth liberating? To complete the ring of peril about these shipwrecked unfortunates, a terrifying phalanx of triangles began to close upon them from seaward. Evans attributed this quick gathering of the sharks to the blood of the wounded in the water. Whatever the cause, a school of these monsters savagely attacked the harried swimmers and gave the final touch of horror to the situation. It was easier to forgive the carnivorous fish than the cowardly Cuban snipers.

Captain Eulate of the *Vizcaya,* bleeding from three wounds and with a crude bandage about his head, had to be hoisted aboard in a chair. He was received not only with every consideration for his condition but also with the honours due his rank. Captain Evans brushed aside the proferred sword and, instead, warmly grasped the hand that held it, while the *Iowa's* men, "crowded aft about the deck and superstructure, . . . cheered until I felt ashamed of myself." Gently placing his arm around his eminent prisoner, Evans assisted him to the cabin, where the ship's surgeons dressed the wounds.

As they were about to step over the hatch combing, Captain Eulate cast a parting glance at his old ship and, "drawing himself up to his full height, with his right arm extended above his head, exclaimed, 'Adios, *Vizcaya!'* Just as the words passed his lips the forward magazine of his late command, as if arranged for the purpose, exploded with magnificent effect." The smoke and débris attained an altitude that seemed as great as the summit of the Cuban hills and was observed at a distance of fifteen miles. Fortunately, none of the life-savers was caught within range of the destructive blast. The perilous business of rescue was completed without an injury to the *Iowa's* men, and a surprisingly large percentage of the *Vizcaya's* crew was snatched from the Cuban snipers and the sharks.

About three hundred Spaniards were taken aboard, a few dead, some thirty-two wounded, and the rest just thoroughly miserable. The dead were buried with the same funeral ceremonies prescribed for Americans of corresponding rank, the prayers being read by one of their own rescued padres and their bodies draped in the flag of the country to which they had given their lives. The wounded were treated by the surgeons with the greatest kindness. The unhurt majority were clothed, fed and regaled with coffee and, in the case of the officers, the finest champagne that the wine chest afforded. Their hosts, however, did not join in the wine sipping. They hoped, in inoffensive and ungloating privacy, to splice the main brace over the victory later. For the time being, they merely cleaned up and stood by, ready for whatever the balance of this eventful day might bring forth.

At twelve thirty, while the chase of the *Colon* was proceeding far to the westward, there was a flush of renewed excitement outside of Santiago. Army transports from the fleet off Siboney were observed scattering in all directions, with smoke pouring from their funnels. The *Resolute* came within hail of the *Indiana* and shouted that a Spanish battleship was about to pounce on these unescorted vessels, which were fleeing like squabs before a hawk. The *Harvard* followed the *Resolute* and confirmed this report. Harry Taylor was sceptical but he was also cautious. With one eye still on the harbour mouth, he again cleared for action and swung towards the source of the terror. A strange man-of-war was indeed climbing the horizon.

The *Resolute* and *Harvard,* galloping on like Paul Reveres to spread the alarm, met the *Iowa.* Evans at first regarded their noisy whistling and their flag hoists as salutations for the victory, but, as they drew closer, he read the signal and grasped the situation. The transports were frantically disappearing in the direction of distant Jamaica (and some never stopped until they reached there). Bob Evans was no less dubious than had been his canny brother-in-law as to the possibility of any Spanish battleship lurking in the vicinity, but Captain Cotton of the *Harvard* was positive in his assurance that the stranger's colours had been those of Spain. Impatient at the *Indiana's* phlegmatic re-action to the tocsin he had sounded, Cotton warned Evans in a tone of the deepest anxiety: "Bob, he has fooled Taylor; don't let him fool you."

The latter, although "confident that there was no Spanish battleship anywhere to the eastward short of the coast of Spain," placed his prisoners upon pledged parole in charge of Captain Eulate, assigned them to places of safety in the event of an engagement, and once more dug his spurs into the sides of the *Iowa*. The call to general quarters revived the weary sailors, who ran to their stations "cheering wildly at the prospect of having a Spanish battleship all to them-selves"—or even of sharing her with the *Indiana*.

Rapidly closing on opposite courses, the ships soon showed up distinctly in each other's binoculars. Sure enough, the stranger was a large warship, and the best pairs of eyes on the *Iowa's* bridge avowed that her flag was indeed Spanish. Evans gave orders to open fire at five thousand yards, and the twelve-inch guns in the forward turret were pointed and trained, with the primers ready.

Then the party was spoiled. Evidently sensing a hostile quality in the manner of the American's approach—pos-sibly in the train of the big forward guns—the stranger sig-nalled: "I am an Austrian," and identified herself as the armoured cruiser *Kaiserin Maria Teresa*. By a narrow margin she had averted an untimely end that would have made her the second *Maria Teresa* to have succumbed within a few hours. This one had been performing duty off the Cuban coast similar to that of the German cruiser *Geier*, constantly annoying the Americans by her unfriendly scrutiny of the blockade. Asking permission to enter San-tiago, she was referred to Admiral Sampson and stood toward the west to meet him.

Years later in the Far East, Evans again met this Austrian cruiser, several of whose officers had been aboard her that day off Santiago. Time had erased all hard feeling and the then Rear Admiral delighted in chaffing those fellows about the dangers of trespassing upon a field of battle.

The *Iowa* fell in to the blockading line which, for the preceding little while, had been held by the *Indiana* and the *Gloucester*.   Everything ashore looked the same as during the weeks before the sortie.   There was the now familiar Morro and Socapa, and inside the channel reposed as for weeks past the wreck of the *Merrimac*.

Aboard the *Gloucester* were crowded some of the officers of the Spanish destroyers and of the *Teresa,* including Admiral Cervera himself.   They were transferred to the *Iowa* to await final disposition, the Commander-in-Chief in an ill-fitting civilian suit given to him by Lieutenant, later Rear Admiral, Huse, and personally escorted by Lieutenant Commander Wainwright.

"As the brave old admiral came over the side scantily clad," wrote Evans, "without shirt or hat, yet an admiral every inch of him, the officers saluted, the marines presented arms, and the buglers sounded the salute for an officer of his rank. . . .   The meeting between the late commander-in-chief, who had with him his son, acting as his flag lieutenant, and the commanding officers of the torpedo boats, and Captain Eulate and his men, was touching and pathetic."

There was something symbolic in this meeting of Cervera and Evans, with their respective sons, both of the latter following in their fathers' professional footsteps.   The curtain was being wrung down upon the stirring finale of the tragedy of Cervera, who deserved a more grateful rôle in the pageant of his country than that of valedictorian of its western empire.

Nothing that lay within the power of the victory-humbled Captain could assuage the grief of this Admiral bereaved of his fleet, yet the sympathetic kindness of Bob Evans during these hours of anguish warmed the old gentleman's heart.   The Captain's cabin was turned into Cervera's guest quarters, where fine old Virginia hospitality was extended with unobtrusive understanding. Before the Admiral would accept any attention, however, he visited his wounded sailors in the sick bay and "had a word of comfort and encouragement for each of them."

Evans rigged up a boat awning for the Admiral, and they spent the evening on deck, smoking together and discussing the memorable battle, in much the same spirit as many years later, after the Australian cruiser *Sydney* had sunk the German raider *Emden* off the Cocos Islands and rescued her survivors, their two captains together plotted out the chart of the engagement.

Occasionally the conversation was interrupted by some Spanish or American officer paying his respects to the Admiral.

When Sampson and Bustamente had met the afternoon that the latter brought the news of Hobson's survival, the prospects for Spain's naval success had looked none too bright, but now there remained nothing upon which to fasten the slightest hope. "Poor Spain" indeed.

The *New York* returned after dark and brought the definite confirmation of the *Colon's* destruction. Poetic justice was having a field day. The Italian-built *Colon* had been driven ashore at the mouth of the Tarquino River, at the very place where, in 1873, the Latin-named *Virginius* had been seized by the Spaniards. Fortunately for the *Colon's* survivors, the captured crews of the two ships received markedly different treatment.

Admiral Sampson's first impulse was to pay a call of courtesy upon his respected adversary, but further reflection and the solicited advice of Captain Chadwick persuaded the conqueror that a meeting at such a time might be painful to the vanquished. Sampson abandoned the idea.

At eleven Cervera retired. His work was done. His responsibilities were ended. For the first time in many an anxious watch, there were for him no decisions to make—

no selection of the lesser of two evils. If he could not sleep, he could at least rest. Captain Evans, however, found himself unable to lie down. He was overstimulated by the excitement of the day, and the presence aboard of so many unconfined prisoners caused him some uneasiness. Up and down the topside he paced all night, leaving the deck only to make occasional inquiries as to the comfort of those of the wounded Spanish officers whose pain made them involuntary sharers of the nocturnal vigil.

One young Spanish lieutenant on deck kept moaning that nothing mattered since he had lost his brother, a naval cadet. Later, Evans found a disconsolate lad, little more than a boy, weeping below for his drowned big brother. Gruffly the Captain ordered this latter prisoner to follow him, and the ensuing reunion was one of Evans' most cherished recollections of the war. He left the brothers that night sleeping in one cot in each other's arms.

The unique rhythm of Old Gimpy's uneven stride seemed to weld him uniquely into the affections of his men, as they heard him ever on duty, after the battle as before. How well he had fought the ship, they alone could really appreciate to the full.

Long after the war and long after he had relinquished command of the *Iowa,* when that ship was in the changed atmosphere of peace and in the remote environment of San Francisco, Fighting Bob received a handsome sword accompanied by the following letter:

"U.S.S. Iowa, First Rate,
San Francisco, California, February 14, 1899.
"Captain Robley D. Evans, U.S.N., Washington, D.C. Sir: The members of this ship's company, who had the high honour of serving you from San Juan to Santiago, beg leave to present this sword as a token of our affection and reverence.

"It had been our intention to make this presentation when you relinquished command, but owing to the disintegration of the crew following our arrival at New York in August last, and our hurried departure, it was not done. Coming at this late day, it will show you, sir, that this action is not from momentary impulse, but that the affection and respect of this crew for you is deep-rooted and lasting, and that the men of the battleship *Iowa* will ever cherish the memory of their beloved commander.

"And with this sword we send our wishes for your health and happiness always. It is an assurance from us that you are *more* than a hero to a *nation—you are a hero to your men.*

Very respectfully,

F. ZULCH,

A. E. MOORE,

J. COLLINS, *Chief M.A.A.*

E. McCORMACK,

H. ENELS HOLT,

Committee"

And bearing deep in their memories the spectacle of Captain Eulate's surrender, these sailors of the *Iowa* had engraved upon the sword these imperishable words:

"To our hero—Too just to take a fallen foe's, we give this sword instead."

When writing his *Log,* he characterized that sword as the most highly valued of "my earthly possessions," and on the afternoon that was to be his very last, his daughter saw the retired Admiral, alone in his den, tenderly fingering the gift so pregnant with memories.

The day following the battle, like that after Gettysburg, happened to be the Fourth of July. The usual ceremonies were conducted, but every effort was made to refrain from any undue jubilation that might have offended the sensibilities of the passenger enemies. Congratulations flashed down the cables from Washington. After dinner in the evening, with appropriate honours, Admiral Cervera was ushered over the *Iowa's* side and sent in one of the converted liners to Annapolis, where he wrote to Sampson a

gracious letter of thanks for the attentions he and his subordinates had received since the hour of their misfortune.
The other Spanish officers and men were transshipped from
the *Iowa* at the same time, and Evans was as glad to be free
of the responsibility of entertaining these prisoners aboard
as he had been to disembark the Chilean refugees from the
Yorktown at Callao.

Now he could give his men, in watches, a chance to clean
up and caulk off, but for him there was still no repose.
Under the Navy Regulations it was incumbent upon each
commanding officer to submit to his superior a report of the
engagement. After the last boat load of prisoners had
shoved off, the Captain of the *Iowa* seated himself in his
reoccupied cabin, where privacy again reigned, and wrote
out his report in longhand with great care. So sparing of
words were these sea warriors that the four-page document
of Evans' was one of the longest that Sampson received.
Half of it was devoted to a detailed accounting of the ammunition expended and the hits sustained, and to words of
commendation for his "magnificent crew" in general and
for certain named individuals, who happened to come under
his personal observation, in particular. The narrative of the
Iowa's part in the battle was a concise summary condensed
into the first two pages.

In his report, Commodore Schley said: "I deem it a high
privilege to commend to you, for such action as you may
deem proper, the gallantry and dashing courage, the prompt
decision and the skilful handling of their respective vessels
of Captain Philip, Captain Evans, Captain Clark, and . . .
Captain Cook."

Admiral Sampson, in his recommendations for honours,
included the names of Captain Evans and the other commanding officers, including Captain Higginson of the unfortunately absent *Massachusetts*.

The sons of *Old Ironsides* had brilliantly added to the
glory of her tradition. Admiral Luce was justifiedly proud

of his boys. This was the same old Navy. There were even two Rodgers among those who had acquitted themselves with conspicuous distinction in the battle: Evans' Executive Officer, Raymond P., whose "coolness and judgment," the former's report said, "deserves . . . a proper reward at the hands of the Government," and the *Indiana's* Executive Officer, John A., the only officer cited by name in Captain Taylor's report.

Toward midnight of this Fourth of July, there were hostile fireworks and Evans watched a display similar to that which had greeted the *Merrimac.* This time the forts were not bombarding the channel but aiming their projectiles at the blockaders. The operations were the reverse of those on the prior occasion. The Spaniards were taking a leaf out of Professor Sampson's text-book on strategy. The old iron cruiser *Reina Mercedes,* whose guns had been conscripted by the Spanish Army defending the city and whose engines had fallen into ruin, had been caught by the beams of the searchlights of the *Massachusetts,* back from Guantanamo and at her old nocturnal duty. The enemy warship was in the narrows near the wreck of the *Merrimac.* The Spaniards had brought her down to block the passage, but they were no more successful in this respect than had been Hobson. The *Massachusetts* and *Texas,* alongside as her support, fired up the notch and soon sank the veteran craft. They were between the *Iowa* and the target so Evans held his fire, which was not needed anyway. The *New York* and *Indiana* moved over to see what was taking place inside the capes, and the latter was spanked on her stern by a mortar, as the punishment for her perfectly proper curiosity.

"At midnight," recorded Bob Evans, "everything was quiet."

The story of Bob Evans' battle would not be complete without the mention of his silent prayer of thanksgiving.

His friend Jack Philip had been carried away by a flood of emotion when the booming of the cannon subsided and the plight of the enemy dulled the keen edge of the joy of victory. His classic injunction has been writ in letters of gold upon the pages of our naval history. It was uttered as a salvo of uproarious encouragement was shouted to the passing *Oregon*. Captain Philip saw the wrecked *Vizcaya* on the other side, with her gory decks and maimed crew. "Don't cheer, men; those poor fellows are dying."

Walking aft, he had all hands summoned and dramatically but most spontaneously invited every shipmate so inclined, to uncover and offer a silent prayer of gratitude to the God of Battles.

A Pennsylvania publisher, who had fought the Spaniards from the press-room of his Williamsport *Index*, seized upon Captain Philip's theistic avowal at the crisis as the text of an editorial-sermon, contrasting that commendable display of religious fervour to Captain Evans' alleged notorious addiction to profanity. Pleased with this high moral journalistic effort, the author wrapped up a precious copy and posted it to Guantanamo Bay, addressed to the rebuked renegade. It was one person's notion of a fitting missive to despatch to a tired hero. Evans dignified the article with a reply and it was one worthy of his pen:

"U.S.S. Iowa
Guantanamo Bay, Cuba
July 23, 1898.

"Dear Sir:

I beg to acknowledge the receipt to-day of a copy of your paper, which you have been good enough to send to me.

I am somewhat at a loss to know whether you sent it for the purpose of calling my attention to the cuss words attributed to me in the newspapers, or to Captain Philip's official show of Christian spirit in announcing to his men on the quarterdeck of the *Texas*, after the battle of Santiago, that he believed in Almighty God. As however, you have seen fit to drag my name in your newspaper, I hope that you will publish this reply that those who have read your issue of July 15 may also read what I have to say about it.

I have never considered it necessary, and I am sure that a great majority of officers in the Navy do not consider it necessary to announce to their crews that "they believe in Almighty God." I think that goes without saying. We, each of us, have the right to show by our acts how much we are imbued by this belief. Captain Philip had a perfect right to show this to his men, as he did; it was simply a matter of taste.

Now for myself: Shortly after the Spanish cruiser *Vizcaya* had struck her colours, and my crew had secured the guns, the Chaplain of the ship, an excellent man, came to me and said, "Captain, shall I say a few words of thanks to Almighty God for our victory?" I said, "By all means do so; I will have the men sent aft for that purpose," and was on the point of doing so when it was reported to me that a Spanish battleship was standing toward us from the eastward. My first duty to God and my country was to sink this Spanish battleship, and I immediately made preparations to do so. When it was discovered that this ship was an Austrian, I found my ship surrounded by boats carrying dying and wounded prisoners, and others of the crew of the *Vizcaya* to the number of 250. To leave these men to suffer for want of food and clothing while I called my men aft to offer prayers was not my idea either of Christianity or religion. I preferred to clothe the naked, feed the hungry, and succor the sick, and I am strongly of the opinion that Almighty God has not put a black mark against me on account of it. I do not know whether I shall stand with Captain Philip among the first chosen in the hereafter, but I have this to say in conclusion, that every drop of blood in my body on the afternoon of July 3 was singing thanks and praise to Almighty God for the victory we had won.

Yours respectfully,

ROBLEY D. EVANS,
Captain, United States Navy,
Commanding U.S.S. Iowa."

21

REAR ADMIRAL

~~~~~~

THE explosion in the *Vizcaya* in response to her captain's "Adios" had been no more remarkable a coincidence than the reception at Fourth of July gatherings around the world of the news from Santiago, the epochal significance of which it required no seer to appreciate.

At the dinner of the American Association in London, for example, which was graced by the presence of Ambassador Hay, James Bryce and many other dignitaries of both nations, the Marquess of Ripon solemnly expressed what all were thinking. A former Viceroy of India and First Lord of the Admiralty, and at the moment Secretary of State for the Colonies, his words were impressive.

"You stand at the parting of the ways . . . the crisis is momentous not only for the destinies of this country, but for the history of the world."

American victory was assured. Our hegemony of the new world was established. Sea power mocked the toiling troops ashore, whose gains were costly and whose achievements were, on the grand scale, inconsequential. The Army had been raised for the most part in days and engaged in combat for weeks. The Navy had been preparing for decades and fought for minutes; but in those minutes history had been made.

The Battles of Manila Bay and Santiago had been won without losing a ship or sparing an enemy's; and the death

346

list contained but one name. Regardless of odds, such over-whelming victories were bound to arrest the attention of the world.

"Mein Gott! it is unheard of!" exclaimed the Austrian boarding officer of the *Kaiserin Maria Teresa,* when Captain Taylor bluntly told him what had happened and showed him through a glass the funeral columns of Spanish smoke along the shore.

Equally amazed was the supercilious young lieutenant of H.M.S. *Pallas* that stood in the following day, who remarked to the American Chief-of-Staff that the Spanish fleet inside the harbour doubtless would also consent to the British cruiser's entry.

Captain Chadwick resented the youth's swaggering man-ner, which bordered on the insolent. He toyed with the situation. The former could be as casual as any English-man. There was no glint of triumph in his expression as he rejoined:

"We sank them all yesterday."

The effect was quite what he had desired. The era of condescension had come to an end.

The navies of Europe looked westward. The French planned a thorough reorganization of their fleet so as to profit by the lessons Spain had learned too late.

The *Petit Journal* commented in a vein typical of the continental press:

"The war would have lasted longer, but the result would have been the same had the American Army not even been in existence. The victory is solely due to the excellent and carefully trained American Navy, but an American Army has yet to be created."

The City of Santiago surrendered in time to prevent General Shafter from exploding with wrath at the fleet for not extricating him from what he erroneously believed but irately denied was a military predicament.

In the final drive for peace, however, the fleet had a few more duties to perform.

All along there had been the possibility of a counter-attack upon Dewey by the portion of the Spanish fleet still in home waters. On June sixteenth, Admiral Camara cleared Cadiz, and statistics, with a wink it is true, cautioned the Department that this relief expedition outclassed our Manila naval force in every physically measurable respect. Commodore Watson was ordered to assemble a squadron at Guantanamo to reënforce Dewey. It was to include the *Iowa* and *Oregon* but, fortunately, their withdrawal from the Santiago blockade was postponed to the last possible moment and they were thus present at the battle, which otherwise might have had a different ending.

Shrewdly it was given out that the new detachment was to attack the coast of Spain. The concatenation of events could hardly have been more propitious. As the Spanish populace became alarmed—as had ours in the spring under the implied threat of a visitation by Cervera—there came the shattering report from Santiago of the second routing of their vaunted naval power. The Battle of Santiago was followed by the immediate recall of Camara, who had just effected his transit of the Suez Canal.

Camara's cruise bids fair to rank as the most fatuous naval expedition in modern history. With sealed orders, that pointed vaguely toward the Philippines but that Captain Chadwick said later really ordered the Admiral just "to go somewhere and do nothing," he had managed with great difficulty to drag his ill-conditioned command the length of the Mediterranean, only to wrangle at Port Said with the British authorities over the international law governing re-fueling of belligerent warships in neutral waters, a contest in which the Admiral could not hope to prevail. While trying to coal ship in the open sea, he was less successful than Bob Evans at performing the "impossible." Writing in the *Marine Rundschau* the following autumn, Rear Admiral

Plüdemann of the German Navy said: "The coaling of Admiral Camara's ships at Port Said was nothing but a comedy." The musical accompaniment, fortunately for the latter's peace of mind, inaudible, was the synchronous gunfire between the mouths of Santiago Bay and the Tarquino River. No sooner had his force emerged upon the Red Sea than it was intercepted by the return summons from the frantic Ministry at Madrid. The canal toll charges in both directions could have built a destroyer.

The Department was promptly informed of Camara's about-face by Ensign William Henry Buck, a young Nathan Hale, who happily was not required to give even his one life to his country, but certainly offered it. Trailing Camara's squadron aboard a foreign yacht chartered in his rôle of a pleasure-seeking English gentleman, he had kept Washington in touch with the movements of the last enemy flotilla.

Our public strategy was altered by this news of Camara's return. Instead of saying we were planning to attack Spain and really reënforcing Dewey, we now announced a gigantic assault upon Porto Rico and arranged for a diversion of part of this naval force for a demonstration at the enemy's gates. The intention of augmenting our Asiatic Squadron was adhered to. The object of everything, of course, was peace. The collapsing morale of the enemy people was already convincing the Spanish Government that it must soon sue for terms. The Navy properly prepared to press home the drive on the Latin depression.

So terrified became the inhabitants of the Peninsula's seaports at the prospect of an American bombardment, that Camara was ordered to hasten his arrival and parade his force "close to the shore, so as to be seen from Spanish cities, exhibiting, when near them, the national flag, illuminated by searchlights."

The statesmen, who after generations of futile negotiations had relinquished the handling of the Cuban problem into the temporary charge of the respective admirals and generals, now obviously were getting ready to again assume the responsibility. The statesmen had made war; the soldiers and sailors of America had about made peace. It was resolved to obtain a completely satisfactory peace, from our point of view. To have Porto Rico in our possession would obviously help at the bargaining table. The expedition to reduce that weakly defended island was pushed along, and the Navy escorted sufficient troops there to take and hold it.

The European-Asiatic situation was to be dealt with by virtually our full naval might. Commodore Watson was to take the *Oregon* and *Massachusetts* and some lesser craft to Manila via the Mediterranean. To dissuade Admiral Camara, now back at his base, from any possible attempt to interfere with the passage of this detachment through the Straits of Gibraltar, Admiral Sampson, as Commander-in-Chief, was reorganizing the North Atlantic Squadron to act as an escorting force past Spanish home waters. The proximity of this powerful armada was expected to arouse any still-dormant peace-loving instincts of the Iberian people.

The *Iowa* was to be included in this covering squadron, without having her whiskers of seaweed and barnacles trimmed from the long-neglected hull.

For many days, the preparations at Guantanamo for the transatlantic voyage must have reminded Bob Evans of those at Key West after the *Virginius* outrage. The ending was destined to be the same as in the former case.

Jules Cambon, one of the two brothers of whom much was heard in the pre-World War days, when one held the post of Ambassador to the Court of St. James's and the other held the corresponding post at Berlin, now represented France at Washington. Through this astute diplomat, who a few years later was transferred from Washington to Madrid, the desperate Ministers of the Queen Regent began to sound out the Conscience. As to Cuba, the Spaniards were reconciled to either independence or American annexation, but in every other respect they naturally wanted the best possible terms. The Conscience could not bring itself to ask for pecuniary indemnity (foreshadowing the spirit of the Fourteen Points) but it might see its way clear to accepting, in lieu thereof, Porto Rico and a Spanish island in the mid-Pacific (foreshadowing the spirit of the Treaty of Versailles). The disposition of the Philippines was to be left to the peace commissioners.

A protocol acceding to an armistice on this basis was signed on August twelfth, just as the other side of the globe was witnessing the capitulation of the City of Manila.

Hostilities were suspended. That night at Guantanamo the *Bulldog* barked a new note. From her masthead there flashed in red and white lights the letters P-E-A-C-E. The bands played "Home Sweet Home," and the last watches in Cuban waters were gleeful with the prospects of heading north. In accordance with tradition, brooms were two-blocked at the yardarms to denote the sweeping of the enemy from the sea.

The following forenoon the fleet got under way. The *Texas* had been sent up ahead for urgent repairs. The *Oregon* was no longer commanded by Captain Clark, whose health had cracked under the reaction that set in after his great cruise and his great battle. The Santiago warriors steamed along, in double column, with the usual drills aboard each ship. The war was over but the efficiency was not permitted to droop. The greatest thrill of the cruise was the burning of lights at night; the release from the constant caution lest a single ray squeeze through a porthole.

Outside Ambrose Light, a packet-boat brought word that New York was preparing a gala welcome, almost impromptu because of the very short notice of the fleet's arrival. In the Lower Bay, a large number of decorated tugs and yachts hailed the warship and puffed alongside the advancing grey column. The *New York,* flying Admiral Sampson's flag, was in the van, followed by the *Iowa, Indiana, Brooklyn, Massachusetts* and *Oregon.* Schley in the *Brooklyn* had recently become a Rear Admiral. At the Narrows, both Fort Hamilton and Fort Wadsworth fired salutes, and thirteen guns that spoke up off Tompkinsville came from the old comrade *Texas,* whose Jack Philip had become Commodore and duly received his eleven guns in reply. The *Texas* fell in astern of the *Oregon* and the column moved through the Upper Bay, the tooting of whistles from the hundreds of craft there to greet the conquerors drowning out the sound of the ship's bands and the salute from Governor's Island. The shores were black with cheering crowds, but they could hardly see the battleships and cruisers, because of the great number of boats of every kind and description flying enormous flags. The *New York* slowed down to pick up a boarding party of dignitaries, who delivered the official welcome of City, State and Nation in platitudes far less impressive than the demonstration of the populace.

The *Oregon* excited the greatest interest of any individual ship and, aside from the two flag officers, the personality that seemed to hold the imagination of the multitude beyond all others was that of the *Iowa's* skipper. The *Tribune's* staff reporter said in his account: "Then came the battleship *Iowa,* and upon her bridge the grim-faced officer who is known and admired throughout the country as 'Fighting Bob' Evans could be plainly seen."

The Battery was jammed to its enormous capacity, and, as the naval parade reached Riverside Drive, it looked as though the entire United States had poured its population into the Park and upon the New Jersey Palisades opposite.

The ships had been painted since the battle, and only the *Brooklyn* showed any scars from enemy projectiles. The war grey and the decks, still stripped of all superfluous gear, alone indicated that the fleet was returning from a business trip. To all who participated in the welcome, it was a marvel that this unscathed squadron could be the one that seven short weeks before had been through the Battle of Santiago.

The column saluted Grant's Tomb and returned down the Hudson to its anchorage off Staten Island. The starboard watch of the *Iowa* rated liberty for the first time in seven months. New York surrendered to the jackies. They swept through Park Row and the Bowery and up to Herald Square, and the freedom of the city that had been tendered in eloquent speeches was for once accepted literally. Where after forty-eight hours the starboard watch left off, the port watch took hold. The officers were less in evidence and more of them were fortunate in being met by their families, but they found New York just as delightful a change from the Cuban blockade as did the bluejackets.

Evans was occupied for some days with his battleship, first showing her to the boat-loads of sightseers and then getting her into the Brooklyn Navy Yard for the long needed docking and overhaul. His old chief Admiral Bunce was Commandant, and it was a pleasure to have the work fall under his supervision. Evans' cruise in the *Iowa,* however, was over. The Navy was being quickly readjusted to a peace-time basis and many of the officers were transferred, including most of the captains.

Bob Evans deserved a rest and a tour of duty on the beach with his family. While the *Iowa* was at the Yard, he was detached.

As he settled down to life in Washington, he reoriented himself in the affairs of the world, from the details of whose daily occurrences he had for some months been quite cut off. There was much to read, see, hear. Hawaii was annexed, the ceremonies taking place two days after the fleet's arrival at New York. He shook his head with misgivings. These islands seemed to be more of a liability than an asset, in the event of a Pacific war. What then of the acquisition of Guam far off in the Ladrones and the talk of keeping the Philippines?

It was gratifying to learn of our new naval program. We were at last going to build not merely some ships but a homogeneous fleet. The plans were being laid for the construction of that armada which nearly a decade later Evans would start upon its voyage around the world.

At the moment, he strove to give the country the benefit of his recent experiences under wartime conditions. He pondered the lessons of the past few months—a period crowded with practical tests of a multitude of previously untried theories and devices. He conferred with his colleagues in the various bureaus at the Department and with the solons at the top. He contributed articles to current periodicals. Orally and in writing, his views always commanded attention and his forceful manner of expression commanded interest.

He emerged from the war with many new convictions and many old ones fortified. Chief among them were: the necessity of having fast cruisers with a large cruising radius and an ample supply of destroyers and supply ships for a well-rounded fleet; the necessity for better inter-ship and intra-ship communication; the necessity for smokeless powder and smokeless fuel; the necessity for a satisfactory range-finder; and the necessity for using only fresh water in boilers. He also learned that properly constructed land fortifications were almost indestructible by naval gunfire.

Many of these needs were sooner or later filled by the inventions of the following period, in which Bradley Fiske was to continue taking a leading part. What Evans learned about our cruiser needs is the doctrine of our General Board to-day that the Treaty of London disregarded.

At one of Bob Evans's recommendations for the new battleships we may be pardoned a smile. Having pronounced his own conning tower "a devilish place," he advocated two, one aft in addition to the usual one forward. The new one would be of use chiefly in a rear-end engagement against a pursuing enemy, and the imagination refuses to picture Bob Evans fleeing from any one or anything.

There was a feeling among certain officers that the turn of the century, striking speed as a key-note, should be reflected by the bestowal of high velocity upon the new battleships. It was the old triangle problem: speed, guns and protection. One could be obtained only by an encroachment upon one or both of the others. Evans believed that cruisers should be swift and that the line of battle should be hard-hitting and long-floating, before it should aspire toward celerity. The weight of his influence was thrown behind this viewpoint. He was unmoved by rumours of fast-moving battleships on the ways of foreign builders.

"If others choose to thin their armour in order to get speed, let them do it, and when the day of battle comes they can run away or get whipped, just as they prefer. . . ."

Thus spake Fighting Bob.

One man and one man only ever implied that the sobriquet was misplaced. After the battle, Chaplain Joseph P. McIntyre of the *Oregon* suffered a nervous break-down and was invalided home to Denver. According to his own story, the extreme changes of temperature endured on the famous cruise around South America, the confessed dread (shared by none of his gallant shipmates) of encountering Cervera *en route,* the tension of the blockade and the strain of the battle, had proved too much for him. A thousand miles of land between him and the nearest seacoast, however, restored his courage, and he proceeded to regale his neighbours with yarns of the victory. To the subsequent annoyance of Captain Clark and his men, the Chaplain accepted an invitation to address an audience for the benefit of the local Y. M. C. A. When the hour approached, he had to be stimulated for the occasion by a shot of some drug, and so

356 FIGHTING BOB EVANS

strong a dose did he take that, he later declared, he mounted the platform with a "whirling brain."

Certainly he gave his hearers something to start their own thoughts spinning. Stripping heroes of their lustre is usually reserved for biographers of another age, but Chaplain McIntyre proceeded to do the job before the victors of Santiago could even return from the theatre of their exploits. Three main charges made the deepest impression: first, that Admiral Sampson had falsely reported his position as nearer to the *Colon* at the time of her surrender than was the fact, in order to share in the prize-money; second, that the *Oregon,* the only western-built battleship in the fight, was the only one that had been built honestly, the others suffering from a corrupt alliance between eastern shipyards and the public authorities, and that the *Oregon* alone had won the victory; and third, that the *Iowa* had run away from the enemy as the *Oregon* was advancing. Several times he sneered at the name Fighting Bob, which was then a cherished one on the lips of everybody. The crowd was dumbfounded. An enterprising woman reporter of the *Rocky Mountain News* turned in an account of the speech, and the public at large became indignant. The poor Chaplain probably had been so terrified in the midst of the battle that he had failed to comprehend what was taking place. He may have supposed quite honestly that the *Iowa's* daring advance upon the flank of the Spanish line, attracting to herself the concentrated fire of all the enemy cruisers, was a retreat because it was on a course that did not parallel the *Oregon's,* which, with her greater speed, she was laying so as to cut off any escape to the westward.

The Department caused a Court-Martial to be convened, and two other chaplains were included in its membership. The Secretary fully approved its findings and sentence, and the President signed the dismissal of the defendant from the Navy.

The Chaplain obviously had never belonged in a man-
of-war, and was to be pitied rather than condemned. His
expulsion from the service was followed by a jilting at the
hands of a very wealthy fiancée. When last heard of, the
Oregon's "sky-pilot" was sipping mineral water at a spring
in California and planning a lecture tour on topics more sacred than secular.

The chief effect of this unpleasant incident was to make
more familiar than ever the name by which Bob Evans was
known. When interviewed upon his return and questioned
for the hundredth time by some reporter as to the derivation,
he said: "I do not like the subject. I have never courted
that kind of distinction in the service. I am simply a captain in the Navy. I am no more of a fighter and no more
entitled to that title than any other officer."

Yet the sobriquet was as much a part of him as his
family name. The *Bulldog* of the Navy was the ship and
he the officer, who were the most colourful to the public eye.
The admirals might be acclaimed for a dozen triumphant
battles and there might be well merited enthusiasm for
Hobson and other heroes of specific feats, but no other
personality stood forth from our picturesque Navy quite
so vividly as did Captain Evans'.

General Nelson A. Miles, the head of the Army, spoke
at a dinner after a compliment had been extended to the
handsome military men.

"The two ugliest men in the United States service are
its two most courageous men, Captain William Wallace of
the Army, and Captain Robley D. Evans of the Navy."

It is odd that those who were not well acquainted with
Bob Evans and were not familiar with his beautiful eyes
and lovable smile, who knew his face only in repose, considered him rather forbidding in appearance.

The *Philadelphia Times,* in a laudatory article about
him, once said: "His is a striking personality. His whole

being breathes force, but he is not what women call a handsome man. His countenance is fierce."

If he looked "grim," as it will be recalled the *Tribune*
had stated, as the fleet stood up the bay, there was a valid
reason. He was suffering one of his chronic attacks—without the knowledge of any of his subordinates. For several
days he had felt it coming on but vowed to himself that he
would not relinquish the active command of the *Iowa* until
she was turned over to the Yard for repairs. The ceremonies attending the arrival were for him a cruel physical
ordeal, but he managed to endure them. The very day, however, that the ship was tied up in her wet slip at the Brooklyn Yard, his body went to pieces. The clinical thermome-
ter showed an alarming fever, and the doctor advised him
to leave at once for the added comforts of a sick-room
ashore. The wardroom and the forecastle were sad that
night. When the "old man" was assisted into a carriage
and driven off, they felt sure that his sea days and perhaps
his land days, too, were over.

They were mistaken, and that error was often to be
repeated before this indefatigable officer would go over the
side for the last time.

The round of dinners and dances had to be omitted, of
course, but within a couple of weeks Bob Evans was back
on his feet, as lively as ever.

On September ninth, he was the guest of honour at a
meeting of the Poughkeepsie Soldiers' Relief Committee.
From up and down the Central Hudson River Valley the
people came to hear his discourse. After a boisterous reception, he limped to the front of the platform and plunged
head first into the topic of the evening.

"Any Government that is worth fighting for should take
care of the men who go out from their families, which is
the hardest part of it, and I hope such a meeting will never
be necessary again." (It wasn't, until the next war.)

After bluntly and effectively stating his irrefutable ideas as to the practical solicitude to which the wounded veterans were entitled, he referred to the recent battle, about which he was well aware the audience was waiting to hear from him.

"I don't know much about it. All I saw was through a narrow slit in a conning tower."

Instead of describing the aggressive and decisive part taken by the *Iowa,* he stressed other phases. The thrill of beholding the enemy fleet emerge from Santiago Bay, he graphically explained.

"If any one could imagine a whole basket of champagne compressed into a single drop and taken in that form it would give some idea of the way we felt."

Then he touched upon the rescue work. It was all very well for him to have said, before the inevitable event, that, if the Dons would come out, he would make Hades reek of garlic, but once he had smelled the real shambles of the "hecatomb," he spoke only with tender pity for the honourable losers. His attitude was that of a surgeon who had been obliged to perform a bloody and painful operation to end a long illness.

Invitations from all sources, from the New York Four Hundred to workingmen's groups, poured in upon him, but he was able to accept very few.

During the next three and a half years, however, that he remained on the beach, with his residence at Washington and at Old Point Comfort, Virginia, where it is said he "squatted" on government lighthouse property from which no one had the temerity to suggest he remove, he got about the country a great deal and extended his wide acquaintance among people of all walks of life. His smile and his stories, his halting tread and his gruff good-humour, became known to many who previously had admired him from afar as a haloed celebrity. More and more he became news. Anything Bob Evans did or said was good copy and this held true for the balance of his life.

At least once a winter, he would go South with his old friend Grover Cleveland and shoot ducks along the Carolina coast. Often there were others in the ex-President's party, but Bob Evans was well known to be his favourite companion. Despite the Captain's dislike of soldiering, he could always handle a rifle or shot gun with the best of them, and, when the day's sport was over, his campfire yarns rarely failed to eclipse the most extravagant story that had been related. Sometimes Cleveland and Evans went fishing together in Lake Erie or a mountain pond. No distance was too great for these two enthusiasts to travel when they heard the call of the wild. Cleveland would order his private railroad car dusted off, wire Evans that he'd pick him up *en route,* and off they'd go, alone or in company with other good fellows; and let the fish or fowl beware!

During the second winter following the war, Evans took his wife and one daughter to Cuba, partly for the pleasure of seeing Old Glory wave over Havana, and partly to escape the rigors of cold weather. The legs were never quite subdued, and now his arms suffered from what he also called rheumatism. Every ache in joint or limb was called rheumatism in those days. He returned with one arm in a sling and soon tried the therapeutic powers of the Arkansas Hot Springs. For two months he remained there at the Army and Navy Hospital, imbibing the healing waters and taking the baths.

Many honours were bestowed upon him during these post-war years. First and foremost was that sword from his old crew of the *Iowa.* Another sword was presented by the State whose name his battleship had brought from cornfield obscurity into world renown.

While he was at Cincinnati on Washington's Birthday 1899 to grace a banquet, the city made him its distinguished guest. In its excitement over the living hero, it almost forgot the great patriot whose anniversary was being celebrated.

In the forenoon there was a reception at the Burnet House, at lunch Captain Evans was fêted by the Chamber of Commerce, there was another reception in the afternoon at the Queen City Club, and in the evening he was the principal speaker at the dinner of the Stamina Republican Club. Throngs hailed him in the streets as though the Battle of Santiago had been fought within the hour.

Living near-by, he naturally was drafted as the principal attraction for the convention of Railroad Master Mechanics at the Chamberlin Hotel, Fortress Monroe. He proved to be an excellent drawing card. Not only was there a splendid attendance of delegates, but many others journeyed from afar to see and hear Fighting Bob. He delivered a stirring address that fulfilled all expectations and the rising vote of thanks was preceded and followed by thunderous applause.

Inane manifestations of hero-worship were distasteful to the plain sailor in him. One day he was waiting for his train at Bath, Maine, after inspecting a new ship under construction for the Navy. Bit by bit, a crowd collected, in silent Northeast fashion, and mutely stared in awe at the Captain pacing up and down the platform with the jerky step that had become celebrated. The cynosure of all these admiring eyes, he began to feel extremely uncomfortable and longed to break the tension. Well, he'd show them he was no royal curiosity but just another chap like themselves. Suddenly wheeling around toward a gaping baggage agent, he barked: "Say old man, gimme a match, will you?" The statue had spoken—and with no Harvard accent.

He was, of course, fully as much at home among the society folk of the big cities as among his humbler fellow-citizens. When Sir Thomas Lipton brought over the first *Shamrock* to challenge the *Columbia*, Evans was in charge of the Navy torpedo boats assigned to patrol the race. As usual, he did his job well. Excursion boats, yachts, craft of all varieties swarmed around the course, but the contestants suffered no interference. Sir Thomas was generous in his praise of this important part of the proceedings. "I want you to put me down as saying that there never was in all the world, not even in England, as clear a course as we had to-day, and I want to add, from the bottom of my heart, that it reflects the greatest possible credit upon the authorities who had in charge the task of keeping it clear."

It was inevitable that Evans should write his memoirs. Mrs. Evans and his friends urged him to put on paper those reminiscences that so often entertained rooms full of comrades and halls crowded with listeners. Finally he agreed to do so, and Appleton's announced *A Sailor's Log*. It appeared in the early summer of 1901, dedicated to his wife, was widely and enthusiastically reviewed, and ran through several editions. Its style was characteristic of the author's racy, picturesque manner of expression. He was still in the service, had many years ahead of him before retirement, and was naturally more circumspect and cautious in his printed remarks than in his intimate oral chats. The raging Controversy was a horrible example of the other extreme. Evans shuddered as he read in the papers, day after day, the anti-Sampson and anti-Schley calumnies and lampoons.

Nevertheless, with all of this self-censorship, he ran afoul of old Secretary Chandler, who read the account of Evans's dismissal from the lighthouse inspectorship with gnashing teeth and the fury of enraged senescence. He protested formally and vehemently. Acting Secretary Hackett may have been actuated by future self-protection or by some sense of having to placate the old ex-Senator or by the mere astigmatism of officialdom. In any event, he tossed off a letter of severe censure to the author, that must have rankled as deeply as had the original injustice of dismissal. It seemed uncalled for from any practical standpoint, and was justified, if at all, only by the most technical construction of the customs of military etiquette, which civilians seem to invoke much more readily than the men in uniform. The letter never injured Evans nor marred his career, but the entire Chandler incident fails to add distinction to the civilian crown of the Department. It was some years *after* this latest affront that Evans appointed Chandler's son to his staff, and nothing in the former's whole life better manifested the innate bigness of the man.

The title page of the book, whose narrative terminated with the return of the fleet from Cuba in '98, described the author as a Rear Admiral. That rank he had attained on March fifth, 1901, as of the preceding February eleventh, by virtue of the Congressional advancement of five numbers for his distinguished services during the war. One other rear admiral was commissioned the same day and it was his brother-in-law Harry Taylor, who had received an equal honorary advancement in grade. Mrs. Evans' two middies of the Annapolis hops were now august Admirals— but not too august to endure around a home of charming simplicity!

1901 was a year of great changes in the American scene, that obviously were bound to affect Evans' career. As an Admiral at the then relatively young age of fifty-five, there lay ahead seven years of active service, which he wanted to be really active. When a vacancy occurred in command of the North Atlantic Squadron, his eye fondly gazed upon the main truck of the flagship, but the Department had other plans.

His intimate co-worker in preparing the service for the war, Theodore Roosevelt, had during the few intervening years been catapulted into the position of Commander-in-Chief of the Army and Navy. Shortly after the return of the fleet, Evans heard his friend's name prominently mentioned for the New York gubernatorial nomination on the

Republican ticket. Roosevelt was a military hero and the most engaging young personage on the political horizon. The nomination duly came in September, election by a close margin in November, and in January the commencement of an incumbency that soon filled with mortal terror the heart of Arch-Boss Platt. The only way to dispose of this irrepressible young statesman, who was not susceptible to the usual baneful influences, was to "kick him upstairs." His nomination for the innocuous office of vice-president of the United States was arranged despite his efforts to defeat the manœuvre. The national campaign, which was fought chiefly on the issue of "imperialism," with Candidate Bryan doing the haranguing and foaming and President McKinley the smiling, was followed by the triumph of the Republicans. Roosevelt had been shelved. He told his friends that he was sentenced to take the veil and that he would study law as a pastime. Then, at the Pan-American Exposition at Buffalo, in September of the inaugural year, an anarchist once more diverted into a new channel the current of history.

It was impossible that Bob Evans should not play a leading rôle in naval affairs during the Roosevelt Administration. At last we had a President who entered the White House thoroughly indoctrinated with the importance of sea power and familiar with our naval organization from within. His messages to Congress, his other public utterances and his personal conversations rang with a demand for adequate national defence and the maintenance of a well-balanced efficient Navy as its first line. The Spanish War gave to the Navy, first, an aroused public interest, and then a President who never permitted that interest to become dormant.

Roosevelt found in Bob Evans the ideal trusted friend and beloved leader in the service, to act as his right hand man in the constant development of the Navy. From smaller assignments to supreme command of our forces afloat, the Admiral was destined to rise during the period preceding his retirement, until the grand climax was attained of the cruise to the Pacific.

The first task was of a quasi-personal nature. The President sought information from a nonpartisan and thoroughly dependable source as to certain conditions in the Hawaiian Islands. The young Territory had displayed marked precocity in learning its lessons in the practical politics of a democracy. Rumours of social and economic maladjustments also trickled into the White House. Roosevelt was at a loss to know whom or what he should believe. He could not ascertain the truth first-hand on the spot and, besides, it would be futile for a President to attempt accurate fact-finding. He could not don false whiskers and run about Honolulu incognito. Bob Evans was a shrewd observer. He possessed the breadth of view of a world traveller. He would be able to see and report. No one would suspect him of being the telescope of the White House nor bother erecting artificial settings for a naval officer apparently engaged in the ordinary course of his duties.

Circumstances dove-tailed nicely. Evans could visit Honolulu upon his return from a Court-Martial in the Samoan Islands. Possibly Roosevelt thought of the Hawaiian mission only after learning of the convening of the Court with Evans as president. It is immaterial. The opportunity was grasped.

From Evans' standpoint, the trip had the merit of taking him away from the nauseating atmosphere of Washington, where the Schley Court of Inquiry was in exhausting session, hashing and re-hashing the events of '98 and breaking the heart and health of his ever reserved and dignified friend, Sampson. From a public standpoint, however, Evans always regarded the Samoan trip as a profligate junket. Somehow, a trial that results in an acquittal rather than in a

conviction strikes many persons as a waste of time.   He
seriously believed in later years that the charges now preferred against Captain B. F. Tilley, the Naval Governor of
Tutuila, were based upon nothing more substantial than the
practically anonymous letter of a woman.   It is true that
the formal specifications were drafted from the contents
of such a letter.   It seems, however, that this complaint, by
a white resident of the Islands, was the final and most convincing of a series that, in one form or another, had been
percolating back from the mid-Pacific.   Missionaries had
accused the Governor of drunkenness and immorality.   The
Navy naturally chafed under this criticism of its uniformed
representative.

     What quite properly offended Evans, when he ascer-
tained the facts, was the readiness of the Department to
link up to such scandalous indictments, the name of an officer whose record had been unblemished, without first in-
quiring into the possibility of being able to prove his guilt.

     Captain Tilley had been administering the affairs of
Tutuila for some time, and was held in high esteem by most
of the white inhabitants there in connection with the meagre
business of the dependency, and was affectionately trusted
by the natives.   To the people he was sent out to govern,
he was eminently satisfactory.   Possibly because of his
reluctance to interfere with Samoan customs as much as
the missionaries believed desirable, the Governor was in the
bad graces of this group, which would have liked to convert
our mid-Pacific coaling depot into a fresh-air evangelist
camp.   These well-meaning but over-zealous spreaders of
the Gospel were free with their aspersions upon Captain
Tilley's official and private deportment, but they refrained
from filing formal accusations.

     Admiral Evans departed in October and, after the long
sail down the latitudes, convened the Court aboard the naval
vessel *Solace* in the harbour of Pago Pago.   At each of six
sessions the gun was fired, the jack hoisted at the yardarm,

and the other ceremonies duly observed. The judge-advocate's case was feeble. His star witness, a physician, faltered under cross-examination, and his other witnesses actually testified in favour of the Governor. The defence called over a dozen witnesses of its own and announced the intention of subpoenaing others from every corner of the archipelago, which, on a library map, looks compact, but, when gauged by facilities for inter-island transportation, is scattered over a considerable surface of ocean. The Court had heard enough to be convinced that the charges had been specious, if not malicious. Its proceedings were halted, and the defendant declared fully and honourably acquitted. The natives were delighted and the air was cleared:

A new governor was, nevertheless, substituted for Captain Tilley. The confused Samoans found the entire proceedings inexplicable. First, an important chief is sent across the seas to rule them, then a group of his white brethren, wearing as much or more gold on their uniforms, arrive to discipline him, then, after elaborate functions aboard a strange ship in the harbour, the beloved Governor is declared to have been free from sin and crime, and lastly he is taken away from them anyway. Is it any wonder that the word of the white man was considered fallible?

Like other visitors to Samoa, Evans was impressed by the splendid physique of the perfect specimens of Polynesians who inhabited the islands, by the harm that they were suffering at the hands of white culture, and by the incessant, relentless, nerve-taxing downpour, which inspired W. Somerset Maugham's story dramatized as *Rain*.

On the way south, there had been a short stop at Honolulu, during which the Captain had been able to see little besides the natural grandeur of the surroundings and the polyglot population that prattled around the water front. After the adjournment of the Court, the *Solace* deposited the members upon the wharf at Honolulu to await the next passenger liner to San Francisco. This gave the presidential investigator about ten days for his confidential task and, without arousing any curiosity among his companions or the citizens he met by any display of undue activity or seriousness of purpose, he lost no time gathering the data. The process was "spending a part of each day and night at clubs and other places where the business men of the city congregated, keeping eyes and ears open, and occasionally leading the conversation into the proper channels by a few cautious words."

This may sound absurdly superficial, but the chances are that Evans accomplished his mission. A trained mind can estimate a situation in a short space of time. The President hardly expected his agent to bring back an elaborate survey, with polychromatic charts and tables of statistics. That was not his function. When he boarded the ship for home, he carried in his head that general perspective of the current conditions that the President had been unable to obtain from the hitherto available sources, each with its own axe to grind.

The report was delivered orally and informally to the President and his Cabinet after a White House dinner. These gentlemen listened attentively to the impressions made by the Hawaiian Islands upon this sophisticated globe-mariner. The region was just emerging from the romantic period of its history into the prosaic but prosperous modern era under American sovereignty, a sovereignty that Congress had accepted as timidly as if the volcanoes themselves were being delivered into the halls of the Capitol. After the picturesque Sanford B. Dole, son of a missionary and father of a revolution, had set up a provisional government, then a constitutional government, and finally had laid the archipelago at the door-step of the United States, just when we were falling heir to Spain's imperial islands near and far, we could hardly refuse this group off our western coast.

The problems of our new wards were chiefly concerned with labour and immigration. All Pacific races met and economically clashed in the fields of Hawaii. The situation was much more acute than in California. Evans saw that the difficulties would not be overcome in a day. As through the cigar smoke he vividly described the mid-Pacific conditions to the Cabinet, he must have realized that these Department heads had become, almost over-night one might say, an imperial council.

Before leaving Honolulu, the Admiral had examined Pearl Harbour, six miles away, where for many years prior to annexation we had possessed the unexploited right to maintain a naval coaling station. The inner basin had a splendid depth of water but the reef that invariably girdles these coral attols barred the entrance. To-day we have a well equipped operating base there but the liminal reef was not dredged until after Evans' retirement. He feared that the low ground around the bay militated against its adequate defence, but he could not, of course, have foreseen the use of aircraft in this connection.

What he realized to the full was the increased responsibility of the Navy in the Pacific. The Pago Pago and Pearl Harbour concessions, which we had acquired to be in fashion, were no longer fads but important potential way stations on the Ocean in which we had a new interest. The Peace Conference had consummated the "purchase" of the Philippines. We were shoulder to shoulder with the European powers in the advance upon Asia. Evans was sceptical as to the advantage of this sudden reaching forth. He was more appreciative of its implications than were the orators of Capitol Hill.

The Admiral had a few remarks to make at the Department anent South Sea's courts-martial, and he carved the Yuletide turkey at the family board.

22

ASIATIC FLEET

~~~~~~

$\mathbf{F}$OR a part of this post-war period on the beach, Evans was recalled to the Lighthouse Board, this time as Chairman. He found the duty as satisfying and enjoyable as ever. Although he indulged in no self-delusion that it was onerous, he never regarded a position in this service as a sinecure. There was always important progress to be made as well as the standard of efficiency in the operation to maintain and raise. He had picked up too many lights at sea to underestimate their importance. While it was a waste to use line officers of the Navy as mere inspectors, they did valuable work on the supervising Board.

Soon, however, after the Admiral's return from the South Seas, there came the day when, after more than forty years under dozens of flag officers, he beheld his own blue symbol of authority broken at the main. The joke was still on those condemned legs.

A special service squadron lay off Staten Island early in 1902, assembled to greet Prince Henry of Prussia. Pursuant to the wish communicated by the Kaiser to the President, there had been designated to act as the Prince's American aide, his old friend of Kiel days.

The plans for the visit had been formulated with most meticulous forethought. It was an international event of high significance. In the first place, the Kaiser sought to propitiate us and regain the good will lost during the Spanish

War, when his naval officers at Manila and off Cuba deliberately behaved in an unfriendly manner. It was peculiarly appropriate that such a mission be entrusted to the chief of the service directly concerned in those *contretemps,* especially when he happened to be the handsome, attractive and intelligent brother of the sovereign. There was also a desire in Berlin to arouse in this country the latent sentiment for the Fatherland among its émigrés and their descendants. The immediate occasion for the visit was the launching and the christening by President Roosevelt's daughter, our own Princess Alice, of the sailing ship *Meteor,* being built here for the Kaiser.

To emphasize the naval background, the royal yacht *Hohenzollern* was despatched in advance of the Prince for use as his wharf-side residence in New York. Here he could dwell and entertain under the German ensign. The United States reciprocally placed at Admiral Evans' disposition, to afford suitable facilities for entertainment afloat in the guest's professional milieu, a squadron of three cruisers and the brand new battleship *Illinois.* One of the cruisers was the *San Francisco,* which had been at the Kiel Canal opening, another was the *Olympia* of Manila fame, and the third was the *Cincinnati.* It was the *Illinois,* then the pride of the Outfit, that first flew the flag of Rear Admiral Evans.

The Prince's visit proved to be a triumph of careful arrangement and astute management, in both of which functions his American aide took a leading part. Although the royal gentleman possessed the simplicity of good breeding, there was no affectation of simplicity in the manner of his reception. The Germans were well aware that his freedom from personal haughtiness would be rendered the more conspicuous and impressive by the ornate trappings with which his entourage was to be surrounded, and the Americans delighted in playing at monarchy and staging a pageant in the purple pomp of European royalty. The publicity was worked up well in advance. The *Hohenzollern,* an imposing craft, duly made her appearance. Titled officers scurried about, perfecting the ceremonial details. The newspapers surrendered their columns to accounts of these glamorous preparations. No item was too unimportant for publication. German Efficiency was in the heyday of its glory and we were treated to an exhibition of it in action, with which Bustling America strove to keep pace. Every want and every pleasure of the visitors were provided for. The republican citizenry was regaled with a description of the brewery wagon, decorated with German and American flags and drawn by four white horses blanketed in the Imperial colours, which was to deliver thirty kegs of lager to the *Hohenzollern* each day, so that the Teutonic thirst would be slaked in the fashion to which it was accustomed.

The German-American singing vereins were rehearsing and the turn vereins were exercising, but their interest in Prince Henry's coming was shared by their fellow countrymen of all ranks and origins. The entire population seemed to be in the scramble for places on the program.

Finally, the royal Prussian arrived on a passenger liner. Despite his familiarity with such goings-on, the prospect of the elaborate reception that extended its fanfares down the bay must have been terrifying. It was with genuine relief and a spontaneous exclamation of joy that he recognized the face and tread of Old Gimpy, hearty and cheeringly plain, coming up the gangway on the heels of the health inspector. The official greeting was reduced to a brevity possible only between two sailors, and then these friends of old forgot, in their personal reunion, the screeching of whistles and the imminence of frock-coated committees.

During the next few weeks and until the visit was brought to an eminently successful conclusion, the Prince and the Admiral were inseparable. They found in each other's sense of humour the essential relief from the tension of crowded schedules and public grimacing. Evans served as a buffer between the sensitive foreigner, intent upon giv-

Courtesy Chicago Record-Herald

ENTERTAINING PRINCE HENRY—"TEN MINUTES IN ST. LOUIS"

ing no offence, and the many ingenious attempts to intrude upon his privacy and to annoy him generally. Together they vanquished boredom and fatigue, struggled through the stupefying banquets of that era, and delightedly frustrated the well-laid schemes of over-ambitious hostesses. Often the Prince would wink at Bob Evans as together they observed the ill-concealed antics of some of these social campaigners, whose tactics were not as subtle as they supposed. The Floyd County mariner had been often enough in the drawing rooms of the élite of all of our large cities and resorts to be able to distinguish at a glance the authentic from the spurious.

There was the torch-light parade up Park Avenue, the launching of the *Meteor,* public and private dinners, dances, all manner of entertainments. The party toured about the East and to the metropolitan strongholds of the Teutonic beer barons in the Middle West. The Prince was still a young man and an avid sightseer, with interests as catholic in scope as those of his more volatile older brother. Before all else he was a naval officer, and Evans' high estimate of his attainments in that profession, originally made at Kiel, was now confirmed. Prince Henry went through the *Illinois* "from double-bottom to bridge. And he saw everything." His inspection of the Academy at Annapolis was thorough. How expertly exhaustive it had been became particularly obvious by contrast when, at West Point, his survey was the polite but superficial one of the ordinary distinguished guest.

Towards the close of the visit, Evans entertained the Prince at a small stag dinner at his own club in New York, the University. Finally the day for the latter's departure came and, although weary from their strenuous activities, the two friends were sorry to say good-bye.

The Admiral wrote an article for *McClure's* about his experiences during the visit and he laconically summarized his net feeling: ". . . we had a good time."

President Roosevelt had been particularly anxious that the Prince's stay in the country be a thoroughly enjoyable one for the guest and a diplomatic success without blemish. He was grateful to Bob Evans for his important part in achieving this.

The latter was tremendously impressed by these events and experiences of the past few weeks. Royalty was nothing new to him but "the cruise around the country" under those unusual conditions was. He devoted a substantial portion of his second volume of memoirs, written many years later, to the Prince's visit.

There were now few important Americans in public or private life who were not personally acquainted with the Admiral. He was better known than ever to the masses, who had become accustomed to seeing his familiar face and form near that of the royal visitor in practically every newspaper photograph and of daily reading of the celebrated Fighting Bob in his new rôle of master of ceremonies.

His duties as commander of the special service squadron completed, he went home to Washington and slept for forty-eight hours. His parting reflection had been that any enemy would "find the German navy a hard nut to crack." He did not live to see this estimate abundantly confirmed. It would have astonished Evans, however, to have been told that the man who was to be the kernel of the nut was not the accomplished royal Prince but his bewhiskered aide, with whom Evans could not have avoided becoming very intimate during the visit, even had he been so inclined, the subsequently famous Admiral Von Tirpitz, then Secretary of the Navy.

Evans and he had "many professional talks" and the former was particularly eager to know why the Germans "were doing nothing about submarine boats." This was only fifteen years before that April of 1917 when the U-boats almost brought Britain to her knees! Perhaps, in those inscrutable chains of cause and effect, the inquiries

and views of the American Admiral turned into their ultimate channels the convictions of that father of ruthless
submarine warfare and *schrecklichkeit,* which brought us
into the World War.

The years ashore were drawing to a close. The orna-
mental special service "afloat," valuable to the country and
interesting to the Admiral, had been performed. Since
Santiago he had had a series of most varied and rich experiences but they had been deviations from the forward
march of his career as a fighting sailor. Now, in the spring
of 1902, President Roosevelt recalled him to active line
duty afloat in the most important zone of operations.

The Far East was trembling between the suppression of
the Boxers and the impending Russo-Japanese War; China
was being exploited with a competitive shamelessness utterly
unprecedented; we were striving to assimilate our new insular dependencies in the Pacific; and the United States was
learning that it bordered on two oceans. We needed more
than nautical flag-carriers in the Orient; we needed a naval
force, whose strength, compared to the other squadrons in
those waters, was commensurate with our interests, and
was headed by an officer of sterling ability.

Robley D. Evans was chosen to assume command of the
Asiatic Fleet. First he was to take over the cruiser division
and then, in a few months, when Rear Admiral Frederick
Rodgers' tour of duty would expire, he was to succeed
Rodgers in the supreme command of the Station. The
orders opened before Evans a vista of stimulating service
and adventure. He was a youngster in spirit as he prepared
to once more visit the Orient, the changed Orient of 1902,
with the responsibilities of this nearly independent
command.

The cruise lasted from the spring of 1902 until the
spring of 1904. It was crowded with new professional
and personal experiences, with the acquaintance of new

places and new people. There were arduous months of active work with his command and there were numerous journeys that carried him to remote interiors, far from the beaten path.

One of the most gratifying features was the presence of his entire family in the East. With his son in the service and a daughter married to a naval officer, it required a most unusual combination of circumstances to enable them all to be together in one remote zone. His son-in-law happened to be Naval Attaché at Tokio and his son also found duty in the Orient. There was nothing to prevent Mrs. Evans and his daughter Virginia from completing the group. They did so, and there were many happy gatherings in those strange ports. The fleet spent its summers at Chefoo in the north of China, was often in Japan and for long periods in the winters based at Manila, so that, with the energy of a sailor's devoted wife, Mrs. Evans managed to be with her husband a substantial part of the time. In these years of constantly increasing dependence upon each other's companionship, long separations were greater hardships than ever. The Admiral found it possible to take Mrs. Evans and their younger daughter on some of his side-trips and no such opportunity was lost.

The family thoroughly enjoyed the transcontinental trip and the Pacific crossing. At Honolulu he was made much of, and the stop-over gave his family the first great thrills of the trip, induced by the gorgeous scenery and the cordiality of their reception.

Evans now might or might not be a prominent figure. His rank and assignment in themselves were not sufficient to require his presence to be made the occasion of gala ceremonies and hearty acclaim. On the other hand, they were adequate to justify such a demonstration if there existed a natural desire to honour him individually. This latter was emphatically the case. Every nation and every important personage in the East seemed to know or want to know

Bob Evans, to honestly admire him and to manifest this
warmth of feeling. Frequently he accepted attentions as
tendered to him merely because of the position he happened
to hold, that were in fact inspired solely by the wish to pay
tribute to the man.

The party reached Yokohama in a downpour but, when
it cleared away, there lay before those western eyes the
twentieth century Japan, decked as of old in the cherry
blossoms of the season. Here the Admiral sustained the
greatest shock of the cruise. He had, of course, come prepared for the wonders of Japan's development, but the
anticipation had fallen far short of discounting in advance
the surprise that awaited an absentee since the seventies.
Evans doubtless recalled Captain Ammen's exclamations of
astonishment at the progress that had been made between
his visits of the fifties and in the *Delaware*. Evans must
have wondered what his old skipper would have said in
1902. Japan's modern awakening was the story of the
tortoise transmuted into the hare. The kingdom had leaped
at a single bound from feudalism to the most advanced industrialism. The net result, Evans felt certain, could have
"no parallel in history."

His first tremendous amazement never subsided. Japan
remained for him the miracle nation, which closer inspection
and extended travels from Hakodate to Nagasaki served
only to render the more wonderful.

When received by the Mikado and asked his impressions
of the changes since the visit of his youth, Evans declared
that only Fujiyama could he recognize.

The entire East looked up at Evans with a different
aspect. There still was curry at Singapore, fortune be
praised, and wintry ice at Vladivostok, but almost everything else along the Asiatic littoral had been altered. Russia
had penetrated Manchuria and squatted at Port Arthur.
France, recovered and boasting the second navy of the
world, was a power gravely to be reckoned with in the

Orient as elsewhere. Portugal and the Netherlands held
their own. The British Empire, with Australia and Canada
well developed on the Pacific and with South Africa at
least politically integrated under the Union Jack, loomed up
larger than ever as the dominant influence. Germany had
come late but at Tsingtao had made up for lost time, as
Evans was to see first-hand. Then, of course, there was the
entry of ourselves into those wide waters. At Honolulu,
Guam, Manila, the Stars and Stripes flew at coaling intervals. The young republic had substituted its zeal, idealism
and inexperience for the lethargy and cynicism of Spain and
for the impotent independence of Hawaii.

The Admiral was not long in Japan before he perceived
the international alignments. The German Minister commenced the long series of cordial entertainments with which
the Kaiser and Prince Henry had instructed their representatives throughout the Orient to brighten Evans' trail.
That nation was playing a lone hand. The British were,
in all activities, alongside of the Japanese. Their squadron
was commanded by Vice Admiral Sir Cyprian A. C. Bridge,
with whom Evans formed a deep friendship. He found the
Russians and French the same cheek-kissing allies as at Kiel,
only out here, with the former's super-ambition, it was not
necessary for the latter to pursue them. Admiral Maréchal
and his subordinates in the French fleet got along splendidly
with the Americans during Evans' command and, while the
Russians seemed queerly obtuse in many professional respects, they were good fellows socially. It required some
slight adjustment for the westerners to accommodate themselves to fraternization with persons whose facial muscles
did not move but, once this habit was accepted, Evans, who
knew the Japanese as of old, found his admiration ripen into
cordial friendships. In short, he was on excellent official
and personal terms with every other naval force on his
station.

At Tokio he not only was received by the Mikado, who

impressed him as a ruler of ability, but, what was of even
greater interest, he met the naval leaders.   There were the
admirals of the past and Admiral Togo of the future, with
his obviously competent assistants.   It later on amused
Evans to hear these diminutive yellow officers spoken of
with contempt by the magnificently stalwart Russians, over
the vodka and staggering banquets in the cabins of their
doomed flagships.

While in Japan, there came the news of Admiral Sampson's death.   Now the hounds which had bayed him to his
destruction would be satisfied!   The officer, who Mahan
said rendered a service to our country *second to none* and
who was beloved by all who came in contact with him, had
died without recognition or thanks by Congress.   Evans
felt a sense of great personal loss and of having sustained a
personal affront.   This sentiment pervaded the Navy.   The
sting of gross and cruel injustice, which only a democracy
can deliver the most poignantly, was dramatically inflamed
by this great Admiral's dignity and serenity, maintained to
the very end.   Schley had not started the Controversy, but
it had been instituted on his behalf and had been fostered
by his attitude, so he could not be forgiven.   His surviving
contemporaries have nothing to say in derogation of his
memory but, as did Evans, they fail to cherish that worthy
creature of unfortunate weakness.   The death of Sampson
closed an epoch, and from then on, as was inevitable with a
man of his age, Evans saw his comrades drop off, one by
one, until many had preceded him into the beyond.   Harry
Taylor died in 1904.

The Asiatic Fleet was a queer organization in those days.
To begin with, the cruiser division was led by a battleship.
The recently commissioned *Kentucky* received Evans as her
new admiral.   He proceeded to gather his flock and wander
over his fold.   Before the summer at Chefoo, he had time
to visit Kobe and Nagasaki and then run across to inspect

Tsingtao, about which he must have heard so much from Prince Henry and Admiral Von Tirpitz in New York. It is inconceivable that during those many hours Evans spent with his German friends in the cabin of the *Hohenzollern*, in carriages, in the dining car and smoking rooms of their special train, in the premier suite of the old Waldorf-Astoria, they did not discuss the acquisition and development of Tsingtao, in which both of these Imperial naval officers had taken a prominent part. This is especially so in view of Evans' knowledge at the time that he was to command the Asiatic Fleet.

Tsingtao was the realization of the Kaiser's dream for a greater Hong Kong. In the spring of 1896, Von Tirpitz was appointed Chief of the Eastern Asiatic Cruiser Division. In his memoirs he bluntly declares: "I took with me from Berlin the commission to seek out a place on the Chinese coast, where Germany could construct a military and economic base." Tsingtao, with its deep-water harbour surrounded by hills' that seemed to have been created for German gun emplacements, its temperate northerly climate and its remoteness from the British zones of activity, seemed the ideal place. The Admiral took time by the forelock and, in his own words, "worked out the form of the lease, so that it looked as little as possible like forceful intervention, and allowed the Chinese to save their face . . ." for which, after all, the Kaiser had no use.

Providence coöperated neatly and promptly. Two German missionaries were slain in Shantung, of which province Tsingtao was the seaport. This double tragedy was not quite as abundant a justification for the imposition of the drafted lease as, for instance, a wholesale pogrom would have been, but the Germans accepted the offering as sufficient for their need. The other powers did not quibble.

The erection of a model metropolis was soon commenced. Evans did not live to see it wrested away by Japan during Germany's colossal folly of 1914 and he died thinking of Tsingtao as a resplendent monument of that "giant among rulers, the Emperor of Germany."

Evans was fêted and lionized by the authorities ashore and the squadron in the bay. He saw where Prince Henry had resided during the superintendence of the early construction work and he was shown the entire elaborate enterprise of establishing a Teutonic Utopia in Asia, built with characteristic German thoroughness, out of the experience and imagination of experts. The Admiral could not but admire the excellent harbour, the wisely-planned commercial district, the luxurious residential section, the healthful seaside resort facilities and the commencement of the railroad into the heart of Shantung. Economics, hygiene and æsthetics had been interwoven as by Plato with a real city to create. The Admiral's professional glances, of course, were the sharpest.

"Its value as a naval base cannot be overestimated; its possession simply puts Germany in a better position for military operations than any other nation, with the single exception of Japan."

Evans foresaw the expulsion of Russia from Manchuria, but no one—excepting possibly some sage minds behind those inflexible, expressionless yellow masks—guessed that the next outpost of power to fall would be Germany's.

Dalny, near Port Arthur, was the Russian project corresponding to Tsingtao. Here, too, was to arise a complete made-to-order city. Evans found the contrast between these places most striking. While listening to the expansive schemes of his Russian guides, his eyes shrewdly detected the pregnability of the place and foresaw the ease with which the Japanese would soon occupy the entire region. The imminent war and its outcome seemed to him as obvious as the Muscovite purblindness seemed inexplicable.

The United States Minister at Seoul invited the Admiral to display a squadron as a moral support for some diplomatically pressed claim again Korea. It is always and nec-

essarily the lawyers of the State Department who call into
hostile demonstration or operation our admirals and generals. Four ships anchored at Chemulpo. Evans looked
forward with eager anticipation to his first tour through the
still independent Empire of Korea. What he saw, however, was a backward shadow of the worst aspects of China,
without any Occidental frosting.

The Emperor appeared to be a fitting sovereign for such
a country. The royal audience was revolting to the Admiral. Alongside of the pompous monarch on the throne,
sat his son, "a half-witted young man who grinned and
giggled incessantly." The two looked like a pair of dressed-
up degenerates, suffering from the ills of the morning after.
The American officers withdrew from this spectacle of
tawdry decadence, with a comfortable feeling of superiority.

Between two pauses at Japan, the Admiral paid his
respects to Vladivostok, where he met the Russian squadron
and a part of the French.

Back at Yokohama he found most of our Asiatic Fleet,
led by his old *New York,* flying the flag of his esteemed
superior, Admiral Rodgers, one of Evans' most cherished
intimates in the service. The *Yorktown* was among those
present, as ready as ever for tropics or icebergs, for friend
or foe.

Before running south, Evans wished to acquaint himself
with conditions in the Yangtze Valley. The press of other
duties might prevent this later on. The patrol of the Orient
covered an enormous beat.

Aboard the gunboat *Helena,* the Admiral and his staff
ascended this mighty river as far as Ichang, eleven hundred
miles from the sea, farther than any vessel of the *Helena's*
draught ever before had ventured. In the remote corners
of this watershed, there were American merchants and missionaries who looked for protection to the flags and guns
of our warships. Evans was received by local Chinese
overlords, and he at once endeavoured to instill a whole-

some respect for his countrymen's lives and to formulate measures for the application of force whenever prestige alone should prove an inadequate nourishment for such respect.

The season was advancing and chased the party downstream ahead of the lowering water, to the waiting *Kentucky* near the mouth. There was a further reason to make haste. At Yokohama the supreme responsibility was awaiting Bob Evans.

Twice in his youth, both times at Singapore, he had attended the transfer of the Asiatic command. Now he was the principal in the ceremony. Into his custody the United States entrusted the projection of its might and of its fair name beyond the cables' ends. Great was the honour. Retroactively it bestowed a full purpose upon the physical suffering since Fort Fisher. As, however, Admiral Rodgers dropped over the horizon, Bob Evans not only felt the heaviness of a friend's departure but also the weight of the added obligation that rested upon his own flag.

As Commander-in-Chief he stood out to sea, bound for the Philippines, that he had not visited since his youth. From a salutation to familiar Hong Kong of those same bygone days, he followed Dewey's course to Manila and passed through the entrance that now was so pregnant with association.

The Islands were in a deplorable state. So fearful had we been of the spectre of militarism, that untrained civilian jobholders had been sent out to take charge before the Army had completed its task of reconciling the inhabitants to the new ownership. So far we had done little to justify our substitution for Spain.

Governor General Taft was struggling with the situation in this most difficult transition period. From the start Evans liked this jovial gentleman and the two remained friends until the Admiral's death during Taft's presidency.

Each of them has left written testimonials of esteem for the other. This does not mean that they never had differences. In the turmoil of insular administration, their respective spheres of authority inevitably collided and the sparks flew. That their cordial relationship never even was scorched bespeaks its incombustible nature.

Only once was Evans really angry at the Governor. The former had transferred to the fleet certain marines long stationed on the beach. The Governor General attempted to nullify these orders upon the ground that he was in supreme authority ashore. The Admiral maintained that all naval personnel in the Far East, wherever detailed, was subject to his disposition as Commander-in-Chief and that he would not waste valuable marines upon what he considered non-naval duty. The marines went to sea.

Evans set forth to inspect the new home waters. He toured through the archipelago, to where it looks at Borneo. He saw a vast conglomeration of turbulent little worlds, at war with one another and with their white rulers. He penetrated the interior of Mindanao, the home of the Moros, those transplanted Mohammedans whose fezes survived several centuries of Malayan environment. At an advanced post he met Captain Pershing and, seven years before the latter's designation as Commander-in-Chief of our Expeditionary Force in France, Evans published an estimate of his soldierly qualities, selecting him of all the Army officers he encountered in the East for the highest praise.

The Admiral was not at all sure that "our beloved flag" in those remote, exotic regions "was not out of place," but "there it was." It is for the State Department to "reason why," as Lord Tennyson expressed it. Accepting the policy of imperialism from those authorized to promulgate it, the Admiral was not inclined toward any half-way measures in reducing the islands to submission. He viewed with impatience the efforts to argue with a bolo-hurling Moro or a head-hunting Igorot. He heard the Dutch and the Eng-

lish neighbours cynically deprecating our novel kind of colonial rule, and he concurred in their misgivings.

The Commander-in-Chief's function with respect to the
Philippines lay, of course, in the realm of their defence in
the event of another assault such as Dewey's. The tables
would be turned and Evans sought to master the lessons
negatively taught by the Spanish predecessors and to apply
sound principles of insular protection to the particular locale and conformation of the Philippines. The fleet tested
out the resources of Subig Bay and worked out elaborate
experiments by actual manœuvres in the other waters about
Luzon. Evans realized that an unfortified Gibraltar is not
an asset but a menace to peace and a source of bloodshed.
One is almost glad that he was spared a perusal of the clause
in the Treaty of Washington relinquishing our right—and
our duty—to fortify the Islands.

The first essential in devising defensive plans is, of
course, an exact knowledge of what is to be defended.
Strange as it seemed to Evans, no one at Manila could point
out to him on a chart the precise boundary dividing those
of the myriad islands to the southwest which Spain had
ceded to us, from those which Spain had not possessed.
Evans volunteered to draw such a line and thus, among
other results, enable Mr. Taft to ascertain of just what he
was Governor. Naturally the latter approved of the idea.
It was even more imperative that a great many uncharted
bays and passages be surveyed. The Admiral organized and
sent out an expedition to perform these tasks.

Landing at an out-of-the-way point to erect a signal
sight necessary in the course of this work, a midshipman
and some sailors were espied by a band of suspicious Moros
and savagely attacked. The Americans were rescued by
shipmates, just in time to avert a massacre, but some of
the assailant's blood was shed in the process. Back through
the jungles and across the water-passages to Manila, there
zig-zagged wild canards of a sanguinary war in which the

Navy had been the unprovoked aggressor. The newspapers published these rumours but the Admiral learned the true story.

"My surprise," he wrote in his memoirs, "can be imagined when I was accused by the press of starting a war with the Moros! In reply I stated what I had done, and added that if this was to produce a war, I could see no better cause for one. If an officer of the navy could not survey waters belonging to the United States in order to secure safe navigation for his ships, I thought the sooner we whipped those holding that view the better."

The Department, properly timid as to the slightest criticism of undue roughness toward civilians of any race or colour, improperly felt constrained to rebuke the Admiral before establishing the facts. The reprimand was based not only upon a false report of what had transpired but also upon the untenable ground that the surveys had interfered with fleet manœuvres, something Evans never would have permitted. He compelled the distant authorities to eat their impulsive words and to concede that in future such matters be left to his undisturbed discretion. Even in the sanctum of the arch-bureaucrats at Washington, it was proving inadvisable to take a misstep with this Admiral.

Evans' next bout was with some customs' officials at Manila and again he emerged the winner. Evidently not warned against treading on the Admiral's toes, one of the civilian collectors of duties attempted to exercise his authority aboard a naval transport lying at anchor. The "old man" waxed "a bit hot," and thereafter that particular agent of the Treasury Department avoided the ships of Fighting Bob's command as if they were an enemy's.

Winter over, it was time to go to higher latitudes. Evans swung over to North Borneo and Singapore, then up the Chinese coast to Hong Kong, Amoy, the mouth of the Yangtze and across to Nagasaki. Here he was amused to encounter a Russian squadron indulging in a display of strength to intimidate the Japanese. Where Evans discreetly smiled to himself, the Japanese "laughed at Russian sea power"—and they were to laugh last, too.

Cholera was still a ubiquitous menace to those Asiatic ports. Evans always stood in from sea wondering whether or not the plague had anchored ahead of him. Finding its yellow flag at Nagasaki, the *Kentucky* departed for Yokohama. The flagship sent many officers and men ashore on leave. Evans took his family and his staff on a short tour to the still unspoiled points of interest.

He and Mrs. Evans planned a trip to Pekin, the most picturesque city of China. The Admiral's official status would be a valuable key to many closed gates. There was an opportunity for such a visit before settling down to the intensive summer program at Chefoo.

When the fleet had assembled, the Commander-in-Chief took his party, including many officers, by rail to Tientsin and thence to the capital. They followed the route of the Boxer relief expedition and almost every mile was deeply interesting to the American naval men. It is not to be doubted that Bob Evans felt a pang of regret at having been absent from this campaign. He relived the march of the international column and the fighting at Pekin. Mrs. Evans doubtless found greater delight in the intrinsic wonders of that historic corner of ancient China.

The climax of the sightseeing was an audience with the Dowager Empress. The Admiral was not missing any of the Oriental sovereigns.

This royal lady found instant favour with him. "She was seated on her throne, beautifully dressed, calm, and dignified. . . . A more striking face, one to be longer remembered, I have never seen." As he gazed respectfully at the daughter of the ancient khans, he was close in experience to Marco Polo and yet beholding the splendid sunset of the last dynasty. The *Kentucky* was of another world, and this stranger behind the sacred portals was deeply stirred by the ineffable contrast. As he solemnly withdrew, however, from the majestic presence on the dais and made his exit through serried ranks of officials and eunuchs, the glamour paled. There was a spurious fringe about the monarch's court, which was to fray its way to the personage that graced the crown.

During the summer there came a report from reliable sources that the Americans in the Poyang Lake district might meet with violence. This was the twentieth century and the Admiral despatched a gunboat. There was no trouble. That is, the threatened Americans had none; the Admiral had plenty. He was asked by our Minister at Pekin why and upon what authority that preventive measure had been taken and was called upon to cite the specific clause of the specific treaty under which he had acted. How Evans loathed these bickerings with his fellow-countrymen! He had no disposition toward drafting a legal brief in support of every move he made. His reply declared that the sending of the warship "was based on the broad principle that wherever the Chinese Government allowed American citizens to reside and engage in business," the right to protect them followed.

It is recalled that, in orally delivering some of his masterful opinions from the bench, Chief Justice Marshall would state "the broad principle" involved and then, deferentially turning toward the more scholarly Justice at his side, would add: "My brother Story will cite the authorities."

In this instance, without Evans being aware of it, the issue between his "broad principle" and the challenging pettifogger was referred at Washington to a learned international lawyer, who was well qualified to "cite the authorities" for the Admiral. In a letter that conclusively settled the controversy, Secretary of State John Hay declared that the sending of the gunboat had been entirely correct. He referred to treaties of which the naval officer had never before heard but which fully justified his action.

Autumn saw another cruise. There was a memorable call at Tsingtao, where an old acquaintance, the former skipper of the *Hohenzollern* during Prince Henry's stay in the United States, was host to the entire squadron of four ships, in royal fashion as if the Admiral had been Prince Robley.

Repairs were planned at Japanese yards and the fleet assembled for the return to Manila. Evans was seized by one of his severe rheumatic attacks. This one confined him to his bed. The doctors were unable to relieve the pain. He could not stand on those legs. Could not? In a crisis?

The crisis struck and awed. The incredulous surgeons beheld their prostrate patient, like the subject of a miracle at a shrine, arise and jump about in the full vigour of his aroused activity.

To the Commander-in-Chief had come an electrifying inquiry as to how soon he could get the *Kentucky, Oregon, Wisconsin* and a squadron of cruisers under way for Honolulu. There was no explanation. Back to Washington sped the reply that the only time needed was that for coaling. Orders came to first dock some of the barnacled ships and then make the crossing. When Evans steamed away, in haste to the eastward instead of leisurely to the southward, he was still "in absolute ignorance" as to what the force would be called upon to do at its destination. Such sudden orders, hailing the big ships of the fleet thousands of miles away from its precincts, might mean a fight ahead. Evans was prepared for any eventuality.

To Mrs. Evans and the other women in Japan it was the old story. They had to shift for themselves and pray that the cables would bring no shocking news. In many cases the wives thus left wondering and alone did not see their husbands again for many months nor until by divers routes they had reached the United States.

The cruisers took a course enabling them to refuel in midocean. We hadn't learned that just that type of warship demands the greatest cruising radius (and our diplomats of 1930 forgot it again at London). The battleships ploughed direct for the Hawaiian Islands through mountainous seas that often hid one from the next in column. The Admiral had seldom made a rougher passage in any part of the world but his big gun platforms maintained station and the rendezvous with the cruisers was duly kept.

The fleet experienced the repetition of one day that results from the eastward bound crossing of the one hundred and eightieth meridian. Most of the ships enjoyed the extended rest of a double Sunday. When the men of the *Oregon* reached port and learned of this, they realized that a sour joke had been played on them. Taking a slight liberty with the navigator's computation, their skipper had completed certain delayed work by decreeing two strenuous *Mondays!*

Twelve days after leaving Yokohama, the fleet anchored off Honolulu in trim to fight. It remained to dance.

Justly proud of his time record and more than ever wondering what was up, the Commander-in-Chief flashed his arrival to Washington. Energetically refilling his depleted bunkers, he eagerly awaited further instructions. The despatch came and contained almost as much of a surprise as the original orders. When ready, the fleet was to return to its Asiatic waters! It was to steam to Manila via Guam. Permission was appended to delay the departure four days, at the Admiral's discretion, to comply with the request of the insular authorities for a gala naval visit.

Years later Evans learned from the lips of Theodore Roosevelt the explanation of this mysterious voyage. We had no fleet on our West Coast and no Panama Canal.

There was trouble—incidentally, over the prospective canal —with certain South American countries on that coast. The President wanted a demonstration of the time it would take the Asiatic Fleet to reach the American zone of the Pacific Ocean and probably he also thought that the availability of this force might be advertised to advantage. The time record, made under adverse weather conditions, was excellent. The President had occasion to rejoice that his friend was in command.

Honolulu has long been noted for its flower-bedecked hospitality and the American Navy has ever been a favourite visitor, before and after annexation. The Asiatic Fleet was an unusual sight. Individual units were familiar enough on their transpacific voyages but now the organization was present in its imposing entirety. The festivities were on a generous scale and, for both the islanders and ship's companies, the stop-over was a spree.

Four days the fleet was there and the Admiral had but three altercations. His average in results was again one hundred per cent. First, he had a general set-to with the Commandant of the Yard, an ancient and well-tried enemy, of whom Bob Evans could boast very few, especially among his colleagues. Then he had sharp and decisive clashes with the local collector of customs and inspector of immigration, respectively. The former quickly found it prudent to yield to the Admiral and the latter he barked off his ship.

The Fighting Bob legend went marching on, during peace as well as war.

Soon the column stood out and the sweep to the Philippines was utilized to visit Guam and other islands *en route* and to sound out the southern approach to Manila. Guam was another trophy of the Spanish War. Evans saw its significance. In time of peace we could procure fuel without owning the island, and in time of war it would be one more outpost to defend—and possibly to recapture after an initial loss. Guam, too, stands unfortified under the provisions of the 1922 Limitation of Armaments Treaty. When Evans stopped there in this autumn of 1903, it was unfortified by reason of sheer neglect and parsimony. What the democratic *conquistadores* in editorial rooms and Congress regarded as a splendid asset, was known by many of the men who in any national emergency would have to do the fighting, as a liability.

The last winter of Admiral Evans' Asiatic cruise now set in. Just as he had become acquainted with the Station, its people and current problems, from the Sea of Japan to the Straits of Malacca, his tour of duty was drawing to a close. It seems like a most uneconomic arrangement but the country can not ask its men to exile themselves for much longer periods and, of course, there are compensating advantages in biennial rotation of command.

When the calendar showed that what in more northern latitudes is called spring had arrived, the *Kentucky* steamed to Hong Kong and cleaned up for the homeward voyage. We still depended upon the Japanese and the British for most of our yard facilities in the East.

When the flagship relinquished the command and headed for New York, the Russo-Japanese War was in full blaze. What Evans had so clearly foreseen had come to pass. Events transpired with the sureness of purposeful destiny. The early and continued blows of the Japanese, that battered the over-extended grasping paw of the Bear, did not in the least astonish Admiral Evans as they did the Americans and Europeans at home.

Looking back upon his first real flag command with the perspective of distance, Bob Evans had every reason to feel satisfied with his performance. What has already been written of his two years in the Orient relates to their superficial aspects. Where he and the fleet had been and the adventures they encountered were of far less importance than the hard routine work of the organization itself. When the President had bade Evans farewell, he had not directed the

Admiral to show his men the ports of Cathay but to "be
sure every night when you turn in that your command is in
better shape for a fight than it was when you turned out in
the morning." The Honolulu trip, without notice and in
battle trim, was proof, far more convincing than a hundred
reviews and a thousand reports, of how well the Admiral
had obeyed this order of his chief. That successful cruise,
a notable one in the history of modern fleet movements,
was the climax of his Asiatic command and a fitting precursor to the epochal cruise around South America that
was to crown the naval achievements of both Roosevelt
and Evans.

The summers at Chefoo and the winters at Manila had
been less picturesque than that grand swing across the
Pacific, but they had made that latter achievement possible.
Evans had taught the fleet all it knew about formation de-
ployment. Starting with small groups and eventually including as many of his heterogeneous units as he could, the
squadron drills had been developed up to fleet manœuvres.
Many a captain, navigator and watch officer learned the
rudiments and some of the finer points of this part of naval
work in the school of the Asiatic Fleet under Admiral
Evans.

The most important progress, however, and progress
that did more than train individuals, that advanced the
science itself, was made in gunnery. The Orient has been
the cradle of ordnance and ballistics. Here the lazy officer
could idle his time and the enterprising one find opportunities for experiment that were not available during the
crowded programs of home service.

The great strides in target hitting that featured naval
development during the first few years of the century, that
reduced the previous high percentage of misses to the previous low percentage of hits, came for the most part as surely
out of the East as did gunpowder itself.

In these waters the late Admiral Sir Percy Scott had

just done his revolutionary work, based on the telescope sight, as Captain of H.M.S. *Terrible,* and it was there that he had inspired the then Lieutenant William S. Sims to introduce modern gunnery to our Navy. The first summer of Evans's intensive drilling at Chefoo, Scott was stalking deer at Balmoral with King Edward VII and enlisting the royal influence to the cause of British naval gunnery. Sims had violated the professional proprieties in a successful effort to bring to the President's attention the deplorable shooting of American crews and was supervising target practise conducted along the new lines.

Less dramatic and less known was the hard work of Admiral Evans and his staff. Possibly it was also less effective than the master strokes of Scott and Sims but it counted. Lieutenants Brittain, McLean and Bristol, all distinguished admirals of a later day, made it possible, by tireless efforts in the employment of ingenious improvisations, to have the equivalent of daily target practise without a proportionate expenditure of ammunition, the cost of which would have been prohibitive. Evans had not heard of Scott's work in the *Terrible* and Sims had had no part in the Admiral's endeavours. All of these resourceful pioneers deserve credit. They refused to accept the standards that had been high enough to achieve Manila and Santiago. Perhaps Evans' most valuable contribution to this progress in gunnery was the adoption of systematic gun-crew training *as a fleet exercise.* The results had shown up gratifyingly when the targets were towed in after the regular full charge firing. Sub-calibre practise had been brought to its apex of usefulness.

These were heartening reflections as the *Kentucky's* wake foamed astern over the Indian Ocean.

There had been, of course, the pin-pricks. Once during the Asiatic cruise the "old man's" temperament, with its proclivity for fiery outbursts, thrust him into a position that he could not fully justify to the Department, whose handling of the incident seems to have been sensible.

Evans insisted upon the proper behaviour of his subordinates on the beach, especially in foreign ports. Of his officers he expected the deportment of gentlemen under all circumstances. If they drank, they must carry their liquor as to the quarterdeck born. The line officers, graduates of the Academy, had a pride in their uniforms that had been acquired as plebes along the Severn and had been more deeply ingrained with every year of active duty. They gave little trouble. Occasionally, however, an officer of the non-combatant corps, a surgeon or a paymaster, would forget himself and his obligations to the dignity of the Navy. At Chefoo, where Evans was particularly anxious to create an excellent impression, so that a more or less regular summer base, with ample accommodations for the officers' families, could be established there, one such occurrence took place.

Assistant-Paymaster Rishworth Nicholson had the misfortune of imbibing too freely and not being able to conceal his over-indulgence. In this condition, it was reported to the Admiral, he had assaulted an elderly civilian. The twist of cowardice in the affair enraged Bob Evans, who wanted to oust the offender from the Navy at once. There are, however, Regulations. A Court-Martial was convened and, at the conclusion of the trial, the accused was duly found guilty. So far so good. The sentence imposed, however, fell short of satisfying the Admiral. The Court reduced the Paymaster five numbers in grade, and three of the members recommended the exercise of clemency by the Convening Authority. To Evans this seemed a disgrace. He saw no room in a self-respecting organization of gentlemen for one who had so flagrantly violated its code. This was no occasion for punishment as it might possibly have been in the case of a bluejacket, for whom greater allowances might be made, but for elimination. The Admiral as Convening Authority could diminish the severity of the sentence but he could not increase it. Frustrated in the exercise of his indignation, he saw but one thing to do and, of course, he did it. The sentence was set aside altogether "as being totally inadequate and insufficient," in a scathing rebuke of the members of the Court whom he declared would "not again . . . be placed in a position of passing judgment on other persons or guarding and maintaining the honour and dignity of the naval service." A protest was made by at least one and possibly two of the officers so castigated, as an unwarranted reflection upon their integrity and an unlawful invasion of their right to independently perform their court-martial duties. Coercion of a court's members smacks of tyranny. The moral justification in any instance is no excuse. "Hard cases make bad law."

The Department was in a quandary as to the attitude it should take. Secretary Moody consulted Secretary of State Elihu Root, recognized as an astute and sober-minded authority on questions of jurisprudence. Finally, after the matter was aired in the press, the Admiral was sustained, but at the same time he was cautioned to be more moderate in his language. Members of courts, it was stated, "are not subject to control." The exact scope of the power of a convening authority was left undefined but the indication was clear that only Evans' personal prestige and the fact that he had been "actuated by high sense of duty and inspired by a regard for the honour and welfare of the service" saved him a formal reprimand. The Admiral had often proved himself an able emergency advocate but he lacked the detached serenity essential in a judge. It is not to be supposed that he cared a fig for anything the civilian hairsplitters at Washington might say! That Paymaster deserved expulsion, the members of the Court a rebuke, and the red-tape surrounding the administration of discipline a mighty slash!

After days of rest and relaxation, the Island of Ceylon

loomed up on the bow and the *Kentucky* landed Admiral Evans at Colombo for a visit, while coal was shovelled aboard and the men given liberty. Of course, he went up to Kandy in the mountains, as all strangers do, and his admiration of the attractions of this place was great.

His old route around the Cape was as obsolete as the ship in which he had followed it. He saw the Suez Canal for the first time and, when once more on the blue bosom of the Mediterranean, felt entirely at home. There was a thrill in revisiting these old haunts. He was eager to see his native land and his family but there was a temptation to pause at every port of his youth, each with its associations of faces and events. The by-gone times came back with a rush.

The *Kentucky* was of the new generation. Unhampered by memories, she pushed steadily westward, interested in nothing ashore but enough coal to proceed. It was necessary to refuel when nearing the longitude of Italy, and not the incomparable bay but the low price of coal drew the battleship to Naples.

The Italians had not been prominent in the East but Evans saw them now in all their glory, entertaining the President of France. The fleets of both nations were assembled for the fiesta. The *Kentucky* felt like an intruder at this Latin reunion and offered to depart at once, but the hospitable Italians wouldn't hear of such a thing and assigned the American flagship to a grand-stand berth next to the French flagship.

The following morning the object of the stop was pursued. "While coaling from lighters on both sides, and with the coal dust so thick that one could hardly breathe," the King of Italy came alongside and paid the Admiral a surprise call. He certainly had no occasion to feel that the ship had been put in royal condition just for him! The sailors "dropped the coal whips and stood at attention." The Admiral "explained the situation" but it was quite superfluous.

The King had a grand time seeing the ship's company at work in dungarees, a rare sight for a monarch.

Victor Emanuel III was then a young man in his thirties and in the full glory of his pre-Fascist reign. He entertained Admiral Evans at a dinner at the palace. The latter was impressed by the toothpicks, served in envelopes bearing the royal coat of arms, but he did not dare use them because he sat between Her Majesty the Queen and a distinguished young diplomat named de Martino, who is now the Italian Ambassador at Washington.

There was a visit to the Rock, almost a second home, coal at Madeira and a high speed run to Sandy Hook; New York at last.

Evans went ashore, believing that his final sea duty had been performed. Back to the lighthouse service he was called, and he settled down to prospective retirement and old age. He forgot, evidently, that Theodore Roosevelt was still Commander-in-Chief.

32

SUPREMACY

~~~~~~

Evans found the Navy in fine fettle. The lingering glamour won during the Spanish War had kept it in the generous graces of Congress, and the election in November had retained Roosevelt at the helm for another term. Growing industry meant expanding commerce and emphasized the vital importance of sea power. One by one, the new battleships were sliding off the ways. Every few months another big vessel, embodying the last word in design and construction, was quietly taking her place in what was still called the North Atlantic Squadron but was soon to be known as the Atlantic Fleet. For we were gathering more than a collection of ships; we were assembling the elements of a unified, balanced, coördinated fighting force. Perhaps, after all, Mahan was a prophet in his own country.

To mould these ships into divisions and the divisions into a fleet whose component parts would respond to the direction of its leader, as readily as the complicated mechanism of a gun obeys the jerk of its lanyard, was the task awaiting the next Commander-in-Chief. Every one in the know, excepting only the Admiral himself, took for granted Bob Evans' assignment to that duty. The President wished it and the Secretary fully approved it. Evans alone was astonished when the orders came dislodging him from the comfortable seat at the head of the Lighthouse Board.

As the grand chief of the hierarchy afloat, as the responsible head of the maturing American battle fleet, Robley D. Evans on March thirty-first, 1905, hoisted his flag on the new *Maine*. It is possible that, in his long career, his greatest service was that now about to be rendered in a period of peace. Given a group of fairly effective units unskilled in joint operations, in three years he was to hurl into the Pacific a fleet of modern excellence, even as measured by the steel line of Togo's that had been tempered at Tsushima.

For the nucleus of his staff, the Admiral naturally rallied around him those able specialists who had helped him modernize the Asiatic Fleet. The ability to surround himself with devoted experts was one of the factors of his success as Commander-in-Chief. Evans was always the leader, yet he left the technical details of administration to the subordinates well qualified to handle them under his supervision. He was an adept executive.

When, off Pensacola, he first ascended the flagship bridge and looked up and down the anchorage, the Admiral found a total of eight battleships, consisting chiefly of the *Maine* and *Georgia* classes. The number was increased during his régime, until finally, before the world cruise, it was exactly doubled. With vertical, tall, slender smoke-stacks and, especially in silhouette, the lines of armoured cruisers, they reminded a veteran of Santiago more of the *Brooklyn* than of the chunky battleships of '98. Contrary to Evans' point of view, these new twelve-inch gun platforms had yielded resistance power to added speed. The available destroyers were really just outgrown torpedo boats, not sufficiently seaworthy or numerous to perform their proper function in fleet operations. Not until during the World War did we lay down enough destroyers of the one thousand ton size that Evans knew and declared he needed in 1905.

The undreamt-of project of the world cruise was three summers and two winters ahead. Every week of this intervening period was squeezed of its hours by the tireless leader, in waters suited by the season to the most intense training. The addition, singly, of the new units with their new complements slowed down the pace of indoctrination. There were also the usual problems of repair and upkeep, the inevitable friction with the yards, the exasperating delays that strained one's faith in the efficiency possibilities of a democracy.

These vexations were as old berth-mates of Bob Evans' as the pain in his legs and failed utterly to distract his attention from the single objective. Day and night he laboured, always with and through his enterprising staff and his fast-learning captains, and a fleet was wrought into being. Every target practise was a real battle test, every cruise was an exacting manœuvre; present opportunities were seized and new ones created.

It was this developing fleet that furnished the imposing moral background to the Russo-Japanese Peace Conference at Portsmouth and was tacitly supporting the other diplomatic advances of the President, consolidating the new world position of the United States.

During this period, the General Board was finding much stimulating reading in the intelligence from across both oceans. Shipwise, there were rumours of fantastic new designs on Lord Fisher's desk at Whitehall. Fleetwise, there was a rumble of approbation over the three unit division of the Japanese battleship force. The blue prints of the future *Michigan* and *South Carolina*, later to be known as our first dreadnoughts, were redrafted and redrafted. As for the division size, there arose the three unit and the four unit schools. Evans tested out matters at sea during his summer cruising. He found that there was, of course, much greater facility in handling signals among three vessels than among four. The ratio was not three to four but two to three, as it was not the number of units but the number of intervals that counted. This advantage of the smaller division, however important, seemed to the Admiral more than offset by tactical considerations that favoured the orthodox quartet arrangement. He urged the latter's retention and, against influential opposition, Evans' view was adopted. Our divisions remained foursomes. European naval practise followed this old standard. The Battle of Jutland was fought out by lines so grouped, as nearly as the available units permitted, and our own battleship fleet is still organized on this basis.

The drilling of the force as a whole was by no means permitted to obscure the internal efficiency and well-being of the individual ships. Evans is still remembered in the Outfit for the dramatic suddenness and the pitiless thoroughness of his inspections. Often an Officer of the Deck would espy the barge coming alongside and almost at the last minute breaking out the blue-starred flag, warning of an official visit by the "old man" himself. Sometimes the entire ship was in for a white-gloved scrutiny that began at the fighting tops and ended in the crank-shaft. Occasionally, to the bluejackets delight, Old Gimpy would announce himself as the guest of the general mess and take his seat upon a bench with the deckhands and firemen, using their gear and partaking of their meal with the most critical judgment of its quality. He was the Admiral of every officer and every jack tar in the organization; of every battleship and every "spit kid" dinghy.

It can not be doubted that to Evans the price of supreme command in some respects was high. It implied his survival afloat of his seniors and his direct contemporaries. After years of service among friends of all ages, it must have occasioned a feeling of loneliness in the bosom of one so devoted to them, to find himself upon the very pinnacle, where there was room for no one else and to which all others in the fleet gazed aloft. The old crowd was gone—dead or

retired or on the beach for ever—gone from the fighting
Navy and the sea. He himself, the Acting Ensign at Fort
Fisher, the follower of such a host of admirals, was now the
dean. The station in life was now attaining an exalted
dignity appropriate to the stiffness of the lower limbs, but
this stiffness never spread above the thighs, in any sense.
And these old legs, like everything else in the squadron,
yielded to the discipline of the master, having their only
triumph in his moments of fiery vocal outbursts caused by
a sudden flash of pain.

The decrepit legs were not necessary, however, to keep
alive the tradition of salty eloquence. Controversies with
landlubbers were quite able to do this unaided. Almost
wherever his nerve-weary and bodily fatigued sailors tumbled
ashore for recreation, the sanctimonious uplifters made felt
their solicitous influence. Rum and reformers, often working at cross purposes and often working in unconscious
alliance, gave the Admiral no end of trouble. In Cuba, on
the Florida coast, in New England, he encountered the pur-
veyors of noxious spirits and the zealots who proscribed
healthful Sunday exercise and mild alcoholic beverages. He
obeyed the laws of each jurisdiction, but he often found it
impossible to reconcile them with his own notions of what
was rational. Speaking of the poison liquor caches near
the Guantanamo target ranges, he wrote: "If we could
have had a canteen where the men could get beer and light
wines, under proper restrictions, all this trouble would have
been spared us. A wise Congress had, however, decreed
that we should not have a canteen, and in consequence we
had to struggle with a much greater evil." Little did he
realize what a momentous experiment was casting its
shadow before.

The summer of 1905 witnessed a strange meeting in
mid-Atlantic of two great American sea fighters, who stood
at opposite ends of the Navy's history. The Atlantic Fleet,

reconnoitring as in a war game, moved off the coast seriatim and intercepted on its westward course a detachment of four ships under Rear Admiral Sigsbee. Upon nearing the latter's flagship, Robley D. Evans saluted the homecoming remains of John Paul Jones. The following April, elaborate ceremonies, worthy of an unknown hero according to later custom, were held at Annapolis, where the body was laid in a special crypt in the chapel.

The story of the disappearance and discovery of Jones' remains is as amazing as it is familiar. The retired terror of the seas had died in Paris neither obscurely nor altogether without honour and there had been a public interment. Thereafter, however, the Commodore's compatriots had seemed less interested in his bones than in his inspiring memory. The grave had been forgotten and lost amid the upheavals and reconstructions of Paris during the full·run of the kaleidoscopic nineteenth century. The glamour and mystery that had obscured his origin and much of his life lent credence to recurring legends, even in recent years, that Jones' body had been secretly removed from France and buried in Scotland, in the Mississippi delta and other widely scattered places.

Then General Horace Porter, with his talented energies unweakened by advancing age, went to France as our Minister. This gallant soldier regarded the laying of wreaths on tombstones as an exercise indispensable to the votaries of heroes. From the mastery of military and business problems, his executive ability had turned to the successful campaign for Grant's Tomb. Settled down in the calm of the Legation, a passion had seized him to behold John Paul Jones suitably buried on American soil. First, however, he had had to find the body. To any one else this would have seemed not merely a hopelessly difficult but an absolutely impossible task. The burial permit had been burned. Tracing the broken thread of circumstance through record-burning conflagrations, revolutions, Latin administrative disorder, vanished and mutilated archives, the General toiled on indefatigably. He devoted his private purse, his every free hour, his rich imagination, his consummate tact, his official influence and his analytical acumen to the quest that to all others seemed—and with good reason—doomed to failure. The ingenuity and perseverance displayed by General Porter were of a classic magnitude. Finally, that burning enthusiasm, driving those other qualities, riding roughshod over obstacles like a caterpillar tank, had carried him to the old submerged burial ground and to the leaden casket itself, within which had been found the well preserved corpse that the most eminent anthropometrists of Paris had positively pronounced to be Jones's.

General Porter had gathered a persuasive mass of affirmative evidence that had corroborated the physical identification and he had also run down to disproof the mythical tales of burial elsewhere. There had survived no reasonable doubt that the remains of John Paul Jones had been retrieved.

Thus Evans saluted Jones. The fleet wheeled about and escorted its progenitor to the Capes of the Chesapeake.

Another and by no means macabre mission of welcome was assigned to Evans a few months later.

On a bleak November morning when, common belief has it, there floated down the Hudson River the ballot boxes whose uncounted contents would have elected William Randolph Hearst the Mayor of New York the previous day, there stood upstream the Atlantic Fleet. With the staunch Fighting Bob in command, the spectacle gave a feeling of national security in contrast to the disquieting news of revolution in Russia and of iniquities in politics and finance at home.

Flying his flag as usual on the *Maine,* the Admiral's force consisted of eight battleships, including the newer ones and his own old *Iowa,* and four armoured cruisers.

They had come from the reception at Annapolis to the
British Cruiser Squadron under Prince Louis of Battenberg.
New York was to have the visitors for a week and in they
stood the day after the arrival of our own fleet. The flagship *Drake*, accompanied by the *Cornwall, Berwick, Essex,
Bedford* and *Cumberland*, anchored near their naval hosts.
From Fifty-fourth Street to General Porter's Grant's Tomb
stretched the line in imposing array. Few who beheld the
smart squadron under the White Ensigns would have guessed
that this call of courtesy to American waters was not to be
repeated for a quarter of a century.

Rather quietly in 1931, Admiral Sir Michael Hodges,
Commander-in-Chief of the Royal Navy's Atlantic Fleet,
brought the mammoth *Nelson* and *Rodney* and the Second
Cruiser Squadron for a gam with our fleet at Panama during
the annual manœuvres. Little was said publicly about the
business aspects of the visit but perhaps much more was accomplished in the direction of coöperative conversations
than during that much more conspicuous entertainment of
1905. Sir Michael demonstrated to the Pacific world that
with American good will he could squeeze his broadest-
blistered leviathans through the Isthmian Canal. His staff
had an opportunity to confer with ours, the newest vessels of
both navies were available for mutual inspection, and after
a few days the Englishmen sailed off.

Prince Louis, on the other hand, partook freely of our
social hospitality. The Four Hundred's strain of Anglo-
Saxon lineage was still sufficiently unmixed to lend to
British aristocracy a glamour that was unique. Although
the visitor had not yet changed his surname to Mountbatten
nor been elevated to the peerage as Marquess of Milford
Haven, he was a *bona fide* Prince (if not of the realm) and
he bore the high commission of the King, which were
ample credentials to arouse New York's Mayfair to a state
of gratified excitement. Arriving upon the birthday of
Edward VII, the Prince graced a banquet worthy of the

finest monarchical traditions. From the hearing chamber
of Charles Evans Hughes' insurance frauds investigation,
the good democrats hastened to forget, in the toasts to His
Majesty's health, the scandalous disclosures of the fiscal
involutions.

Fifth Avenue seemed to take even more enthusiastically
to the German Prince Louis in a British uniform than it
had, three years earlier, to the German Prince Henry in a
German uniform. The brewery magnates were not in
prominence upon this later occasion, the ceremonies remaining under the supervision of those normally supreme in the
responsibilities of Society.

The Rear Admiral was charming and a recognized
leader in his profession. Ashore and afloat, Evans found
himself in the Prince's company a great deal, and he enjoyed the association and the friendship it engendered. The
round of the exclusive ballrooms led him over familiar
territory.

Manhattan's mansions and clubs vied with one another
in staging elaborate entertainments. The Prince reciprocated
at a resplendent dance aboard his flagship, the *Drake,* now
moored alongside the Cunard pier. Not even a cold autumn
wind, lashing against the protecting canvas, could chill the
gaiety of this occasion as those fortunate enough to have
survived the pruning of the guest lists crowded over the
cruiser's festooned decks. Admiral and Mrs. Evans with
their daughters headed the American naval contingent.
Preserving the nautical atmosphere, supper was announced
by a boatswain's pipe. The Prince gave his arm to Mrs.
Evans, and Lady Townley, wife of the Counsellor to the
British Embassy, was escorted by Bob Evans.

While this evening was to Mrs. Astor's cohorts the
climax of the week, the Prince and Evans took most delight
in the memorable night at Coney Island when the American
bluejackets, at their own expense, gave a dinner and vaude-
ville show of their own arranging for the enlisted men

of the British squadron. Scorning proffered champagne, the two Admirals joined the tars in splicing the main brace in homely, wholesome beer. An average of over ten bottles apiece was emptied.

As the party rose to its height, there was only one joy-restraining influence: the expiration of the British liberty at seven a. m. Two members of the American sailors' committee pressed toward the Prince to beseech an extension for their guests. Neither the remonstrance nor the command of several of their officers halted their advance until only their own Fighting Bob stood between these intrepid petitioners and the Prince.

"What do you men want?" demanded Evans. He explained that no such request as was contemplated would be in order. But Prince Louis overheard the colloquy, and a megaphone boomed out the announcement that all British liberty was extended until the following noon. A deafening shout arose and, when seven o'clock in the morning came, the festivities showed no sign of abatement. It took many of the guests a couple of days to find their way back to their ships. The British squadron's departure had to be postponed pending the tardy return of many of Prince Louis' most jovial men, but a different reason was officially assigned for the delay.

Finally the visit came to its end. The Prince and his staff, in full uniform, set forth from the old Hotel Netherlands in electric hansoms and were met by Admiral Evans' barge at the foot of West Seventy-ninth Street. There was a brief ceremony of leave-taking on the *Maine*. Said the New York *Herald:* "The meeting lost all its formality at once, for the two are warm friends and the words of parting were stripped of the terms ordinarily used."

Bound for Gibraltar, the British cruisers slipped down the bay, and Admiral Evans despatched his ships to various yards for winter overhaul and docking.

There followed a winter of hard work in the West Indies, with strenuous manœuvres *en route* in both directions, a spring of overhaul and leave, and a summer of more hard work and more manœuvres in northern waters. These unpicturesque months of toil beyond the horizon were bearing fruit, and even if editors, Congressmen and the general public were unappreciative, there was always the observant eye peering seaward from the White House or Sagamore Hill to inspire the best effort. The target practise of the summer in Cape Cod Bay was witnessed by the President from Admiral Evans' bridge.

At Guantanamo the following winter there were sixteen battleships, four complete divisions. For some time this constituted the battleship force, old units being dropped as new ones reported for duty.

It was during Evans' régime that wireless telegraphy took its miraculous place in fleet communication, involving such revolutionary changes in tactics. Back in 1904, President Roosevelt had appointed an inter-departmental board to consider the entire question of wireless telegraphy in the service of the national government and had named Evans as a member, representing the Navy. At first the novelty was regarded chiefly as an emergency device but its general utility was quickly recognized. Evans experimented for years with its practical possibilities and, when he relinquished command in 1908, radio was an accepted and well understood element of fleet operations. He was not unique in his appreciation of the adaptability of this invention to naval purposes, but he is remembered, and justly, as the American officer who put it to use in our fleet.

One memorable event of that year interrupted the routine of drill.

When on his last visit to Singapore, Admiral Evans had been royally entertained by the Governor, Sir Frank Swettenham, who insisted upon his visitor even lodging at

Government House. The invitation had come at a time when it was sure to be appreciated, as the flagship was coaling and the hotels were crowded. Evans rested, ate that famous curry for which he had not lost any of the fondness developed during his first cruise to the East, and spent many delightful hours chatting with the young Governor, who was a product of the Indian service and a thoroughly charming Englishman. "I have never," wrote Evans, "enjoyed a visit elsewhere as much as I did this one to Government House, Singapore." "Never" in a career like that of Evans is a big word, but he meant it.

On the morning of January fifteenth, while the Admiral was temporarily aboard the battleship *Alabama* at Guantanamo Bay, an orderly brought him a despatch. He read it with an expression of horror and handed it to Rear Admiral Davis, commanding the second division, of which the *Alabama* was the flagship.

"You are the man for this job," said Evans, "and I want you to prepare to get under way."

The message was the first word that had reached the fleet of the terrific earthquake at Kingston, Jamaica, the previous afternoon, and was a request for help, transmitted via Havana, where the British Consul had been appealed to by the Governor of the stricken island. The catastrophe had been a grave one from any standpoint and had left the City of Kingston and its environs in a pitiful state of devastation.

A great agricultural conference had been convened to which had come delegates from many parts of the Empire, including several prominent men of public affairs. Such diverse celebrities as Sir James Ferguson, a celebrated veteran of the Crimean War and later an administrator in the Dominions and India, and Earl Dudley and Hall Caine were there. Most of the visitors arrived on Friday the eleventh and devoted the week-end to sightseeing trips.

On Monday the fourteenth the convention was opened.

It was a beautiful day. At about three thirty, the foundations of the city suddenly reared up without the slightest warning of any kind and violently upset the entire community, buildings, pavements, people and all, as a child might pull a cloth from under a table set for dinner. There was one omnipotent shock, which seemed to toss the earth itself and respect nothing upon its surface. A large passenger steamer moored alongside her wharf was hurled out of the water and dropped back with a resounding splash, luckily escaping the pier. There had been no warning tremors, usual in severe earthquakes. Before any one knew what had happened, it was all over. The city was a wreck. Structures collapsed in a way to jeopardize neighbouring ones still standing, the large Myrtlebank Hotel was a pile of ruins, the streets were no longer thoroughfares, fires were breaking out, panic seizing the populace, and those not killed or injured were standing about dazed, unable to grasp the situation or know what to do. The flames along the waterfront spread rapidly and the whole warehouse district was going up in smoke. The military hospital was burned to the ground. Those homes which had not fallen apart were dangerously unstable.

As soon as the reality made itself evident to the populace, the survivors rushed about in terrorized anxiety, seeking their families and friends. The men made their way as best they could from the commercial section to the sites of their homes. Others, away from their stores and offices when the tremor occurred, stumbled over the débris to ascertain what, if anything, remained of their places of business. The agricultural convention was a shamble; Sir James Ferguson and many other delegates were dead.

To cope with the situation, there were only the few police and the small garrison of troops, altogether an utterly inadequate force to maintain order in the shattered city.

The cables had been snapped, but on the next day, after a night of unspeakable misery, with the dead lying about in the open, the wounded uncared for, thousands of homeless shifting for themselves as best they could, and the fires raging unchecked, the American Consul succeeded in getting a laconic message through to Washington. The world was shocked and horrified. President Roosevelt immediately wired his profound sympathy to King Edward and Secretary of State Root offered every aid to Sir Edward Grey, the Foreign Secretary, and to the Chargé then the senior at the Embassy—none other than Esme Howard, a generation later the Ambassador.

Practical assistance was, of course, the first essential and, before the Department could direct Admiral Evans to send all possible help, he was, as has been shown, characteristically acting upon his own initiative. Admiral Davis was requisitioning all available medical supplies and food from the fleet and loading them aboard the *Alabama* and *Indiana*. These battleships, however, lumbering hulks for such an emergency, were not fast enough to satisfy the spirited Commander-in-Chief, and he signalled to the swiftest of his destroyer greyhounds to "prepare for a full-speed run at sea." This was nine thirty, within a few minutes of the receipt of the Havana despatch.

The *Whipple,* to which the flag-hoist signal had been directed, was in the outer harbour engaged in flotilla manœuvres. An hour and a quarter later the lithe destroyer was slicing the Caribbean with her knifelike bow, headed for Jamaica, with a full cargo of first-aid material and three surgeons from the fleet. She taxed her boilers and the propellers were whirled at their highest possible rate of revolutions per minute despite the roughness of the sea. Early that evening she picked up the Island ahead and soon reached the channel leading into Kingston Harbour. Already she could perceive the effects of the earthquake. In the distance, the sky was crimson from the continuing conflagration and here at Plumb Point the lighthouse was on its beam ends. Buoys had been unmoored or displaced.

The former aids to navigation were now worse than useless. A couple of pilots came aboard but flatly refused to take the *Whipple* through such a hazardous channel. Very well. The skipper, Lieutenant Commander Anderson of Cienfuego's cable-cutting fame, brushed aside these timorous civilians and felt his way safely into Kingston. The spectacle there was appalling. The city was a burning wreck.

The surgeons commenced their relief without having to be told what to do, while Anderson reported his arrival to the Governor and informed him that Admiral Davis was following with many more supplies and men. The Governor was active in the relief work, going from spot to spot and supervising everything.

In the meantime the battleships had completed sailing preparations and Evans, bidding Davis God-speed, gave him *carte blanche* to extend all possible assistance to the Governor.

"You will find him a charming man," said Evans, "because he is a brother of Frank Swettenham, my friend in Singapore. Any brother of his must be a good fellow."

The following day the relief squadron was sighted off Kingston. Admiral Davis delivered Admiral Evans' respects, and placed himself, his ships, his men and his supplies at the disposal of the Governor, who was by then exhausted from his sleepless labours amid the havoc and whose secretary indicated that he was thankful beyond words for the succour at hand.

The hospital corps turned to and distributed the bandages, drugs and other material, all sorely needed. The crews sent details ashore to feed the starving masses, who had been without nourishment or shelter since the upheaval. Other sailors were rushed to quell a mutiny at the jail, rebuild the lighthouses, clear the streets, tear down dangerous walls, recover dead bodies and attend to the innumerable tasks that very naturally were beyond the limited facilities of the colony. They prevented looting and ac-

tually caught some thieves in the act of carrying off a
safe from a collapsed shop. The populace was as grateful
for the timely and friendly coöperation of these trained men
as they were for the supplies they had brought with them.

A Jamaican describing the disaster has written: "Fortunately the American Navy . . . put in an appearance,
bringing prompt help and sympathy from the American
people, which was greatly appreciated."

Order was being brought out of chaos. The Governor
was able to get a little rest. Then, on the day following
Admiral Davis' arrival, while he was tirelessly directing the
ministrations of mercy by his men, always under the general leadership of the local authorities, there was delivered
to him one of the most amazing documents that can be
found in the files of the British Colonial Office. To be adequately appreciated, it must be read in full:

January 18, 2 p. m.
"Dear Admiral Davis,

"I thank you very much for your kind letter of the 17th
(delivered to me this morning), for your kind call, and for
all the assistance you have given, and have offered us. While
I most fully and heartily appreciate your very generous offer
of assistance, I feel that it is my duty to ask you to reëmbark
your working party, and all parties which your kindness has
prompted you to land. If, in consideration of the American
Vice-Consul's assiduous attention to his family at his country
house, the American Consulate may need guarding in your
opinion (he was present, and it was unguarded one hour ago),
I have no objection to your detailing a force for the sole purpose of guarding it, but that party must not have firearms or
anything more offensive than clubs or staves. I find your
working party this morning helping a tradesman to clean his
shop; the tradesman is delighted to get valuable work done
without cost to himself, and if Your Excellency were to remain
long enough, I am sure that almost the whole of the private
owners would be glad of the Navy to save them from expense.
It is no longer any question of humanity; all the dead died

days ago, and the work of giving them burial is merely one of convenience. I should be glad to accept delivery of the safe which the alleged thieves were in possession of from the jeweller's shop. The American Consular Agent has no knowledge of it; the shop is close to a sentry post, and the officer in charge of post professes profound ignorance of the incident, but there is still on the premises a large safe which has been opened by the fire. I believe police surveillance of no city is adequate to protect private property. I may remind your Excellency that not long ago it was discovered that thieves had lodged and pillaged the town house of a New York millionaire during absence of owner for the summer. But this fact would not have justified a British Admiral in landing an armed party to assist the New York Police.—J. A. Swettenham."

Admiral Davis was flabbergasted. He found the Governor and was then curtly told to his face what he had been unable to believe in black and white. Not only that but he was informed that the American warships were unwelcome and that their prompt departure was desired! The whole proceeding was so absolutely incomprehensible that the stunned Admiral, who at last encountered a form of hostility he did not know how to meet, could say nothing. The remainder of the supplies was unloaded and delivered to the authorities, the crews reëmbarked and the squadron withdrawn. The populace, totally unaware of what had transpired, cheered their sailor friends with nothing but gratitude in their hearts, and the diplomatic wires buzzed with expressions of British appreciation.

Admiral Davis came over the side of the fleet flagship at Guantanamo and saluted his chief. Silently they walked together to Evans' quarters. In the privacy of the cabin, Davis looked at his superior and said:

"Admiral, I have met the brother of your Singapore friend. You may select good fellows for some of your friends but I will be damned if you can select one for me!"

The narrative of what had occurred at Kingston made

Evans' blood boil. It was a sorry sequel to his good intentions, the reckless dash of the *Whipple* and the tireless efforts of his squadron. "A more disgusted set of officers and men I have never seen." At least, however, they had the gratitude of Fighting Bob, who lauded the work of one and all on the relief expedition.

"I not only approved the conduct of Admiral Davis in the whole matter, but I heartily commended him for the wonderful coolness he showed under most trying conditions."

The Department and the President and the British press joined in this chorus of praise.

When Davis left Evans alone, the latter must have reflected upon the inexplicability of the operation of the human mind. Probably his memory carried him back to the deck of the *New York* at Trinidad the day of the great fire. Now he knew why Admiral Meade had been so cautious about landing the fire and rescue parties!

The Government at London learned of the affair with embarrassed astonishment. Lord Elgin, the Colonial Secretary, was not the Minister to trifle with such a situation. He cabled a brusque inquiry as to the accuracy of the letter as reported in the newspapers and added:

"If such a letter is correctly attributed to you I must observe that both in tone and expression it is highly improper, and especially unbecoming to His Majesty's representative in addressing the officer of a friendly Power engaged upon an errand of mercy. I must further require you to withdraw forthwith and unreservedly any such letter, and to express your regret for having written it. Your withdrawal should be telegaphed to me at once, when it will be transmitted to the Government of the United States through the proper channels.— Elgin."

On January twenty-third came Swettenham's reply admitting that he had sent the letter in question. We do not know what Lord Elgin then cabled, but on the twenty-fourth there were two despatches from Kingston. One read:

"The GOVERNOR to the SECRETARY OF STATE.
(Received 8:10 a. m., January 24, 1907.)
  "I respectfully request that following telegram may be sent on to American Admiral, Davis, Cuba, from me through the proper channel: —
     "At the instance of the Secretary of State for the Colonies I desire to fully and unreservedly withdraw my letter of 18th January, and express regret that I   . wrote it."
                                              —Swettenham."

The other:

"The GOVERNOR to the SECRETARY OF STATE.
(Received 8:10 a. m., January 24, 1907.)
  "Respectfully apply for permission for retirement on account of age, forthwith to be relieved.—Swettenham."

The summer of 1907 is remembered in the Navy by its valiant but futile struggle for a lost cause. It was the year of the much-advertised Jamestown Ter-Centennial Exposition on the shores of Hampton Raads. There was celebrated the establishment, at an unhealthful, swampy point up the James River, of the first British colony in the new world. That here was also the scene of the introduction to America of negro servitude was not commemorated. Handicapped by the administrative ineptitude and the fatuous procrastination of its managers, the Fair required much more than the coöperation of the Federal Government and foreign nations, which was bestowed upon it in generous abundance, to escape dismal failure. It did not escape. Like so many other recent exhibitions, the official opening found the grounds resembling more closely a construction camp than the widely circulated pictures and nothing in readiness for the occasion except the oratory. Those in charge never caught up with their pretentious program and, from beginning to end, the enterprise was a disappointment. There were, of course, redeeming features and, outstanding among these, was the brilliant and ever changing spectacle afforded by the presence of squadrons of the world's naval powers, presided over by Bob Evans.

Ten days before the April twenty-sixth opening he led his fleet into Hampton Roads in the *Connecticut,* his new and destined to be his last flagship. When the big day dawned and the *Mayflower,* carrying President Roosevelt, steamed around Old Point Comfort, the salute of the *Connecticut* was echoed by the guns of many ships of many nations. The event must have reminded Evans of the ceremonies at Kiel so long before. To the horror of the strident pacifists, according to one of their tracts, ". . . the peculiar devil of the American breast, the admiration of bigness and force," was "fed to its full with the census of the iron monsters . . . from . . . every quarter of the globe." Three great lines of these "iron monsters" stretched along the famous man-of-war anchorage. We had our full Atlantic Fleet of sixteen battleships and, in addition, five cruisers, six destroyers, five torpedo boats, two auxiliary cruisers and four station ships, including the veteran *Brooklyn* and Jack Philip's old *Texas.* There were British, Brazilian, Chilean, German, Austro-Hungarian and Argentine vessels in the Roads. Later there arrived squadrons or single ships of Japan, Portugal, France, Norway, Sweden and the Netherlands. Flying the flag of Rear Admiral Sir George Neville was the *Good Hope* which, in 1914, was to sink in a heavy sea with Sir Christopher Cradock off Coronel, between a setting sun and the merciless guns of Graf von Spee. Also in the British squadron was the cruiser *Hampshire,* on whose submerging decks Lord Kitchener was to be last seen alive. At the Jamestown Exposition she was commanded by Captain Sir Robert Arbuthnot, who, as Rear Admiral, was to perish gallantly in the thick of the fight at Jutland.

Important and interesting naval personages shared Evans' social activities of these weeks and the entertainments were almost daily. The Duke D'Abruzzi, commanding the Italian squadron, the son of the King of Sweden aboard a picturesque corvette, Vice Admiral Ijuin of Japan, who outranked the Senior American Naval Officer Present, and the many other naval visitors of distinction, poured their wine at splendid dinners aboard the various ships and then moved on. Evans had to remain and smile. These professional associations, some new and some renewed, were the pleasant part of his stay as the Fair dragged its mediocre way through a hot Virginia summer.

There were constant demands upon the fleet and the Admiral always responded. One day there would be landed battalions of bluejackets and marines for a parade ashore, another day the Admiral would perspire through interminable speechmaking, on another the crews would hold cutter races, and the electrical displays on the ships after dark would feature night carnivals. Over the battleship's decks tramped thousands of curious feet.

The vehement objections of the Exposition officials notwithstanding, Evans sent his divisions off to sea in rotation lest they stagnate and become demoralized by the weeks at anchor. After all, these divisions were not mere gunboats showing the flag in a Chinese harbour but constituted our battle fleet.

"The time finally came," wrote Evans, "when the Exposition closed, and candour compels me to say that every officer and man in the American fleet was glad when the flags came down and the gates were closed."

Later the flags were again hoisted and the gates reopened. The grounds had been turned over to the Navy for what became its model wartime Operating Base. In Smith Basin, between the two handsome Government piers connected by the graceful arching bridge, where the barges and gigs of all nations had landed during the Fair, Evans would have been astonished to see taking off the dozens of seaplanes of the Naval Air Station. To him, as the *Connecticut* stood out in 1907, the Exposition was an interlude to forget in the joy of once more restoring his fleet to normal duty.

There were elaborately organized and excitingly executed war games before the ships were ordered to their home yards for the big job ahead.

24

THE LAST CRUISE

~~~~~~

WITH the assurance engendered by her recently war-won laurels, Japan was vigorously protesting against the anti-Asiatic immigration policy of our western states when, with a dramatic boldness characteristic of the man, President Roosevelt confirmed the report that the American battle fleet was to move into the Pacific Ocean. The world gasped. What would Japan say? What did she say? Officially, nothing. Unofficially, a great deal.

The Canal being uncompleted, the cruise was an ambitious project under any circumstances, but, at this particular time, it was daring; many said reckless. The military expert of the *Berliner Tageblatt* openly proclaimed it "the greatest experiment ever undertaken by any nation in time of peace." Would it break the peace? Did the President intend it should? What was his real purpose?

At first the voyage was alleged to be mere naval routine. Secretary Metcalf announced it as "a substitute for the comparatively short cruising and the harbour work which the fleet has engaged in for the winter season of the last six or more years. . . ." The press of both hemispheres speculated without restraint upon the diplomatic implications and possible complications. Then, within a fortnight of the scheduled departure, the President's message was read to Congress.

"No fleet of such size has ever made such a voyage, . . ." it declared. "This trip to the Pacific will show what some of our needs are and will enable us to provide for them. . . . The United States Navy is the best guarantee the nation has that its honour and interest will not be neglected, and in addition it offers by far the best insurance for peace that can by human ingenuity be devised."

On that same day, Viscount Aoki, Japanese Ambassador to the United States, announced his sudden departure to deliver a mere routine oral report to the Foreign Office at Tokio. Two could play at this routine business! To emphasize, as it were, the intended transparency of the explanation, a scant three days were permitted to elapse before a new bulletin declared that the Viscount was going home not to return, his post being assigned to Viscount Takahira, then at Rome. This was an inoffensive but effective manner of expressing Japan's dissatisfaction with the American situation.

Japanese stewards, dropped from the preparing American battleships, denounced the cruise as a step towards a coldly calculated war, but the authorities explained that these discharges were in obedience to a regulation against the reënlistment of foreigners.

The public everywhere took increasing notice of the situation, which became more tense as the date of departure approached. There was influential disapproval at home and not only abuse but ridicule abroad. The London papers characterized the cruise as a "Brobdignagian expedition," a "fluttering of the American eagle's wings" and a "piece of American bombast." For all Theodore Roosevelt cared, these critics might just as well have saved their breath and their ink.

Through the late summer and the autumn there were accelerated target practise, a cramming of squadron drills and an unprecedented racket of hammers in the yards, as the battle fleet was being put into shape for the record-breaking ordeal.

Evans was in poor health. It was the same old trouble, centring in the legs, and steadily growing worse. Old Gimpy was unmistakably becoming gimpier, but the spark burned as brightly as ever. To all suggestions that some more robust officer be entrusted with the responsibility of supreme command during the exacting test ahead, the President turned an impatient ear. Rather a decrepit Bob Evans, if need be, than any Herculean substitute!

The two friends formulated their plans on the wide porches at Sagamore Hill and there was plain talk as to what the Admiral was to do should the peaceful state of our foreign relations become vexed while he was *en route*. To him was left the choice of route and he decided upon the Straits of Magellan in preference to the Suez Canal. The Anglo-Japanese Alliance was in effect, for one thing, and the Mediterranean was a British lake. On the South American course, the fleet could always round the Horn if the Straits seemed too confined for comfort. Evans had braved them once in the *Yorktown* in those pre-wireless days when Chile might have been an unknown enemy, and it was not likely that a Power several thousand miles northwest of Cape Pillar would frighten him away now.

As the big ships were being overhauled and docked at the East Coast yards, the people caught occasional glimpses of the Commander-in-Chief. On the last day of November, the football crowd cheered him in Philadelphia, where Evans saw his Alma Mater win an exciting game from the Army. More than ever was he the personification of the fleet. Against any and all possible foes would they trust Fighting Bob.

At the Lotos Club in New York, where he was tendered a farewell banquet, the Admiral gave his famous promise that "You will not be disappointed in the fleet, whether it proves a feast, a frolic or a fight." His listeners were sure of that. Chauncey Depew delivered one of his celebrated post-prandial discourses.

". . . and, speaking of trouble," said the latter upon this occasion, "it is the distinction of the Admiral that he has never avoided it anywhere and has always beaten it. . . . In no stress of weather during his long life has our open-minded, open-hearted and red-blooded guest ever been a lamb or fooled by a lemon."

Throughout the nation, Monday, December sixteenth, was hailed as an impromptu holiday. Everywhere, the departure of the Atlantic Fleet that morning was the stimulus for a spontaneous celebration possessing the thrill and fervour of an adieu to fighters going to the front without the dread gloom of warfare.

At Hampton Roads the armada swung at its anchor chains in two long lines, sixteen powerful battleships. The oldest of them had been commissioned since the Spanish War, and the promise of continued replacements was signalized by the laying that very day of the keel of the newest dreadnought, *North Dakota.*

The naval community thronged Norfolk and Old Point Comfort. The old Chamberlin was crowded with officers' families. The excitement increased as the last night passed into the awaited day. The previous summer's Exposition had seen nothing so bustling in the Roads as the final scurrying back and forth of the running boats.

In the cabin of the *Connecticut,* Evans bade good-bye to his family. Taylor, now a lieutenant and a watch officer of the *Louisiana,* was also sailing with the fleet.

Evans tried to conceal the painful condition of his legs, but his daughter-in-law accidentally brushed against one and there escaped from the old gentleman a howl of anguish. His heroic endurance never had been displayed more dramatically than it was to be upon this cruise. Much of the time he was to spend in his bunk, often in his quarters and often in a little emergency cabin on the afterbridge, but he was always on duty.

The *Mayflower* hove into view with the President's flag at the main. Barges and gigs sped towards her gangway from each of the battleships, the Commander-in-Chief's first. There was a reception on the quarterdeck of the yacht. The real business was transacted in a five minute conversation between Roosevelt and Evans, during which the former spoke earnestly and rapidly in a carefully pitched undertone, while the latter concentrated upon every syllable. With many an important mission had Roosevelt entrusted Evans in the past. Now he was handing into his care the security of the nation.

The destroyers, an absurd handful, had gone ahead. The skies had cleared. The boats and booms had been hoisted in, the chains had been hauled short, all was set.

On the signal halliards of the *Connecticut* flew the hoist "Get under way." Down snapped the flags and, with them, the ensigns and jacks, as the former broke out in the sunshine on the gaffs aloft. The water stirred about eight steel hulls, the first squadron's anchors were out of the ground, its two divisions were under way, they had way upon them, the cruise had begun! Smartly the second squadron fell in astern. The column was in perfect formation, the ships spaced as exactly as lamp-posts along a boulevard, a mighty procession three miles in length.

The President took the parting salute of each ship as she passed the *Mayflower,* and he proudly watched the rigid line disappear in a smudge of smoke beneath the eastern horizon. Outside of the Capes, the enterprising fiancée of one of the officers, who had provided herself with a yacht for a last farewell, approached close to the flagship. The strains of *Auld Lang Syne* were heard across the water, and then home was behind. For the last time, Bob Evans had passed out between Cape Henry and Cape Charles.

The Admiral deployed his force in columns of divisions abreast, the columns sixteen hundred yards apart and the ships at the standard interval of four hundred, a mighty rectangle, sweeping south in solid phalanx, ready for "a feast, a frolic or a fight."

That night the country received this radio message: "Fleet at eight o'clock forty miles northeast of Hatteras. Northwest wind. Smooth sea. Heading south. Ten knots."

Thirteen thousand miles ahead stretched the course to California.

Blue water brought on regular drills, constant attention to business, all the while the engineering forces and the Officers of the Deck concentrated on the precise and unflagging maintenance of station. A few yards of error in position in a tossing sea seldom escaped the notice of that experienced drill master on the *Connecticut*, whose uncanny eye seemed almost as accurate a judge of distance as a stadimeter.

Down through temperate and then tropical waters marched the squadrons until, at the southern edge of the Caribbean, Trinidad welcomed them for their first halt and Christmas liberty.

The Admiral was royally entertained by Governor General Jackson, an old friend. Port-of-Spain had long since lost all traces of the great fire but Evans vividly remembered that exciting occasion.

The sailors enlisted as shipmates a large flock of many-hued and many-toned parrots and developed a familiarity with the potent "green swizzle." They owned Trinidad that Christmas, and Trinidad owned the fleet. In the wardrooms and forecastles passed the word: "There's nothing of Swettenham about Jackson. He's all right!"

On Christmas the ships were decked with foliage from smoke-stacks down.

The next leg of the voyage was around the elbow of Brazil to Rio.

To stimulate engineering efficiency, fuel conservation

tests and competitions were decreed. The rivalry was keen. Most of the ships managed very well but one of them seemed a glutton for coal. When she asked for more, the Admiral signalled back: "You will get no more coal; we'll tow you to Rio if necessary." The black gang blushed beneath the soot on their faces and the ship held her proper station until safely anchored in the shadow of Sugar Loaf.

One day as Evans stepped out of the cabin on the after-bridge, he heard a stream of profanity flowing from the lips of one of the sailors. With a serious mien, he snapped: "Don't you know I'm the only one privileged to cuss on this bridge?"

"Aye, aye, sir," responded the abashed tar, "I'll go aloft, sir!"

New Years Eve and the Line-Crossing ceremonies enlivened the run. Two of the officers in the *Louisiana* who never before had forsaken northern latitudes were Taylor Evans and the son of Captain Osterhaus of the *Connecticut*. Neptune Rex signalled from the *Louisiana* to the Commander-in-Chief that these two fellows were among those due for initiation. Back came the reply, signed "Evans and Osterhaus":

"We are delighted that our sons are at last real sailors. . . . Soak 'em, boys!"

As soon as the hooks went down at Rio, two thousand bluejackets eagerly piled into the liberty boats to taste the allurements of this most gorgeous of seaports. In blue streaks they scattered along the boulevards. An American sailor seated at a café table was hurt by a bottle thrown during a fight between two native negroes. A riot developed. The police cried for help. Evans hoisted the general recall. There was gloom on every ship because it was taken for granted that there would be no more shore leave in that place. Perhaps the Admiral recalled that other occasion in Rio when his midshipmen in Russian uniforms had run afoul of the authorities. In any event, there was a surprise in store for all hands. Orders were issued the next day that, instead of two thousand men being allowed on the beach, there would be liberty for four thousand! To each crew was published a personal appeal from the Admiral. He trusted his men to behave themselves for their own sakes but, if they couldn't do that, to behave themselves for his sake. Their conduct was exemplary.

The fleet was most heartily received by the Brazilians, who made of the visit a gay carnival, resplendent in the manner of such fiestas down there. Because of the circumstances surrounding Evans' pleasant little stay in Chile during the hectic days of '92, it had been deemed best to omit Valparaiso as a port of call and, because of lack of sufficient water in the harbour for the battleships, Buenos Aires was likewise to be skipped by all except the auxiliaries, thereby leaving Rio the only one of the three greatest South American seaports on the itinerary of the big divisions. The days and nights in Rio were crowded with entertainments of all kinds. The city distinguished itself by its lavish generosity and warm hospitality. Evans, however, was suffering from one of his bad spells and had to decline all official and social invitations. It was as much as he could do to keep himself in touch with the daily activities of his command, but this he did most diligently.

The Brazilian Navy, which had guarded the visiting fleet against rumoured hostile anarchists and other possible molestation and injury, acted as escort upon the departure. The American ships steamed out amid a swarm of applauding craft that rivalled in number and enthusiasm the welcoming crowd in New York Harbour upon the return from Cuba.

Far out off the wide mouth of La Plata, a squadron of olive green Argentine men-of-war were met by radio arrangement so that that nation also might salute the Northerners. There on the high seas, courtesies were exchanged as the United States Atlantic Fleet paraded along in extended column.

Just because of the fears of many of his fellow country-men that Evans' leadership of the fleet would reopen old international sores in Chile, the truly friendly greeting that awaited him there, in the isolation of the Straits of Magellan, was to the Admiral perhaps the most touching feature of the voyage.

It was necessary to coal at Punta Arenas. Arrangements had been so handled that, without giving offence and without the slightest embarrassment or discourtesy, Chile could have refrained from taking any but the most perfunctory notice of the fleet. At Rio there were messages that the reception was to be whole-hearted. As the ships were not scheduled to stop at Valparaiso, Punta Arenas would play host for the nation. When the column felt its course through the Straits and finally anchored off Sandy Point, there was seen the Chilean gunboat *Chacabuco*, flying the flag of Rear Admiral Simpson, an officer of British Royal Navy ancestry and an old friend of Bob Evans's. This was a Chilean handshake of genuine warmth. Also aboard the gunboat were the Assistant Secretary of the Chilean Navy, the United States Minister and other dignitaries from Valparaiso and Santiago. The town of Punta Arenas had obtained from New York a shipment of two hundred thousand American flags and had made elaborate preparations to ensure the enjoyment of the visitors while refuelling. Punta Arenas provided every conceivable kind of entertainment and for those hours brought Times Square to the southernmost city in the world.

The "old man" chuckled with delight. Chile had forgotten '92.

The climax of the festivities was a party given on the *Chacabuco* for as many of the American bluejackets as could be accommodated aboard. The Chilean officers, insistent upon contributing to the hospitality, provided and poured the wine, their own delicious pisco, a rapid-fire beverage if ever there was one. Upon most of the men it had the effect of stimulating uproarious fraternization with their hosts, but there was one marine from the *Louisiana,* a handsome fellow with an exemplary record——.

The following day, Evans was huddled up in pain when Captain Wainwright of the *Louisiana* was announced on an official call. That officer doubtless felt more dread at the coming interview than he had when, in the *Gloucester,* he had awaited the emerging Spanish torpedo-boats at the mouth of Santiago Bay, and doubtless also expected an explosion louder than the one he had survived in the *Maine.* He reported to the Admiral that one of the *Louisiana's* finest marines, previously a sober soldier, had run amuck, that an investigation had disclosed an over-indulgence of pisco at the *Chacabuco's* party and—now he came to the reason for this special call—a grave violation of discipline on the Chilean man of war. Evans frowned. Of all places for such an occurrence! The hitherto model marine had so far forgotten himself as to assault a Chilean officer. The American Admiral was becoming angrier as Wainwright proceeded. The Chileans, it seemed, had been determined that nothing should mar the party and, although their officer had been knocked down, the marine's apology had been accepted and the pisco had continued to flow. Then, down had gone a second Chilean officer at the hands of the same marine. This time it had been deemed prudent to remove the fighting sea soldier to his ship, and back he was rowed, singing all the way.

What Bob Evans said had best be recorded in asterisks. The cabin rang with his old-fashioned expletives. How the papers at home would assail Fighting Bob's bellicose return to Chile! The fleet under his command couldn't even touch the tip of that country without causing trouble! Of all spots for such an unfortunate breach of discipline and good manners to have occurred, this was the worst!

The Admiral consulted his staff. They shook their heads and deplored. A letter was drafted and its phrases polished, containing an abject apology to Admiral Simpson. It was speedily transmitted. What attitude would the Foreign Office at Santiago take? Would there be an international incident?

The Chilean barge approached the *Connecticut*. Admiral Simpson, in full dress, came over the side and was received with due honours. Evans was in his bunk. He sat up stiffly, in tense anxiety, as the caller stepped over the hatch-combing.

"Admiral Evans," the latter began, "you have done me the honour this morning to send me a letter of apology for some disturbance by your men which you say took place on my ship yesterday."

Evans nodded and waited. He had, in his distress at the incident, not reckoned upon the affection with which the Chilean Admiral regarded him personally.

"I think," continued Simpson, "you have been misinformed. I have made the most diligent inquiry and I find that there was no disturbance of any kind on my ship yesterday. I can not accept your apology and I beg leave to return to you your letter in person."

The face of Old Gimpy broke into its smile and his eyes shone with delight.

"Simpson," he shouted, "Simpson, by God, you're a brick!"

This entire affair became known outside of the fleet only after Evans' death in 1912. Officially, the incident never occurred. No report was ever made to either Government. The log of the *Louisiana* records merely that a certain marine sergeant was restricted as to liberty because of having been "drunk and disorderly aboard ship." The violent assault of an enlisted man upon two officers of a friendly foreign navy would have been indignantly denied, had any story of its happening leaked ashore.

The personality of Bob Evans, far from having provoked the trouble, completely assuaged its effect, and another tale in the legend of Old Gimpy was added to naval lore.

Arrangements were made for a nonstop salute of courtesy off Valparaiso and the fleet advanced through the Straits, escorted by the *Chacabuco*.

This was the critical part of the entire cruise. The whole of American sea power moved slowly, cautiously, through the gorge, the very hugeness of its units here increasing the hazards and difficulties of piloting. Wild rumours of Japanese floating mines in those narrow passages had alarmed some of the citizens at home. The sixteen battleships tiptoed through the swirling currents between the glacier mountains, but they maintained their standard intervals and let nothing break the formation. Clouds of mist rolled down. The fog became opaque. The land, so close on either side, was totally obscured and not even the next ship astern or ahead was visible. The *Connecticut* led the tortuous way along, the men in the chains singing out the fathoms of depth. It was a delicate operation for cumbersome battleships, this transit of the Straits in rigid column through such thick weather, but the elements had to yield to the schedule of the Atlantic Fleet. At last the broad bulk of the flagship rose and pitched under a strong ground swell. By that alone the Admiral, unable to see beyond his jackstaff, knew that the open sea had been reached. He had brought his command safely through the perilous cleft in the Andes and the President's plan of sending the battle fleet to the Pacific had been executed. No comparable armada had ever before negotiated the Straits of Magellan. The *Connecticut's* bow swung around toward the North and the fleet was pointed back toward home waters.

The citizens of Valparaiso seemed to have no recollection of 1892. If the North American armada would not come to them, they would go to it. In dense throngs they crowded the hillsides and watched the long column steam by, close to shore, each band playing Chile's national anthem as the ships passed in review before the President of Chile. There was a naval spectacle never before and never since equalled in that part of the world. The President took his salutes, one after the other, in perfectly timed cadence, from the deck of the picturesque training ship, an auxiliary square-rigger, the beautiful *Jeneral Baquedano*. She was full-dressed and her yardarms on both masts, as well as her rails, were manned, a picture that reminded Evans of days for ever gone in his own service.

This harbour was the scene of that tense visit of the *Yorktown* sixteen years before. Now, not only was this ceremony of friendship conducted on the part of the United States by that Captain of the *Yorktown,* but on the part of Chile by President Pedro Montt, younger brother of the very Jorje Montt, leader of the anti-Balmacedists in the Civil War, who had accused the American Navy of interfering against them. The despair felt by Evans at Punta Arenas upon hearing of the disgraceful episode at the *Chacabuco's* party must now have been supplanted by extreme elation at this demonstration of complete rapprochement. This one incident alone vindicated his retention in command by Roosevelt. With no one else on the flagship bridge could the exchange of courtesies have been so convincingly symbolic of the burial of the hatchet, national and personal. Virtually the entire population of Valparaiso and the vicinity watched and cheered in the background as the guns barked out and the bands played on the long, immaculate line of white hulled fighting monsters. Their majestic swing past the harbour mouth after their long cruise and their unhalting march past this leading port on South America's west coast, must have been impressively suggestive of their latent strength and the urgency of their mission.

The crowds marvelled particularly at the fortitude of the little destroyers in having undertaken such a trip.

The battle force stood by in the same imposing array in which it had left Hampton Roads. First came Evans' own division, consisting of the fleet flagship in the van and then the *Kansas, Vermont* and *Louisiana;* then Rear Admiral Emory's second division, the *Georgia, New Jersey, Rhode Island* and *Virginia,* then Rear Admiral Thomas, commanding the second squadron and the third division, flying his flag on the *Minnesota,* followed by the *Ohio, Missouri* and *Maine;* and finally Rear Admiral Sperry's fourth division, the *Alabama, Illinois, Kearsarge* and *Kentucky.*

Steaming evolutions had to be minimized because of fuel limitations, but the strain of maintaining station at four hundred yard intervals was felt by every captain, navigator and watch officer in the fleet. Through heavy seaways and dense mists the squadrons had for days pressed ahead with formation unrelaxed. Internal drills were held with unfailing regularity and rigour. The fleet was ever ready for "a feast, a frolic or a fight." It had had its feast and its frolic and, if there was to be no fight, there was plenty of hard work. To his last hour of service, Bob Evans sustained and ever raised the standard of battle efficiency.

Once he decided to burn up a little surplus coal and see how prepared were his ships for emergency orders. It was on a quiet Sunday afternoon, when no one expected any interruption in the usual routine. Suddenly a flag hoist broke out on the yardarm of the *Connecticut.* The division rear admirals and their thousands of subordinates snapped into activity. Impromptu manoeuvres were ordered; they were commenced; the big ships swung out of column by squadrons, by divisions; the fleet was deployed in this organization, in that; smartly the signal commands were obeyed; not a ship had been caught napping. The Admiral was satisfied. "Present exercises discontinued" flew in conclusion, and the force was once more cruising North in regular formation.

The next destination was Callao, about as far from

Punta Arenas as are the British Isles from North America.
This visit of the fleet was a great event in the history of
Peru. The nation expended its full energy in recognition of
that fact. From the greeting at sea by the cruiser *Bolognesi*
until the parting fleet review by President Pardo from the
cruiser *Almirante Grau,* there were nine midsummer (February) days and nights, dedicated by the people of Peru to
the officers and men of the Atlantic Fleet. The near-by
capital, Lima, took on the appearance of a United States
naval headquarters. Down at Callao the enormous fleet
crowded the harbour and daily despatched on the tramway
to Lima every one who could possibly be spared aboard.
Into the great central Plaza the sailors poured and then
scattered in all directions through the handsome Spanish-
looking and Spanish-feeling metropolis, which had been
extravagantly bedecked in their honour. The sights, in and
around the city, they saw, the cafés they frequented, the
amusements they sampled. A special gala program was
arranged at the bull ring. The sailors filled the seats and
overflowed onto the roof of the stands. The toreadors
paraded and went through their elaborate preliminary ceremonies. Then there were bull fights of a calibre to delight
the most expert Madrid enthusiast, the general excitement
of which communicated itself to the gay spirits of the men
on liberty, who cheered as if in the bleachers at a baseball
game.

Some of the men took trips on the Oroya Railroad up
over dazzling heights in the surrounding mountains.

There was much to see and to do. The bluejackets and
their officers drained the cup of Peru to its dregs. An unforgettable abundance of adventure and experience was
packed into that visit.

Another long leg of the voyage lay ahead, three thousand
miles to Magdalena Bay, Mexico. As on the extra day of
that Leap Year the guns boomed farewell on the *Almirante
Grau,* Bob Evans took the last salute of his career from a

foreign nation and a foreign man-of-war. His health was breaking down, day by day, and his devoted juniors realized that not even Old Gimpy would be able to make those legs perform much more active duty.

At Magdalena Bay a month was devoted to intensive target practise, the results of which proved that the fleet was actually in better fighting condition than when it had left Hampton Roads, a prodigious and unspectacular feat, which was the crowning achievement of the career of the Chief that was now obviously drawing to its close.

Evans was surrounded by admirals, captains, aides, men who followed him with a confidence, enthusiasm and devotion few other modern military or naval leaders have inspired. To his particular intimate friends among these fell the duty of persuading their "old man" to abandon the struggle, at least temporarily. He sorrowfully resigned himself to a course of treatment at the Paso Robles Hot Springs, north of Santa Barbara, where the baths were supposed to be of therapeutic value in cases of chronic rheumatism and similar ailments. The physicians there found a badly and irreparably damaged human machine but they patched it together so that at least there might not be denied to the Admiral the personal delivery of his fleet to its destination within the Golden Gate.

In his absence, the ships were painted and led to San Diego and to San Pedro, near Los Angeles, and all was ready for the climactic approach to San Francisco.

The President sadly learned of the almost complete physical collapse of his friend. The international atmosphere had cleared a great deal. The much discussed transfer from ocean to ocean had been effected. Robley D. Evans' work had been done. Nothing remained but the valedictory. In a stirring letter of commendation and regret, the President relieved the Admiral of active duty upon his arrival at San Francisco. Several times in the past, Evans had astonished his friends by his almost miraculous recovery of health. This time, however, he was nearing the age limit, and he was irrevocably through with the fighting Navy and the sea.

Outside the harbour entrance, the battleships *Nebraska* and *Wisconsin* joined the Atlantic Fleet. Inside there were found the armoured cruisers of the Pacific Fleet. The flag of Rear Admiral Evans, senior American officer afloat, was now flying within signal distance of the nation's assembled sea power.

25

LANDLOCKED

~~~~~~

T HE exit was in all respects worthy of the career.

Nothing else in his life equalled Bob Evans' reception at San Francisco. The city realized that even the long awaited and historic arrival of the battle fleet was secondary in importance to the retirement of the chief. Every ship, every sailor, every mascot had a place in the welcome but, by universal accord, the prime guest of honour was the Commander-in-Chief, not because of the rank but because of the man, the hero in war and in peace.

The anchoring of the squadrons was the achievement of an epoch making cruise. Old Gimpy had led them from Hampton Roads and, intact and readier than ever for any exigency, he led them into the harbour of their destination. It was his last effort afloat.

Mrs. Evans and Mrs. Marsh were there, waiting with a wheel chair, detested symbol of the end. His wife and daughter made the Admiral comfortable at the St. Francis Hotel in a suite of regal proportions, assigned, by those in charge of the arrangements, to the king of the festivities. His son being also there, the family circle was complete excepting for Virginia. Far away, she was in tragic distress. Robley Evans Sewall, her little boy, the adored grandson of the Admiral, had succumbed to an illness. The news was too dreadful to disclose to the old gentleman during this very trying week. Mrs. Evans and Mrs. Marsh managed to keep their bitter secret. Kind editors, whose columns and special naval supplements were crammed with anecdotes of the Admiral's past and every scrap of fact concerning him, excluded from their papers any mention of this untimely death. Not until he was on the train for home did the grandfather, whose career had ended, learn that the budding career of his namesake had been cruelly snipped off at the same time. This was the most crushing grief of his whole life. He never recovered from the effects of the blow. His sorrow, however, did not obscure from his appreciation the remarkable fortitude that had been displayed by the equally smitten grandmother and by the others of his family in San Francisco. He eventually sought to fill the gap in his life by having the boy's sister Dorothy take his place as well as her own. The unusual mutual devotion of grandfather and granddaughter was known to all acquainted with the family.

Secretary Metcalf arrived to review the fleet and this he did in the old *Yorktown* of treasured memory. There was a colossal parade of the sailors, marines and the soldiers from the Presidio, through the streets of the city, colossal not for the marchers but for the ecstatic acclaim of the multitudes of onlookers. They wanted to see and cheer Fighting Bob. He insisted upon participating in the procession but no one believed his condition would permit of that.

At eight in the morning three hundred cadets from Salt Lake City, delegated as a personal escort in honour of the Admiral's appointment to the Naval Academy from that place, lined up before his hotel. Sure enough, out he came, and entered a car with Mayor Taylor.

Asked how he felt, he smothered the pain and replied with a jovial "Fit as a fiddle." He had thrust aside the proffered crutches. "Did you expect to find me a stuffed monkey?"

The parade proved a triumphal procession for Robley D. Evans. So busy was he kept bowing that he hardly had an opportunity to behold the rows of modern structures that had sprung from the ashes of the great fire.

"The people cheered the bluejackets wildly, but they went mad over Admiral Evans. . . . Although thousands of men marched in the parade there really was only one man in it—Fighting Bob Evans. All the others were a mere escort."

Thus wrote Franklin Matthews, a newspaper man who accompanied the fleet, in his two volume narrative of the cruise.

The night of the eighth a banquet was tendered to Secretary Metcalf and the officers of the fleet at the St. Francis. The Commander-in-Chief was in his room, too ill to attend, and his absence cast a gloom over the gathering. · The Mayor arose and rapped for attention. He proposed a toast to the health of the beloved Admiral upstairs. Glasses were raised when, with a dramatic timeliness none present will ever forget, the banquet hall doors flew open, revealing in his wheel chair, his face deeply lined with suffering but illumined by his smile, Bob Evans himself.

The aghast diners jumped up. The walls shook with their applause as the chair was rolled to the speakers' table. The noise suddenly stopped. The Admiral was somehow forcing himself to stand once more on those old legs.

"If you gentlemen will kindly be seated I'll talk a little."

It was a breathless moment.

In characteristic phrases, the familiar voice expressed gratitude for the wonderful welcome to the fleet. Noticing in the audience one who had criticized the new battleships as lacking adequate armour belting, he pitched into that subject.

"That is a great fallacy—the belief that our ships are not properly protected. And more, I care not how well they are armoured if they have not the right fellows to man them. The man who shoots the straightest and fights the best wins all the battles, no matter if there is an armour belt of leather, wood or eggshells."

There were cheers. Looking about he saw the blue uniforms of his faithful juniors of the service but also the black and white evening dress of civilian celebrities, governors, senators, judges. This was his last official utterance while on active duty. To-morrow night he would be an ex. This was the last rallying cry of the Brethren of the Brood. The very last of them was to turn their Navy over to another generation. Rising in all the might of his prestige, he plunged with stupendous simplicity into the brief peroration. The final sentences echoed through the nation.

"If you wish to preserve the peace of the world give us more battleships and fewer statesmen."

Every man present leapt to his feet and cheered. Handkerchiefs were waving and voices were shouting as the chair was wheeled from the hall.

The ceremonies in the fleet on the following day were without his presence. He just could not make it.

A farewell message was read aloud to every ship of his command at a special muster. It was a tender farewell but couched in his usual plain seamanlike words. The salty tars had tears in their eyes. The Admiral's devoted steward broke down on the flagship and wept. Old Gimpy was saying good-bye to each and every one of them.

On the *Connecticut,* the Chief-of-Staff followed the reading of the message with the reading of the detachment order. As the last syllable was uttered, out flashed the first gun of the salute—the very last. One after the other they flashed and banged, thirteen in all. Sadly the Chief-of-Staff stepped to the halliard leading to the main truck, where flew the Admiral's flag. Slowly it made the long descent and lay upon the deck, a crumpled bit of blue bunting.

The Brood of the Constitution had passed into history. Old Gimpy was on the beach forevermore.

His officers called at the hotel to pay their respects and now, when no misconstruction could be placed thereon, to express without restraint their affection and devotion. Late that night a train starting East carried the family toward Washington.

The fleet was to remain for some time on the West Coast and then cruise back to its regular haunts via Australia and the Suez Canal.

In the train the Evans family was alone with its grief. The grandfather strove to readjust himself to the sudden shocking change in his world. It all seemed utterly irrational. At stations along the way, cheering crowds, unaware of the personal tragedy, hailed the Admiral and wrung from him smiles of acknowledgment for the ovations.

The arrival at Washington was a doleful homecoming.

At such a time, formal reward shrank to insignificance. To the nation at large, however, it was important that this closing career be accorded some especial recognition. A spontaneous demand had arisen that Robley D. Evans be retired as a Vice Admiral. President Roosevelt urged such a measure upon Congress and undoubtedly it would have been approved with enthusiasm by overwhelming majorities in the House and Senate. When Roosevelt had mentioned the matter to Evans on the eve of the world cruise, the latter had estimated the situation shrewdly and had not expected the promotion. That case of Rear Admiral Rowan years before had been a miracle; miracles do not happen twice. Evans had never compromised with sincerity in his dealings with politicians. His failure to repress certain views and to bridle his temperamental candour in advocating them would never, he believed, be forgiven by a couple of the influential members of the Senate Committee on Naval Affairs. He was correct. To overcome an adversary in a bitter fight may sometimes be condoned if the winner was espousing a wrong cause, but it takes an opponent of rare generosity to excuse one who was on the right side. By vir-

tue of the committee system, the plan to honour Evans by
elevation in rank was throttled practically in camera on the
flimsiest of pretexts, obscuring the particular proposition in
a maze of unconvincing generalities. As Commander-in-
Chief of the Asiatic Fleet and later of the Atlantic Fleet,
there had been well performed the duties of a full four-star
Admiral. Sampson had died a Rear Admiral. The elevation
of Dewey to the exalted rank of Admiral of the Navy
seemed to have exhausted the generosity of Congress with
respect to naval promotions. What mattered the retirement grade excepting a few dollars more or less in the pay
checks?

There remained several weeks before the professionally
fatal sixty-second birthday would transfer Evans to the
inactive list. At Admiral Dewey's suggestion, he was
appointed to the General Board of the Navy. Soon, however, the descent of hot weather upon the capital made it
necessary for the invalid to seek relief from the climate.
The family and the physicians recommended Lake Mohonk,
that beautiful mountain resort west of the Hudson River.
There he spent a restful summer.

On the shore of that gem of a little lake, in the groves
and summer houses, in the hotel lobby, the Admiral in his
wheel chair became a familiar presence. The outstanding
celebrity and the dominant personality of the place long associated in the public mind with international arbitration
conferences, was this weary warrior.

August eighteenth, his birthday, was marked by greet-
ings from far and near, from great and humble. That night
the other guests assembled in the parlour to celebrate the
occasion. Five hundred people were packed in the room
when the chair was rolled in. There were speeches and,
with manifest affection, the presentation of a loving cup.
The guest of honour must have realized that these chance
acquaintances constituted but a cross-section of his fellow
countrymen. Gratitude and appreciation are exquisite to

old age. Evans was deeply touched. Necessarily still seated, he expressed his deep thanks and made a few gracious remarks of an appropriate nature, with a reference to his old Outfit.

"It was borne in upon me," he told these visitors to a spot consecrated to councils of peace, "that the worst use you could put a navy to was fighting, and the best, keeping the peace."

The remaining years he spent mostly in Washington, constantly plagued by his ailments, fulfilling occasional assignments to miscellaneous duties by the Department, and writing on naval subjects and his own adventures. His interest in his profession was keen to the very end. Always he threw himself into a naval controversy on the side of progress. Never did he degenerate into a mossback.

He became a frequent contributor to magazines. Sometimes he retold incidents of his life; mostly he discussed professional topics in terms that were interesting and clear to the lay reader.

The critic of the Navy, whom he had answered face to face at the San Francisco banquet, was the celebrated marine artist Henry Reuterdahl, who now was supplementing his classic paintings of naval subjects with charges of structural inferiority of our ships compared to the vessels of foreign navies. His pen was less skilled than his brush. The form and colour of a battleship lashing through a seaway he could grasp with exceptional insight, but the technicalities of her design naturally involved factors beyond the limits of his training. The repeated animadversions, however, tended to shake popular confidence in the efficiency of the fleet. Bob Evans raised his voice of authority, admitted what weaknesses he conceived there were and disspelled the doubts that were unfounded. In a series of articles in *Hampton's Broadway Magazine* he joined issue with Reuterdahl and met his accusations point by point. It was, of course, a debate between unequal adversaries but the artist who had entered the unfamiliar lists, uninvited and unqualified, encountered only the opposition and the defeat he deserved.

Evan's contributions to *Hampton's* were by no means confined to this refutation. He dealt with a broad variety of naval subjects. Most of his contentions have withstood the test of time but a few have not. For example, he failed to anticipate the great range at which future engagements would be fought between capital ships and hence the high angle at which projectiles would strike, with all the consequential structural implications. On this topic Reuterdahl proved to be correct.

In 1910 Evans published *An Admiral's Log*, the sequel to *A Sailor's Log,* bringing his autobiography from the close of the Spanish-American War to his retirement. In a volume of about the same size as his former one, he covered a period less than a quarter as long. Much of it was devoted to the exposition of his views upon many matters encountered in his experiences as a flag officer. So far as was possible, he excluded accounts of controversies and any unpleasant personalities. The book is very interesting and is indispensable to a study of modern naval history. One wishes, however, that Old Gimpy had drafted it with less restraint, that he had dictated it in the sparkling flow of his conversation, as Lord Fisher did his memoirs, profanity and all.

Quietly the months slipped by with his wife and among his friends. The legs were sometimes more painful, sometimes less, but never well.

Disgusted with "all sort of remedies and cures" he took himself in hand, abstained from alcoholic beverages and adhered to a rigid diet. Whatever the cause, his legs did improve and he threw away the crutches. Meeting an acquaintance who was delighted to see the Admiral walking with only a cane for support, the latter proudly described the self-imposed regimen.

"I just made the doctors walk the plank," he said.

The Taft Administration moved along in its slow tempo. Under its ægis the country was experiencing what it pleases to regard as a normal period. Washington was wholesome and dull.

The Navy kept pace with the general advance, steady but not rapid. Evans saw the early units of the American dreadnought fleet come into being. The *Wyoming* and *Arkansas* were launched and the keels were laid for the first of our battleships mounting fourteen-inch guns, the *Texas* and *New York*. Naval aviation emerged from its infancy, the automobile torpedo was being elaborately developed, and enlarged destroyers were finding their important function in fleet organization. A decade later, one of the ships of this type was to be given Evans' name and to be christened by his beloved Dorothy, then grown up.

The Admiral's last duty as a retired officer was performed as President of the General Court-Martial that was convened at the Norfolk Navy Yard for the trial of Captain Austin M. Knight. The latter was the internationally celebrated author of the textbook on seamanship which occupies the position in the era of steam that Luce's work did in that of sail.

A Court of Inquiry had recommended that Knight be tried on a charge of negligence in connection with the loss of the monitor *Puritan* at Norfolk during explosive tests. The Special Board on Naval Ordnance, of which he was President, had been studying nitro-glycerine at the Department and had gone to Norfolk to conduct certain experiments. A two hundred pound charge had been set off near the *Puritan*. The Board had wanted to see what would happen. The ship sank and in a depth of water rendering salvage difficult.

There was adverse criticism of the unnecessary selection of such a place for the test. Captain Knight declared that the Commandant of the Yard had been responsible for the arrangements but the latter insisted that the entire affair had been in the hands of the Board which Knight headed. The Court of Inquiry adopted the latter view.

The General Court was an appropriately imposing one. With Evans presiding, there sat six other rear admirals. From March ninth to seventeenth, 1911, the sessions were held. Lieutenant Commander Ridley McLean, Evans' former aide, who had been Judge Advocate of the Court of Inquiry, filled that office before the Court-Martial. The accused was ably defended by Major Leonard of the Marine Corps.

Knight was senior on the list of captains and due for promotion when the unfortunate incident occurred. The *Puritan* had been a valuable ship in dollars and cents. The service was stirred by the exhibition of "buck-passing" on the heights. The case was a *cause celebre* and attracted attention in Congress and among the general public.

The Department received the Court's decision on March eighteenth and an announcement was awaited, anxiously by some, eagerly by all. No announcement was forthcoming. Instead, there emanated a flood of rumour. It was reported that the Court had honourably acquitted Captain Knight but that the Judge Advocate General of the Navy had prevailed upon the Secretary of the Navy to withhold his approval of the finding. The accused remained under arrest. Finally, gossip had it, a ninety-page document was transmitted to Admiral Evans requesting the Court to reconsider the case upon the original testimony. Among the arguments therein advanced against the justice of the determination was said to be a challenge of Knight's credibility, based upon an alleged excess in one of his travel vouchers, amounting to ninety-six cents!

Official silence continued to prevail. Time passed and

Knight quietly reëntered upon the performance of his duties and soon after appeared in the uniform of a flag officer.

Despite every pressure, the Court had stood by its original determination. Word passed through the service: "Evans saved Knight."

No Court-Martial Order ever has been issued and hence the papers in the case have remained automatically in the secret files of the Secretary of the Navy. Even to-day the veil will not be lifted.

Christmas and New Year's passed. On January third, 1912, there was a happy family luncheon at home. Admiral and Mrs. Evans, Mrs. Taylor Evans, and Mr. and Mrs. Sewall were there. The Admiral was in the gayest of moods, laughing and joking throughout the meal.

Then he withdrew to his den, where his many trophies and souvenirs were housed.

His thoughts of that moment were his last. Suddenly stricken with what was diagnosed as acute indigestion, he reminded Mrs. Evans that it was the second such attack he had sustained within a year.

"I must be getting old," he gasped.

The physician, who had responded to the hurry call, left the house assuring the family that the Admiral would soon be himself. This, however, was not to be. He sank rapidly. Within a few hours Robley D. Evans joined the vanished hosts of *Old Ironsides'* alumni. His family could not believe he was gone. Mrs. Evans secluded herself in an adjoining room, completely prostrated by her grief. Mrs. Marsh and Taylor Evans were summoned home.

The news spread quickly. Reporters notified the distinguished men of the time, asking for comments. Instead of stereotyped tributes, there came tears. Admiral Dewey was dumbfounded and could not speak for some minutes. Editors rearranged their front pages and were stimulated to the drafting of heartfelt editorials. As the flag on every

ship and station of the Navy was half-masted, there passed
from cabin to forecastle the sad word that Old Gimpy was no
more.

The country mourned and well it might. Never since
has there been a naval officer whose hold on popular affection and imagination has equalled that of Bob Evans.
Not even our greater modern Navy nor our greatest war
sufficed to produce his equal in that respect.

From all over the world came messages of sympathy
and testimonials of regard. The Kaiser permitted himself
to take unprecedented action. Besides sending a cable to
Mrs. Evans, he directed the German naval attaché at Washington to attend the funeral as the Kaiser's personal representative and to lay upon the coffin a wreath of flowers
tokening the final gift of friend to friend. The leaders of
affairs recognized that a great American career had come
to an end, and from countless people, whose names were not
celebrated, there came expressions of deep sorrow.

The funeral services at All Souls Unitarian Church,
brief and simple as the Admiral would have wished, were
impressive. There were the usual ceremonies but they
seemed unusually meaningful. In deference to the Admiral's injunction, there was no eulogy. The honorary pall-
bears were not only distinguished contemporaries but real
friends. Devoted juniors carried the casket. In the group
of mourners were the personages of the day from President
Taft down. The words and gestures of bereavement that
are cheapened by common employment were upon this occasion patently pregnant with sincerity. Outdoors, in a
rainy, near-zero cold stood throngs of nameless admirers,
many of whom followed the procession to the Arlington
Memorial Cemetery.

Bob Evans, in his coffin draped in the American flag
flown by the *Iowa* during the Battle of Santiago, was borne
back across the Potomac to his native soil of Virginia. The

Rev. Dr. Wellbourn, an Episcopal Minister of Tokio and an old friend, said a last good-bye.

The stone that marks his grave is not large nor particularly well hewn. It bears the inscription:

"The path to duty was the way to glory."

INDEX

INDEX

"Blanco Encalada," Chilean Ship, 211
Blaine, James G.
Defeated for presidency, 138-9; Compared to Harrison, 142; Secretary of State during Chilean crisis, 146, 52, 9, 63; Handles Bering Sea Controversy, 174
Blake, Admiral Robert, 98
Blake, Captain George S.
Commands Naval Academy, 31, 3, 6
Blockade of Germany in World War
See "World War"
Blockade of Havana, Cuba
See "Havana, Cuba"
Blockade of South in Civil War
See also "Gulf of Mexico" and "Fort Fisher"; Importance, 43-5; Proclamation, 45; Extent, 45; Operations, 46-50, 3-6; Effect upon Lee's Army, 44, 6, 77; Illegality, 46; In 1863, 46; Running, 47, 8; Evans' services in, 50-1; Off Wilmington, 54-6, 63; Reference to, 226
Blockade Running
See "Blockade of South in Civil War"
Blockades
See "Sea Power"
Blue, Lieutenant Victor, 299-300
Board of Inspection
Praises condition of Congress, 128; Inspects Indiana, 214
Boat-Racing
Evans' interest in, 88; Boat of Congress wins championship of Mediterranean, 116; Boat of Congress defeats Brooklyn's, 125-6; Evans names boat of New York for Kaiser's daughter, 209; Indiana's cutter defeats New York's, 215; At Jamestown Exposition, 420
Boca Chica, Manila Bay, 261
Boca Grande, Manila Bay, 261, 3, 4
Boetticher, Dr. Karl Heinrich von, Prussian Minister, 201, 10
Bolivar, Simon, 221

"Bolognesi," Peruvian Ship, 436
Bonaparte, Napoleon
See "Napoleon Bonaparte"
Borneo, 385, 7
Borntraeger, William
Superintendent of Carnegie Steel Co., 140
Boston, Mass., 106, 27
"Boston," S. S., 34
"Boston," U. S. S.
Wildes commands, 30; Under construction, 139; At Manila, 261
Boxer Uprising, 388
Brazil
Piscataqua at, 81-2; Emperor and Empress of, at opening of Centennial Exhibition, 127; Becomes republic, 146; U. S. fleet at, 428-9
Brazilian Navy
Case of spontaneous combustion in, 239; At Jamestown Exposition, 419; Escorts departing U. S. fleet, 429
Breese, Lieutenant Commander K. R.
Porter sends to ask Sherman for aid, 64; Leads naval brigade at Fort Fisher, 78
Brethren of the Brood
See "Brood of the Constitution"
Bridge
Evans inspects steel for, 138
Bridge, Vice Admiral Sir Cyprian A. C.
Quotation from, 43; Evans friend of, 379
Bridger, James, 17
Bridgetown, Barbados, 188
Brig
Evans confined in, 50
Brillat-Savarin, Anthelme, 113
Bristol, Lieutenant Mark L., 395
British Army
Officers at Gibralter, 99, 117; At Hong Kong, 99; At Malta, 118
British Colonial Office
Communications with Governor of Jamaica, 417-8
British Empire
In Orient in 1902, 379

BRITISH GUIANA, 186

BRITISH NAVY
Constitution's campaigns against, 22-3; Confederacy's hopes for aid from, 49; Fights with liberty parties of *Powhatan*, 52-3; Officers engaged in blockade-running in Civil War, 56; South African base, 83; Singapore base, 84; Officers at Hong Kong, 85; Profits by lessons of Civil War and Battle of Lissa, 97; Officers in Mediterranean, 99; Impressions of Spanish Revolution upon officers of, 99; Officers at Malta, 118; Evans meets old friends in Mediterranean, 131; Reference to 1914 battles, 154; Entertains Evans in London, 199; Effect of torpedo upon, 211; *Royal Sovereign* class, 213; Case of spontaneous combustion in, 239; Fleet commands in, 247; Asiatic Fleet commanded by Bridge, 379; Gunnery development, 394-5; *Dreadnought* class, 1, 402; Visit of squadron to New York, 407-9; Visit of squadron to Panama, 407; At Jamestown Exposition, 419-20

BRITTAIN, LIEUTENANT CARLOS B., 395

BROOD OF THE "CONSTITUTION"
At Naval Academy, 30-1; Lee beaten by Navy of, 77; Evans and Taylor two of, 94; At Manila, 259, 61; At Santiago, 321; Evans delivers valedictory of, 442; Evans last of, 442

BROOKLYN, N. Y.
See "Navy Yard, U. S."

"BROOKLYN," U. S. S. (OLD)
At Fort Fisher, 59; Boat of *Congress* defeats, 125-6

"BROOKLYN," U. S. S. (NEW)
Cook commands at Santiago, 30; Reference to turn of, at Santiago, 156; Availability for war, 251; In Flying Squadron, 253; Coal supply on May 26, 1898 of, 295; Signals return to Key West, 296; Sights Cervera, 298-9; Coals during bombardment, 300; Leads Schley's division, 309-10;

Position before Battle of Santiago, 319-20; *Teresa* plans dash at, 319; In Battle of Santiago, 324-34; In victory parade, 352; At Jamestown Exposition, 419

BROOKS, PRESTON, 11

BROOME, SIR FREDERICK NAPIER
Governor of Trinidad, 191

BROTHER OF EVANS, 27-8, 41-2

BROWN, REAR ADMIRAL GEORGE, 149

BROWN, JOHN, 11

BRYAN, WILLIAM JENNINGS, 220, 364

BRYCE, JAMES, 346

BUCK, ENSIGN WILLIAM HENRY, 349

BUCHANAN, COMMANDER FRANKLIN, 35

BUCHANAN, PRESIDENT JAMES
In White House, 7; Handling of Mormon crisis, 19; Close of Administration, 25; Condition of Navy under, 45

BUENOS AIRES, ARGENTINA, 153, 429

BUFFALO, 13, 170

BUFFALO, N. Y., 364

BUFFALO BILL, 14

BULL FIGHTS
In Spain, 100; In Havana, 233; In Lima, 436

"BULLDOG, THE"
See "*Oregon,* U. S. S."

BUNCE, REAR ADMIRAL T. M., 211, 353

BUOYS
Electrically lighted, 141

BUREAU OF ORDNANCE, 167

BURIAL OF EVANS, 450-1

BURNET HOUSE, CINCINNATI, 361

BUSTAMENTE, CAPTAIN, 307-8, 18

BUTLER, GENERAL BENJAMIN F.
See also "Fort Fisher"; At and near Annapolis, 32-4; In first attack on Fort Fisher, 56-79, 60-2; Before Congressional Committee, 64

"BUZZARD," H. M. S., 189

BUZZARD'S BAY, MASSACHUSETTS, 185

NICARAGUA
Evans seeks employment by company organized to construct canal through, 142; Difficulties in, 186
NICE, FRANCE, 103, 9, 17
NICHOLAS II, CZAR
French overtures to, 196; Attitude toward France and Germany in 1895, 201; Expresses displeasure at French behavior at Kiel, 209
NICHOLSON, ASSISTANT PAYMASTER RISHWORTH, 396-7
NILE, BATTLE OF THE, 265, 86
NORFOLK, VA.
Evans at Naval Hospital at, 74-6; Fleet departs from, 425; Sinking of *Puritan* at, 447
NORFOLK NAVAL HOSPITAL
See "Naval Hospital, U. S."
NORTH AFRICA, 117
NORTH ATLANTIC OCEAN
Evans crosses, 96; *Shenandoah* crosses, 106; Evans runs line of soundings across, 131; *New York* crosses and recrosses, 197, 210; Cervera crosses, 279, 81-2
NORTH ATLANTIC SQUADRON
New York with in 1894, 185-8; Prepares for war, 251; On Porto Rican expedition, 267-73; To blockade Cuba, 277; *Oregon* joins, 282; In Battle of Santiago, 320-36; To escort Watson past Spain, 350; Returns to *New York*, 351-3; Evans aspires to command of, 363; Evans commands, 400; Evans moulds into a fleet, 400-2
NORTH CAROLINA, 54-6, 7
NORTH PACIFIC SEALING CONVENTION, 183
NORTH SEA
Mine barrage across, 47-8, 238; Kiel Canal connects with Baltic, 194
NORWAY
Mine barrage in World War from Great Britain to, 47-8; Navy of, at Jamestown Exposition, 419
"NOSTROMO," 147
NOVA SCOTIA, 282

NULLIFICATION, ORDINANCE OF, 25

"OHIO," U. S. S., 435
OLD CALIFORNIA TRAIL, 11, 5
OLD GIMPY
Evans' nickname, 73-4, 6, 165
"OLD IRONSIDES"
See "*Constitution,* U. S. S."
OLD POINT COMFORT, VA.
See also "Hampton Roads, Va."; "Fortress Monroe, Va."; Evans resides at, 359; Evans delivers address at, 361; During Jamestown Exposition, 419; Fleet leaves from, 425
OLD SALT LAKE TRAIL, 11, 5
"OLYMPIA," U. S. S.
At Manila, 30, 260-5; Ready for sea, 192; At Hong Kong, 237; In Evans' special service squadron, 371
"OMAHA," U. S. S., 281
"OQUENDO," SPANISH SHIP
Cruise to Santiago, 281-5; Rapid-fire guns, 317; Leaves Santiago, 320; In Battle of Santiago, 322-9, 31
ORANGE FREE STATE, 230
ORANGE RIVER, SOUTH AFRICA, 83
ORDINANCE OF NULLIFICATION, 25
ORDNANCE
See also "Bureau of Ordnance," "Torpedoes," "Rifles," "Gunnery"; Evans performs ordnance duty at Washington Yard, 79; In European navies in 1873, 97; Evans works with cables and forgings at Washington Yard, 133; Fourteen inch guns, 447; Special Board on, 447
OREGON, 13
"OREGON," U. S. S.
Clark commands, 30, 321; Authorized, 212; Nick-named *Bulldog*, 250; Cruise around South America, 282-3; Reaches Santiago, 302; Searchlight duty, 310; Position before Battle of Santiago, 320-1; In Battle of Santiago, 323-33; To join squadron to reenforce Dewey, 348, 50; Signals "Peace," 351; Clark relinquishes command, 351; At New York, 352; Chaplain Mc-

PHILADELPHIA, PA.
Evans at, 76; Evans at Yard at, 79; Evans at Centennial Exhibition, 126-8; *Saratoga* at, 132; *Indiana* at, 214; Army-Navy game at, 424
"PHILADELPHIA," U. S. S., 23, 118, 21
"PHILADELPHIA PUBLIC LEDGER, THE," 127
"PHILADELPHIA TIMES, THE," 357
PHILIP, JOHN W.
At Naval Academy, 30; Evans relieves, in command of *New York*, 185; Evans hails in *Texas* re Schley's signal, 296; Coals *Texas* off Santiago, 297; Commands *Texas* in Battle of Santiago, 321; Schley praises, 342; Famous injunction of, 344; Victory prayer of, 344-5
PHILIPPINE ISLANDS
Evans first visits, 85; Weyler's service in, 227; Spanish squadron in, 252; Governor of, 258, 9; Camara vaguely ordered to, 348; U. S. acquisition of, 351, 4, 69, 79, 86; Evans revisits, 384-7; American administration of, 384; Evans plans return to, 390; Evans ordered to return to, 391
PICKETT, GENERAL GEORGE EDWARD, 70
PICKETT'S CHARGE, 70
PILLAR, CAPE, STRAITS OF MAGELLAN, 424
PINAR DEL RIO PROVINCE, CUBA, 224
"PISCATAQUA," U. S. S.
See also "*Delaware*, U. S. S."; Evans aboard, 80-1; Cruise to Asiatic Station, 81-4; Cruises about Orient, 85-7, 90; English relieves Ammen in command of, 89; Renamed *Delaware*, 90; Rolling propensities, 98; Fitted out at Portsmouth, 128
PISCATAQUA RIVER, 80
PITTSBURGH, PA., 138
PLATT, SENATOR, THOMAS C., 364
PLATT AMENDMENT, 230
PLATTE RIVER, 11, 3
PLÜDEMANN, REAR ADMIRAL, 348-9
PLUMB POINT, JAMAICA, 413

"PLUTON," SPANISH SHIP
Cruise to Santiago, 281-5; Leaves Santiago, 320; In Battle of Santiago, 330-1
POINT LOBOS, CAL., 2
POLITICS AND POLITICIANS
Evans' conflicts with, 136-7, 443-4
POLK, PRESIDENT JAMES K., 4, 7
POLYGAMY
Among Mormons, 18-9, 20
PONY EXPRESS, 12, 4
POPE, 244
PORT ARTHUR, CHINA, 378
PORT AU PRINCE, HAYTI, 143
PORT ETCHES, 179
PORT HUDSON, BATTLE OF, 263-4
PORT MAHON, MINORCA, 116
PORT-OF-SPAIN, TRINIDAD
Fire at, 189-92, 417, 91; Fleet at, 427
PORT-OF-SPAIN "GAZETTE," 191
PORT ROYAL, S. C.
Congress returns to, 125; *Indiana* docked at, 215
PORT SAID, EGYPT, 348-9
PORT TOWNSEND, WASH., 169, 80
PORTER, COMMODORE DAVID
See also "Porter, David Dixon"; In *Essex*, calls at Cape Verde Islands, 110
PORTER, DAVID DIXON
Mississippi campaign, 46, 56; Inspection of Malakoff Fortress by, 58; First attack on Fort Fisher, 56-63; Second attack on Fort Fisher, 63; Lee beaten by Navy of, 77; Orders Breese to lead naval brigade at Fort Fisher, 78; Ammen under at Fort Fisher, 79; Sampson follows example of, 316
PORTER, GENERAL HORACE, 405-6
"PORTER," U. S. S., 267, 70, 4
PORTO GRANDE, CAPE VERDE ISLANDS, 110, 4
PORTO RICO
Spain grants autonomy to, 229; Cervera's logical destination, 266; Capture of, 350; U. S. acquisition of, 351
PORTSMOUTH, N. H.
Piscataqua at, 79; *Congress* put out of commission at, 128; Peace Conference at, 402

INDEX